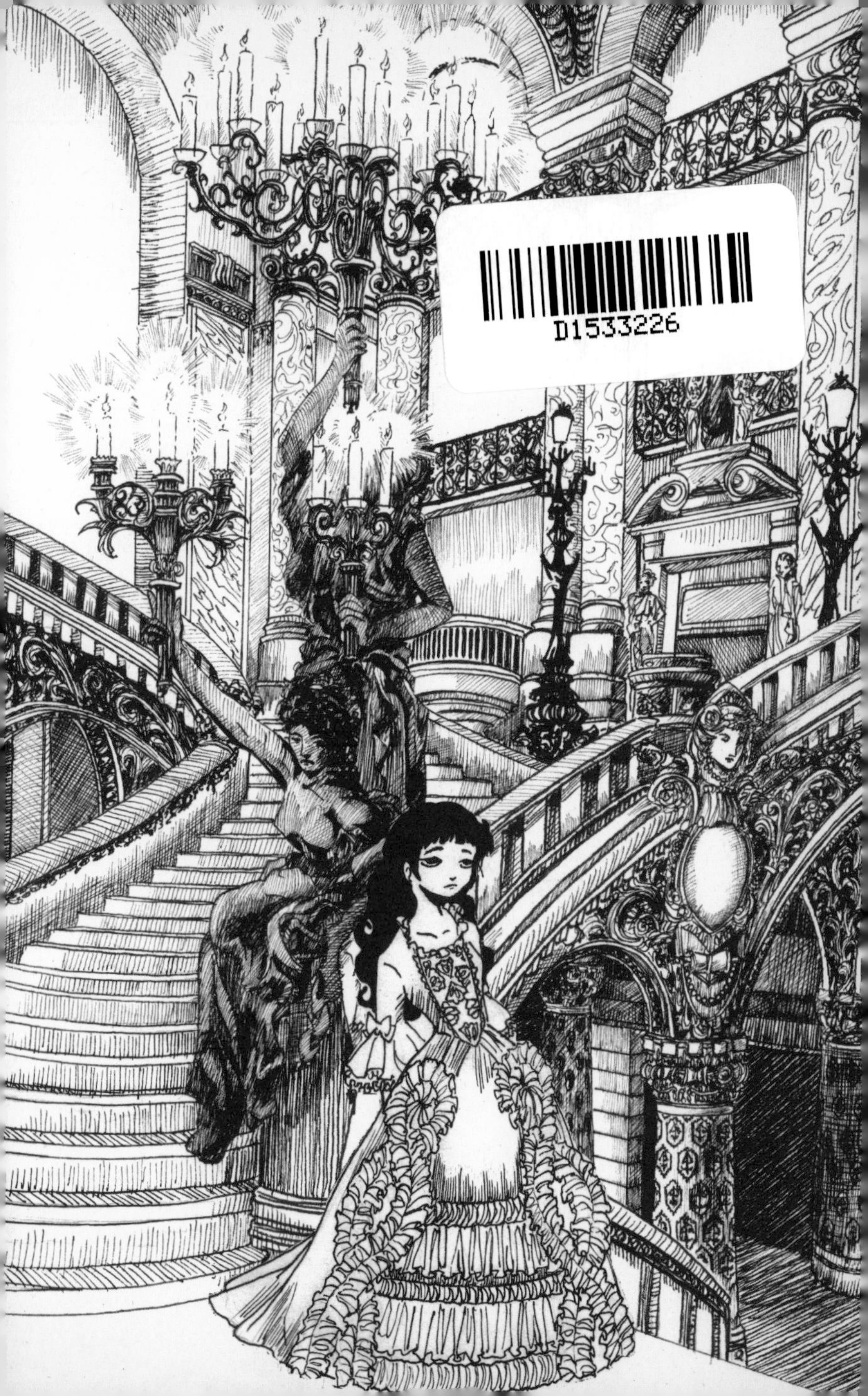

Bizenghast Volume 1
Created by M. Alice LeGrow

Development Editor - Jodi Bryson
Layout and Lettering - Rob Steen
Toning - Catarina Sarmento
Production Artist - Chris Anderson
Cover Artist - M. Alice LeGrow
Cover Design - Raymond Makowski

Editor - Aaron Suhr
Digital Imaging Manager - Chris Buford
Production Managers - Jennifer Miller and Mutsumi Miyazaki
Managing Editor - Jill Freshney
VP of Production - Ron Klamert
Publisher and Editor-in-Chief - Mike Kiley
President and C.O.O. - John Parker
C.E.O. - Stuart Levy

A  Manga

TOKYOPOP Inc.
5900 Wilshire Blvd. Suite 2000
Los Angeles, CA 90036

E-mail: info@TOKYOPOP.com
Come visit us online at www.TOKYOPOP.com

ISBN: 1-59532-743-6

First TOKYOPOP printing: August 2005
10 9 8 7 6 5 4 3 2 1
Printed in the USA

Volume 1

By M. Alice LeGrow

HAMBURG // LONDON // LOS ANGELES // TOKYO

Bizenghast

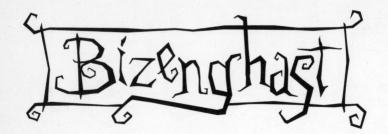

Contents

TRAGIC AUTO ACCIDENT IN DRURY

Drury, Pa.- The sudden bursting of a tire on a Honda Civic caused the vehicle to swerve head-on into oncoming traffic on Route 32, killing two of three passengers Thursday night.

"I just don't understand how it happened," said firefighter Neil Redman. "The busted tire we found was brand new with no defects or puncturing. It didn't even burst in the way you'd expect a tire would. It had a tiny puncture in it like a dart."

Police are still investigating the scene for signs of foul play. The victims, Catherine and Jonathan Wherever and their eight year old daughter Dinah, were rushed to nearby Jonas Mercy Hospital. The adults were pronounced dead upon arrival, but Dinah survived with only minor bruising and abrasions.

Child-care representatives for the state have confirmed that the child will be given over to the care of her maternal aunt, Jane Addison, who stands to inherit substantial property in Bizenghast, MA from her sister. The property is reported to be a defunct lot of buildings called St. Lyman's School for Boys. Ms. Addison's attorney has stated that as soon as custody of the child is turned over to her, she will have the former school renovated into a home,

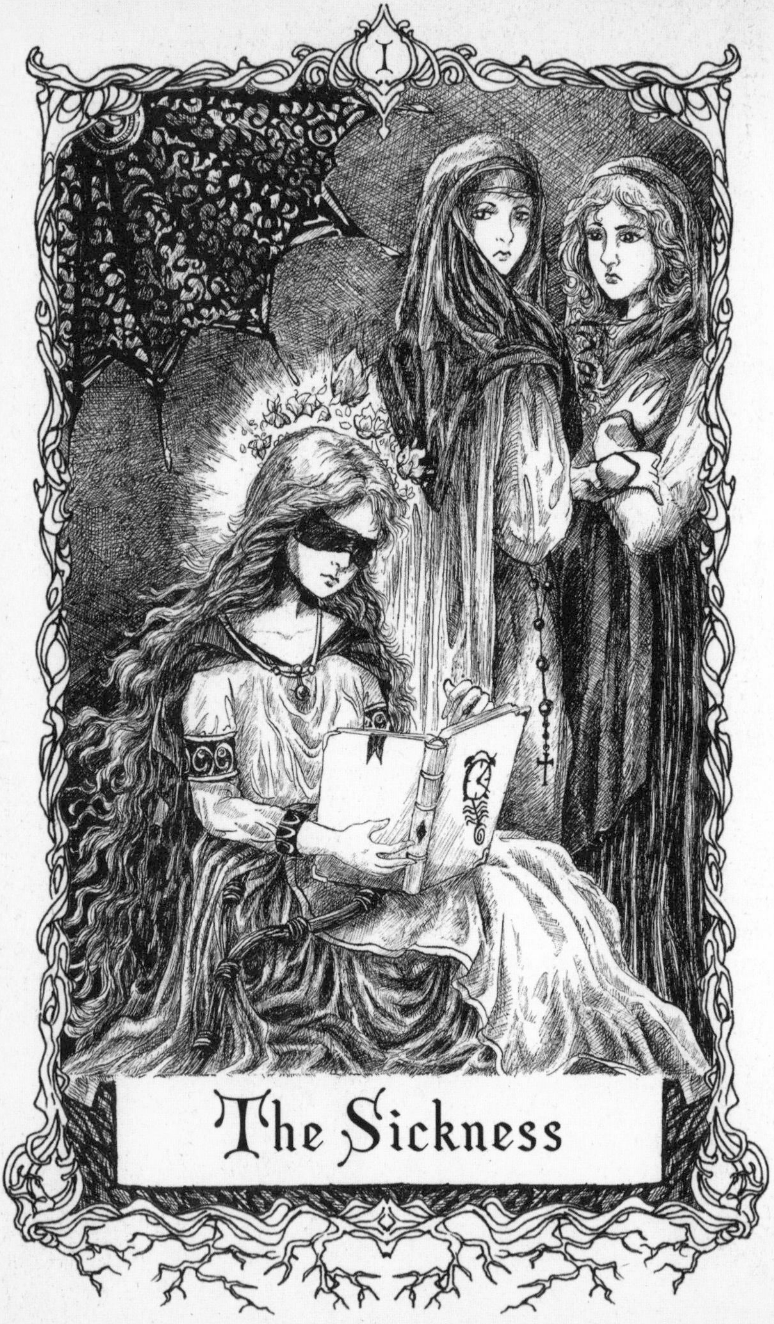
I
The Sickness

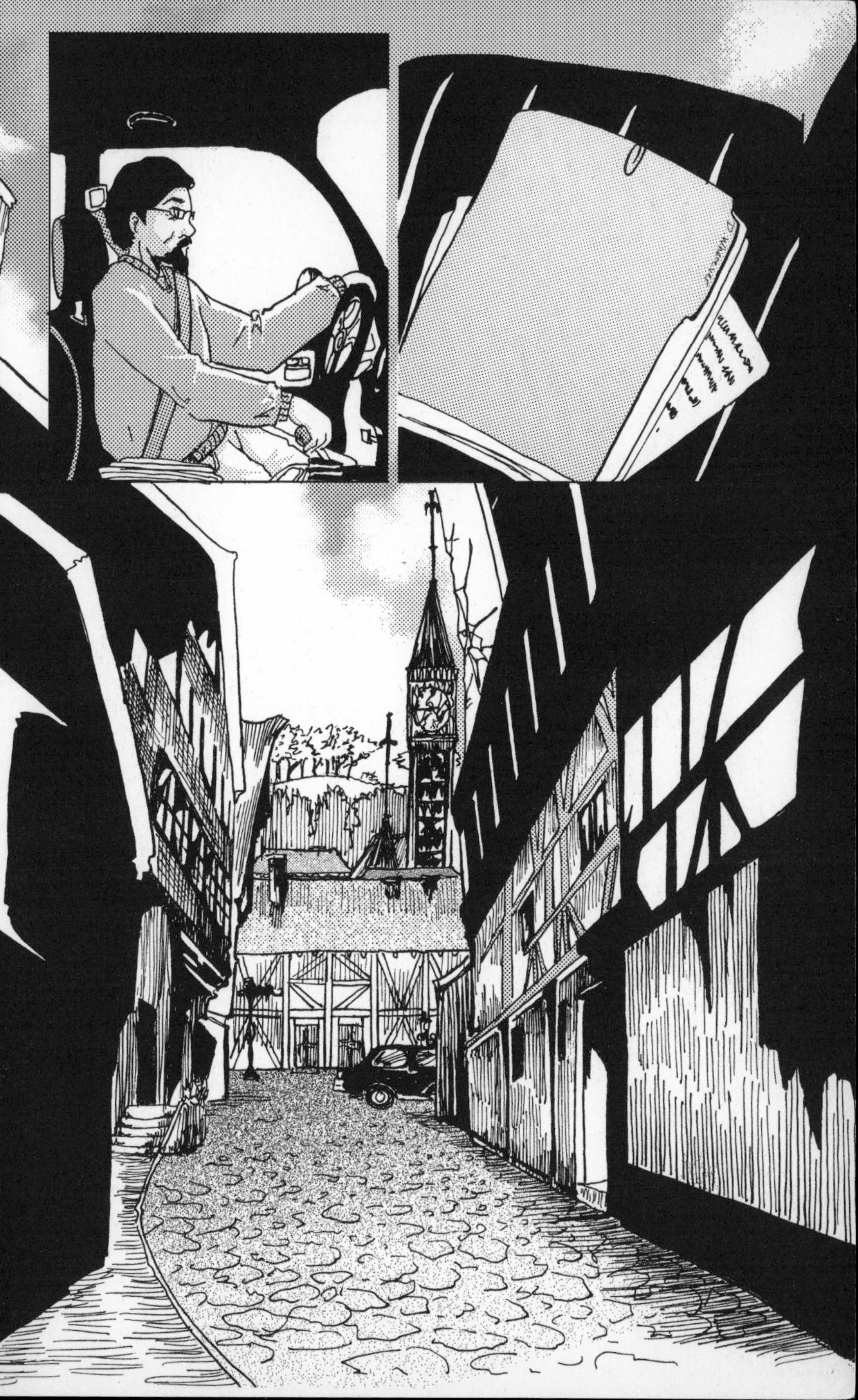

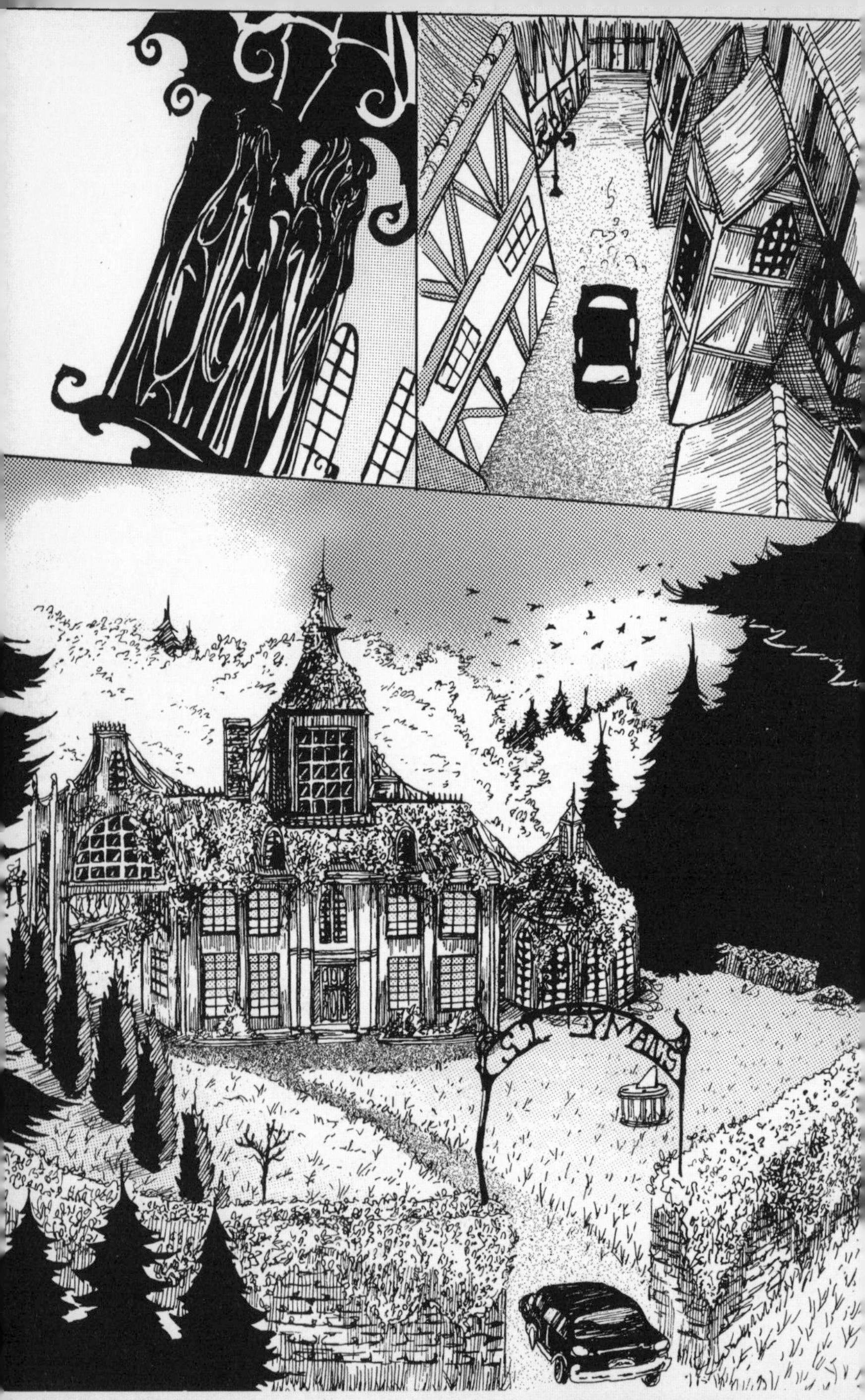

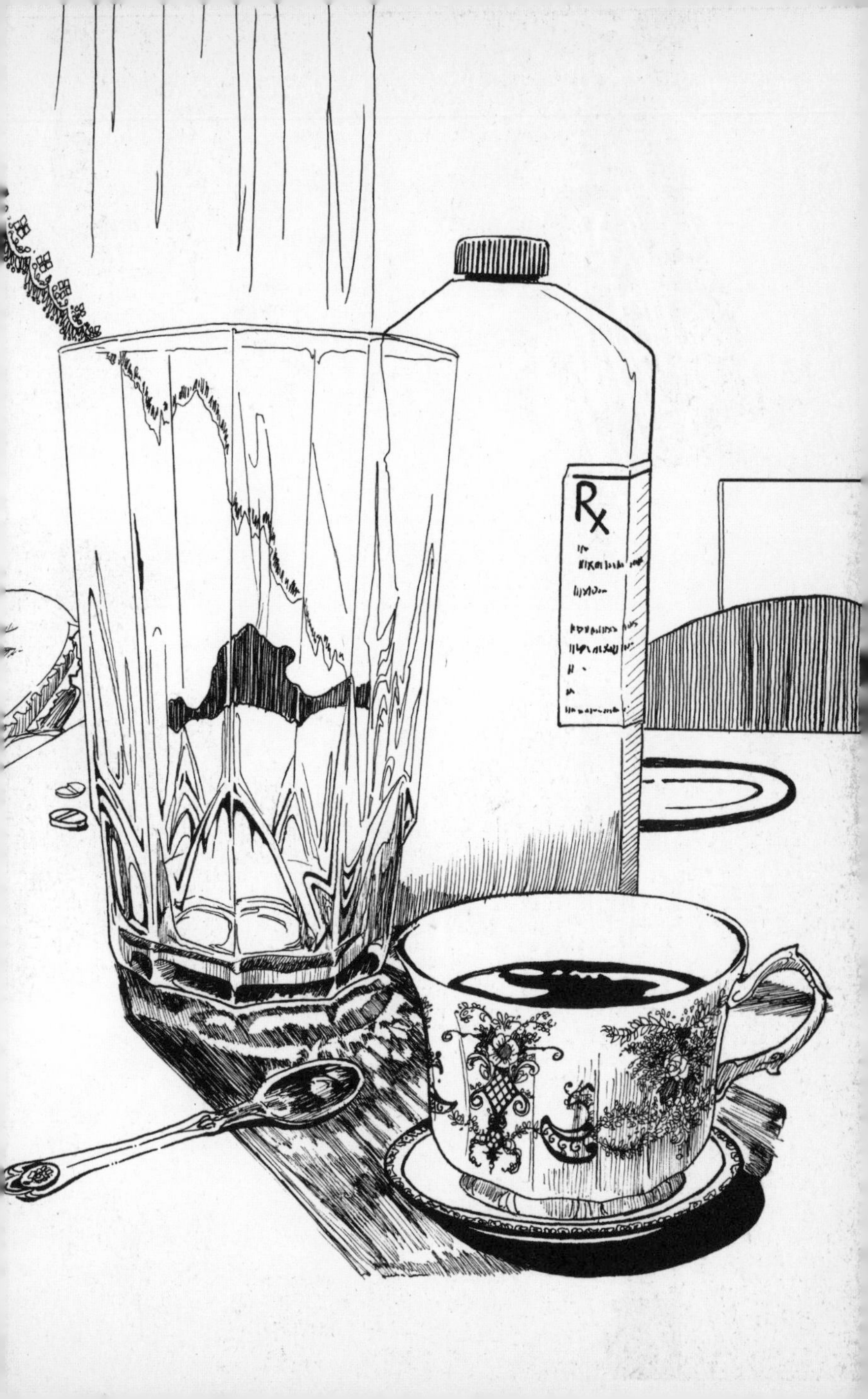
Rx

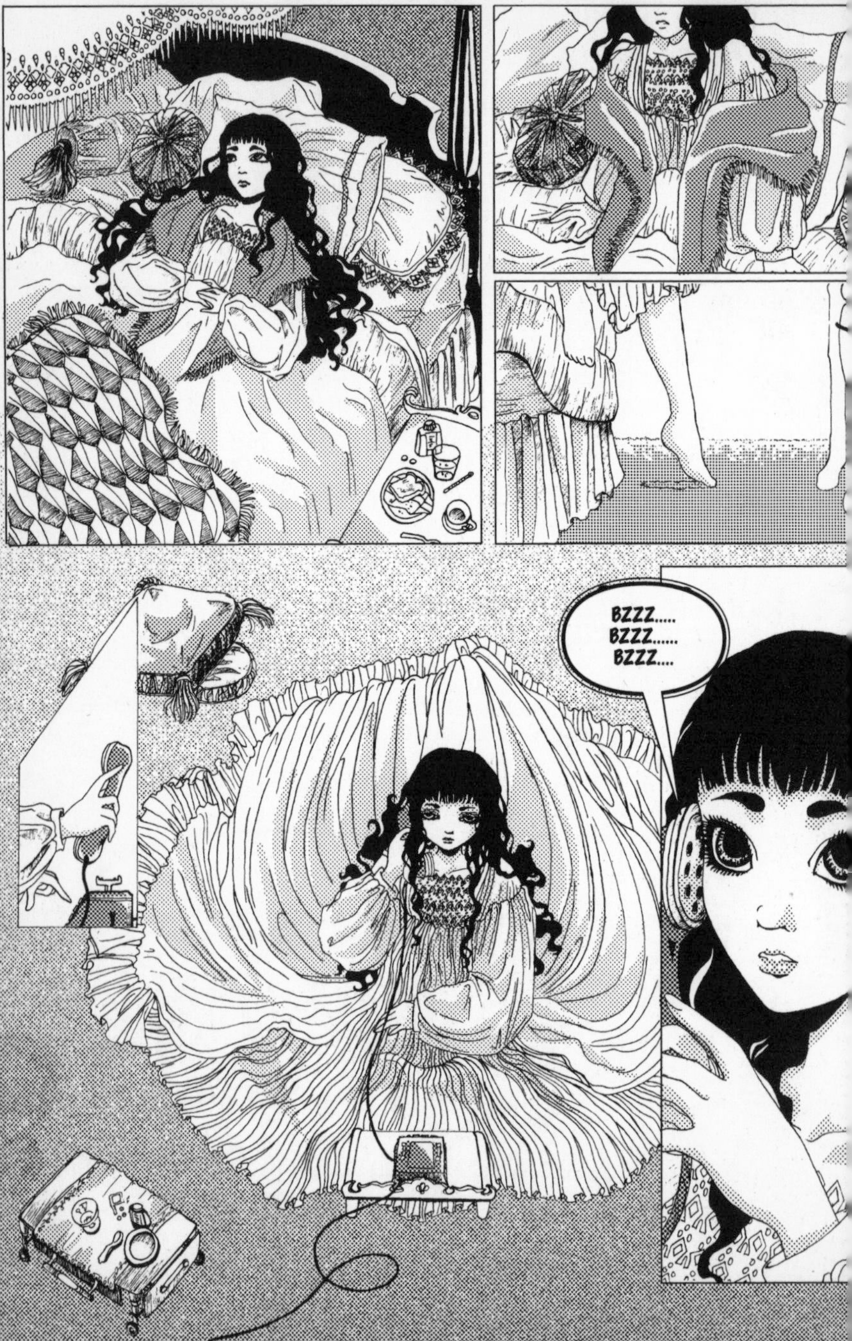
BZZZ..... BZZZ...... BZZZ....

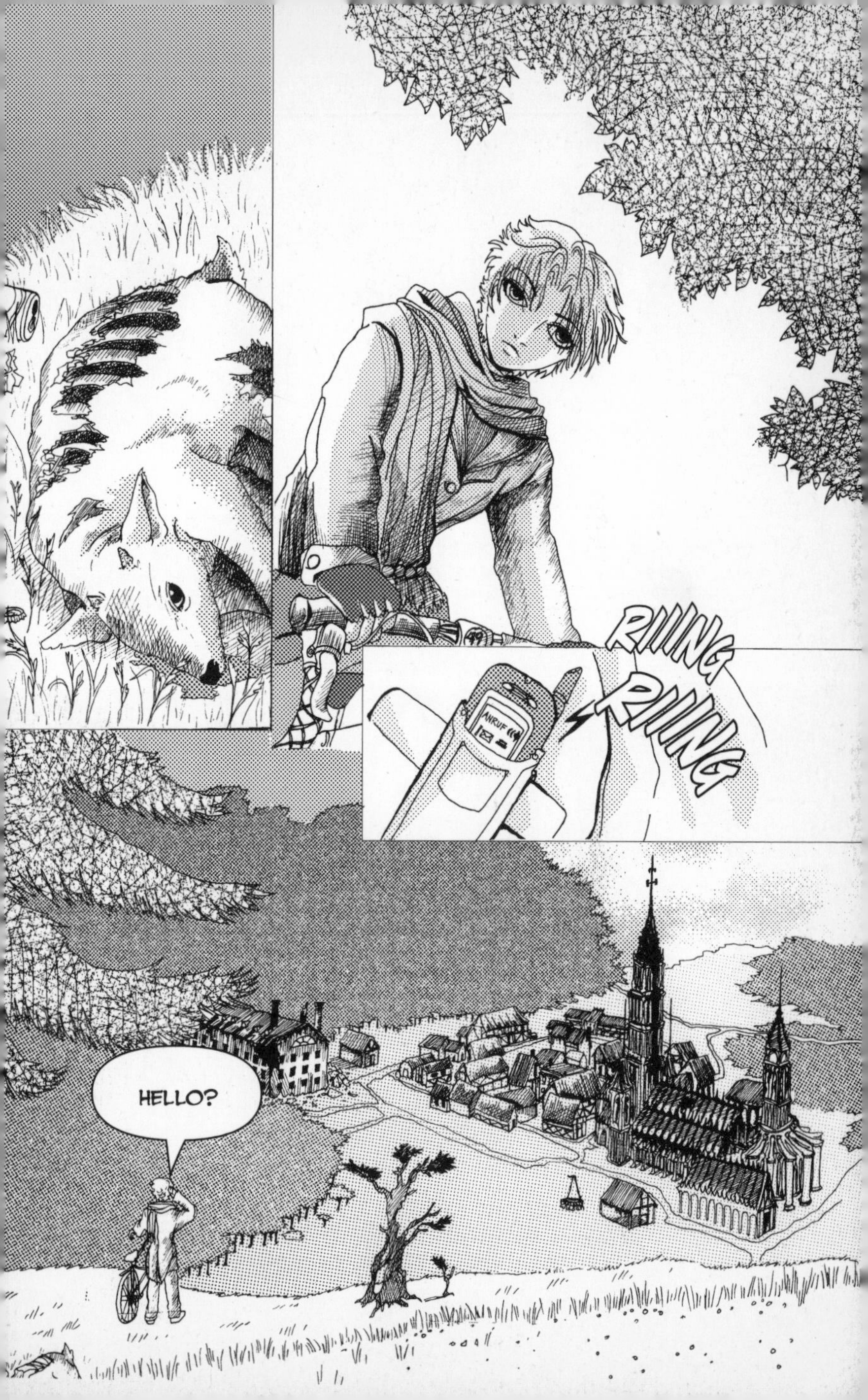
RIIING
RIIING
ANRUF
HELLO?

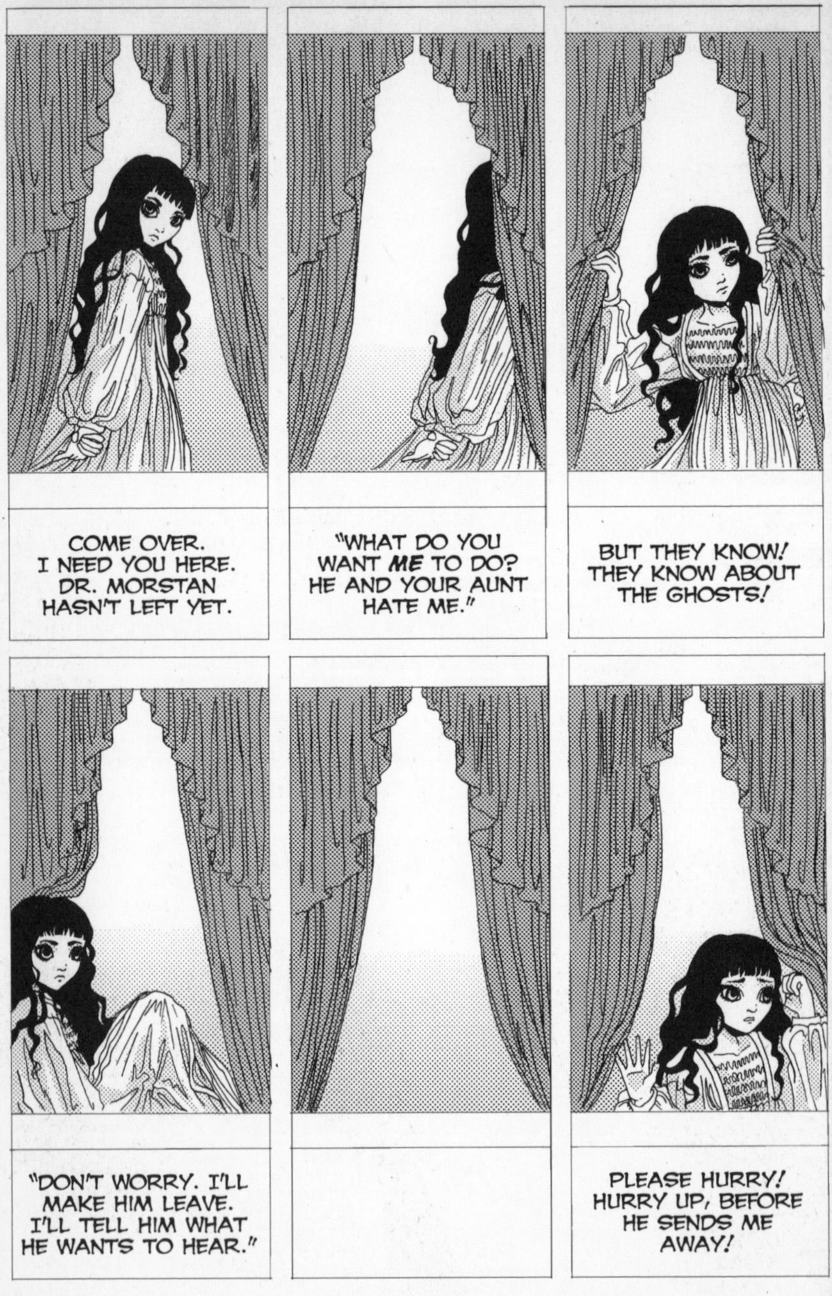
COME OVER. I NEED YOU HERE. DR. MORSTAN HASN'T LEFT YET.
"WHAT DO YOU WANT ME TO DO? HE AND YOUR AUNT HATE ME."
BUT THEY KNOW! THEY KNOW ABOUT THE GHOSTS!
"DON'T WORRY. I'LL MAKE HIM LEAVE. I'LL TELL HIM WHAT HE WANTS TO HEAR."
PLEASE HURRY! HURRY UP, BEFORE HE SENDS ME AWAY!

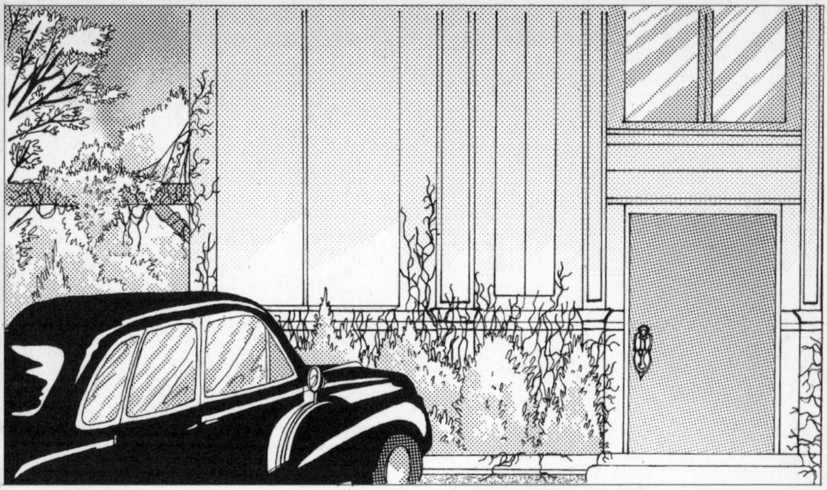
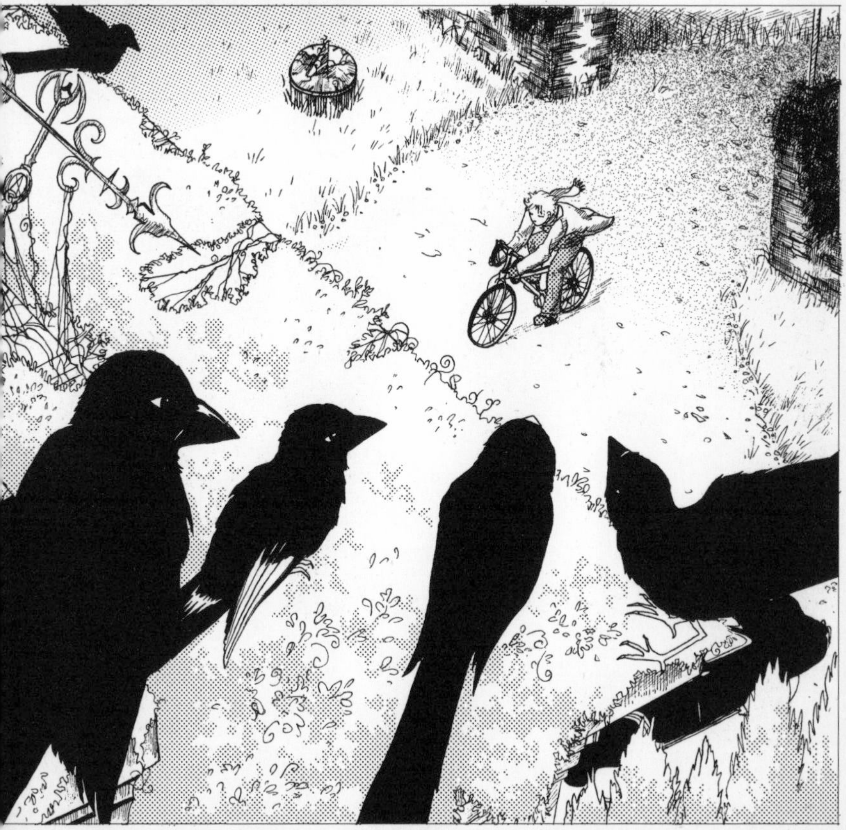

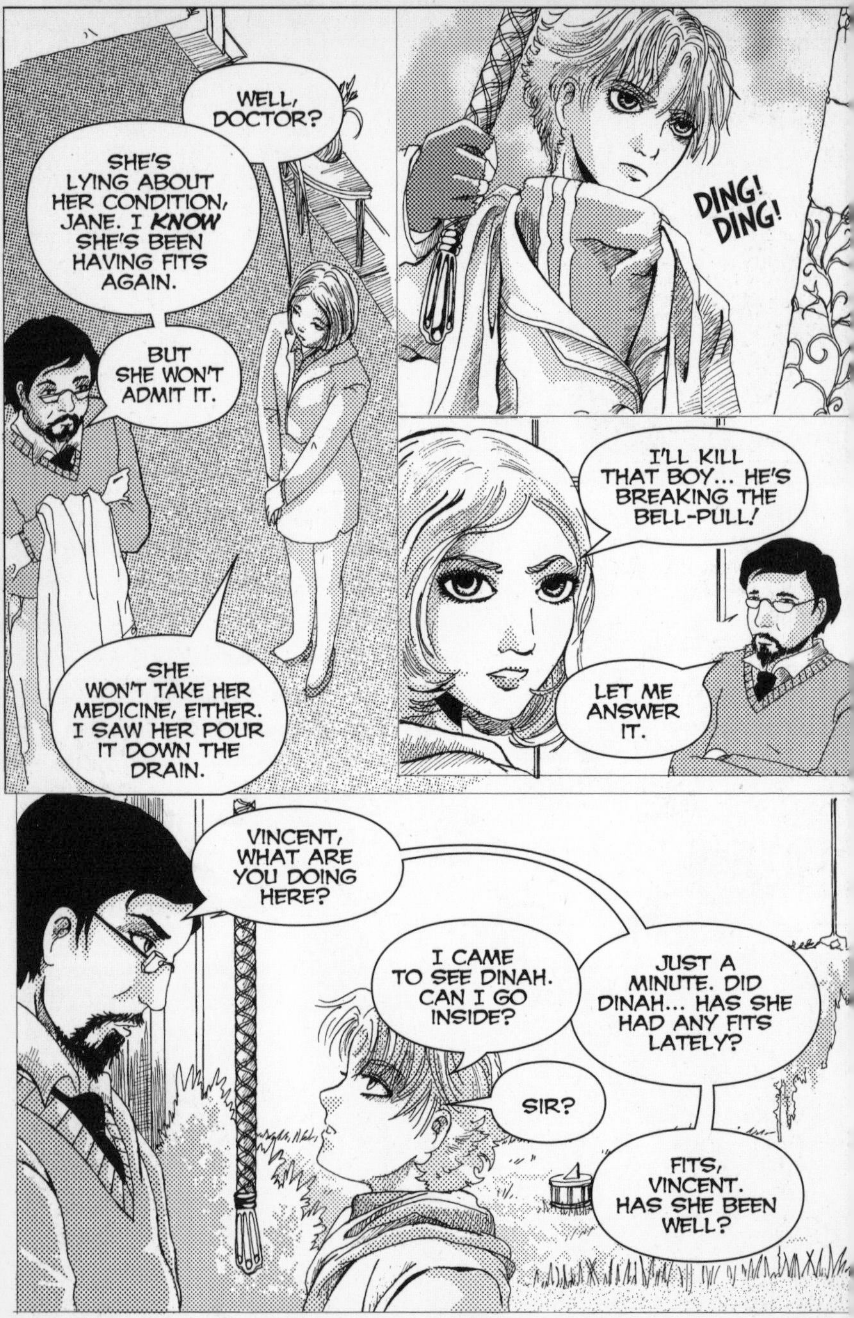
WELL, DOCTOR?
SHE'S LYING ABOUT HER CONDITION, JANE. I *KNOW* SHE'S BEEN HAVING FITS AGAIN.
BUT SHE WON'T ADMIT IT.
SHE WON'T TAKE HER MEDICINE, EITHER. I SAW HER POUR IT DOWN THE DRAIN.
DING! DING!
I'LL KILL THAT BOY... HE'S BREAKING THE BELL-PULL!
LET ME ANSWER IT.
VINCENT, WHAT ARE YOU DOING HERE?
I CAME TO SEE DINAH. CAN I GO INSIDE?
JUST A MINUTE. DID DINAH... HAS SHE HAD ANY FITS LATELY?
SIR?
FITS, VINCENT. HAS SHE BEEN WELL?

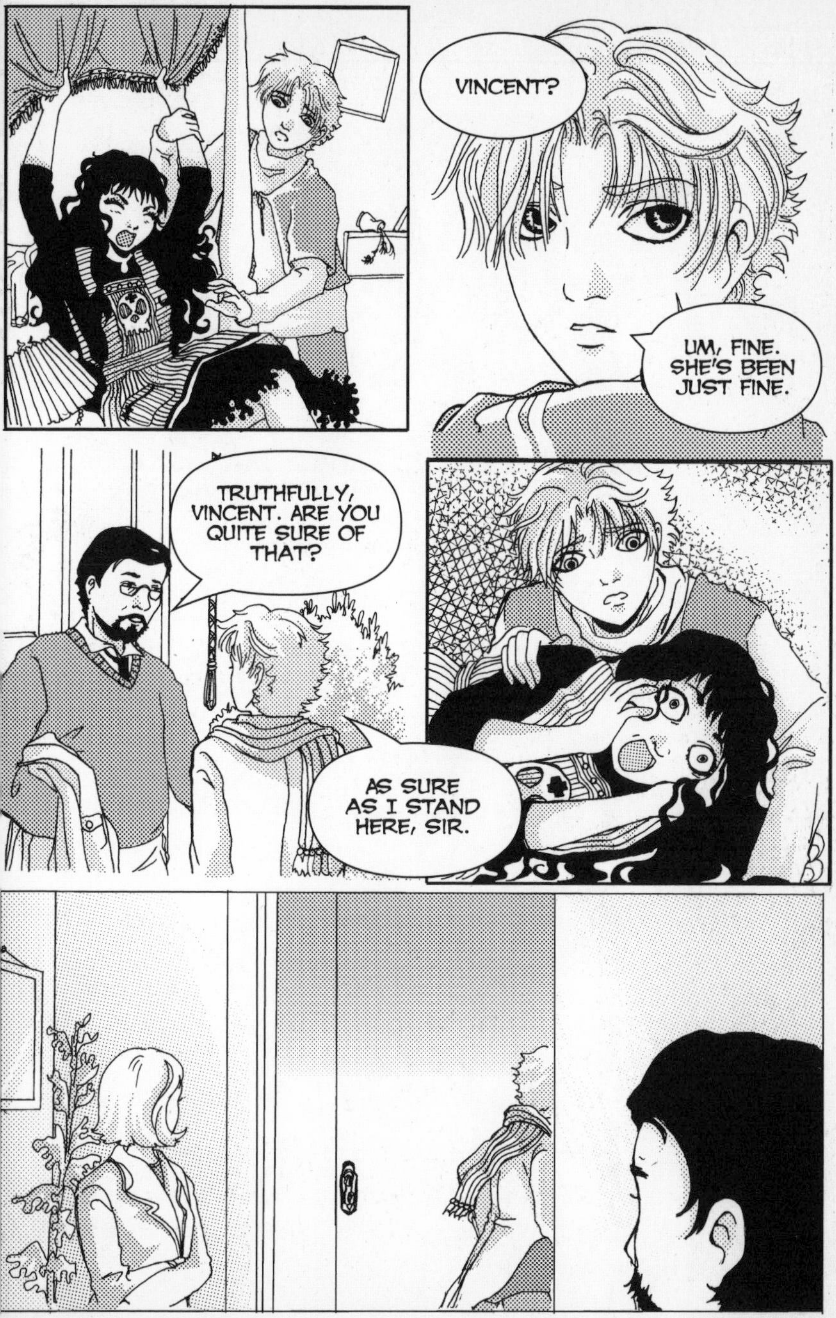
VINCENT?
UM, FINE. SHE'S BEEN JUST FINE.
TRUTHFULLY, VINCENT. ARE YOU QUITE SURE OF THAT?
AS SURE AS I STAND HERE, SIR.

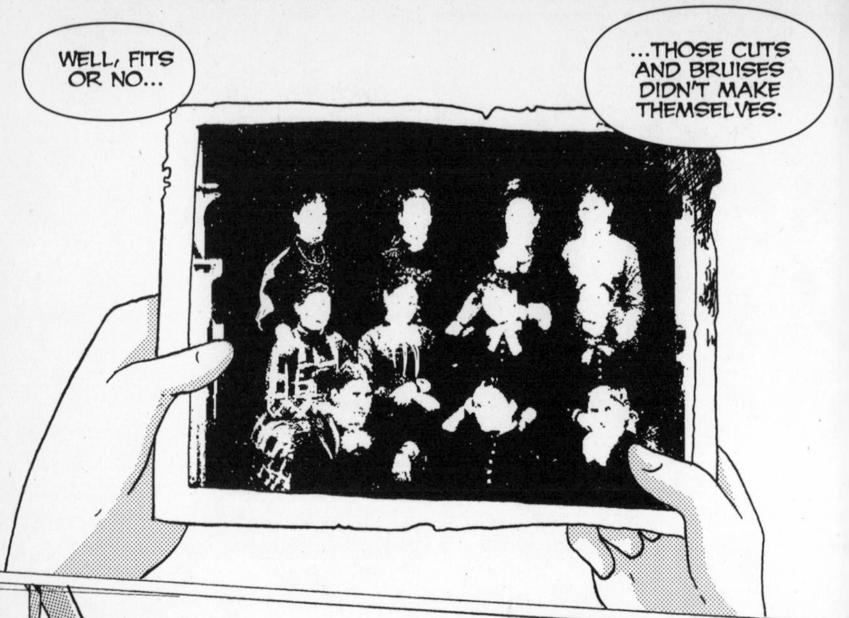
WELL, FITS OR NO...
...THOSE CUTS AND BRUISES DIDN'T MAKE THEMSELVES.
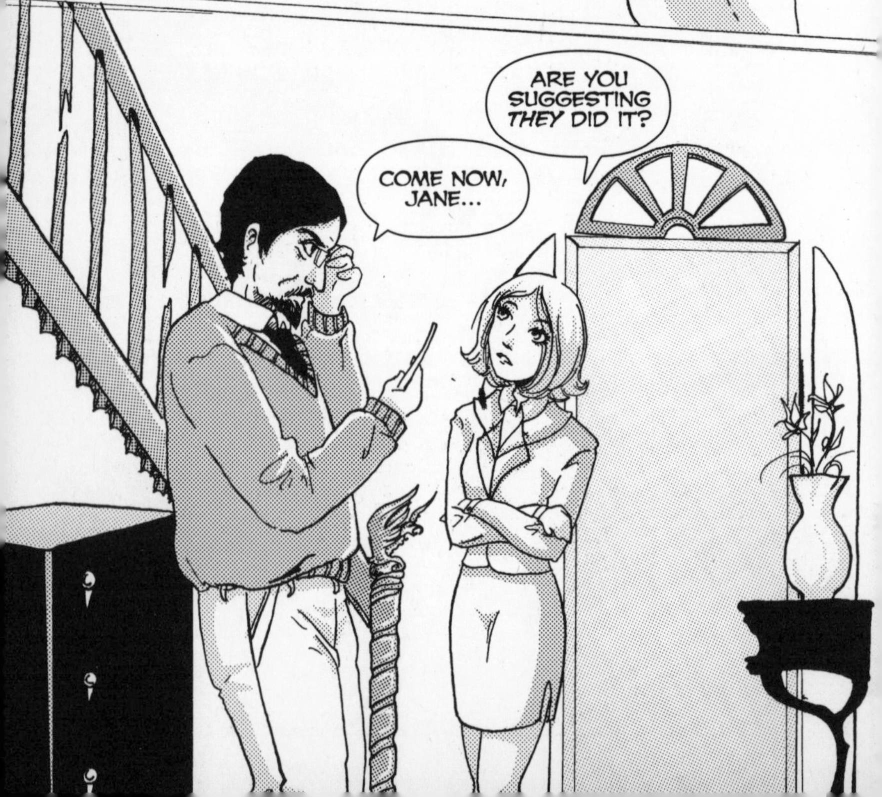
ARE YOU SUGGESTING *THEY* DID IT?
COME NOW, JANE...

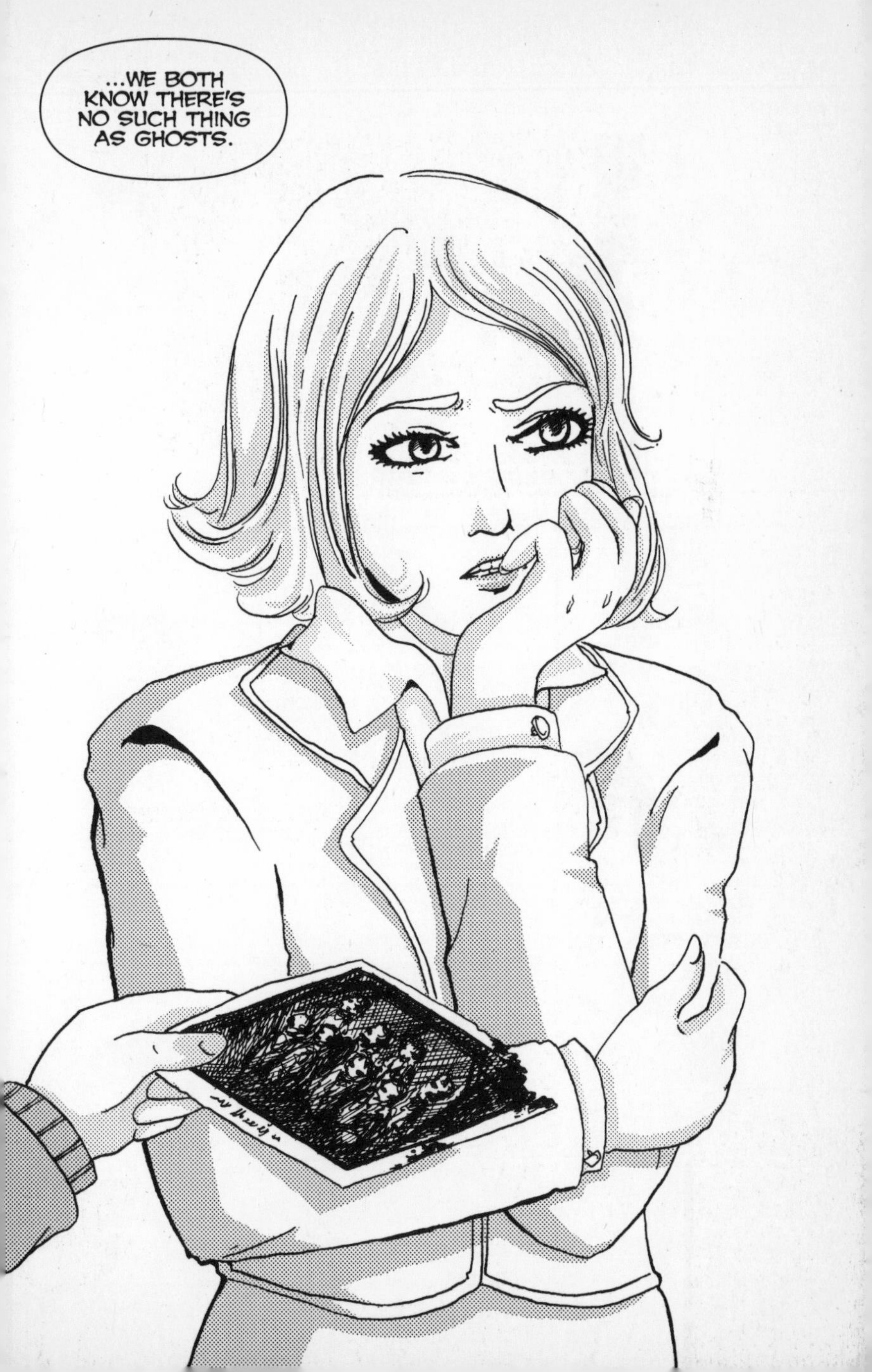
...WE BOTH KNOW THERE'S NO SUCH THING AS GHOSTS.

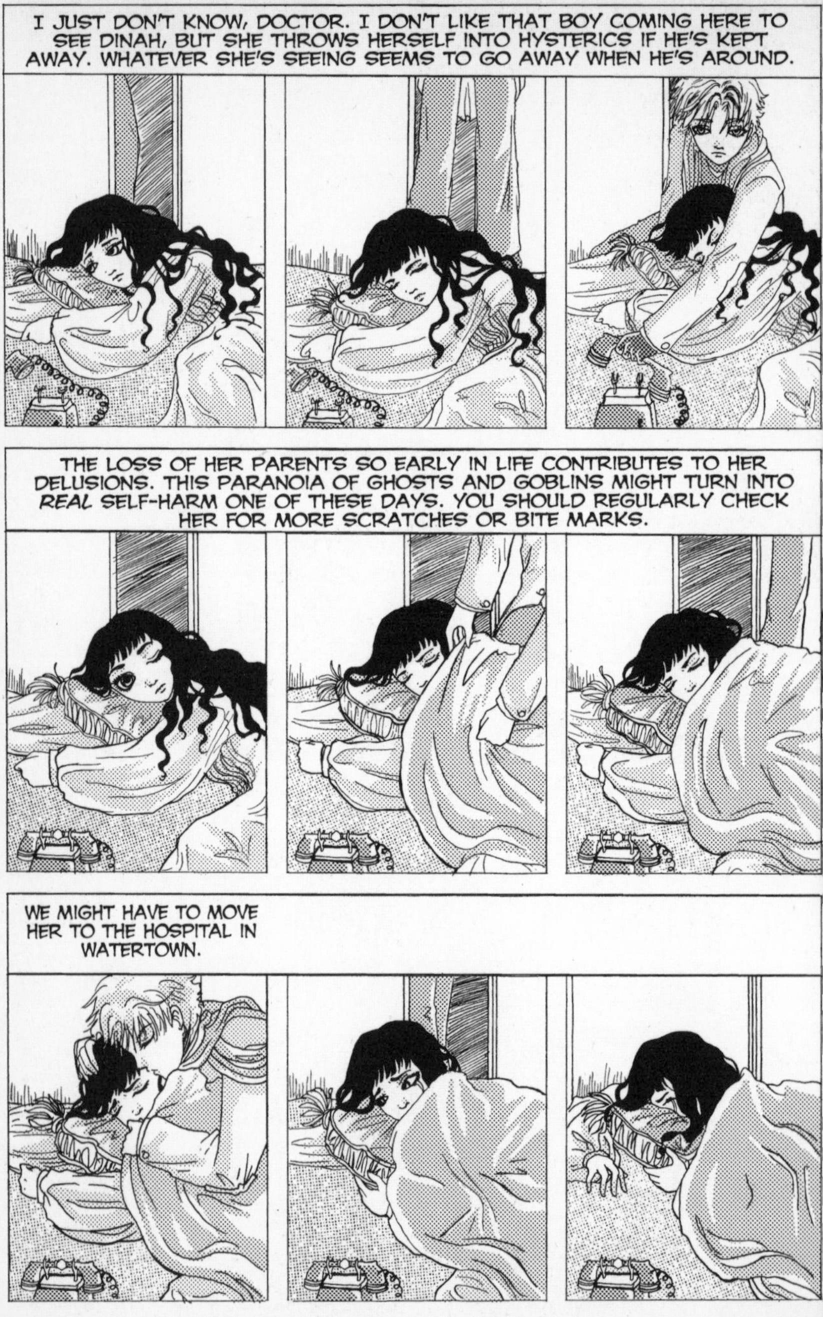
I JUST DON'T KNOW, DOCTOR. I DON'T LIKE THAT BOY COMING HERE TO SEE DINAH, BUT SHE THROWS HERSELF INTO HYSTERICS IF HE'S KEPT AWAY. WHATEVER SHE'S SEEING SEEMS TO GO AWAY WHEN HE'S AROUND.
THE LOSS OF HER PARENTS SO EARLY IN LIFE CONTRIBUTES TO HER DELUSIONS. THIS PARANOIA OF GHOSTS AND GOBLINS MIGHT TURN INTO *REAL* SELF-HARM ONE OF THESE DAYS. YOU SHOULD REGULARLY CHECK HER FOR MORE SCRATCHES OR BITE MARKS.
WE MIGHT HAVE TO MOVE HER TO THE HOSPITAL IN WATERTOWN.

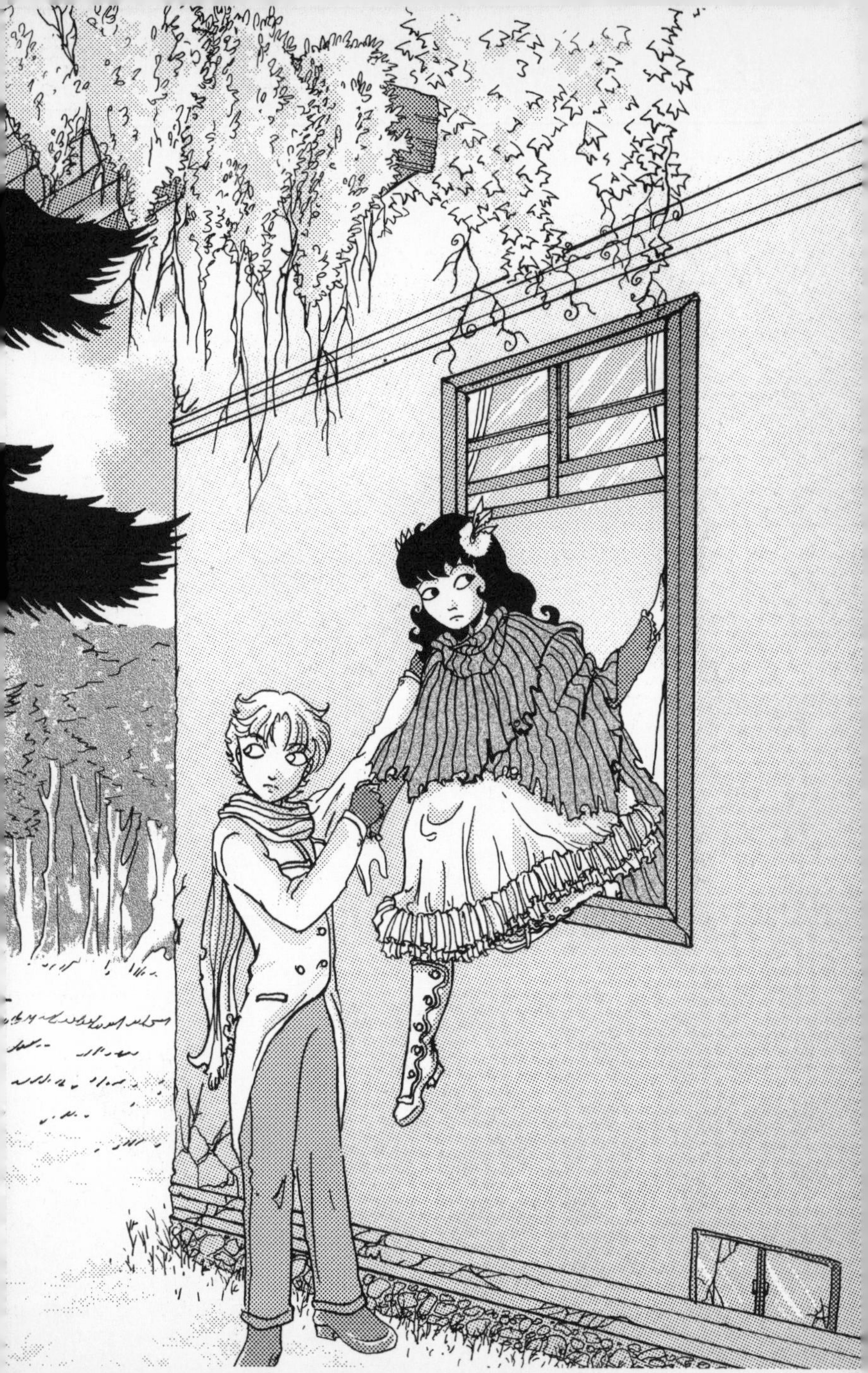

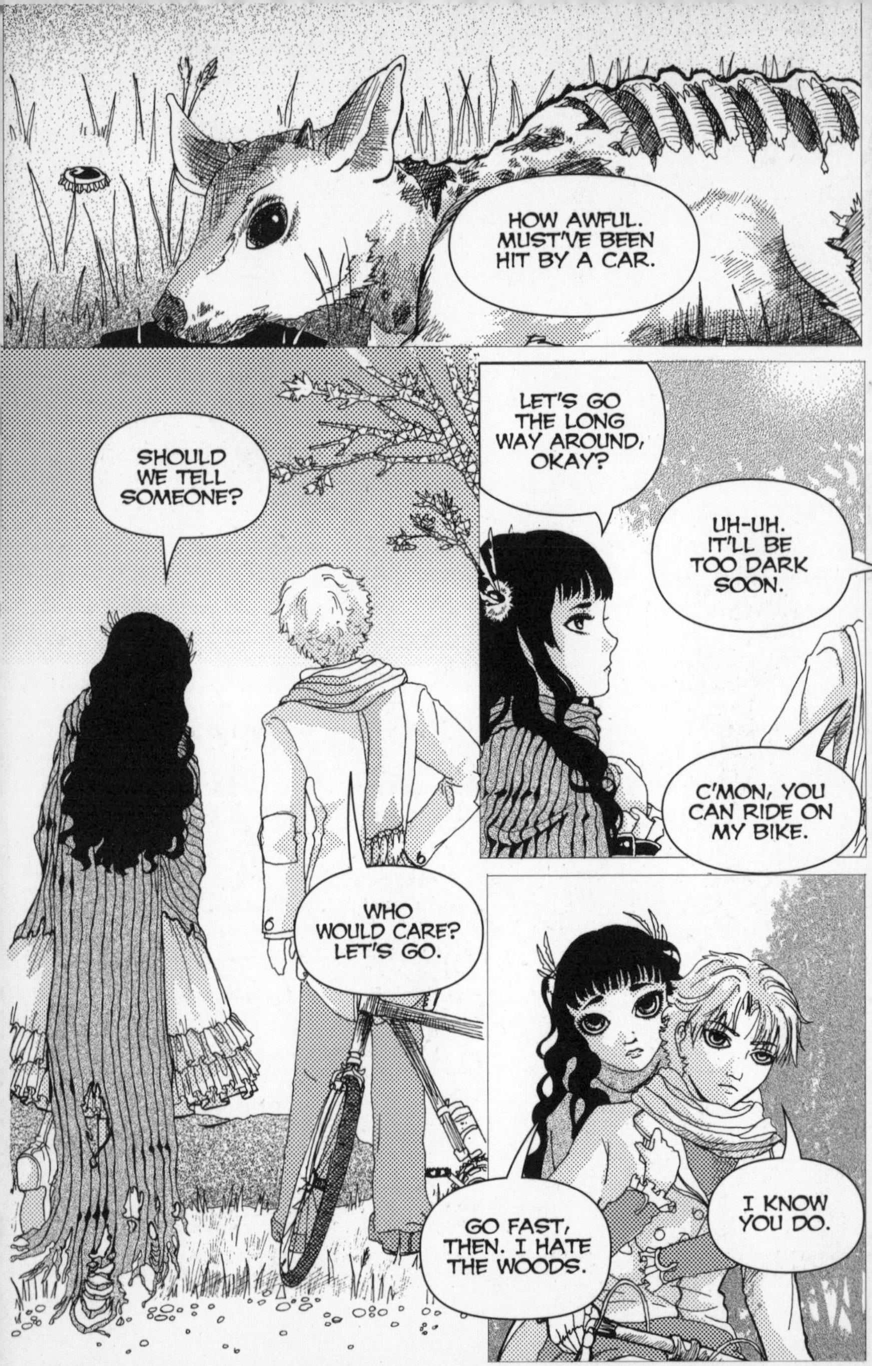
HOW AWFUL. MUST'VE BEEN HIT BY A CAR.
SHOULD WE TELL SOMEONE?
WHO WOULD CARE? LET'S GO.
LET'S GO THE LONG WAY AROUND, OKAY?
UH-UH. IT'LL BE TOO DARK SOON.
C'MON, YOU CAN RIDE ON MY BIKE.
GO FAST, THEN. I HATE THE WOODS.
I KNOW YOU DO.

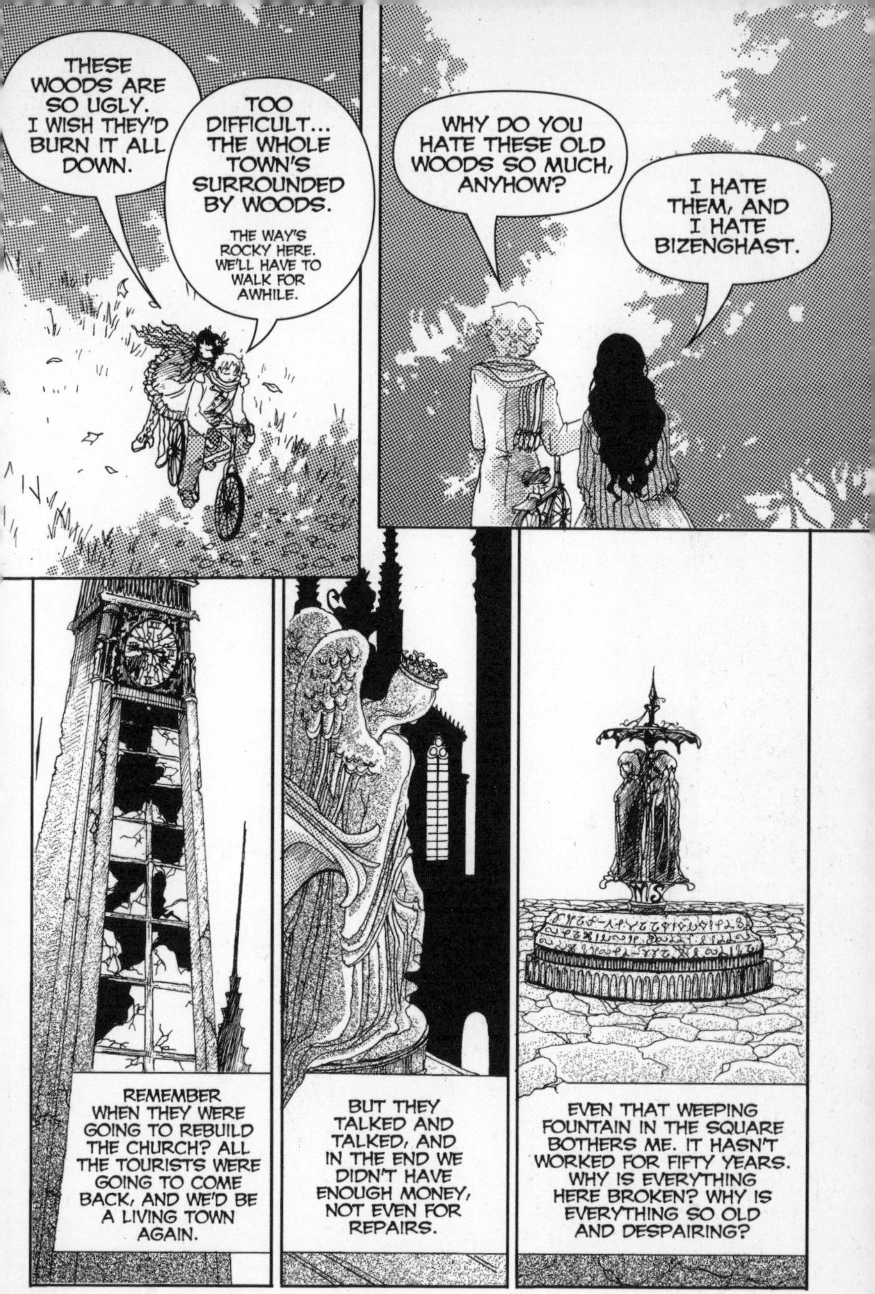
THESE WOODS ARE SO UGLY. I WISH THEY'D BURN IT ALL DOWN.
TOO DIFFICULT... THE WHOLE TOWN'S SURROUNDED BY WOODS.
THE WAY'S ROCKY HERE. WE'LL HAVE TO WALK FOR AWHILE.
WHY DO YOU HATE THESE OLD WOODS SO MUCH, ANYHOW?
I HATE THEM, AND I HATE BIZENGHAST.
REMEMBER WHEN THEY WERE GOING TO REBUILD THE CHURCH? ALL THE TOURISTS WERE GOING TO COME BACK, AND WE'D BE A LIVING TOWN AGAIN.
BUT THEY TALKED AND TALKED, AND IN THE END WE DIDN'T HAVE ENOUGH MONEY, NOT EVEN FOR REPAIRS.
EVEN THAT WEEPING FOUNTAIN IN THE SQUARE BOTHERS ME. IT HASN'T WORKED FOR FIFTY YEARS. WHY IS EVERYTHING HERE BROKEN? WHY IS EVERYTHING SO OLD AND DESPAIRING?

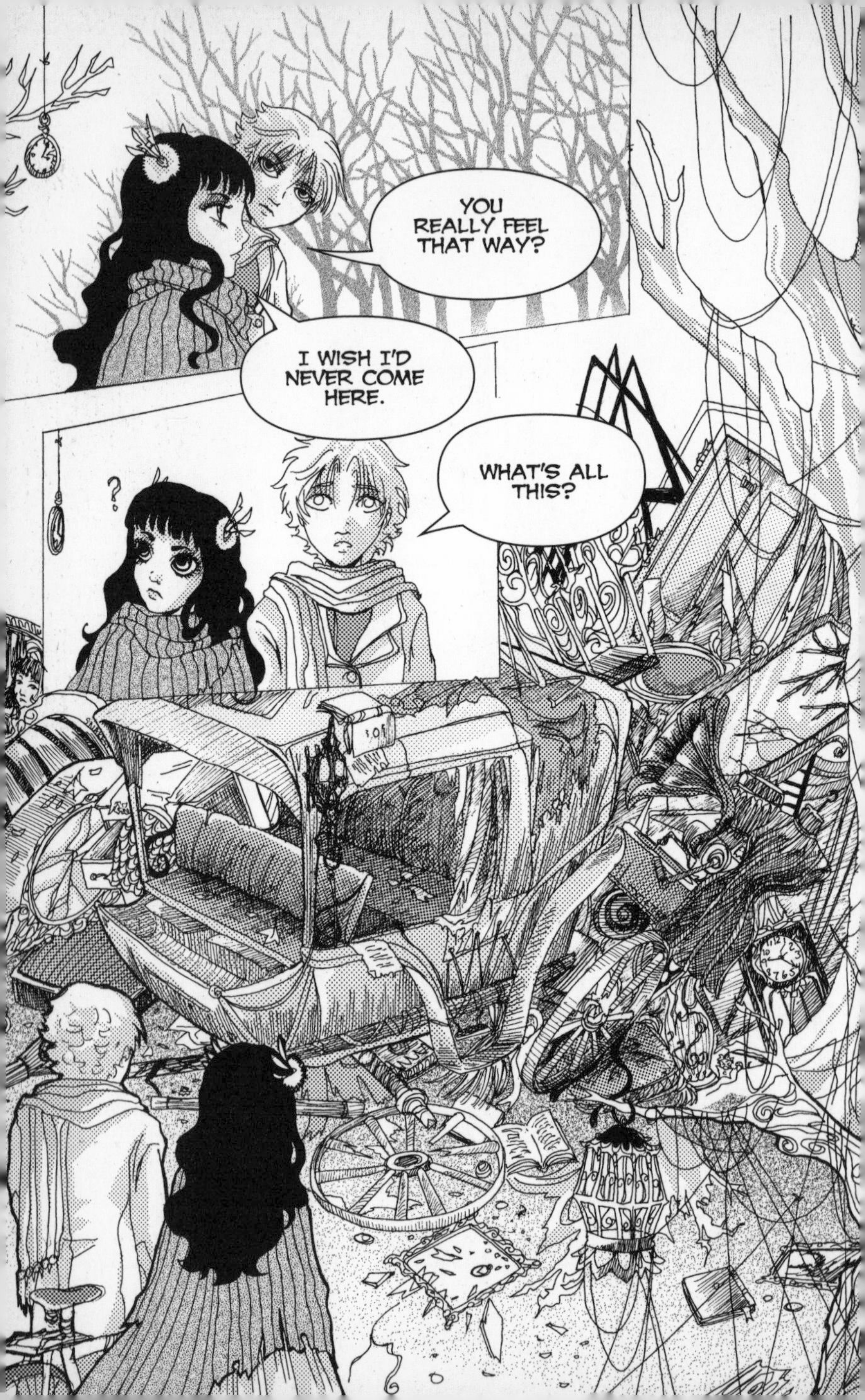
YOU REALLY FEEL THAT WAY?
I WISH I'D NEVER COME HERE.
WHAT'S ALL THIS?
?

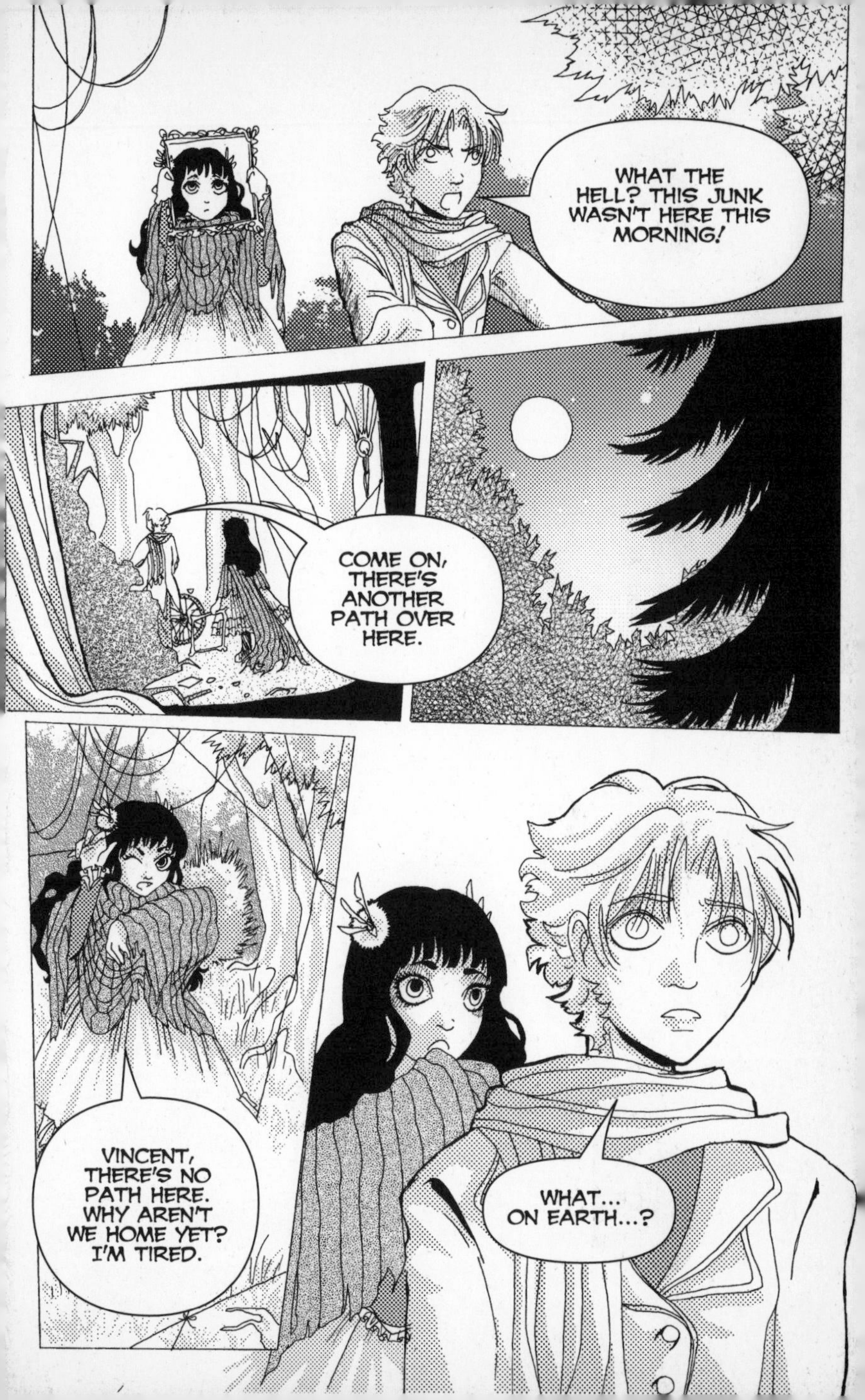
WHAT THE HELL? THIS JUNK WASN'T HERE THIS MORNING!
COME ON, THERE'S ANOTHER PATH OVER HERE.
VINCENT, THERE'S NO PATH HERE. WHY AREN'T WE HOME YET? I'M TIRED.
WHAT... ON EARTH...?

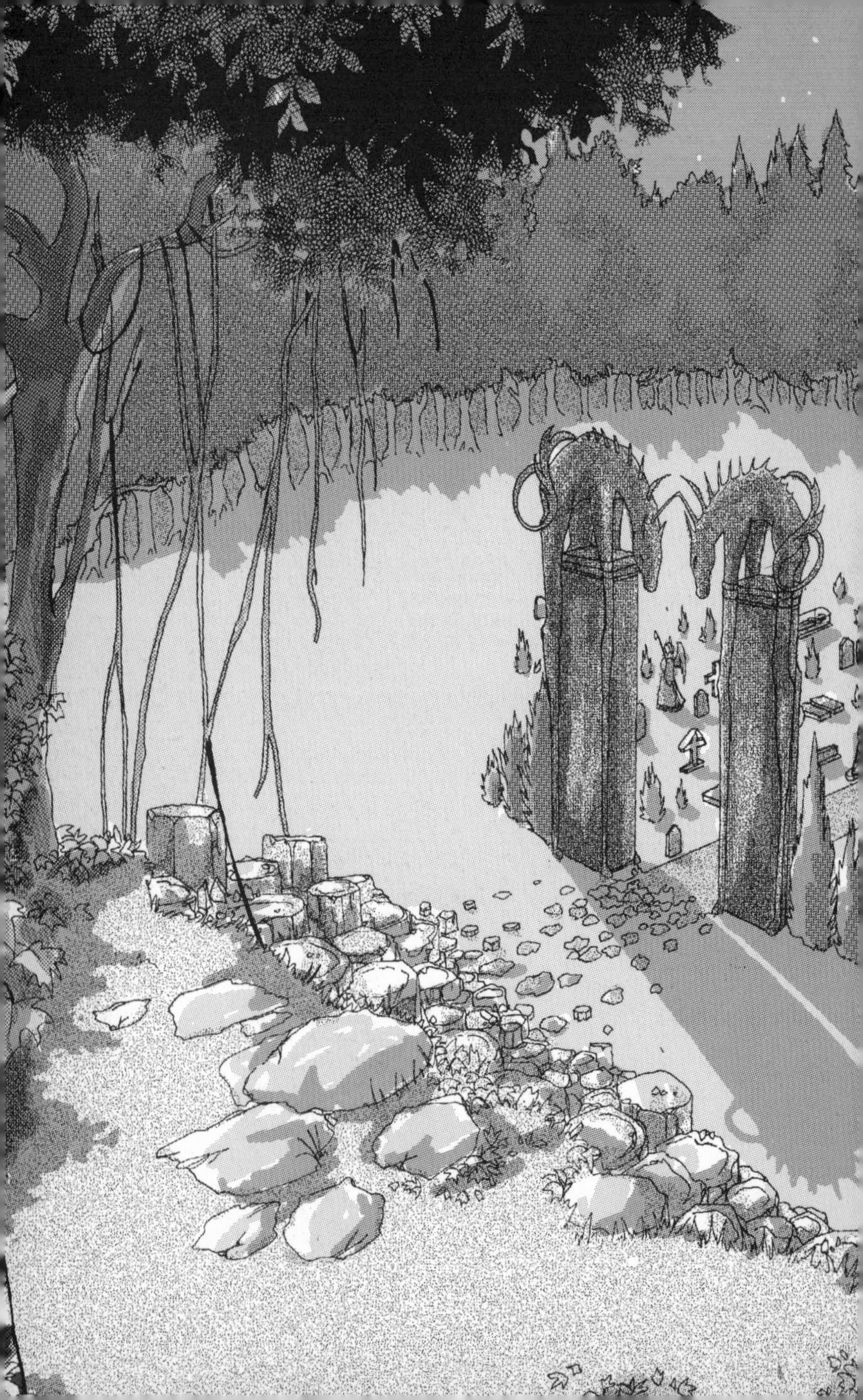

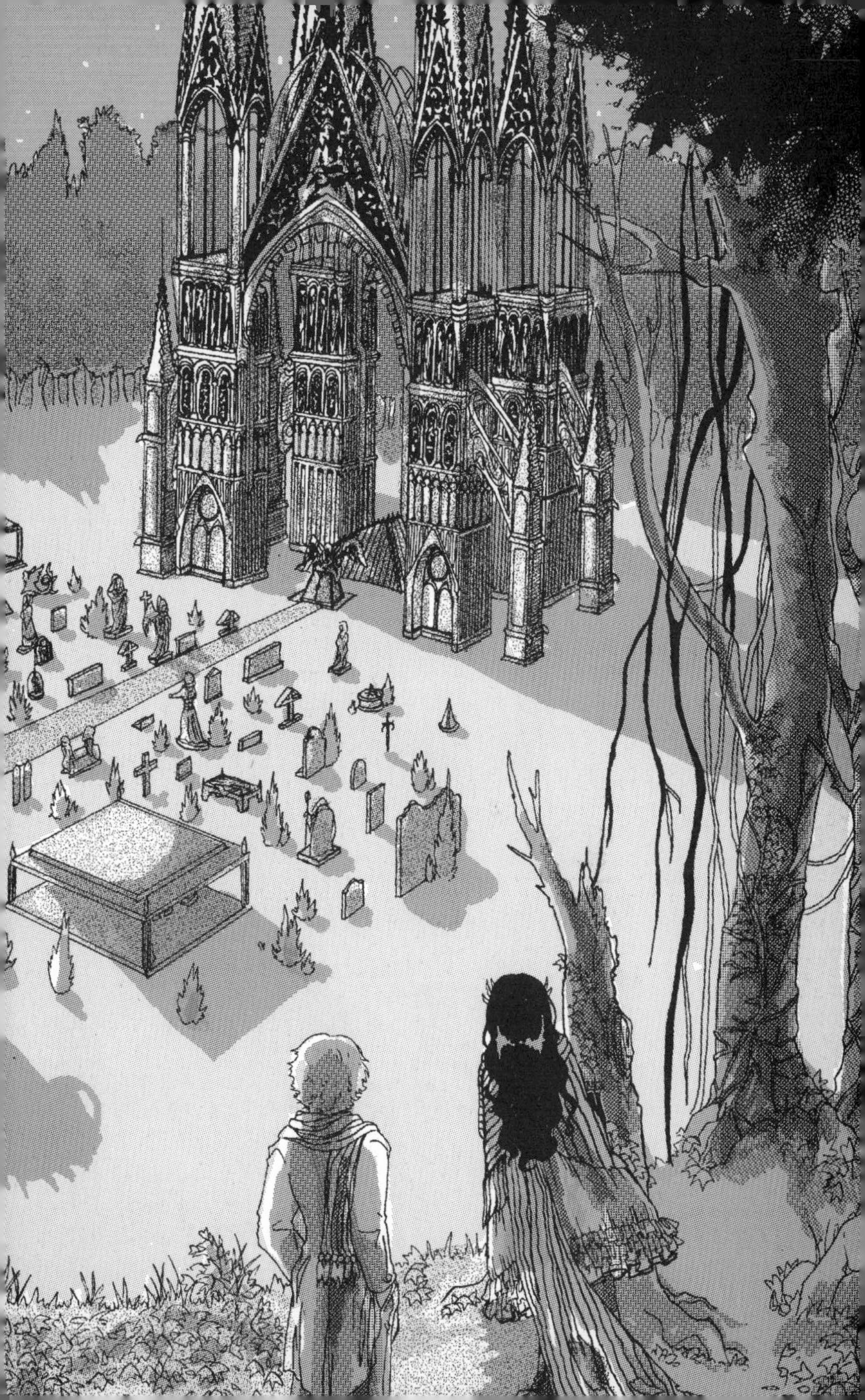

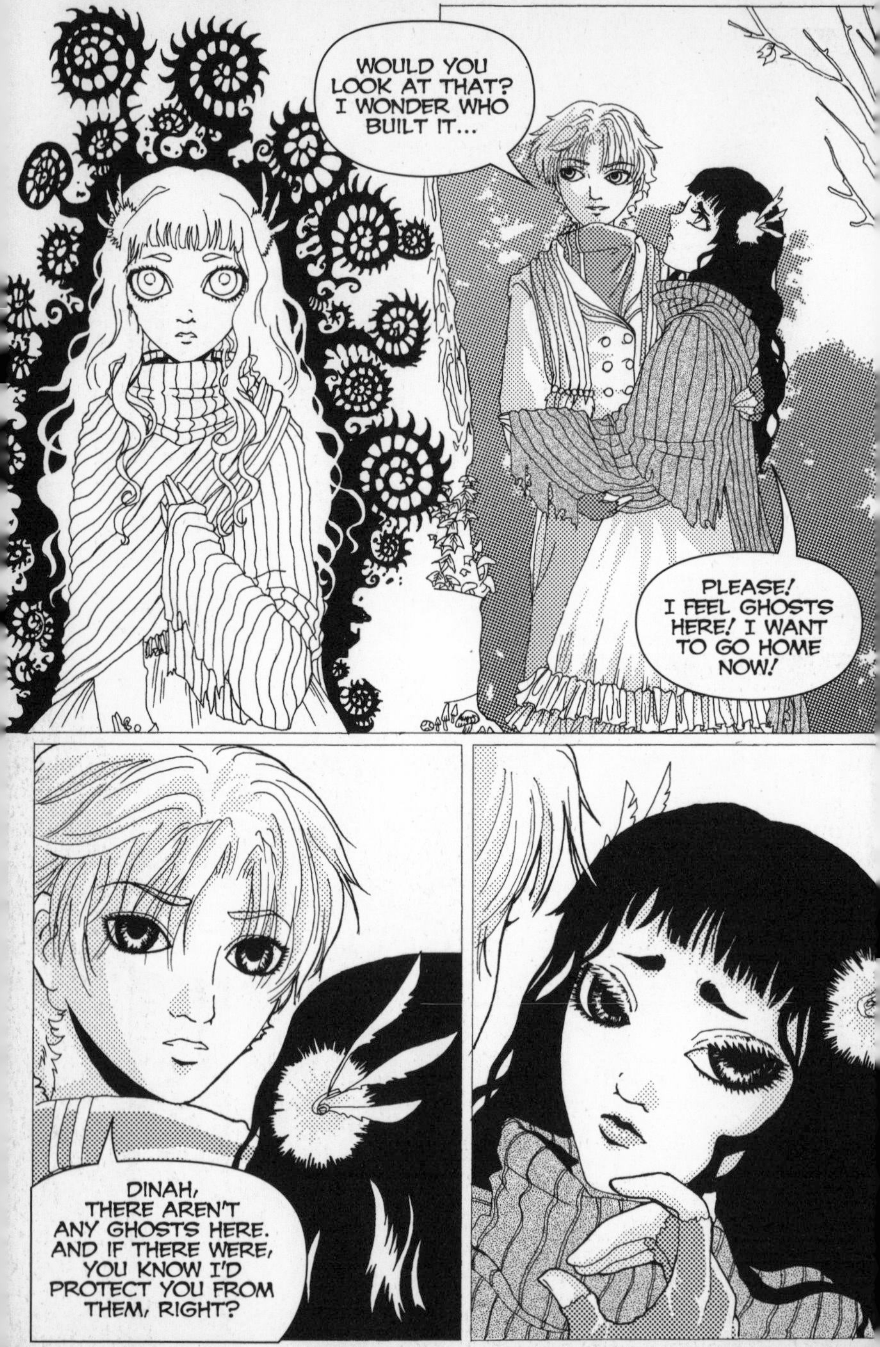
WOULD YOU LOOK AT THAT? I WONDER WHO BUILT IT...
PLEASE! I FEEL GHOSTS HERE! I WANT TO GO HOME NOW!
DINAH, THERE AREN'T ANY GHOSTS HERE. AND IF THERE WERE, YOU KNOW I'D PROTECT YOU FROM THEM, RIGHT?

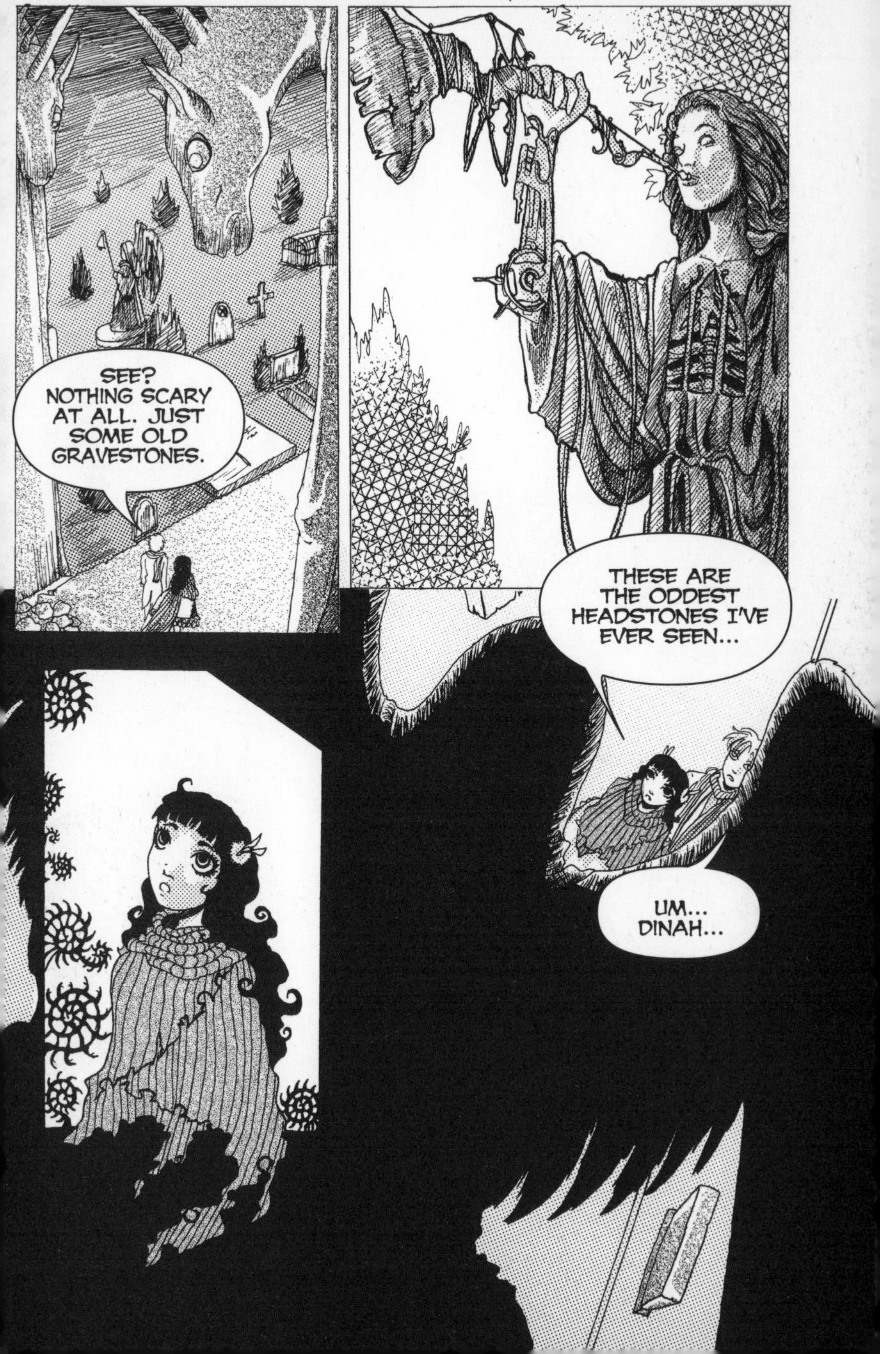
SEE? NOTHING SCARY AT ALL. JUST SOME OLD GRAVESTONES.
THESE ARE THE ODDEST HEADSTONES I'VE EVER SEEN...
UM... DINAH...

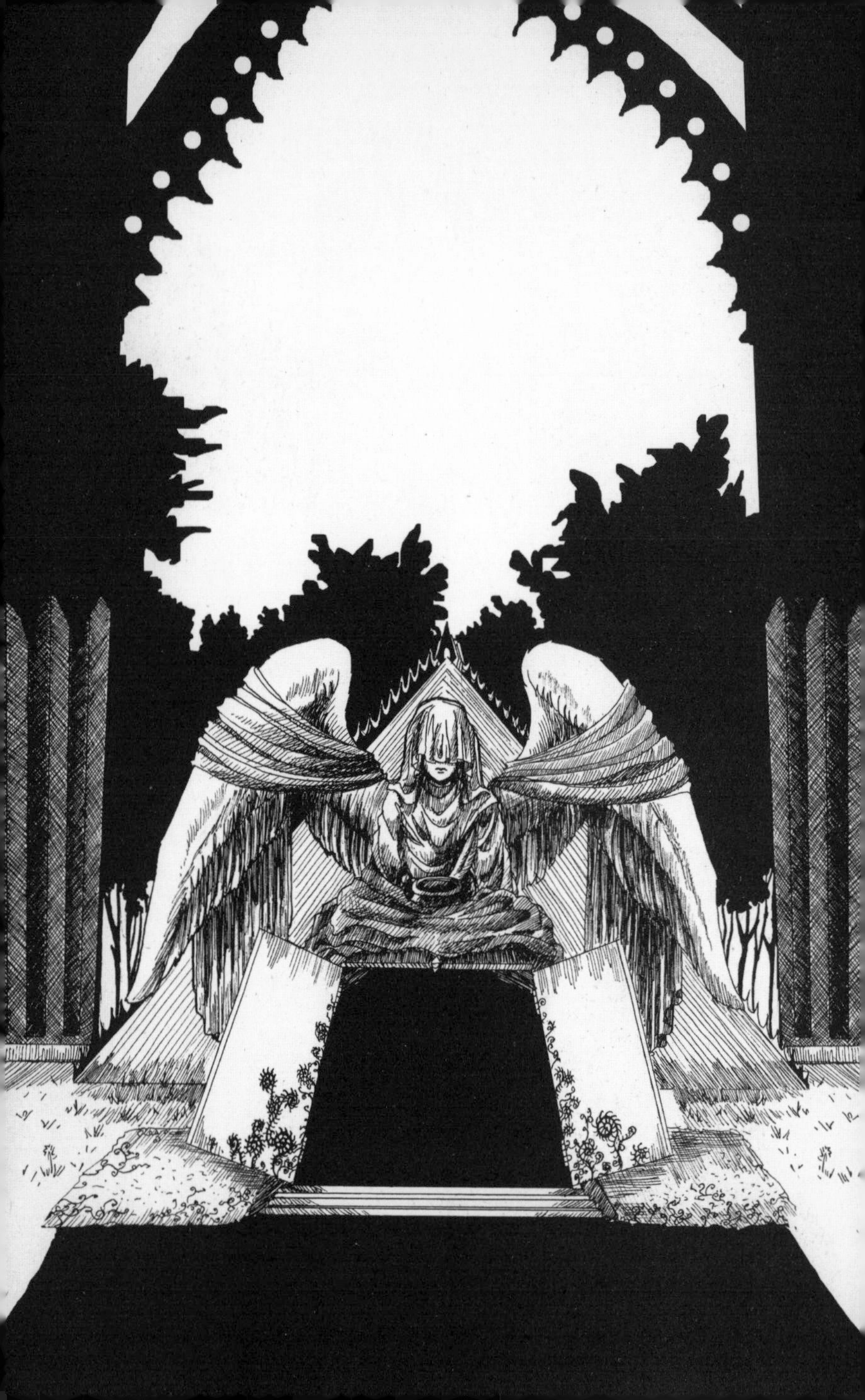

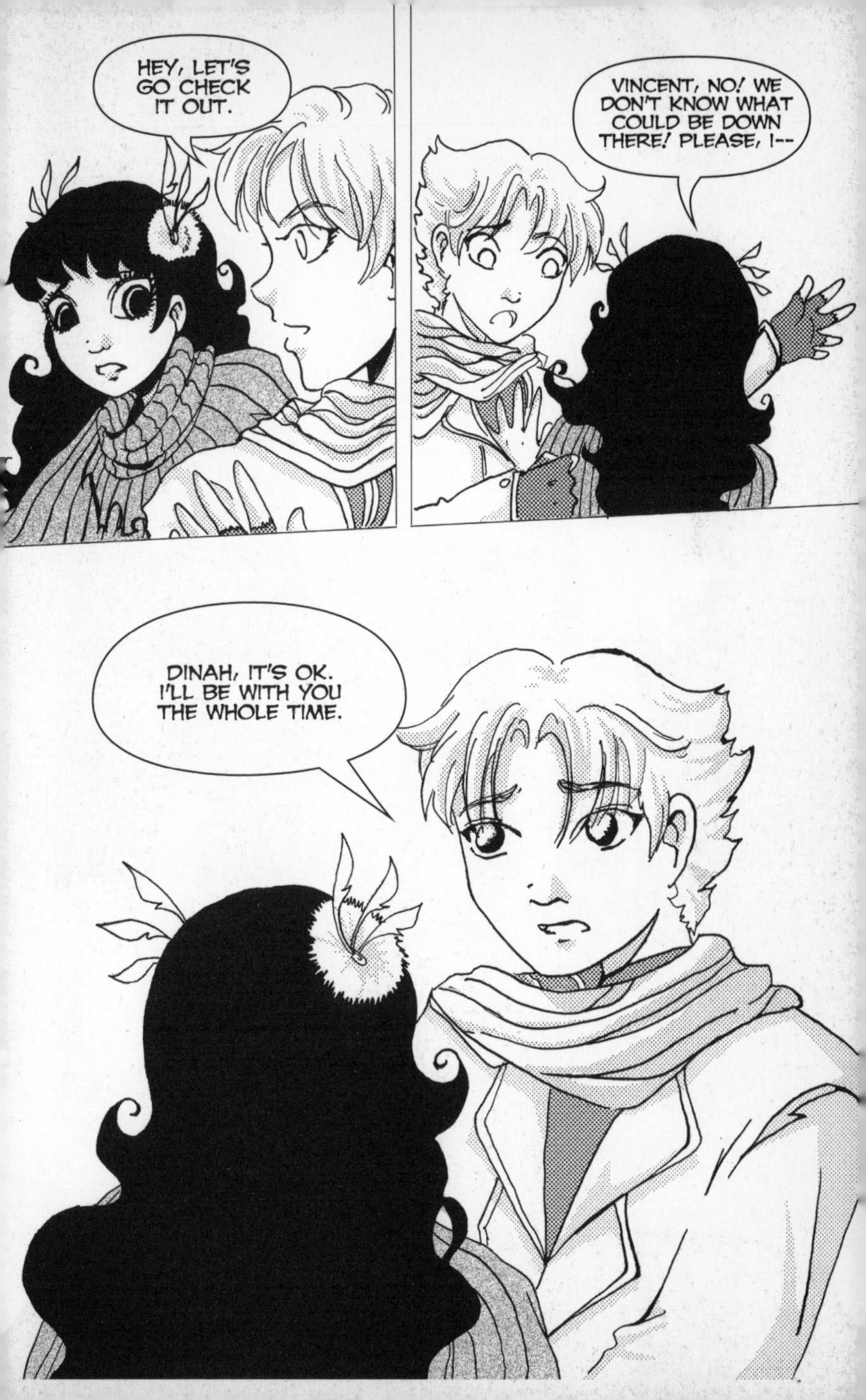
HEY, LET'S GO CHECK IT OUT.
VINCENT, NO! WE DON'T KNOW WHAT COULD BE DOWN THERE! PLEASE, I--
DINAH, IT'S OK. I'LL BE WITH YOU THE WHOLE TIME.

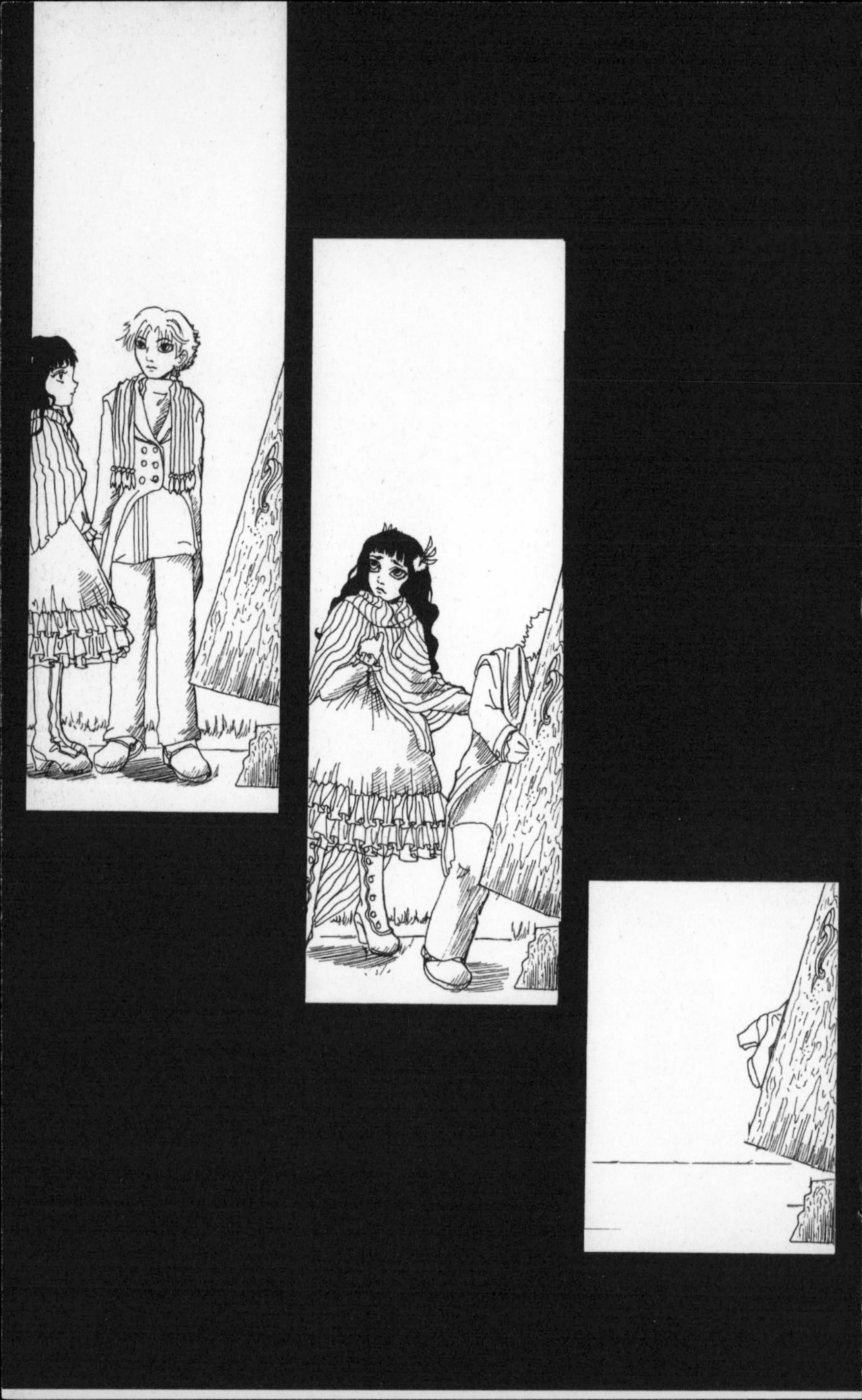

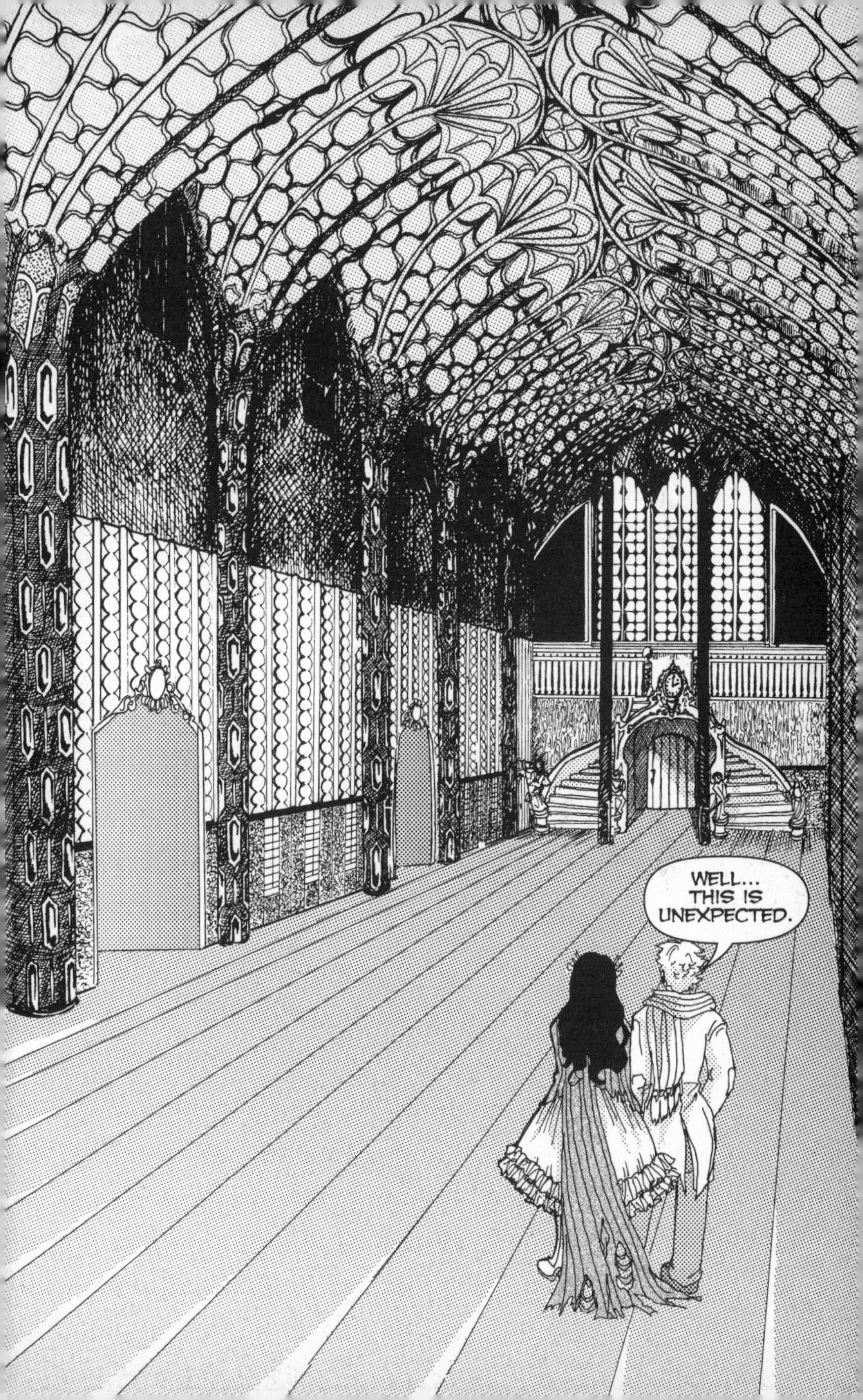
WELL... THIS IS UNEXPECTED.

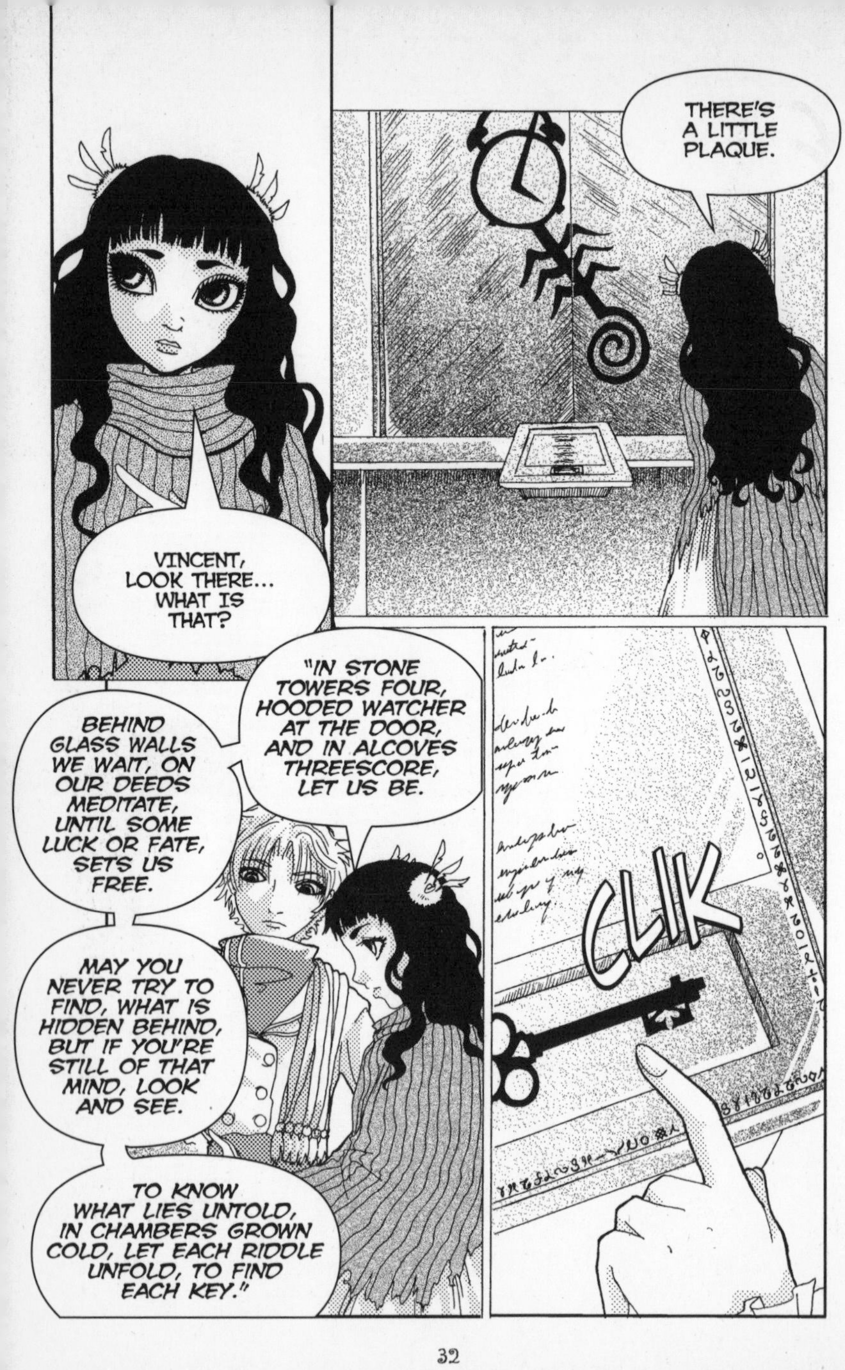
VINCENT, LOOK THERE... WHAT IS THAT?
THERE'S A LITTLE PLAQUE.
"IN STONE TOWERS FOUR, HOODED WATCHER AT THE DOOR, AND IN ALCOVES THREESCORE, LET US BE.
BEHIND GLASS WALLS WE WAIT, ON OUR DEEDS MEDITATE, UNTIL SOME LUCK OR FATE, SETS US FREE.
MAY YOU NEVER TRY TO FIND, WHAT IS HIDDEN BEHIND, BUT IF YOU'RE STILL OF THAT MIND, LOOK AND SEE.
TO KNOW WHAT LIES UNTOLD, IN CHAMBERS GROWN COLD, LET EACH RIDDLE UNFOLD, TO FIND EACH KEY."
CLIK

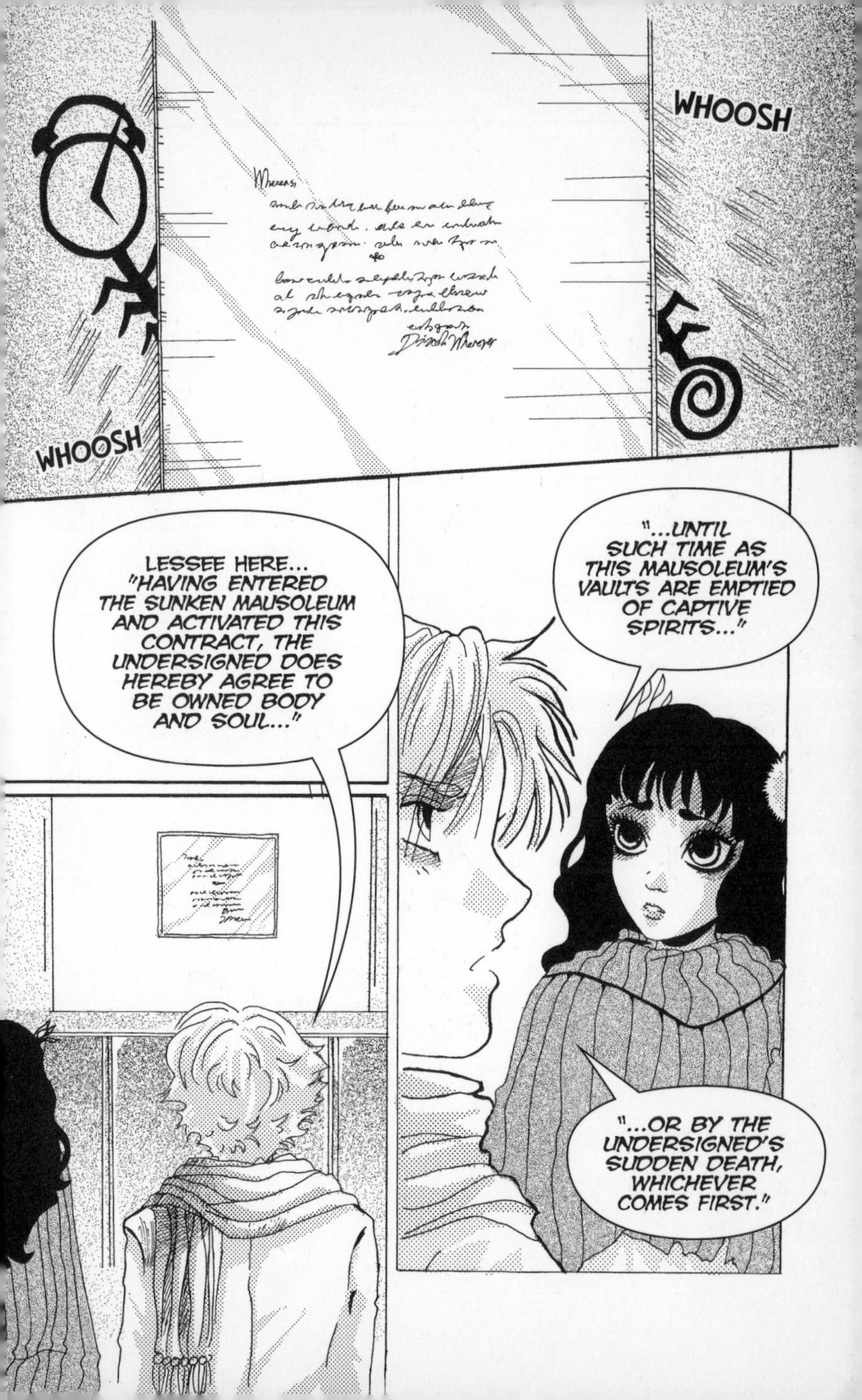
WHOOSH
WHOOSH
LESSEE HERE... "HAVING ENTERED THE SUNKEN MAUSOLEUM AND ACTIVATED THIS CONTRACT, THE UNDERSIGNED DOES HEREBY AGREE TO BE OWNED BODY AND SOUL..."
"...UNTIL SUCH TIME AS THIS MAUSOLEUM'S VAULTS ARE EMPTIED OF CAPTIVE SPIRITS..."
"...OR BY THE UNDERSIGNED'S SUDDEN DEATH, WHICHEVER COMES FIRST."

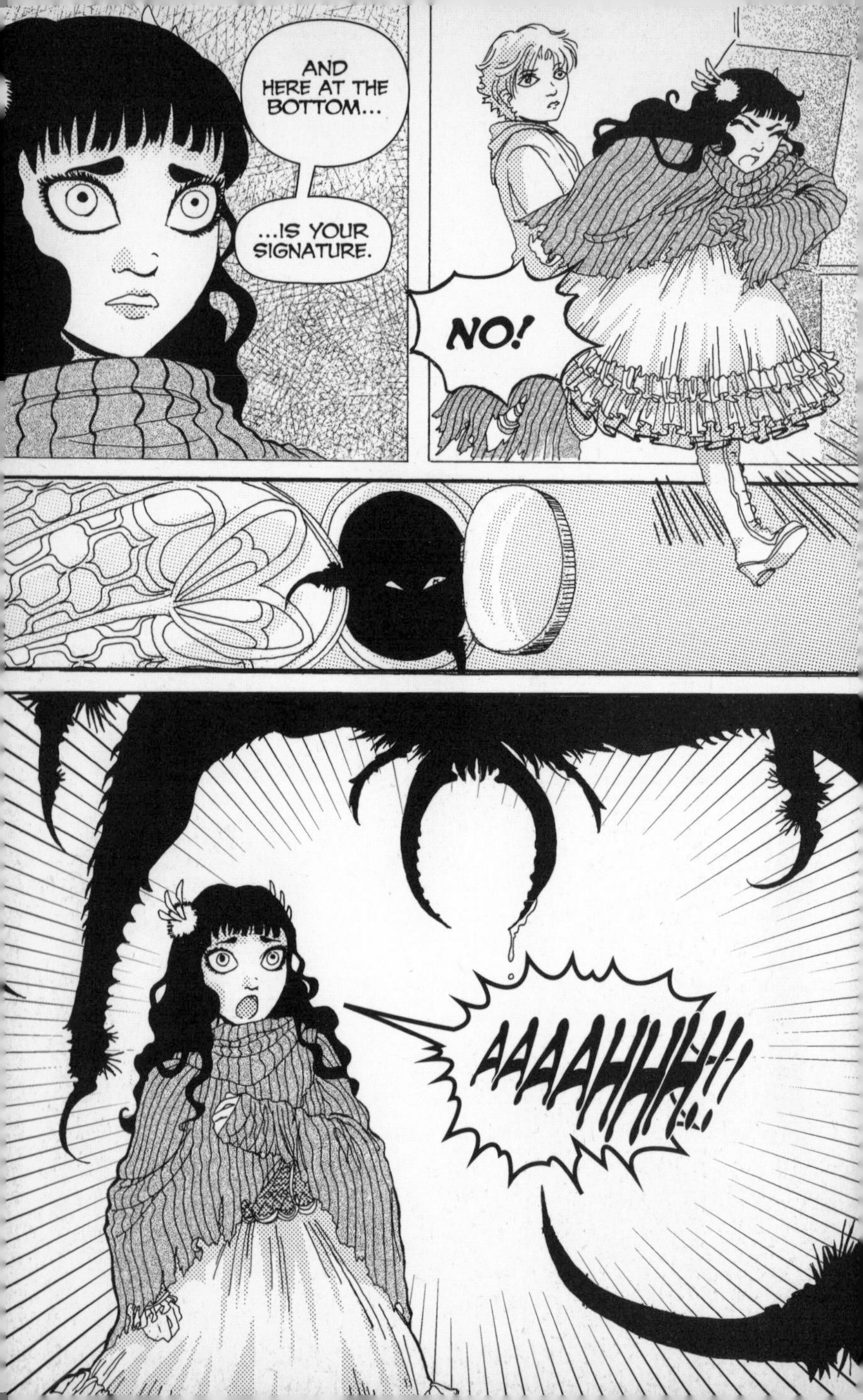
AND HERE AT THE BOTTOM...
...IS YOUR SIGNATURE.
NO!
AAAAHHH!!

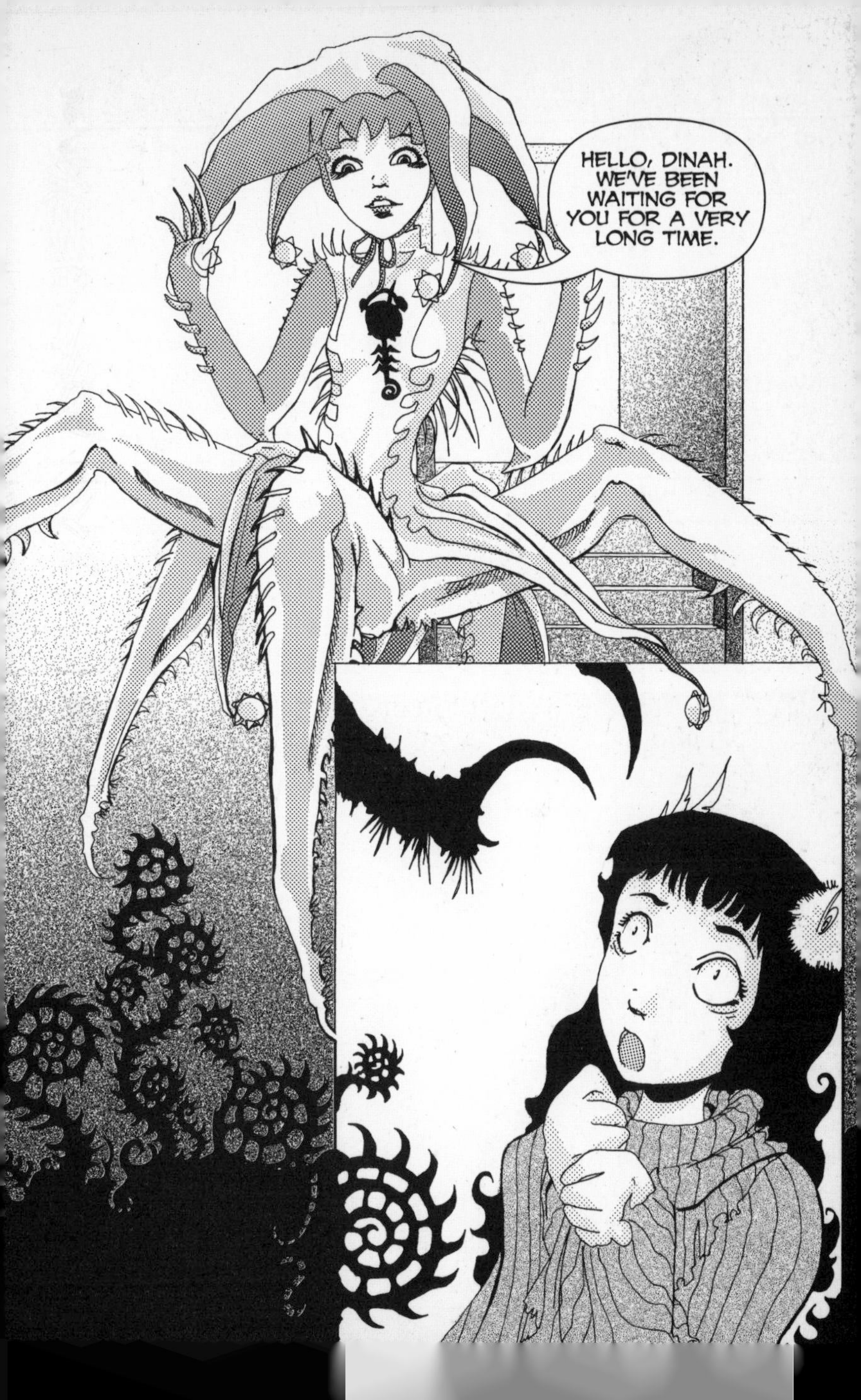
HELLO, DINAH. WE'VE BEEN WAITING FOR YOU FOR A VERY LONG TIME.

'SECOND GRAVEYARD' THEORY STILL DISPUTED

Recent investigation into the town records of Bizenghast (a small mill city outside of Watertown) has left historians stymied, as a large number of death certificates officiated in the town between 1701 and 1950 do not match up to any of the plots in the residential graveyard.

This apparent lack of bodies to match the certificates was for a long time only the concern of local genealogists. Recently however... vistors from the nearby suburbs have begun to take long hiking trips through the woods of Bizenghast on a quest to find what has now become known as Bizenghast's Graveyard, an alleged second cemetery that historians claim must exist, in order to contain the missing bodies. To add to the confusion, many vistors to the antiquated town claim to have found the graveyard in the woods, only to mysteriously lose it again.

"My husband and I were out hiking in the woods when we found this enormous place, right in the middle of a field." Maryann King told the Daily Eagle. "It was like a huge graveyard with really big towers that looked kind of like horses or something. We had no idea anyone was looking for it until we got back to town and asked the manager of the inn about it. We came back later with [sister] Joyce and [brother-in-law] Robert, but we couldn't find it again. We went right to the spot it was in, but it wasn't there. And all the pictures I took came out overexposed."

"I don't want them anyhow," added King. "That place gave me the creeps."

Similar stories have appeared on the Internet, so many that the town of Bizenghast has promised to issue an official statement on its website, advising visitors not to enter the woods without a guide, as sudden cliffs and drop-offs near the coastline represent a risk of injury to inexperienced hikers. Unfortunately for the town, its remote location and unexplained electrical storms have taken the town's official website offline for months.

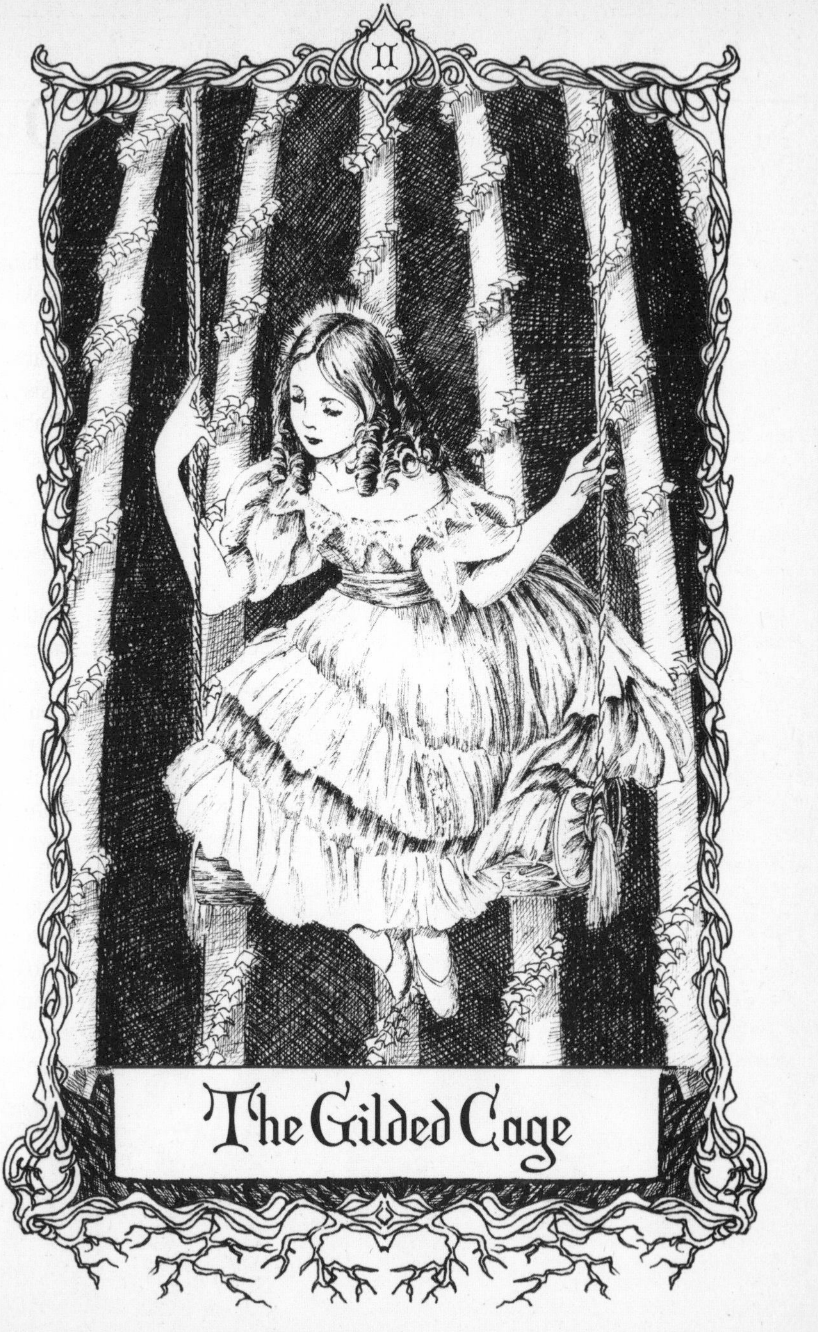
II
The Gilded Cage

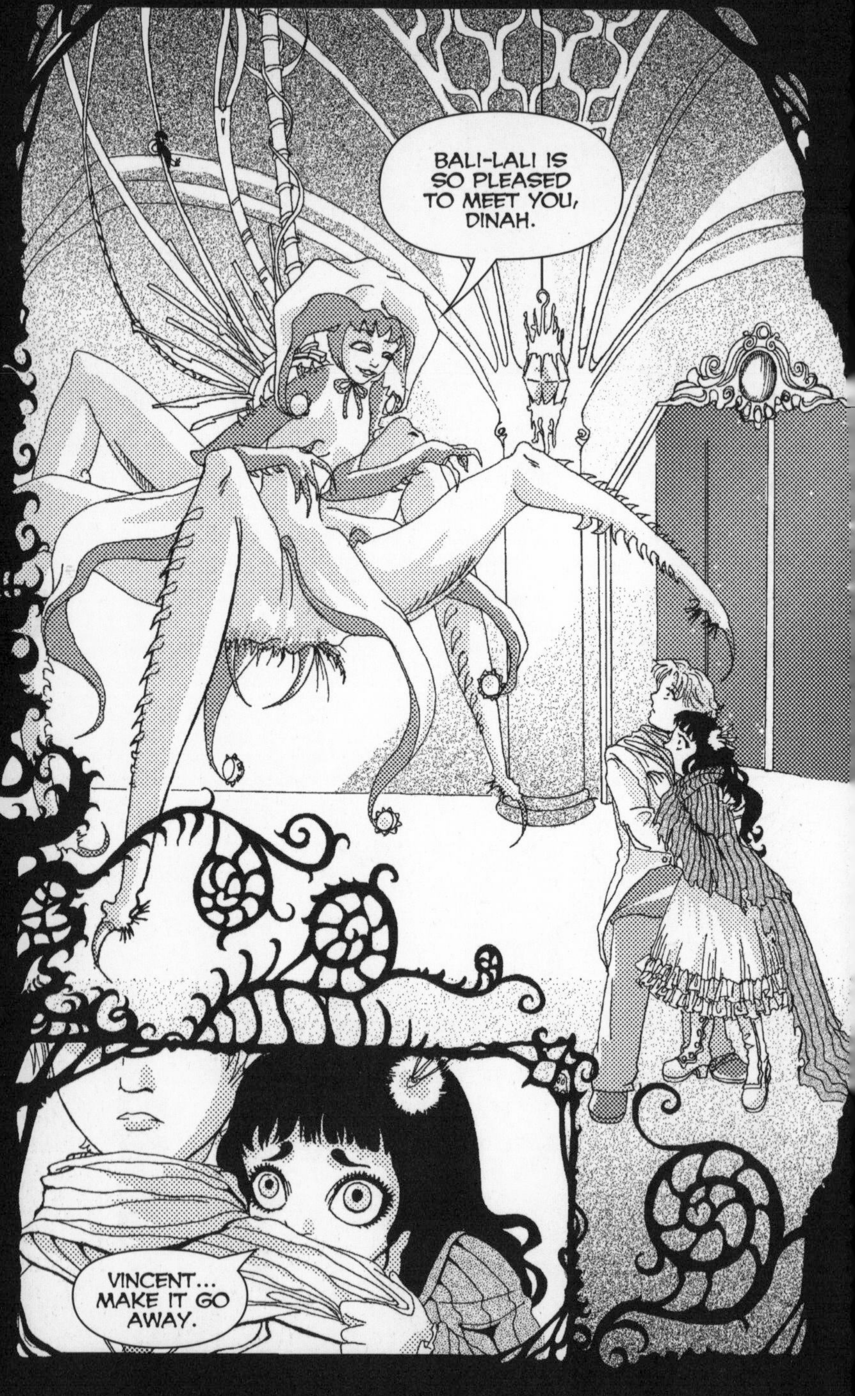
BALI-LALI IS SO PLEASED TO MEET YOU, DINAH.
VINCENT... MAKE IT GO AWAY.

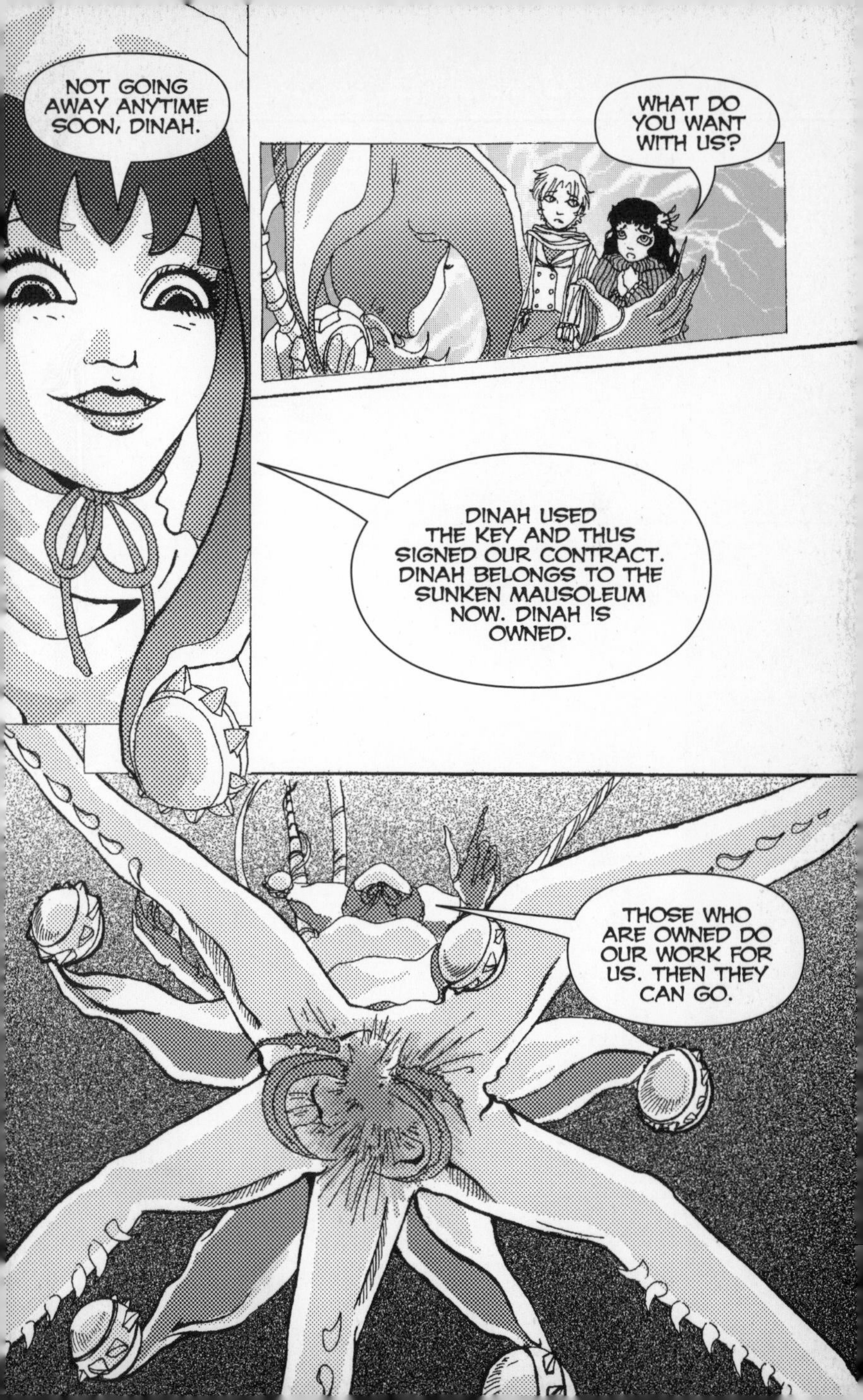
NOT GOING AWAY ANYTIME SOON, DINAH.
WHAT DO YOU WANT WITH US?
DINAH USED THE KEY AND THUS SIGNED OUR CONTRACT. DINAH BELONGS TO THE SUNKEN MAUSOLEUM NOW. DINAH IS OWNED.
THOSE WHO ARE OWNED DO OUR WORK FOR US. THEN THEY CAN GO.

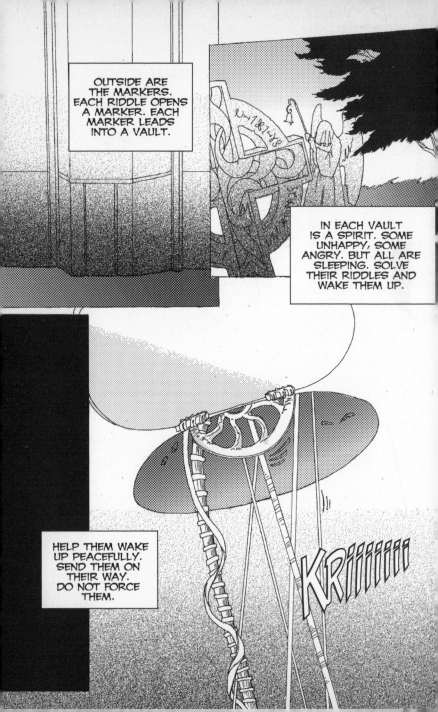

OUTSIDE ARE THE MARKERS. EACH RIDDLE OPENS A MARKER. EACH MARKER LEADS INTO A VAULT.

IN EACH VAULT IS A SPIRIT. SOME UNHAPPY, SOME ANGRY. BUT ALL ARE SLEEPING. SOLVE THEIR RIDDLES AND WAKE THEM UP.

HELP THEM WAKE UP PEACEFULLY. SEND THEM ON THEIR WAY. DO NOT FORCE THEM.

KRiiiiiiii

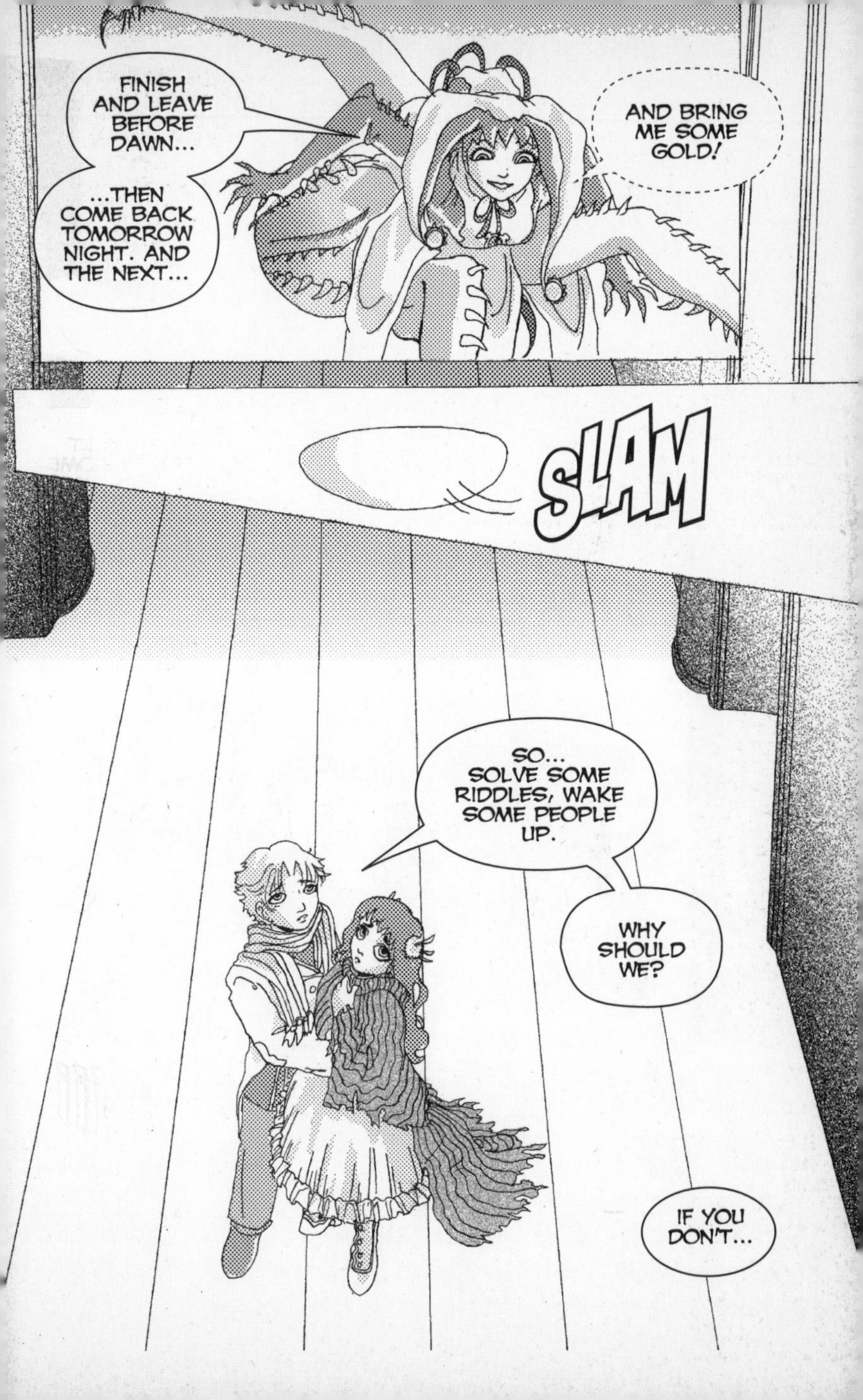
FINISH AND LEAVE BEFORE DAWN...
...THEN COME BACK TOMORROW NIGHT. AND THE NEXT...
AND BRING ME SOME GOLD!
SLAM
SO... SOLVE SOME RIDDLES, WAKE SOME PEOPLE UP.
WHY SHOULD WE?
IF YOU DON'T...

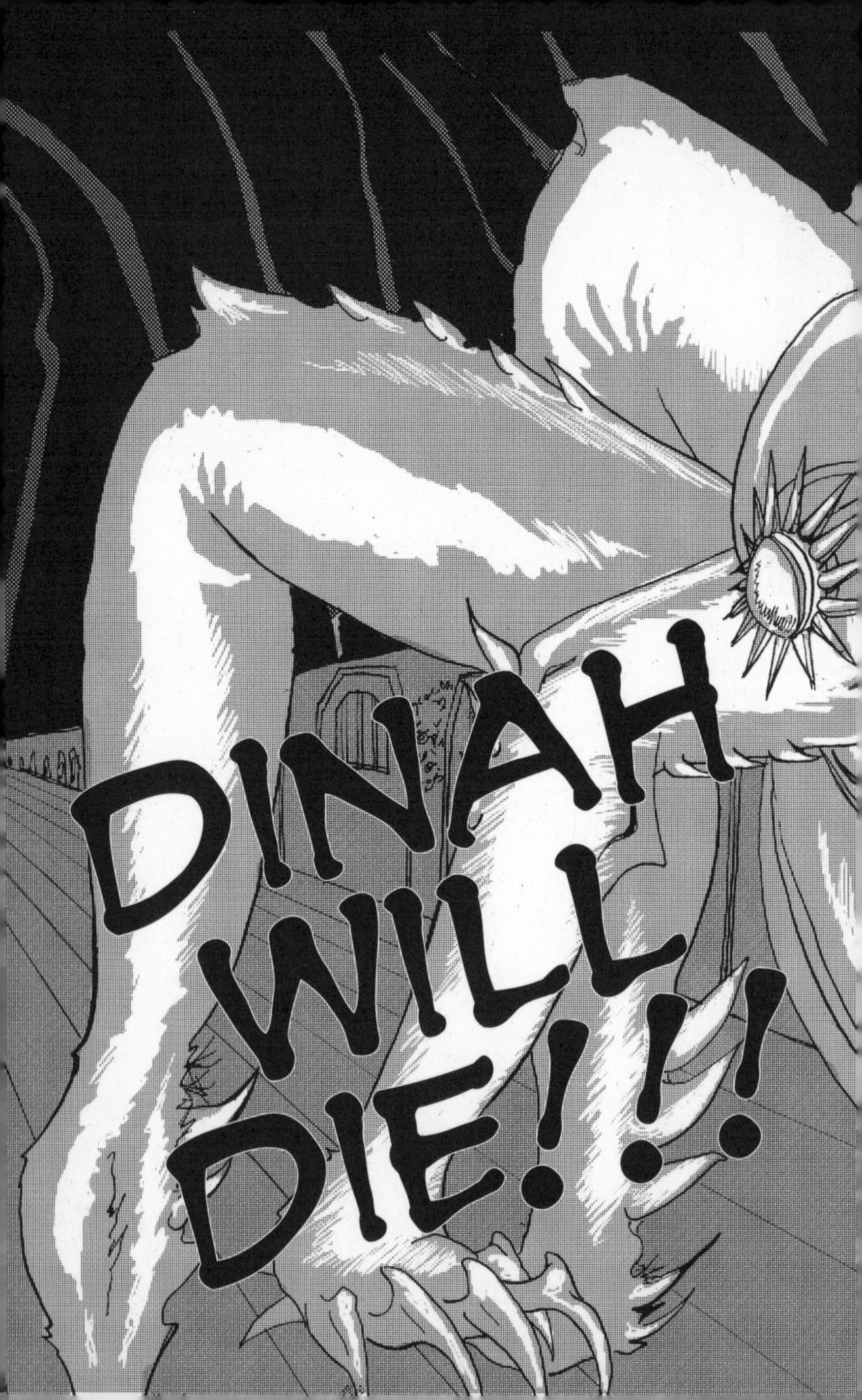
DINAH WILL DIE!!!

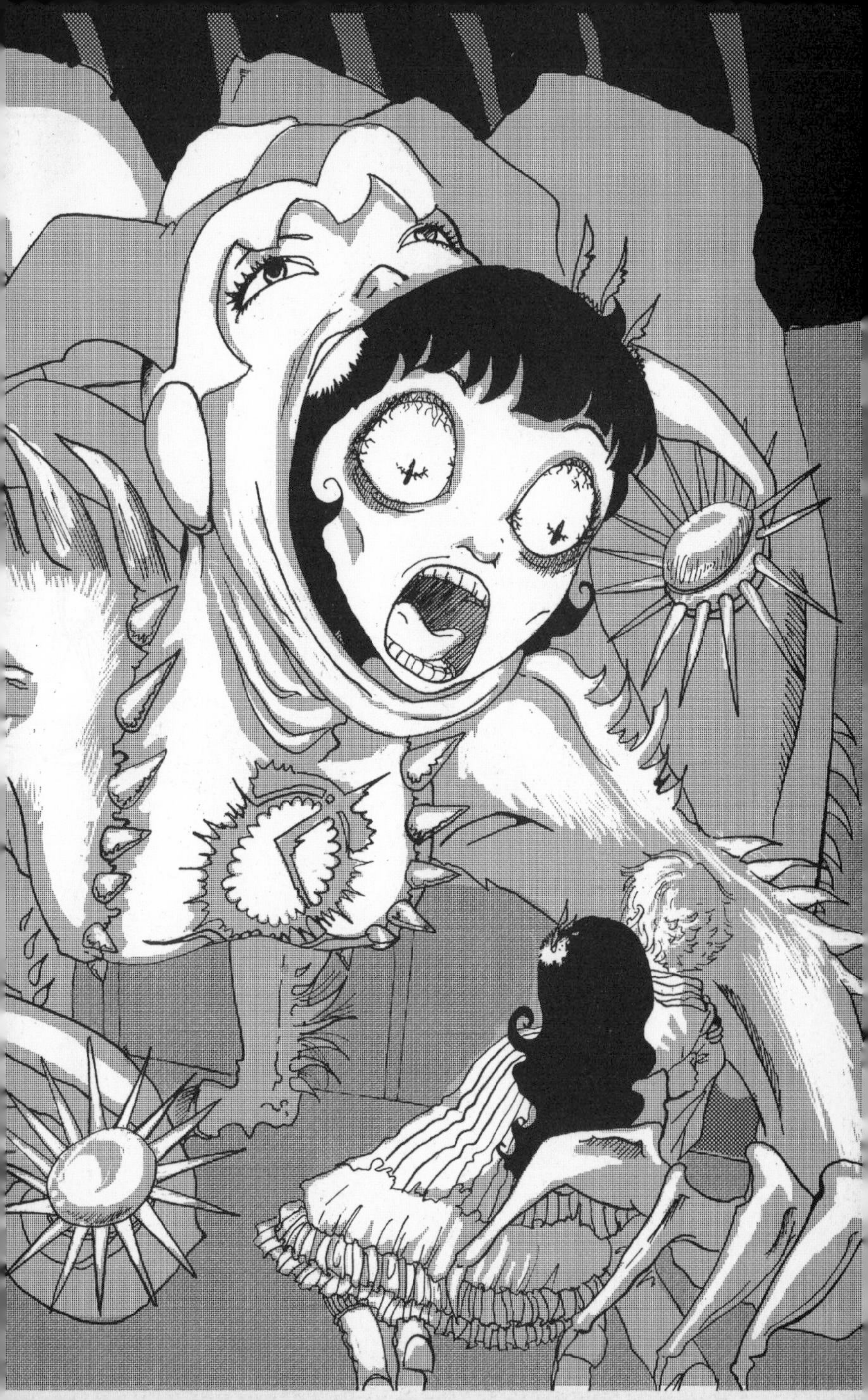

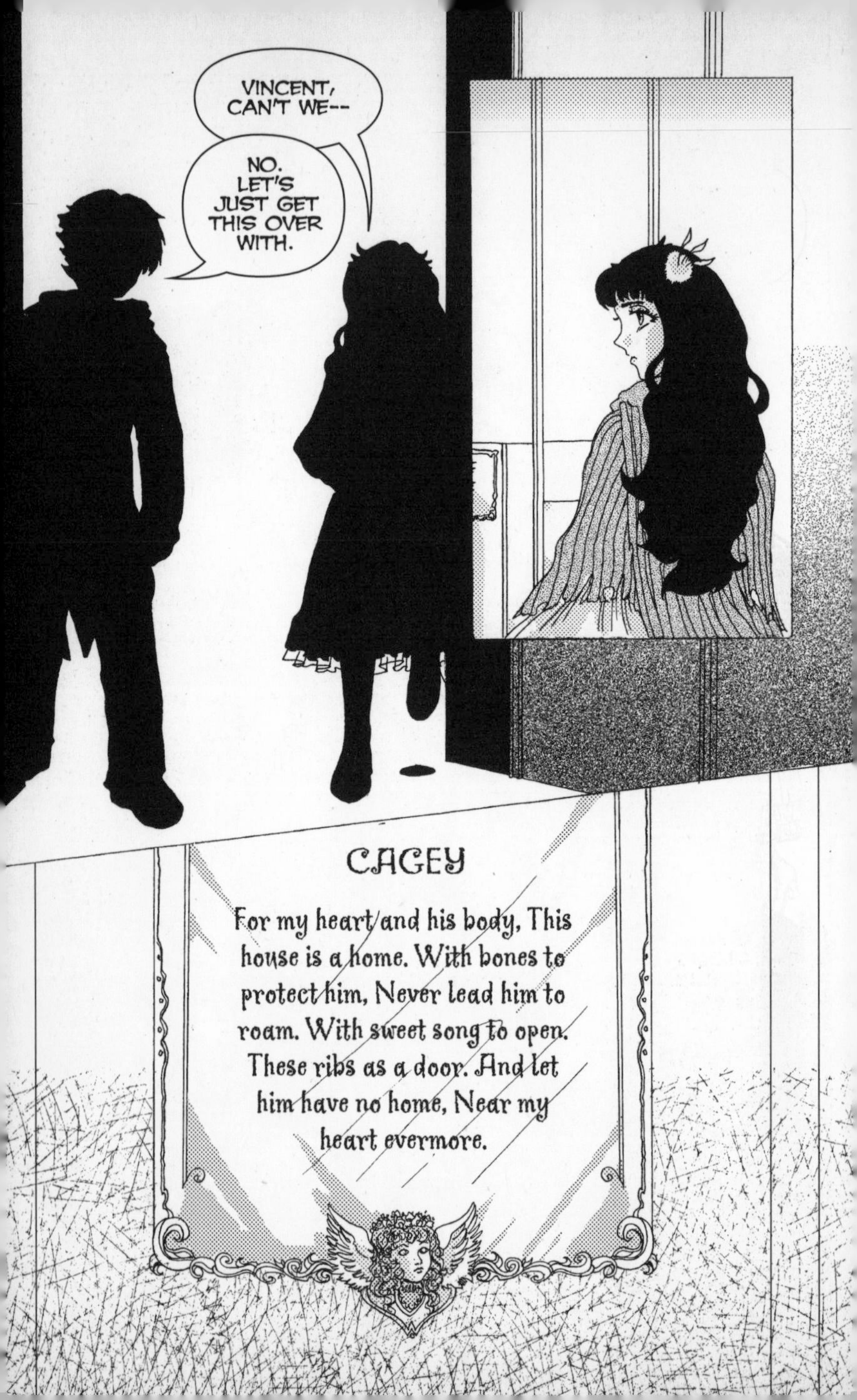
VINCENT, CAN'T WE--
NO. LET'S JUST GET THIS OVER WITH.

CAGEY

For my heart and his body, This house is a home. With bones to protect him, Never lead him to roam. With sweet song to open. These ribs as a door. And let him have no home, Near my heart evermore.

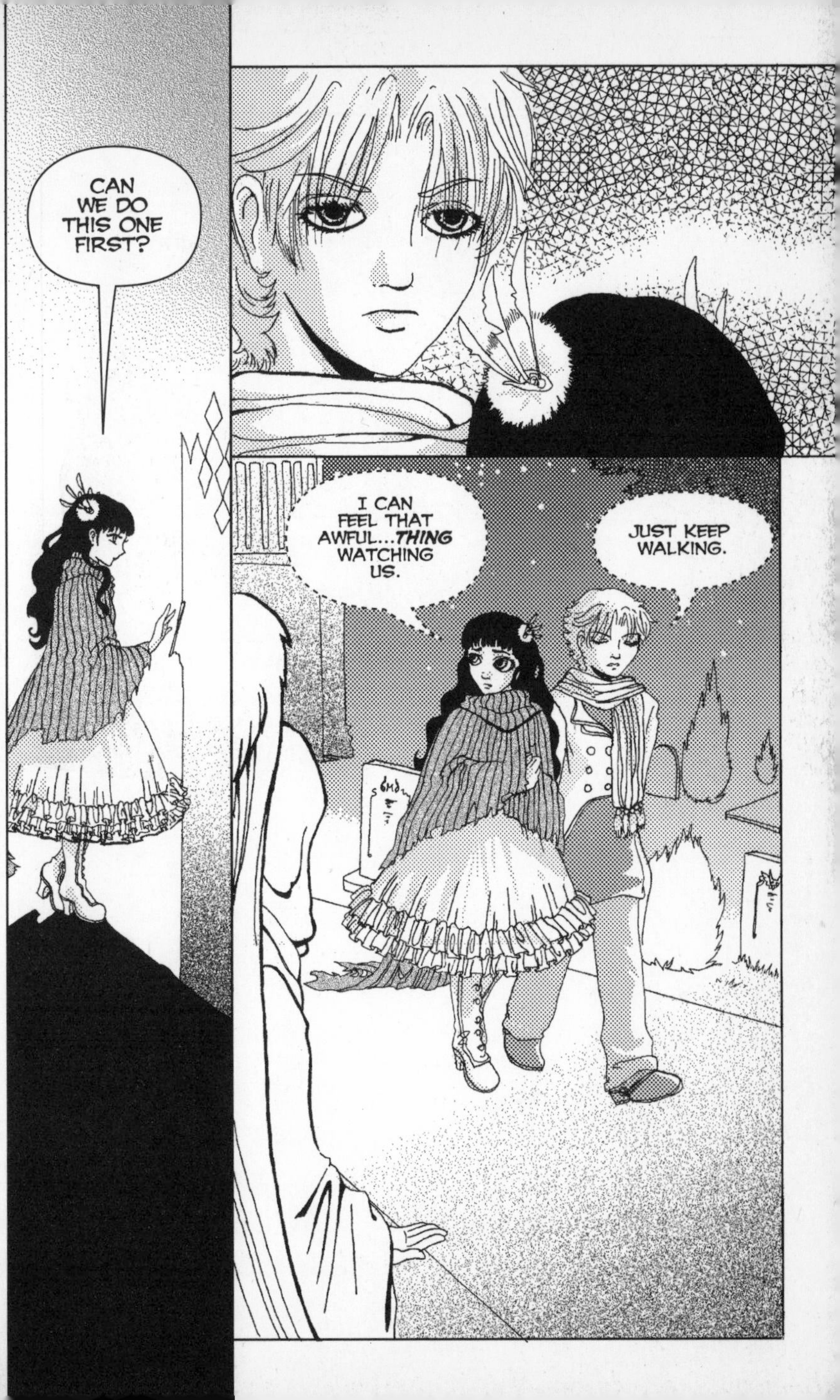
CAN WE DO THIS ONE FIRST?
I CAN FEEL THAT AWFUL...*THING* WATCHING US.
JUST KEEP WALKING.

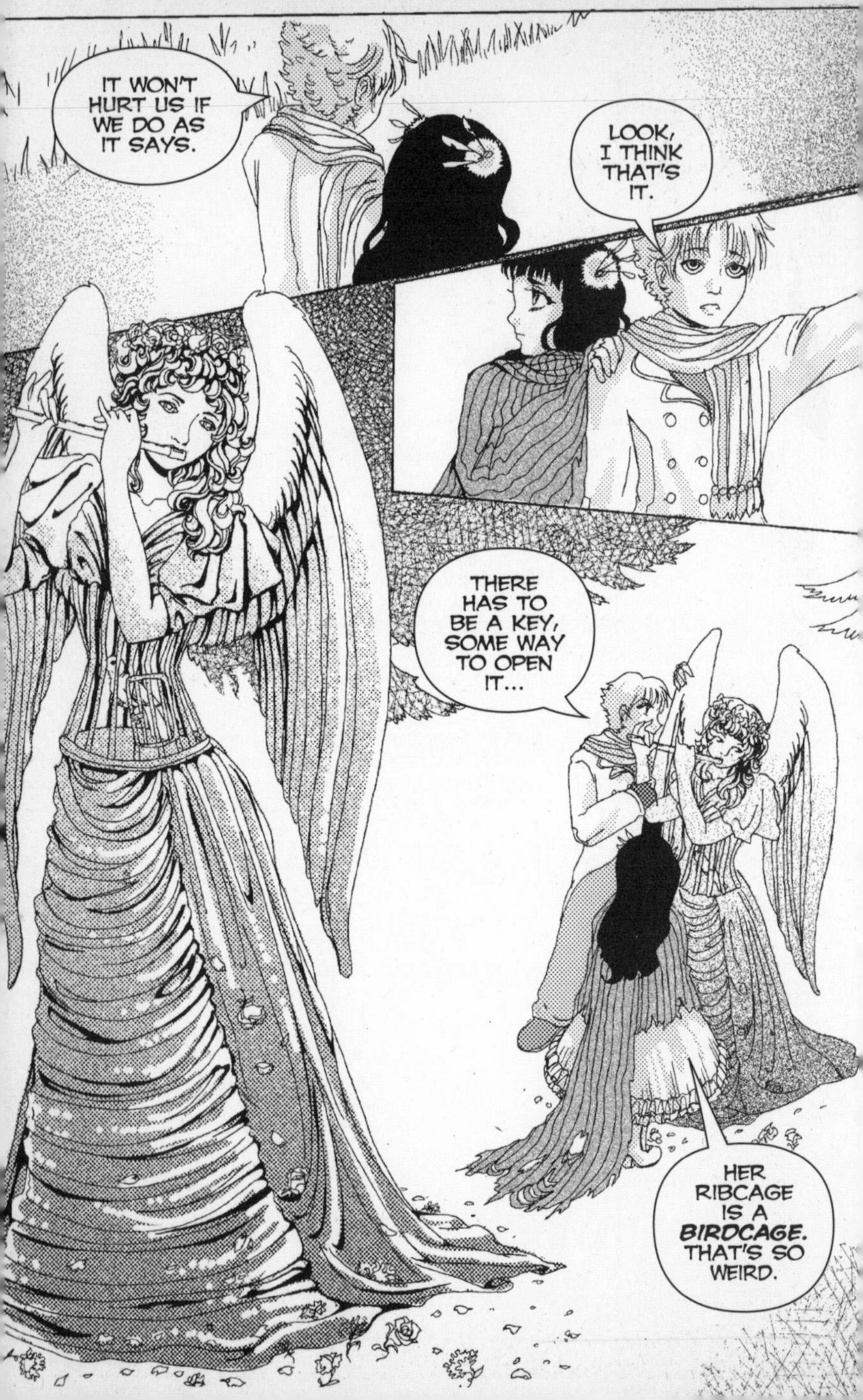
IT WON'T HURT US IF WE DO AS IT SAYS.
LOOK, I THINK THAT'S IT.
HER RIBCAGE IS A *BIRDCAGE.* THAT'S SO WEIRD.
THERE HAS TO BE A KEY, SOME WAY TO OPEN IT...

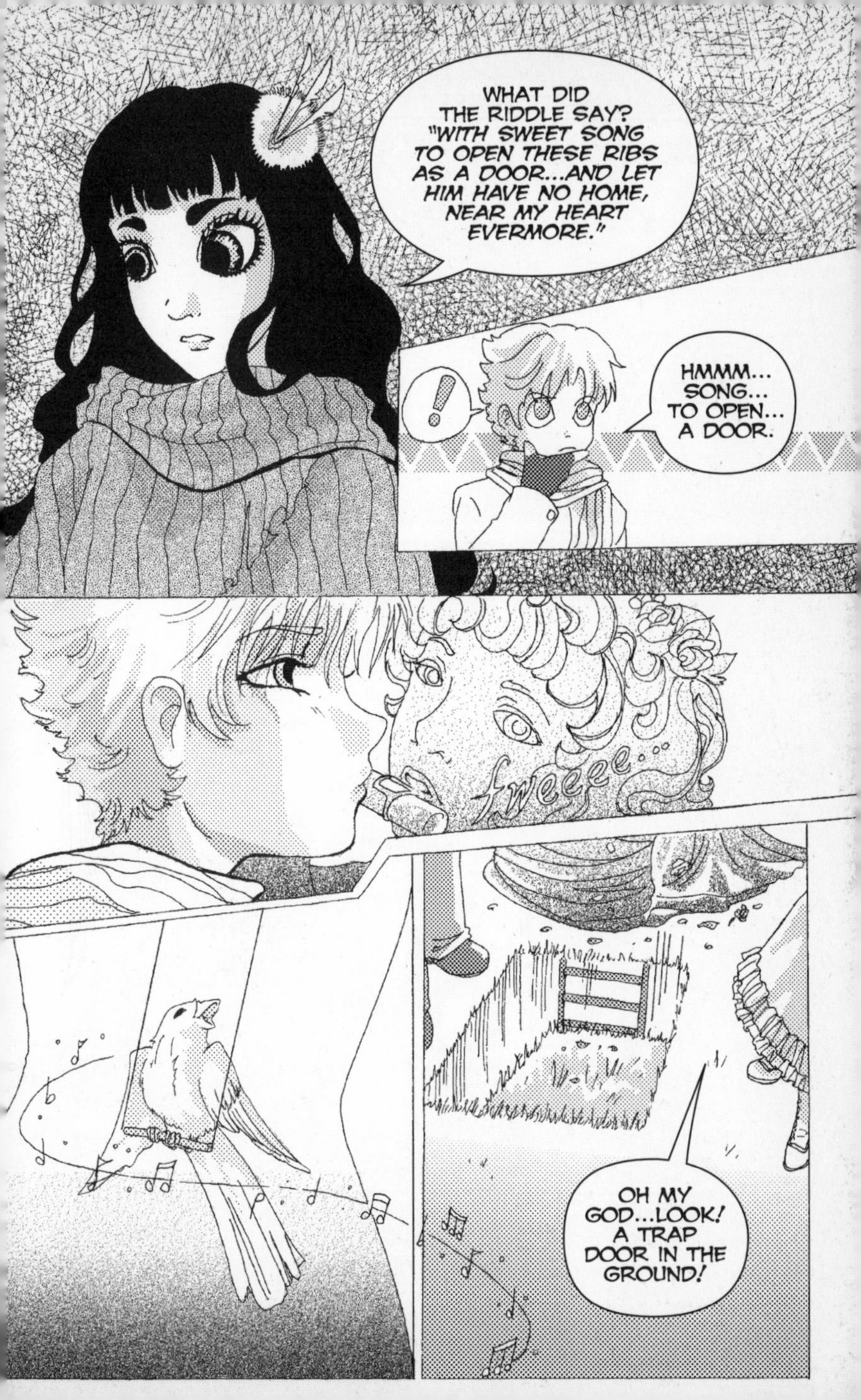
WHAT DID THE RIDDLE SAY? "WITH SWEET SONG TO OPEN THESE RIBS AS A DOOR...AND LET HIM HAVE NO HOME, NEAR MY HEART EVERMORE."
!
HMMM... SONG... TO OPEN... A DOOR.
fweeee...
OH MY GOD...LOOK! A TRAP DOOR IN THE GROUND!

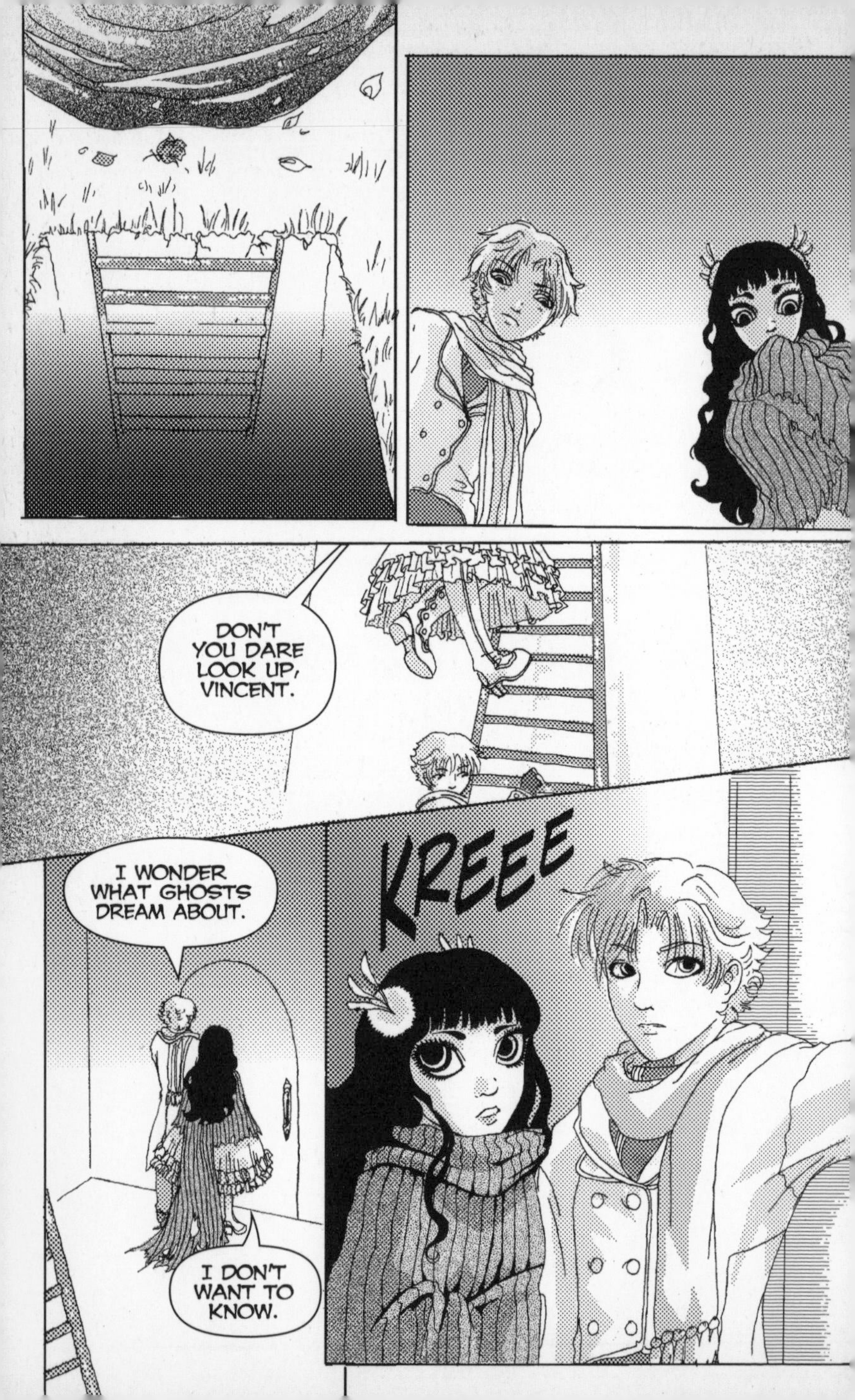
DON'T YOU DARE LOOK UP, VINCENT.
I WONDER WHAT GHOSTS DREAM ABOUT.
I DON'T WANT TO KNOW.
KREEE

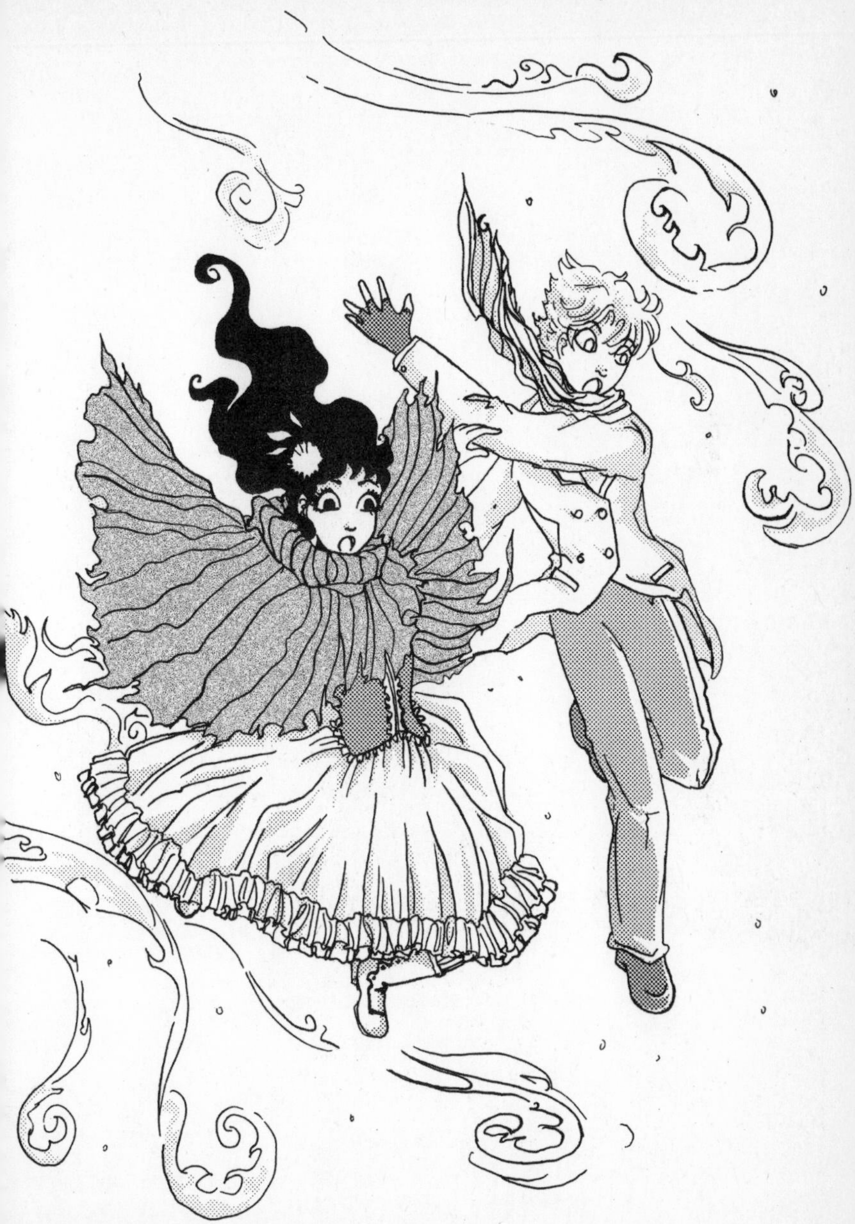

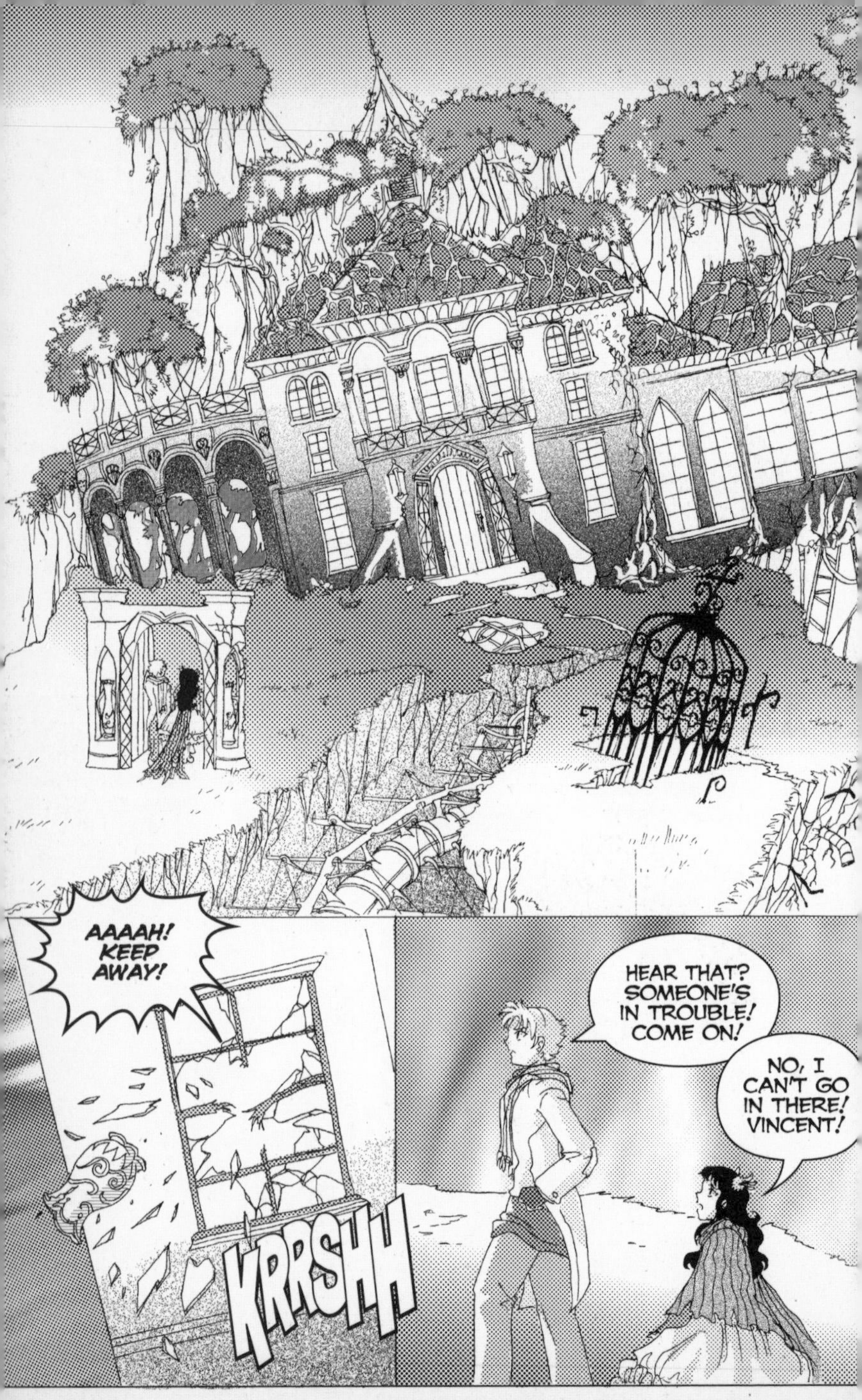
HEAR THAT? SOMEONE'S IN TROUBLE! COME ON!
NO, I CAN'T GO IN THERE! VINCENT!
AAAAH! KEEP AWAY!
KRRSHH

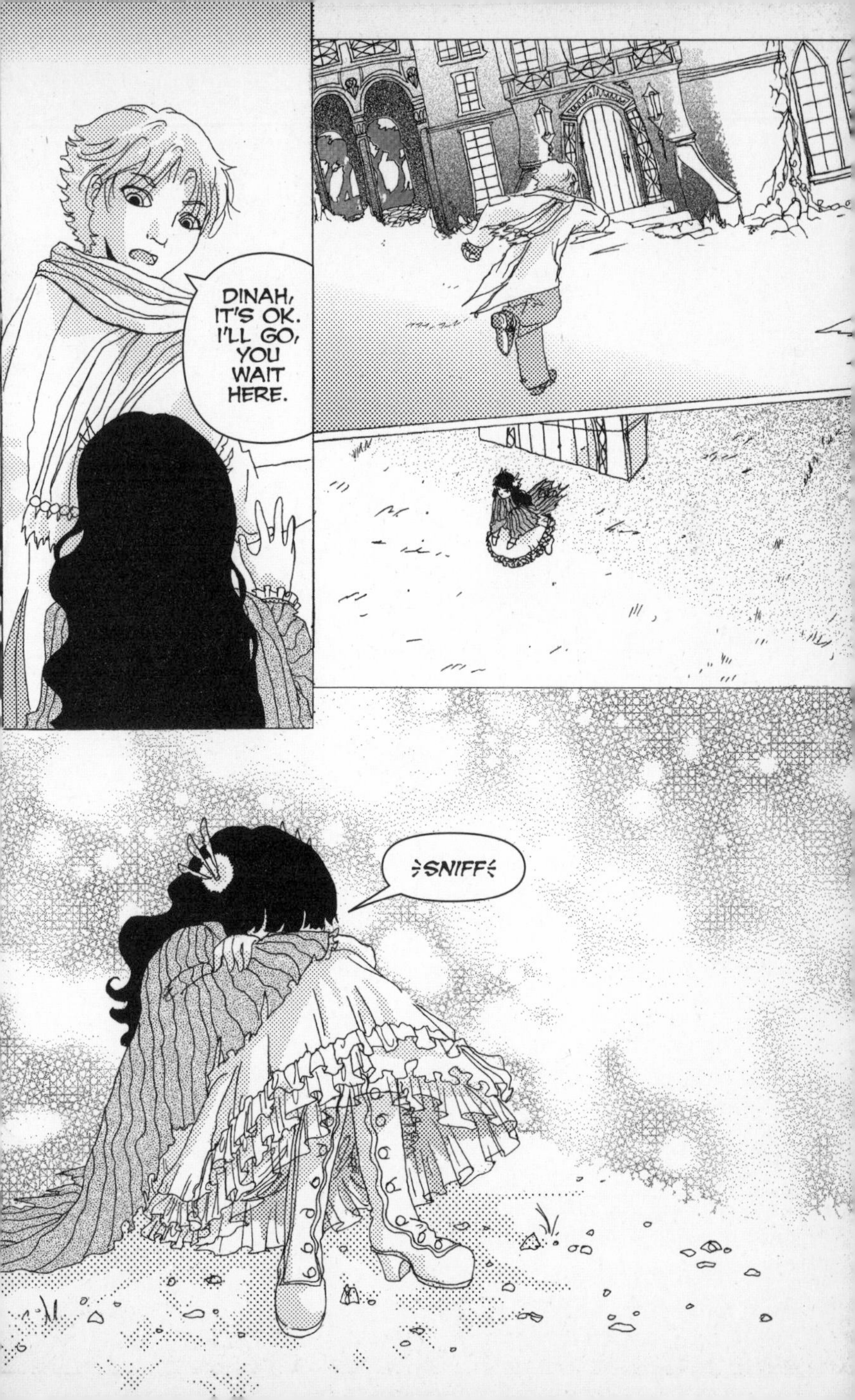
DINAH, IT'S OK. I'LL GO, YOU WAIT HERE.
SNIFF

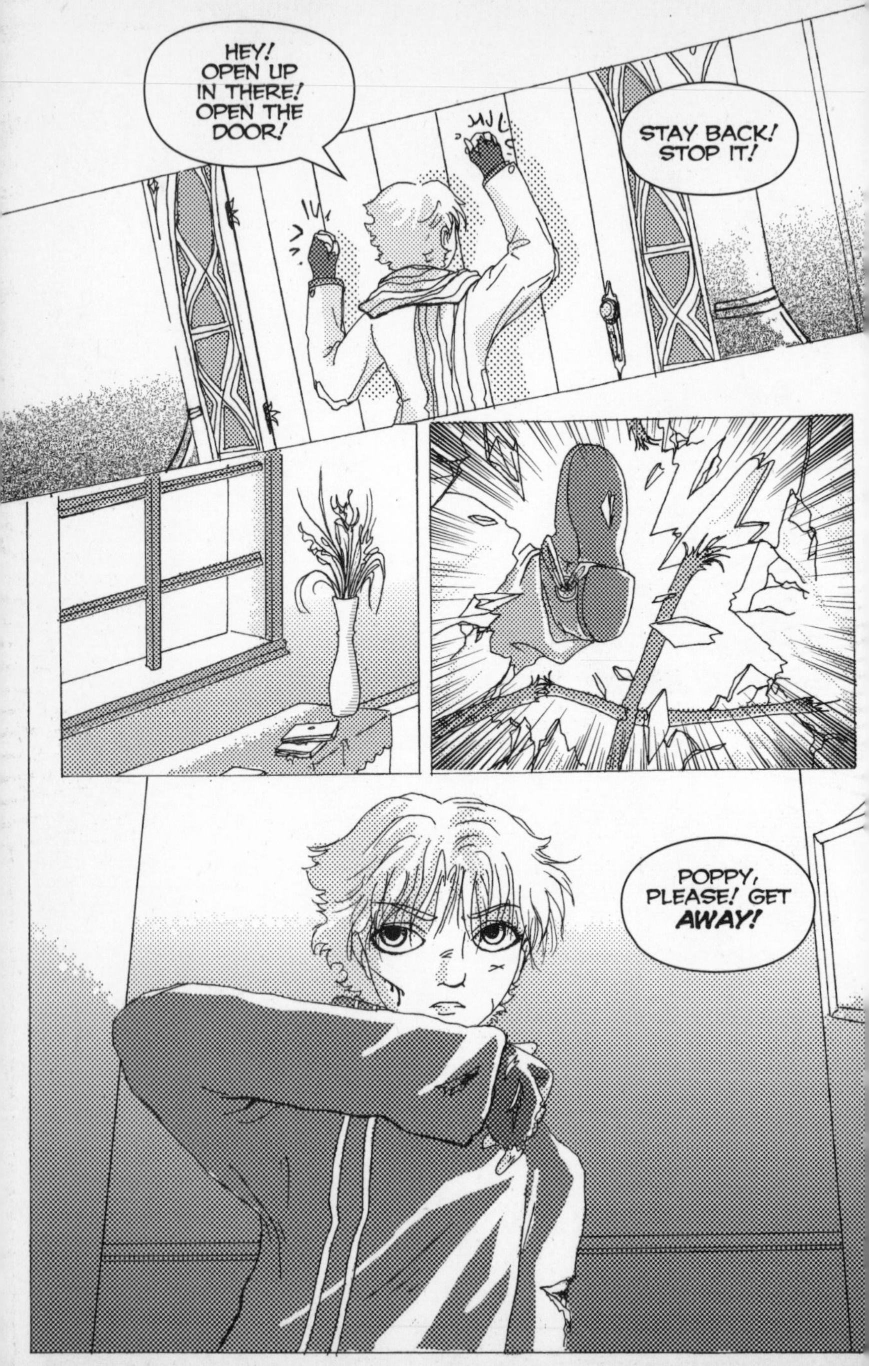
HEY! OPEN UP IN THERE! OPEN THE DOOR!
STAY BACK! STOP IT!
POPPY, PLEASE! GET AWAY!

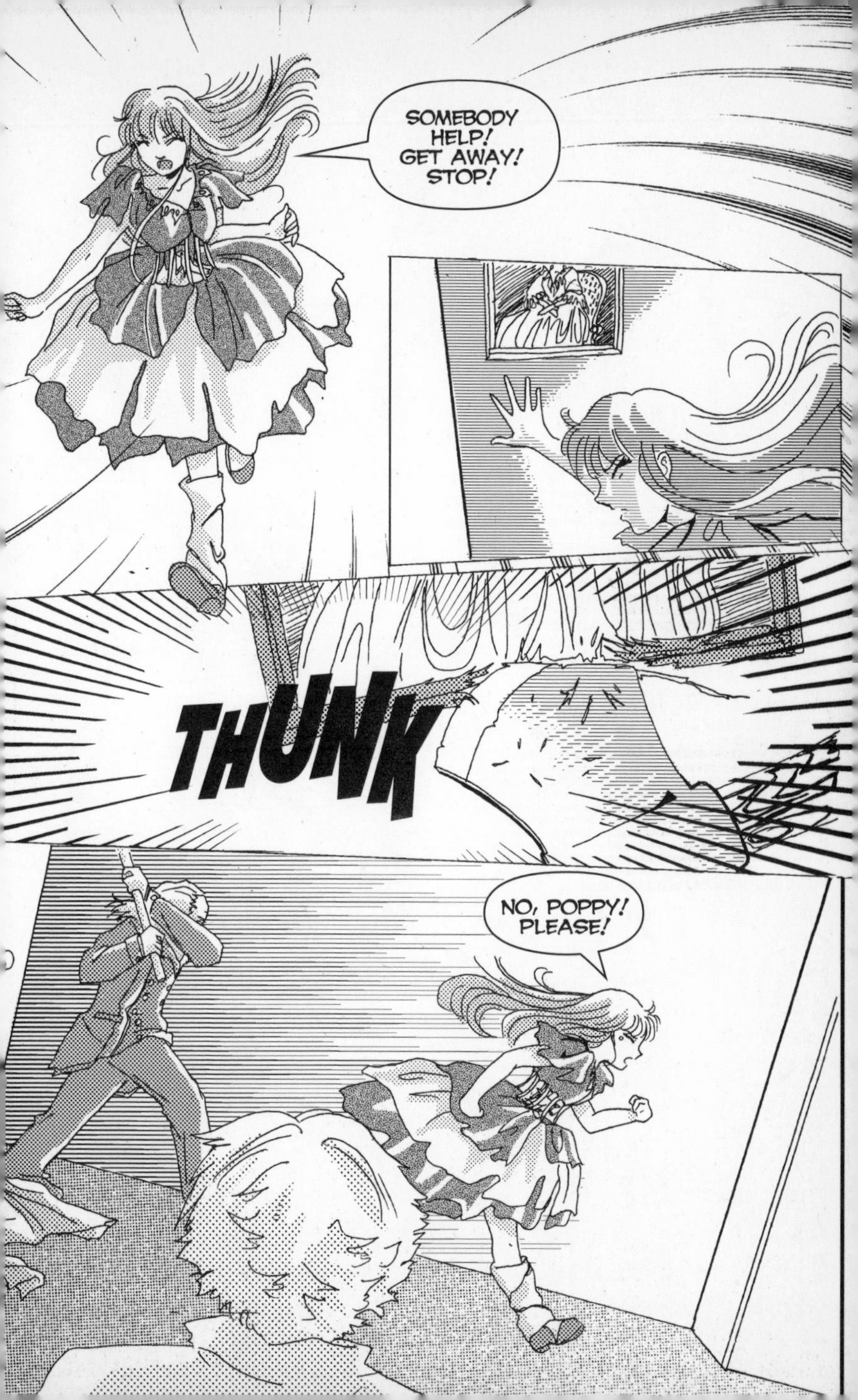
SOMEBODY HELP! GET AWAY! STOP!
THUNK
NO, POPPY! PLEASE!

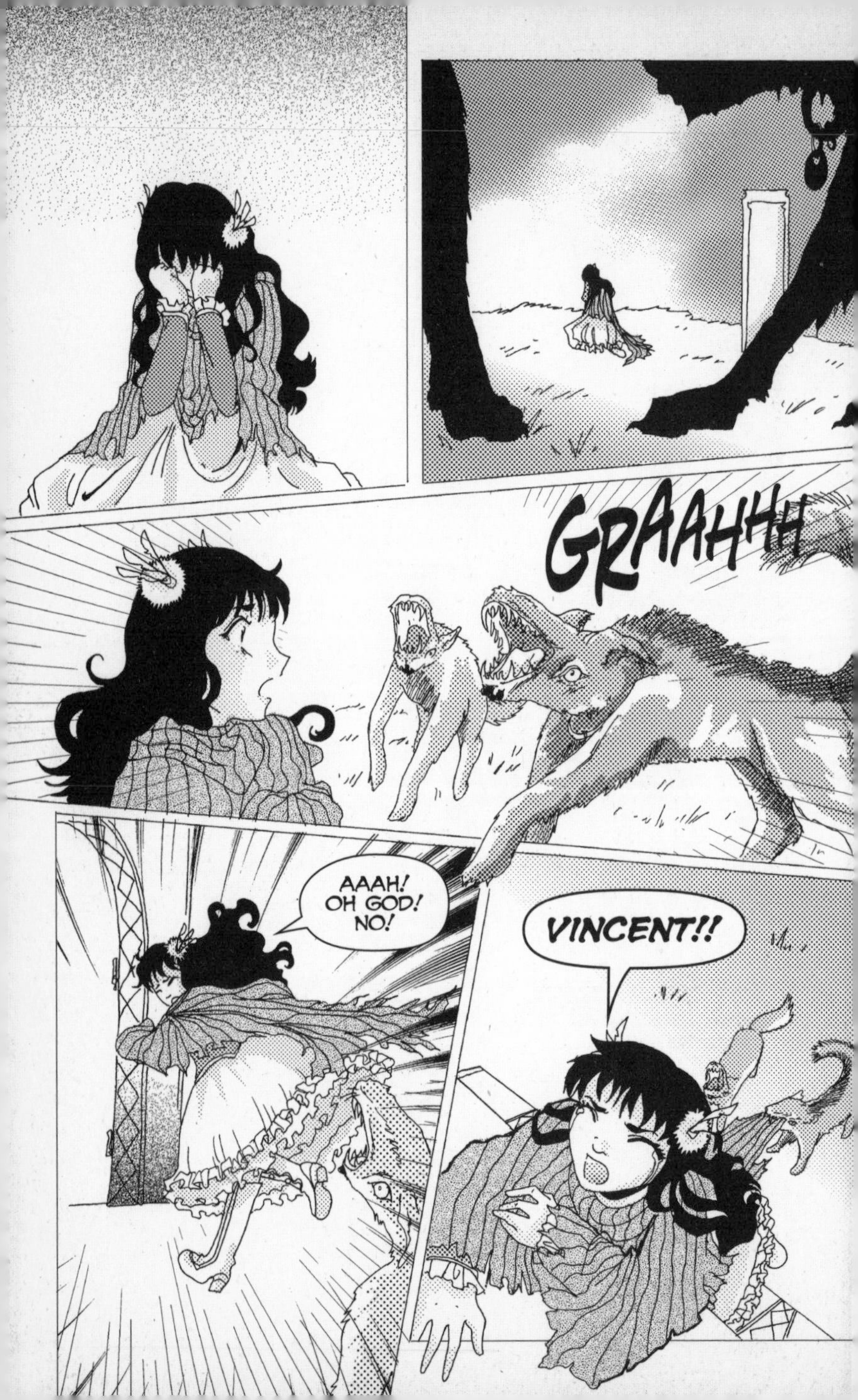
GRAAHHH
VINCENT!!
AAAH! OH GOD! NO!

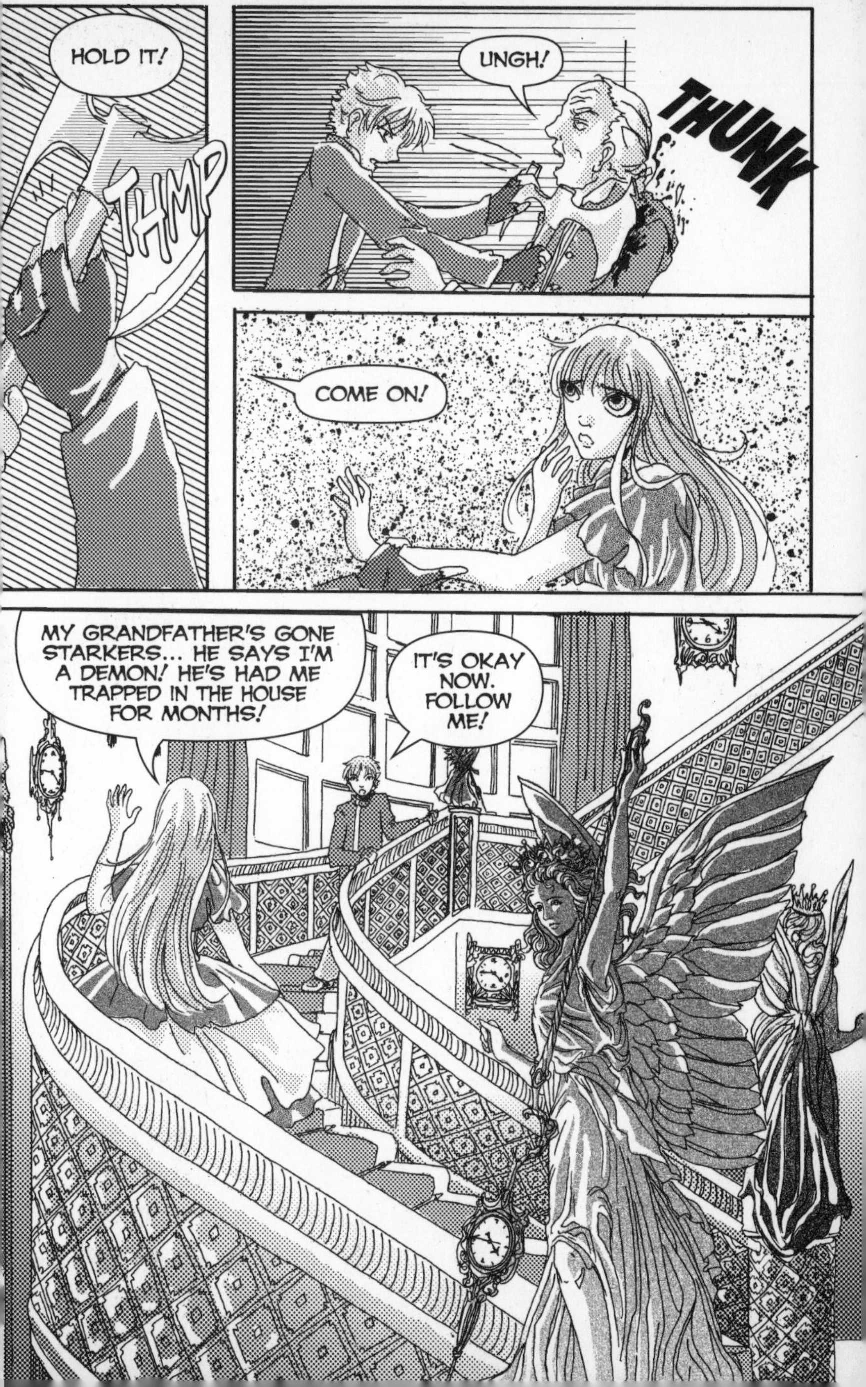
HOLD IT!
THMP
UNGH!
THUNK
COME ON!
MY GRANDFATHER'S GONE STARKERS... HE SAYS I'M A DEMON! HE'S HAD ME TRAPPED IN THE HOUSE FOR MONTHS!
IT'S OKAY NOW. FOLLOW ME!

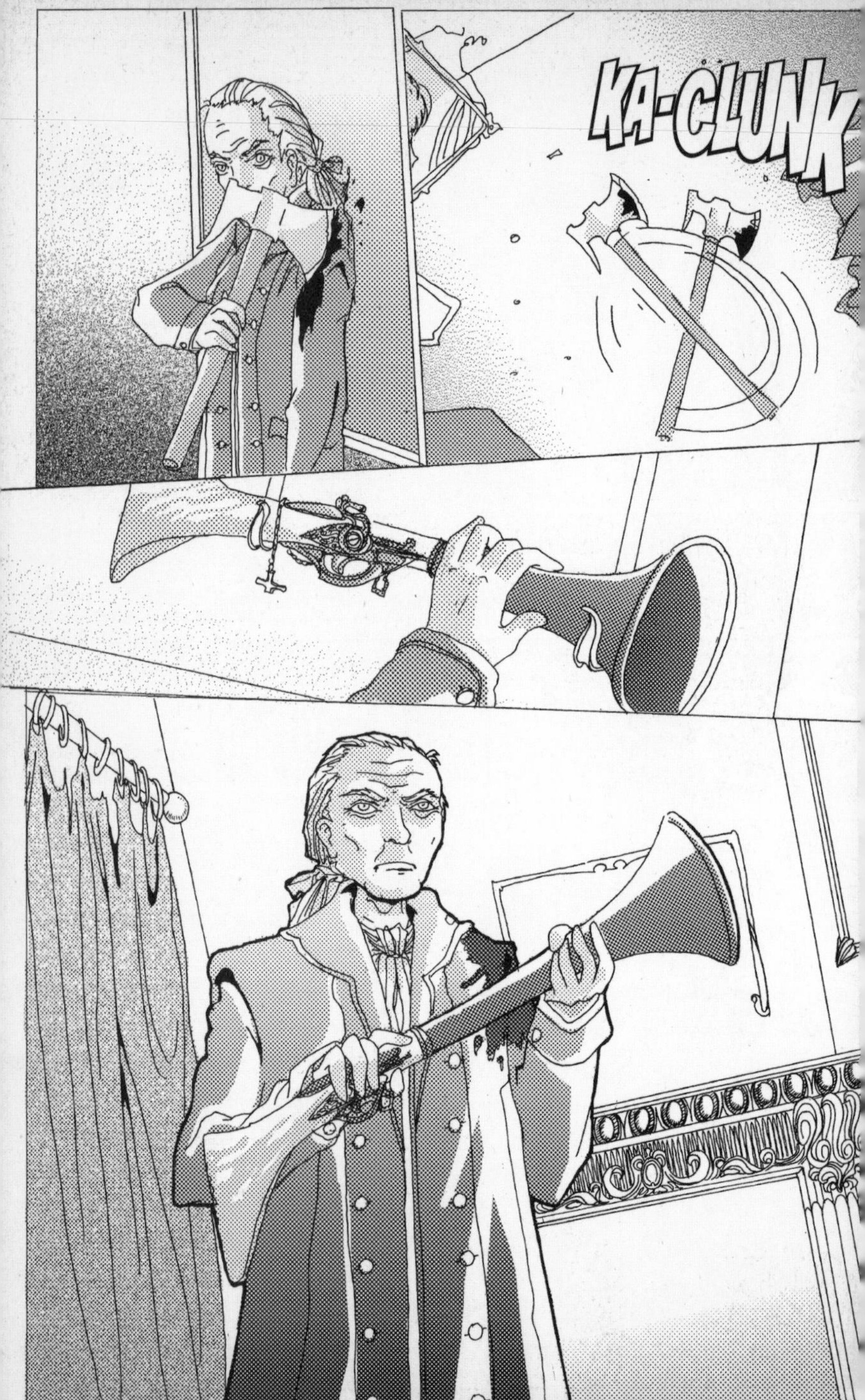
KA-CLUNK

...WE'RE ON... THE ROOF?

I THINK I GET WHAT BALI-LALI WAS TALKING ABOUT...

IT'S TIME FOR YOU TO BE FREE, CAGEY.

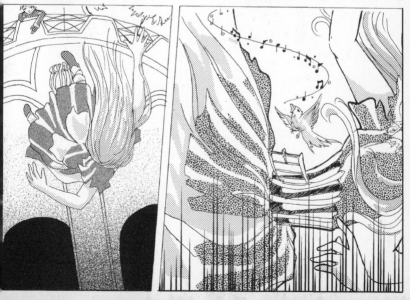

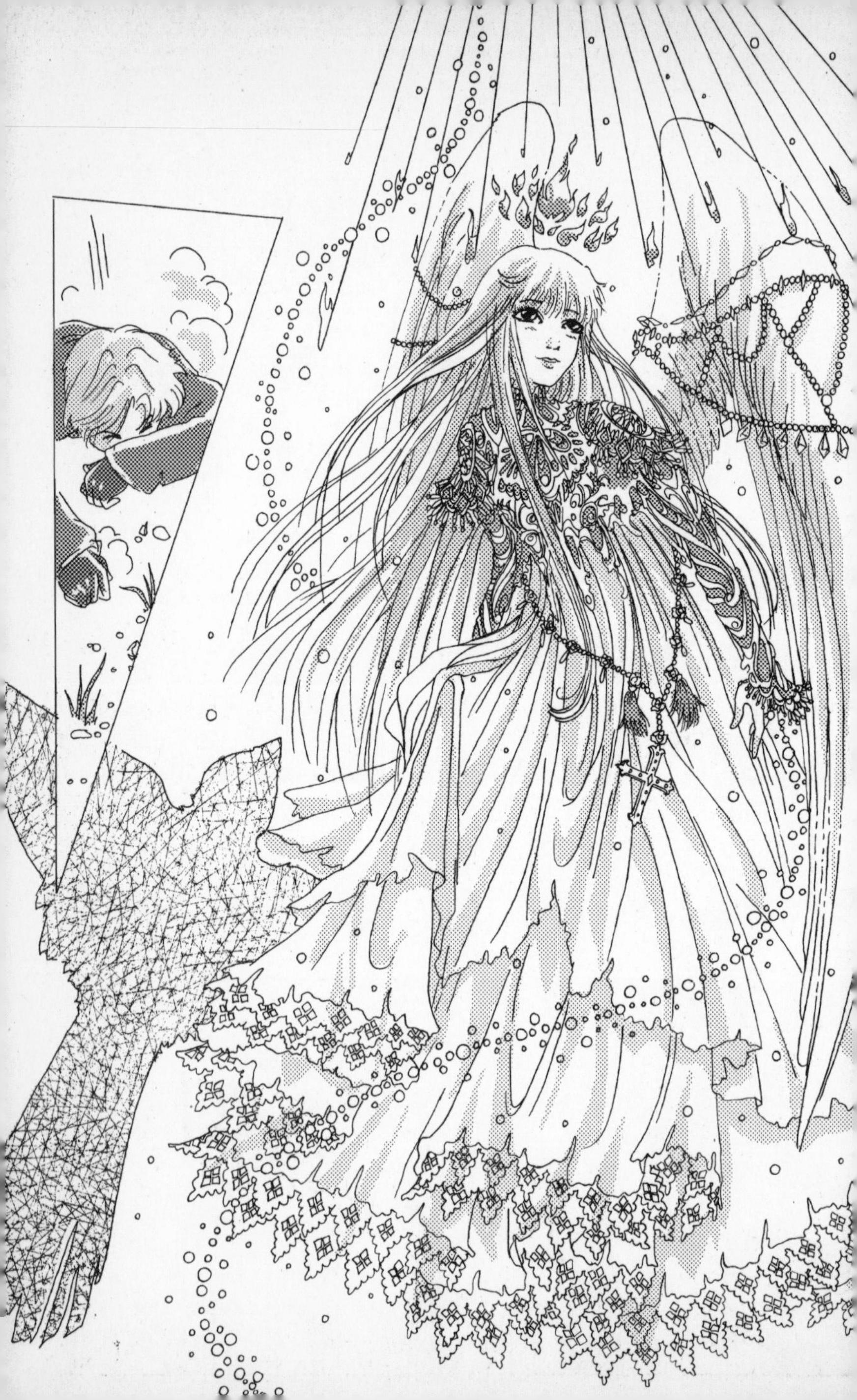

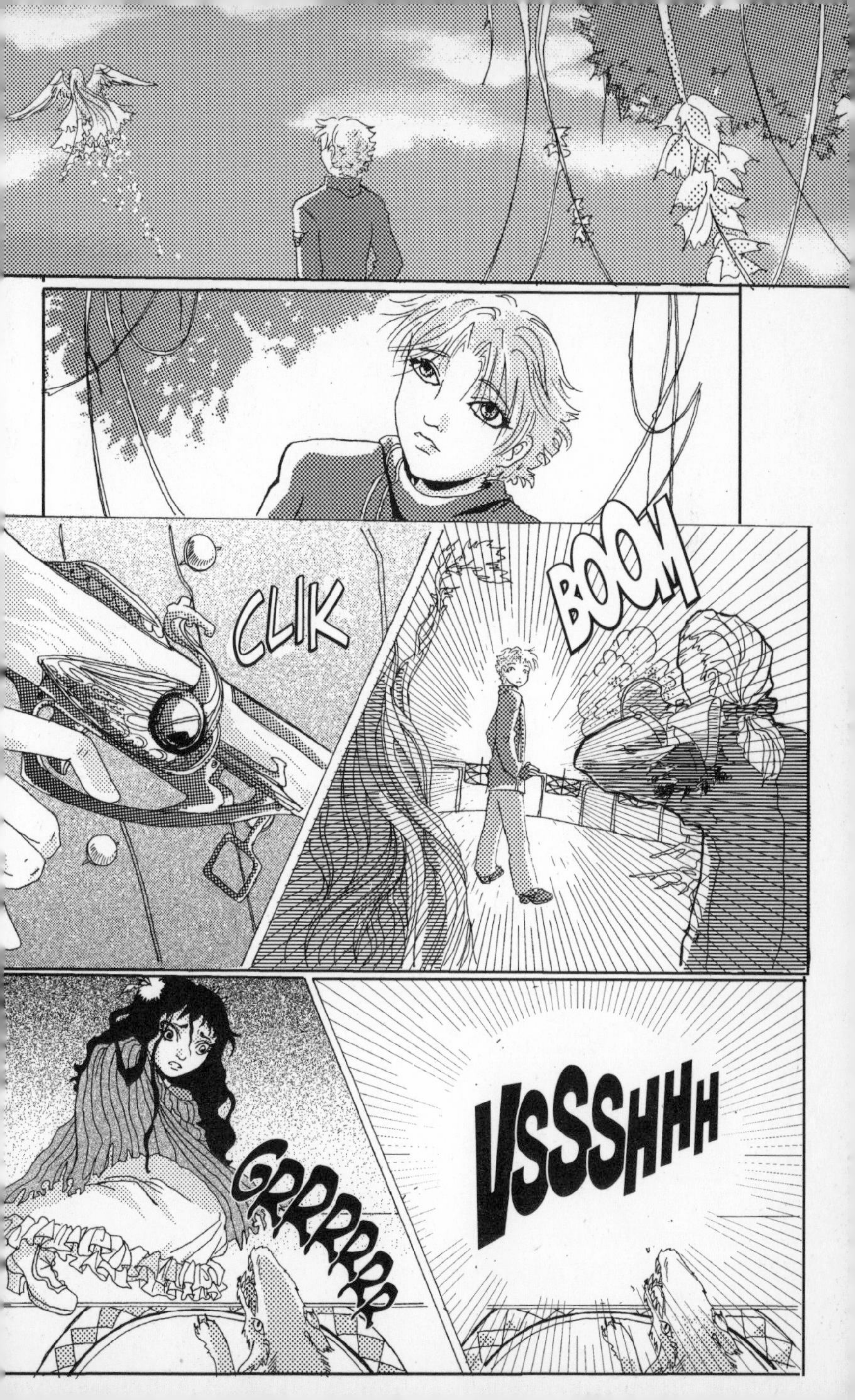
CLIK
BOOM
GRRRRRR
VSSSHHH

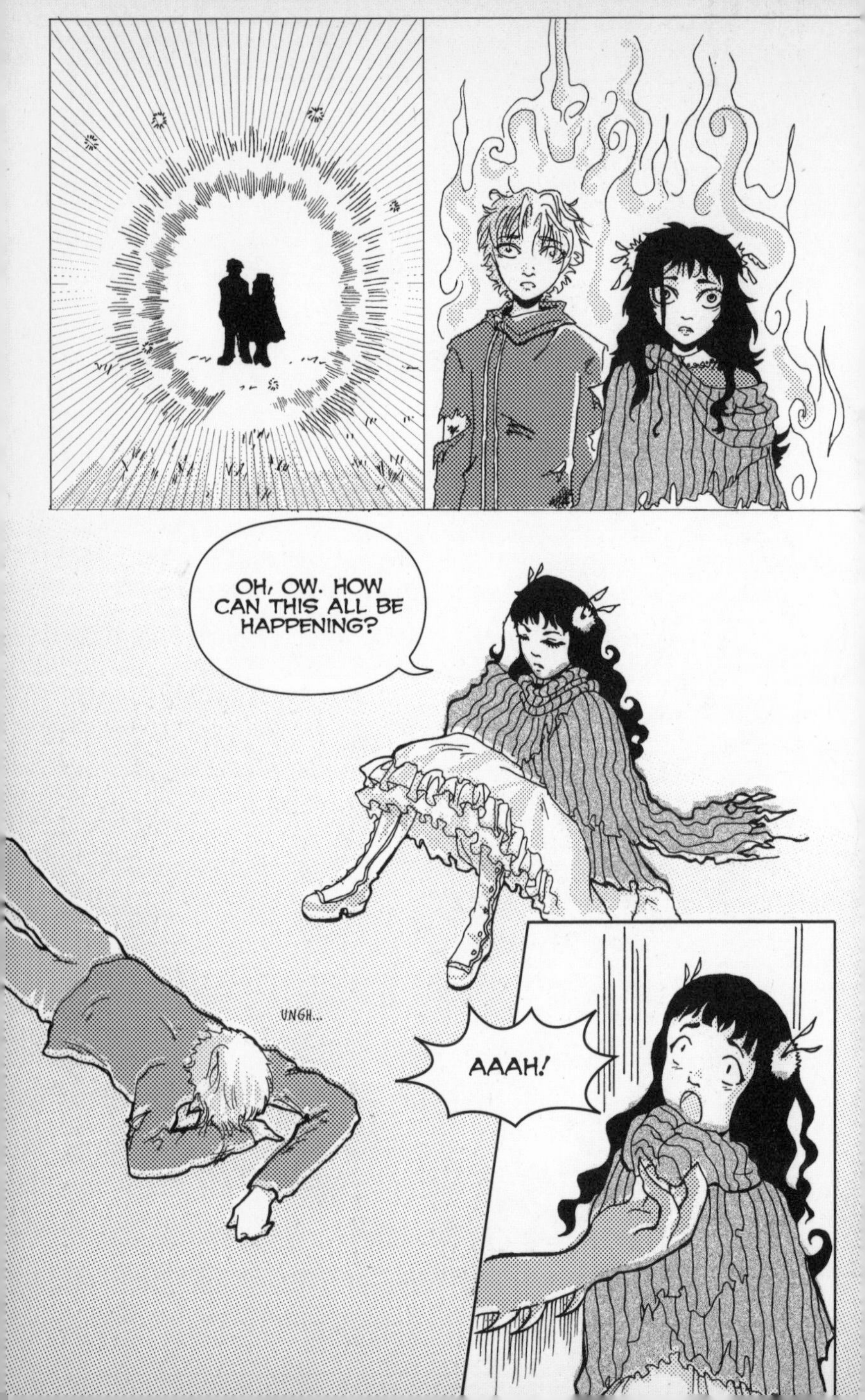
OH, OW. HOW CAN THIS ALL BE HAPPENING?
UNGH...
AAAH!

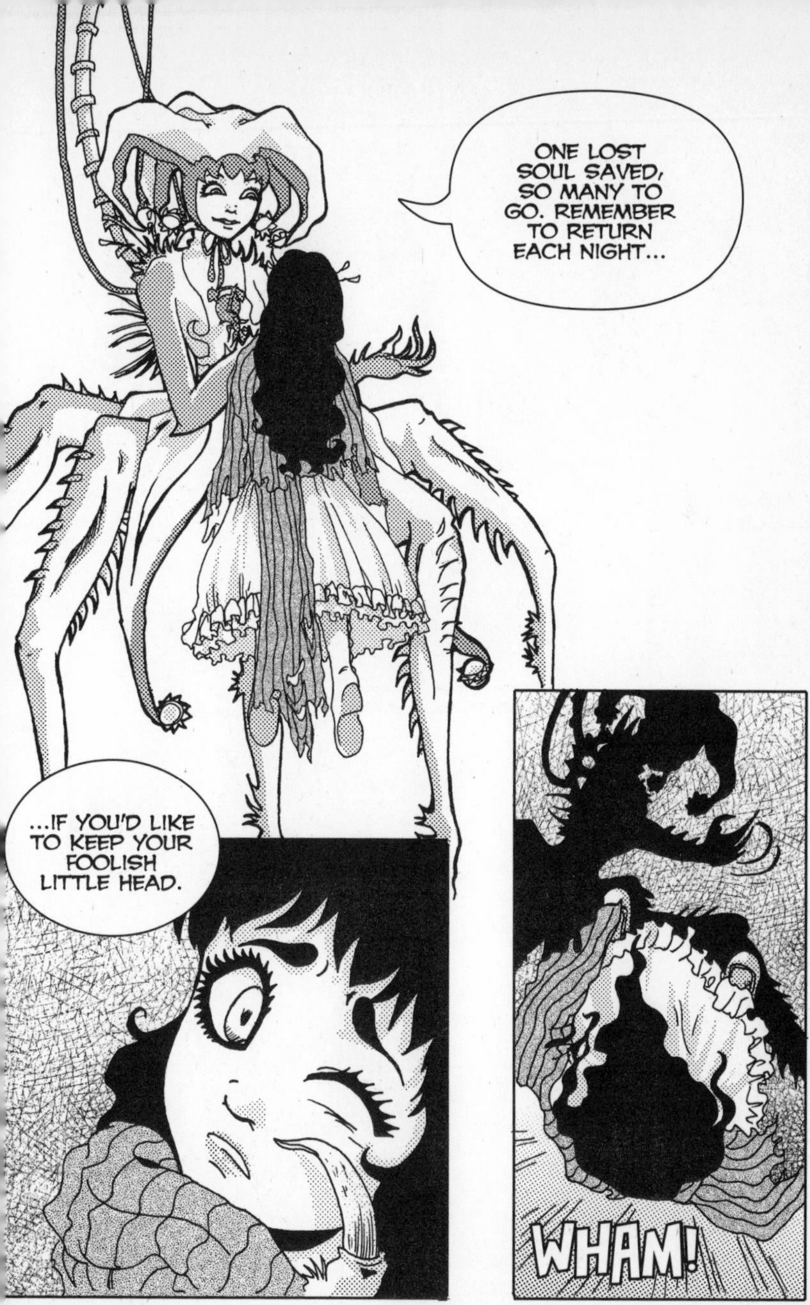
ONE LOST SOUL SAVED, SO MANY TO GO. REMEMBER TO RETURN EACH NIGHT...
...IF YOU'D LIKE TO KEEP YOUR FOOLISH LITTLE HEAD.
WHAM!

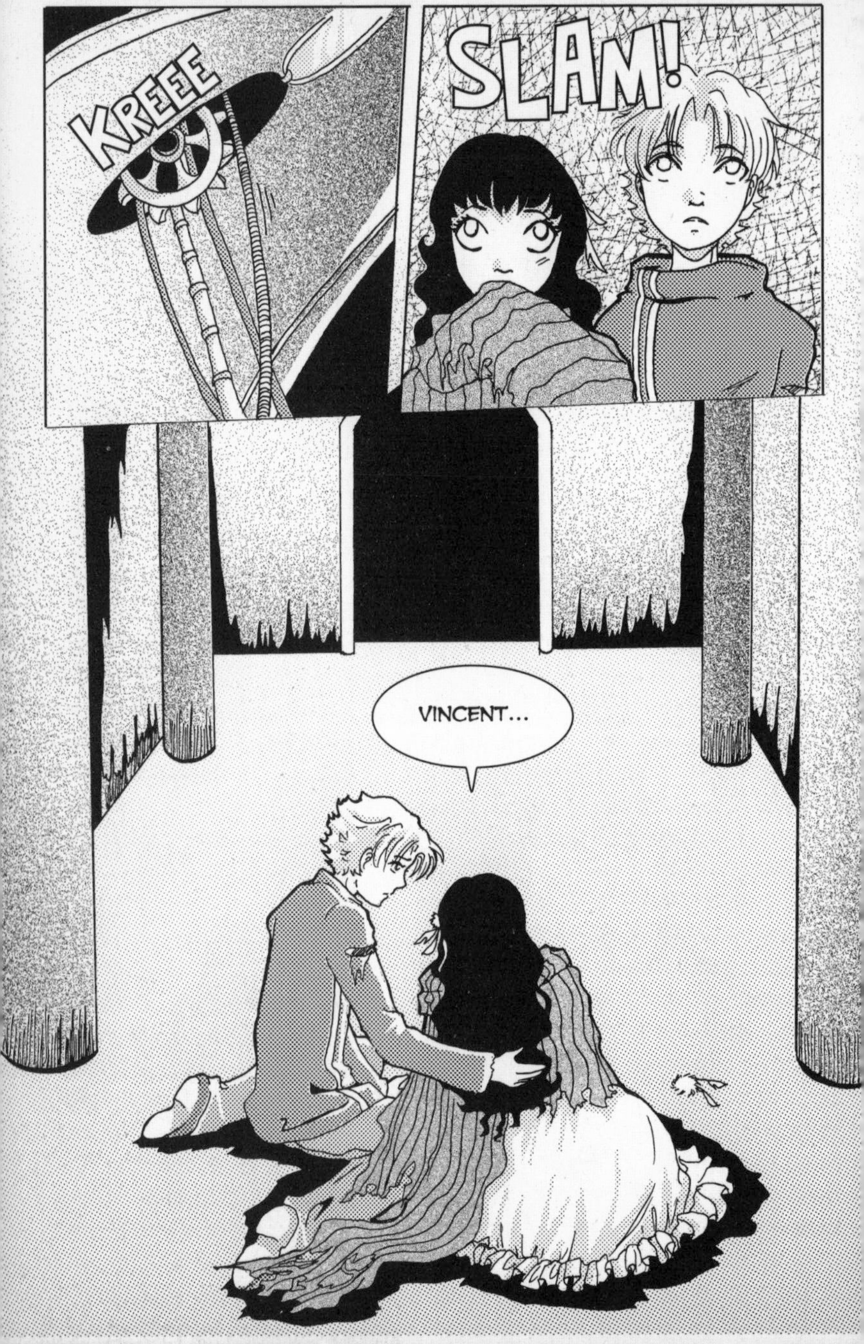
KREEE
SLAM!
VINCENT...

ST. LYMAN'S SCHOOL BURNS

An overturned lamp was the small spark that ignited a massive fire at St. Lyman's School for Boys Tuesday night. Although the main house was largely untouched, the other buildings on the school grounds were burnt to cinders in a matter of hours. The school was evacuated when smoke was noticed coming from the shed, but as of this afternoon, seven boys and one teacher are still unaccounted for.

The cause of the conflagaration is said to have been an unattended oil lamp burning in the shed, although no one can say who left it there or why, as the school had electrical lines laid several years ago. This summer's unusual heat left the grounds in a dry, flammable state that contributed to the spread of the fire from building to building. Only the main building still stands.

Established in 1848 as part of the 1832 Massachussetts law requiring the separation of the mentally feeble and the criminally ill, the original State Reform School of Massachusetts now comprises three branches which split from the original structure and went their separate ways-Flagg Farm (now located in Berlin), The Lyman School (now located in Westborough) and St. Lyman's, now located in Bizenghast. St Lyman's in Bizenghast was the only branch not specially constructed, but instead took over a small plot of land and buildings from a local asylum known as Blackrow House.

This is the second fire related to the original State Reform School. The Westborough branch also suffered through a mysterious blaze three years ago.

Police are investigating the remains of the destroyed buildings at St. Lyman's for any trace of the missing students. Officials on the Board of Health, however, are calling for a more thorough report on the conduct of the school, suggesting that the missing students had been killed long ago by overzealous discipline on the part of the teachers. One in particular, Miss Addie Clark (age unknown), is wanted for questioning.

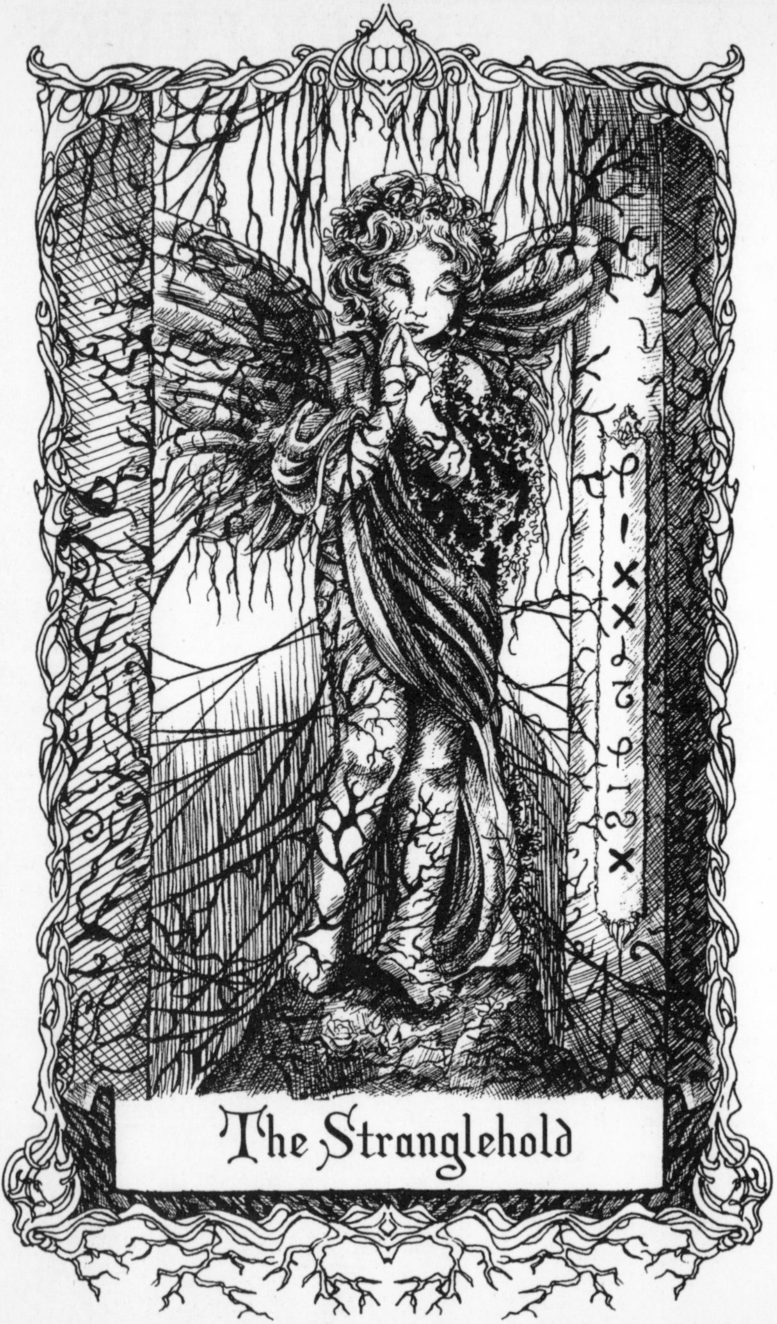
III
The Stranglehold

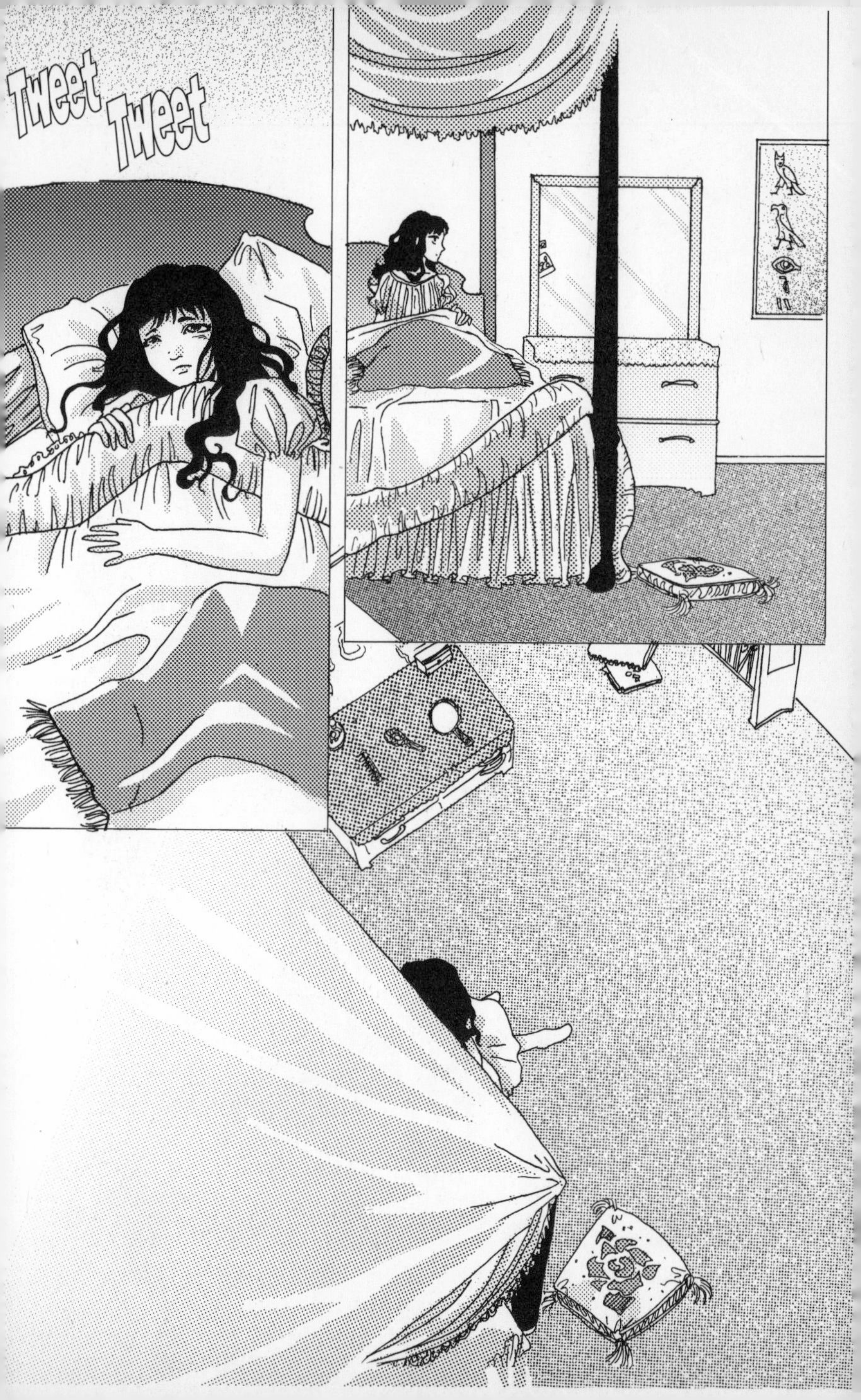
Tweet
Tweet

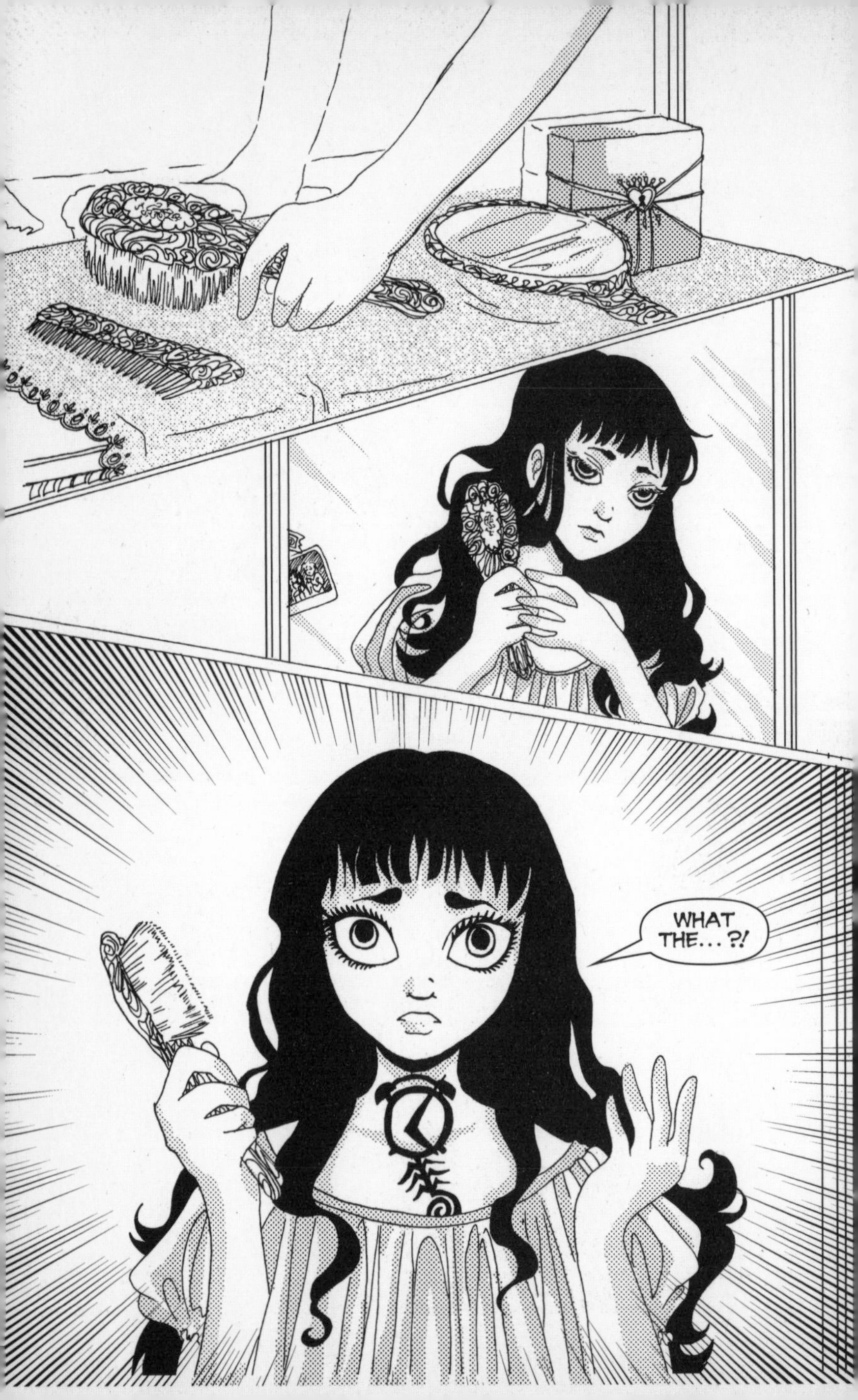
WHAT THE...?!

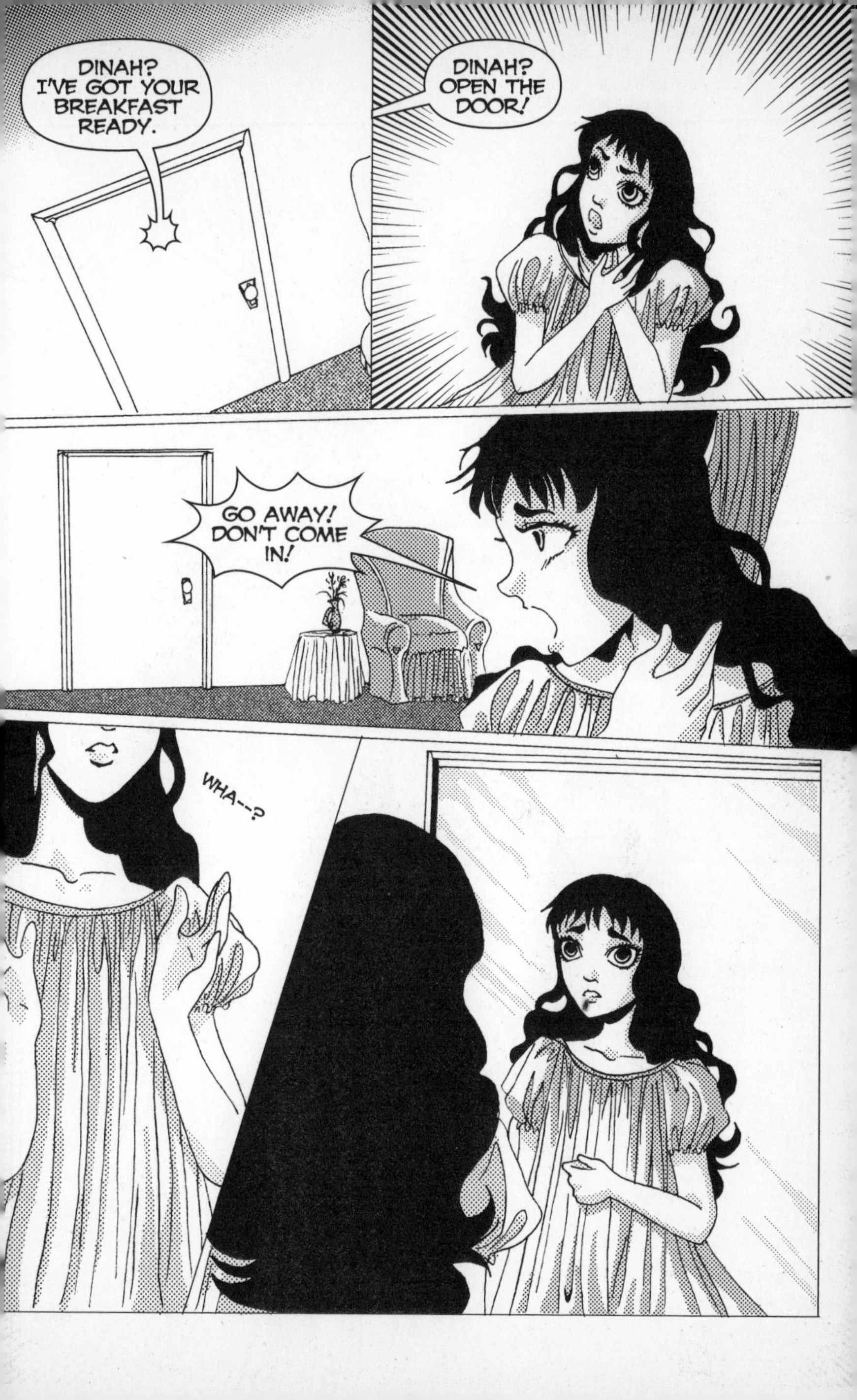
DINAH? I'VE GOT YOUR BREAKFAST READY.
DINAH? OPEN THE DOOR!
GO AWAY! DON'T COME IN!
WHA--?

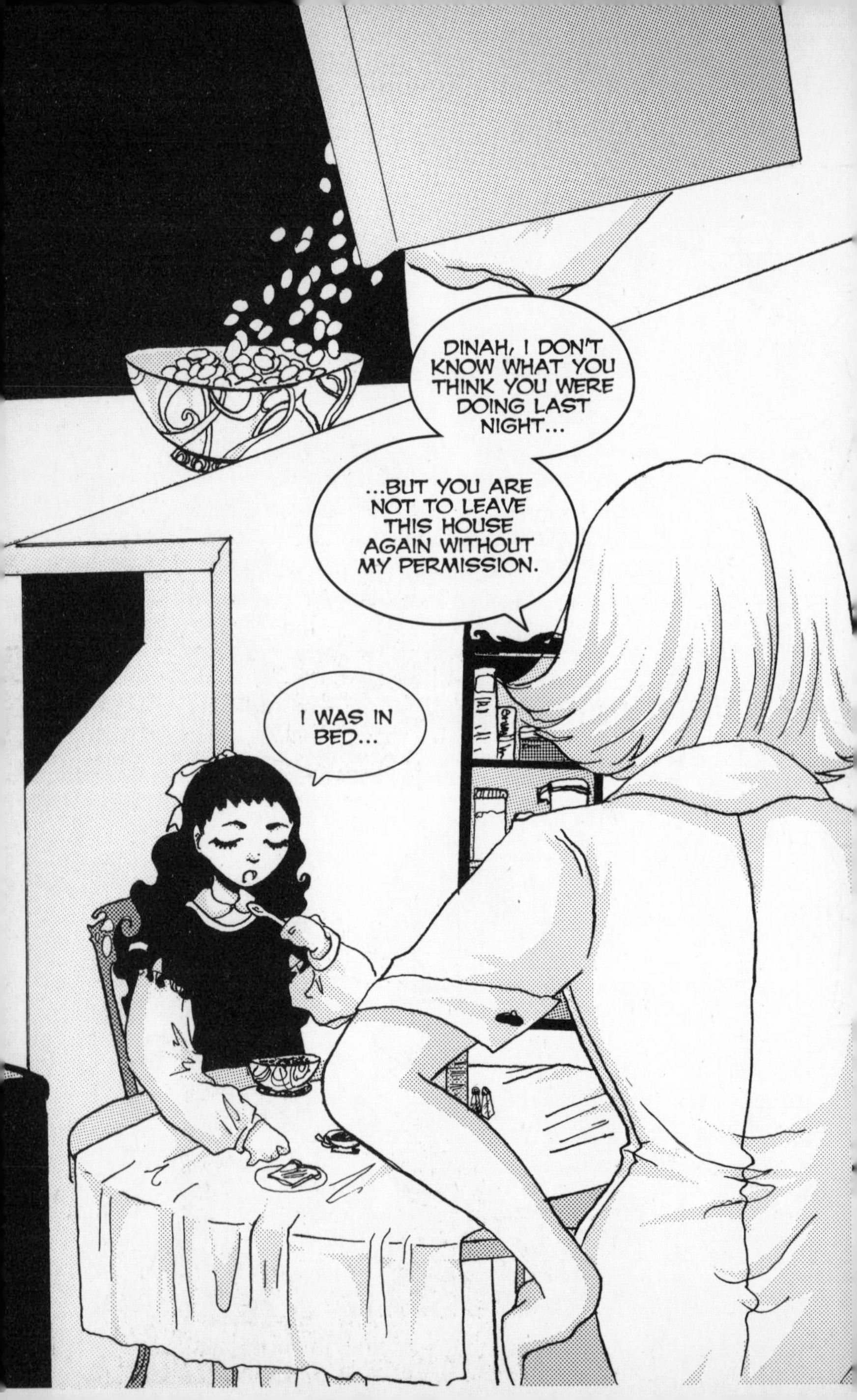
DINAH, I DON'T KNOW WHAT YOU THINK YOU WERE DOING LAST NIGHT...
...BUT YOU ARE NOT TO LEAVE THIS HOUSE AGAIN WITHOUT MY PERMISSION.
I WAS IN BED...

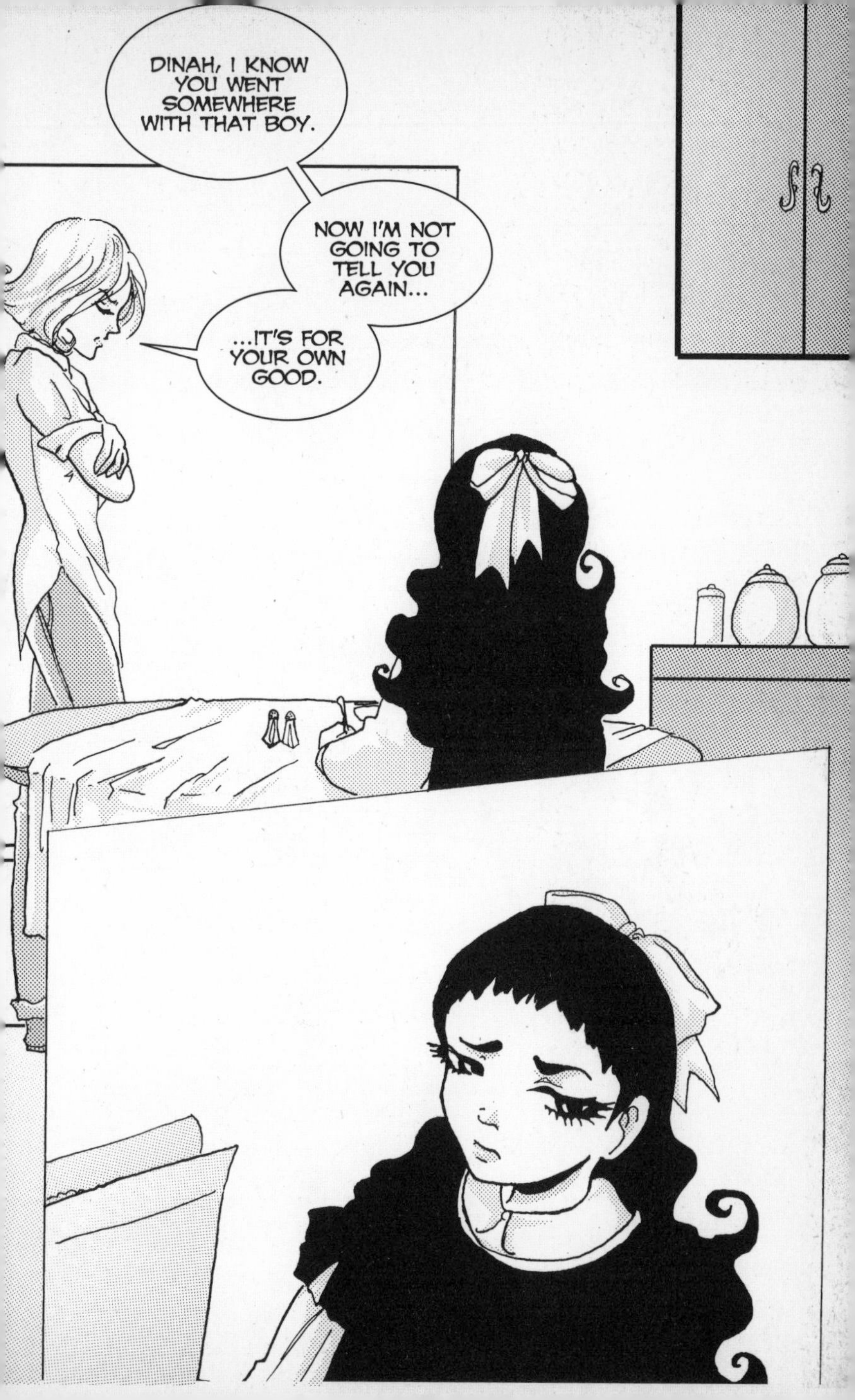
DINAH, I KNOW YOU WENT SOMEWHERE WITH THAT BOY.
NOW I'M NOT GOING TO TELL YOU AGAIN...
...IT'S FOR YOUR OWN GOOD.

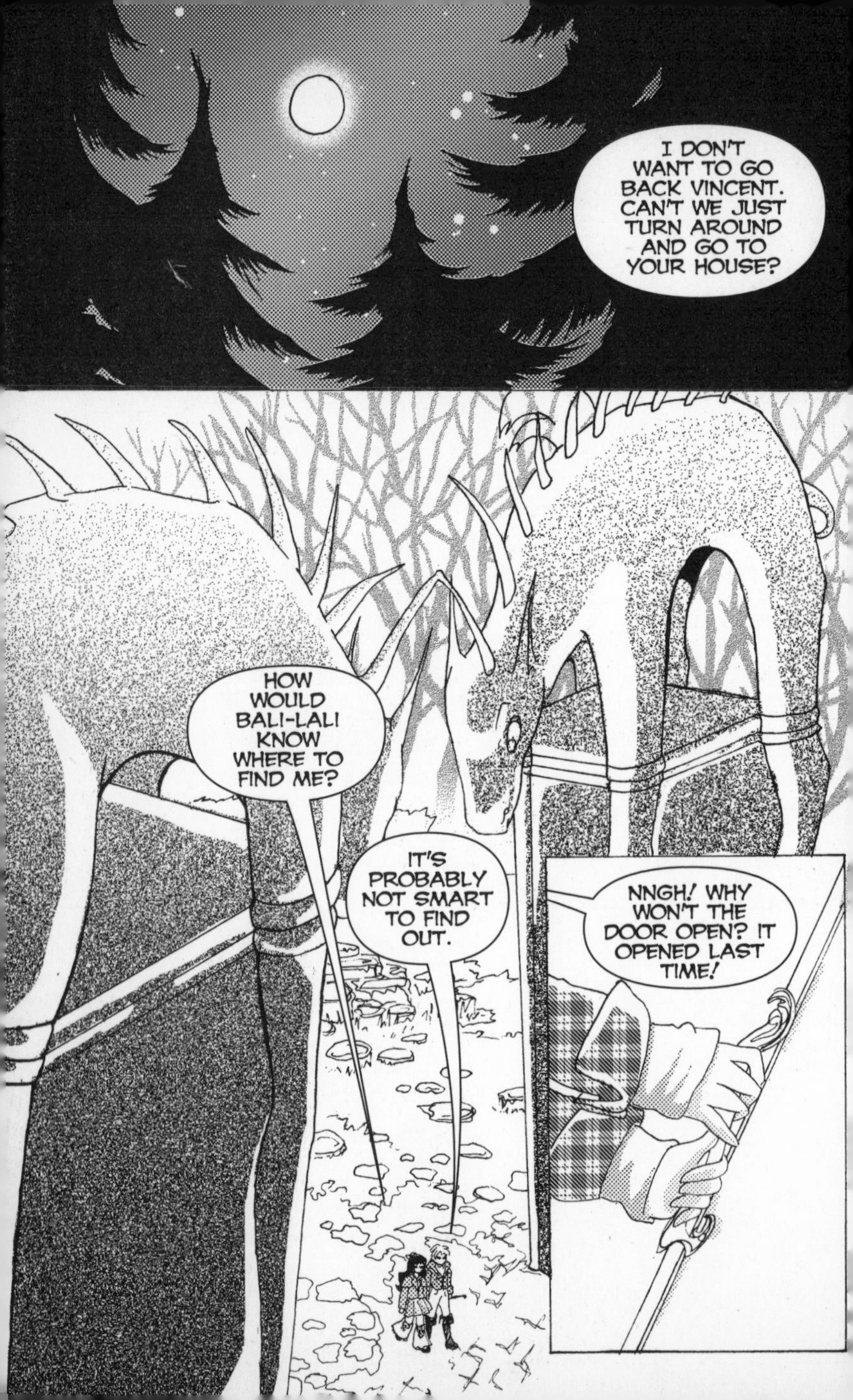
I DON'T WANT TO GO BACK VINCENT. CAN'T WE JUST TURN AROUND AND GO TO YOUR HOUSE?
HOW WOULD BALI-LALI KNOW WHERE TO FIND ME?
IT'S PROBABLY NOT SMART TO FIND OUT.
NNGH! WHY WON'T THE DOOR OPEN? IT OPENED LAST TIME!

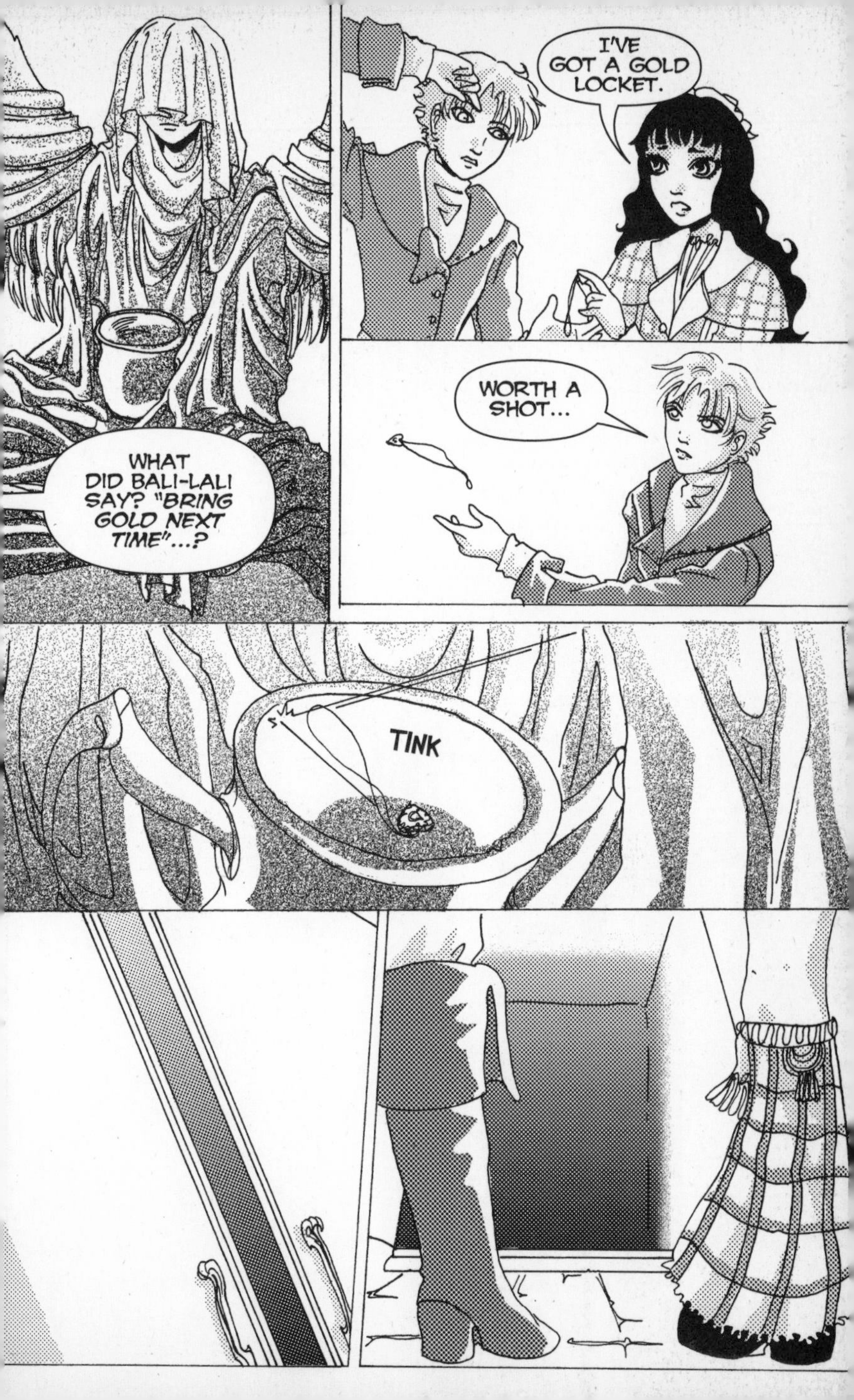
WHAT DID BALI-LALI SAY? "BRING GOLD NEXT TIME"...?
I'VE GOT A GOLD LOCKET.
WORTH A SHOT...
TINK

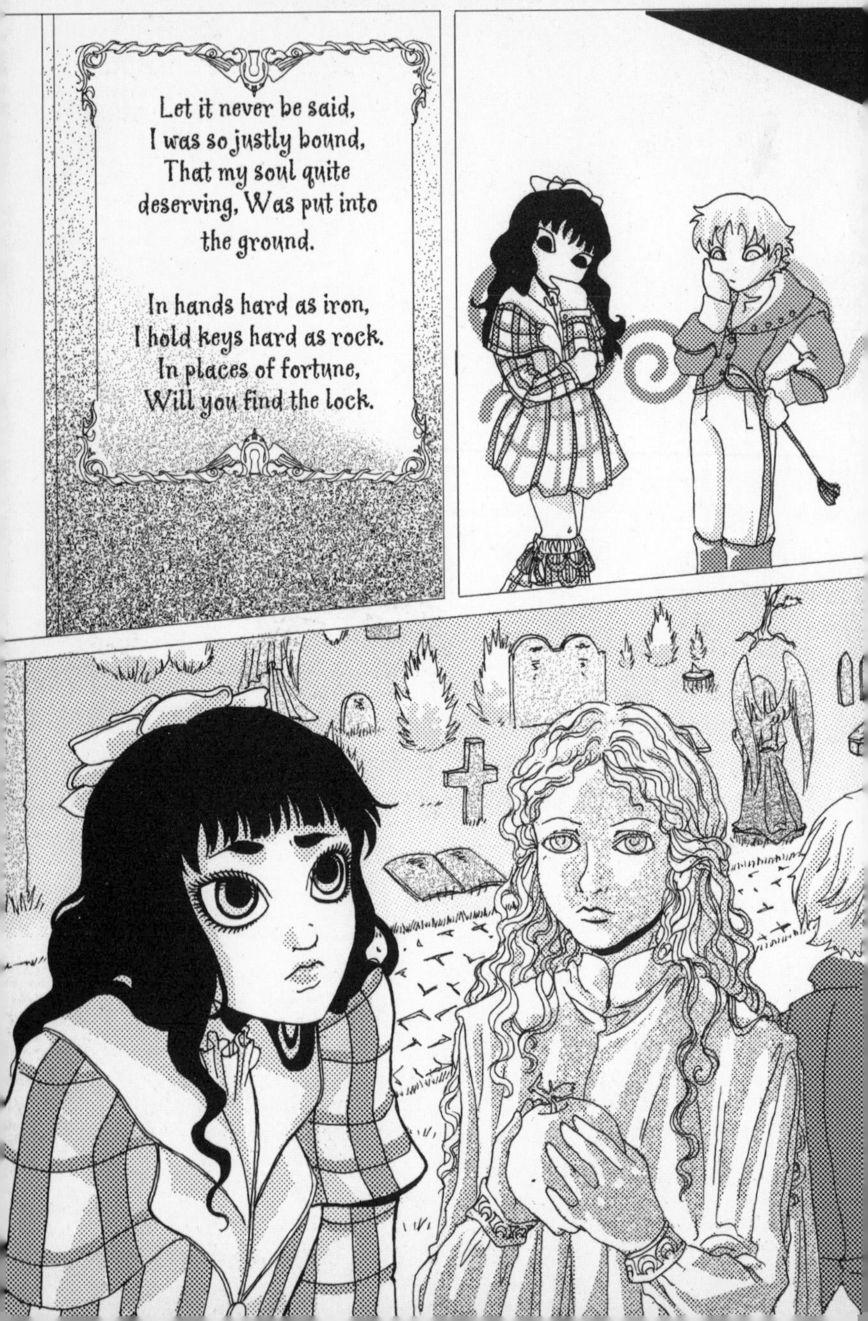
Let it never be said,
I was so justly bound,
That my soul quite
deserving, Was put into
the ground.
In hands hard as iron,
I hold keys hard as rock.
In places of fortune,
Will you find the lock.

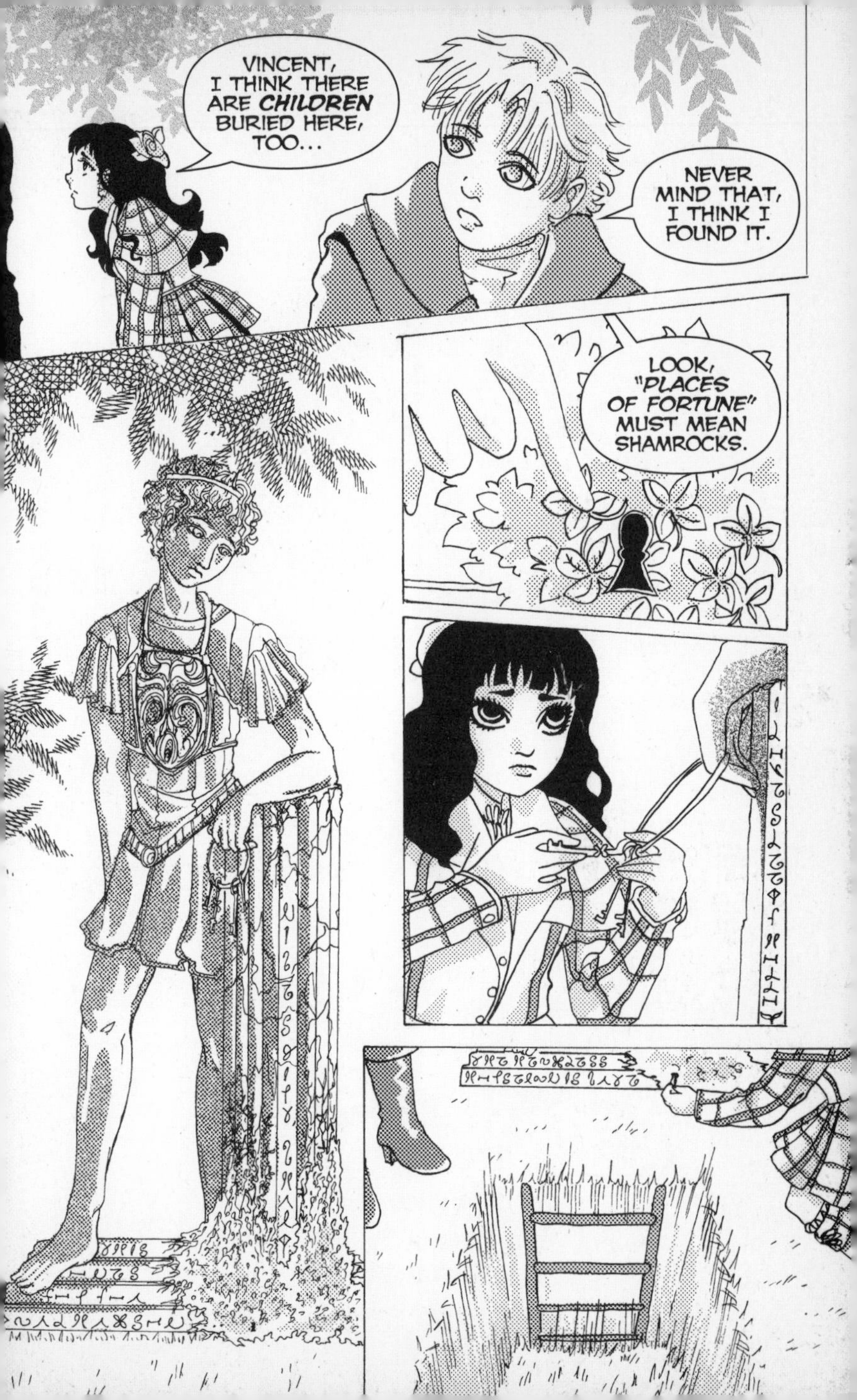
VINCENT, I THINK THERE ARE *CHILDREN* BURIED HERE, TOO...
NEVER MIND THAT, I THINK I FOUND IT.
LOOK, "*PLACES OF FORTUNE*" MUST MEAN SHAMROCKS.

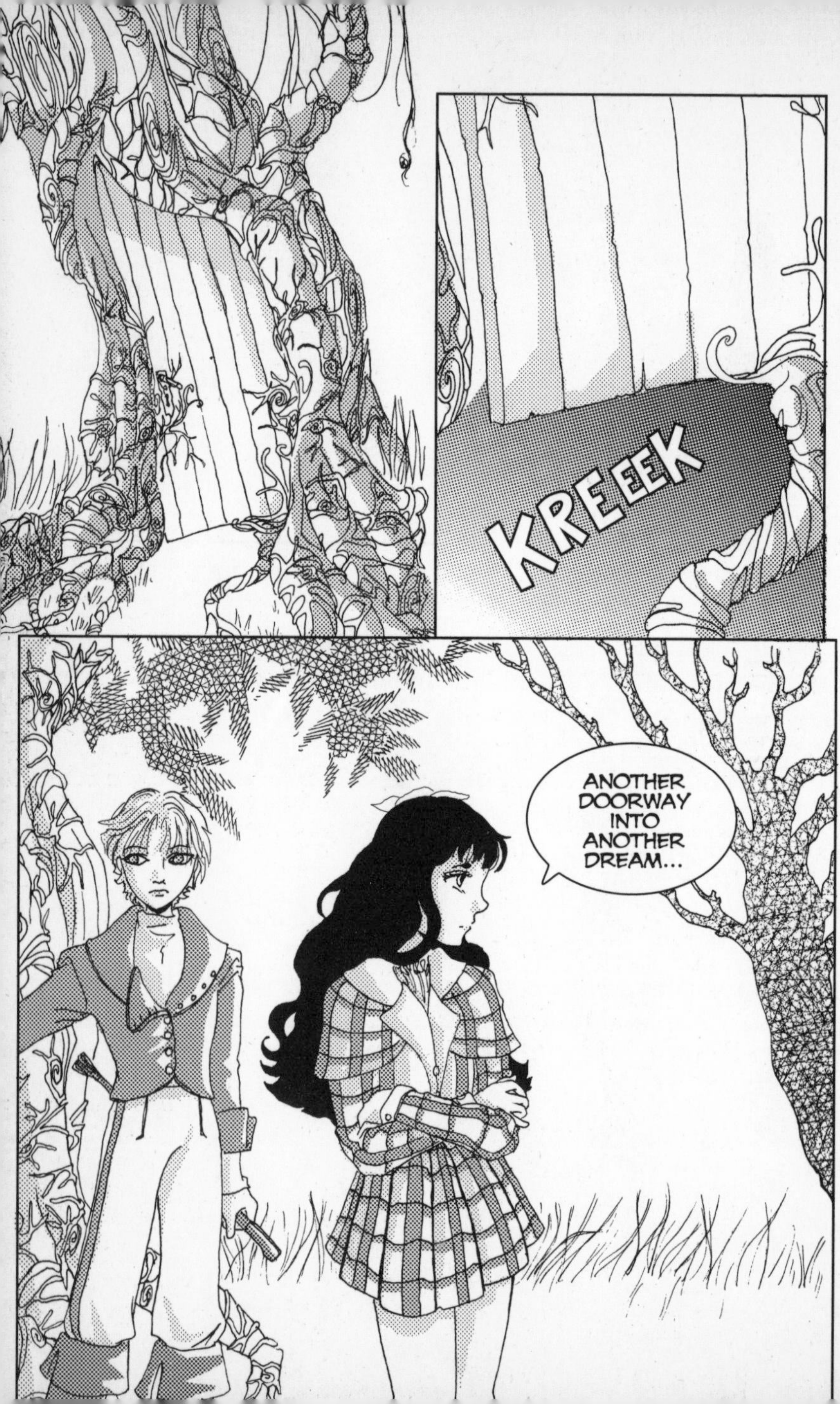
KREEEK
ANOTHER DOORWAY INTO ANOTHER DREAM...

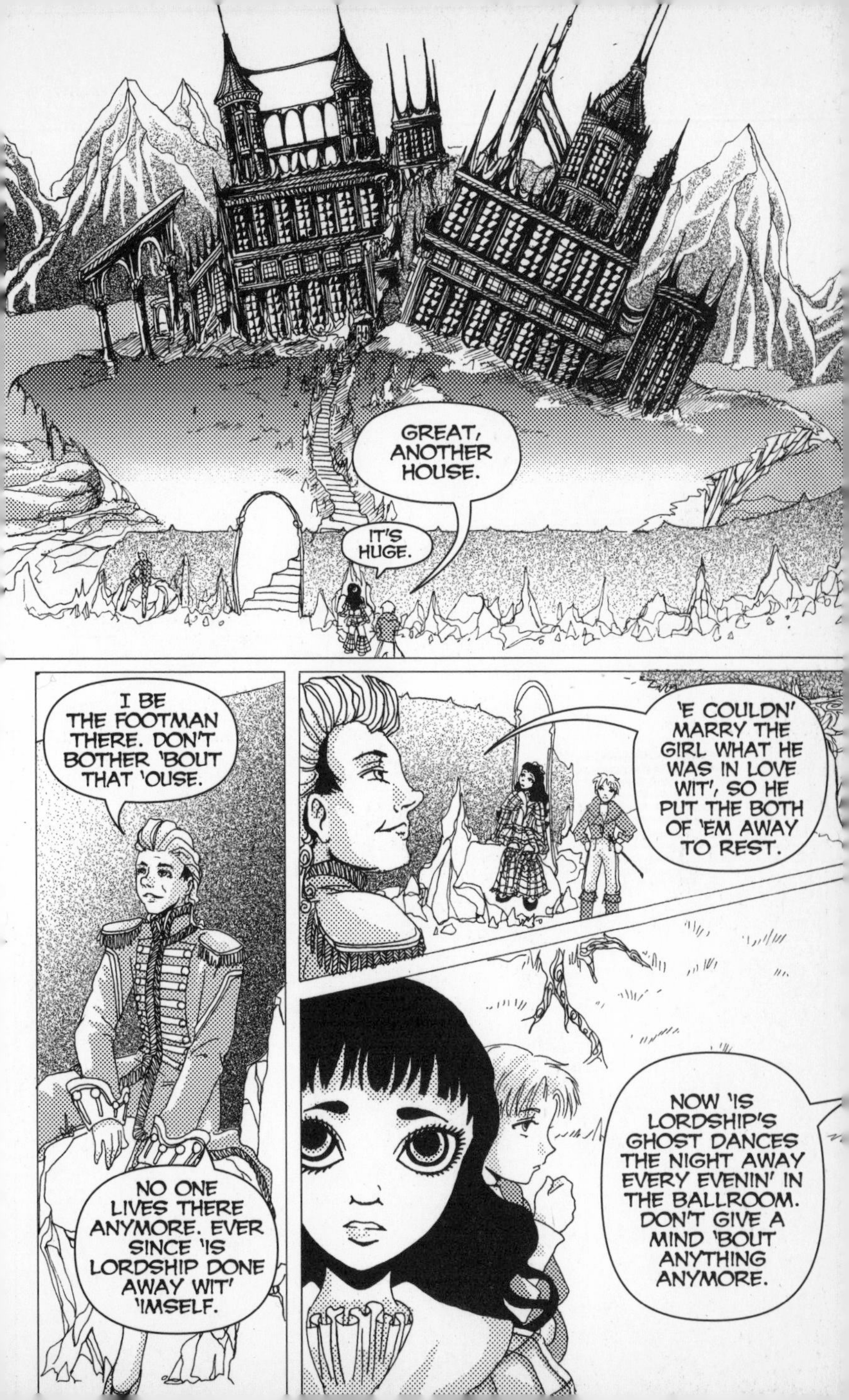
GREAT, ANOTHER HOUSE.
IT'S HUGE.
I BE THE FOOTMAN THERE. DON'T BOTHER 'BOUT THAT 'OUSE.
NO ONE LIVES THERE ANYMORE. EVER SINCE 'IS LORDSHIP DONE AWAY WIT' 'IMSELF.
'E COULDN' MARRY THE GIRL WHAT HE WAS IN LOVE WIT', SO HE PUT THE BOTH OF 'EM AWAY TO REST.
NOW 'IS LORDSHIP'S GHOST DANCES THE NIGHT AWAY EVERY EVENIN' IN THE BALLROOM. DON'T GIVE A MIND 'BOUT ANYTHING ANYMORE.

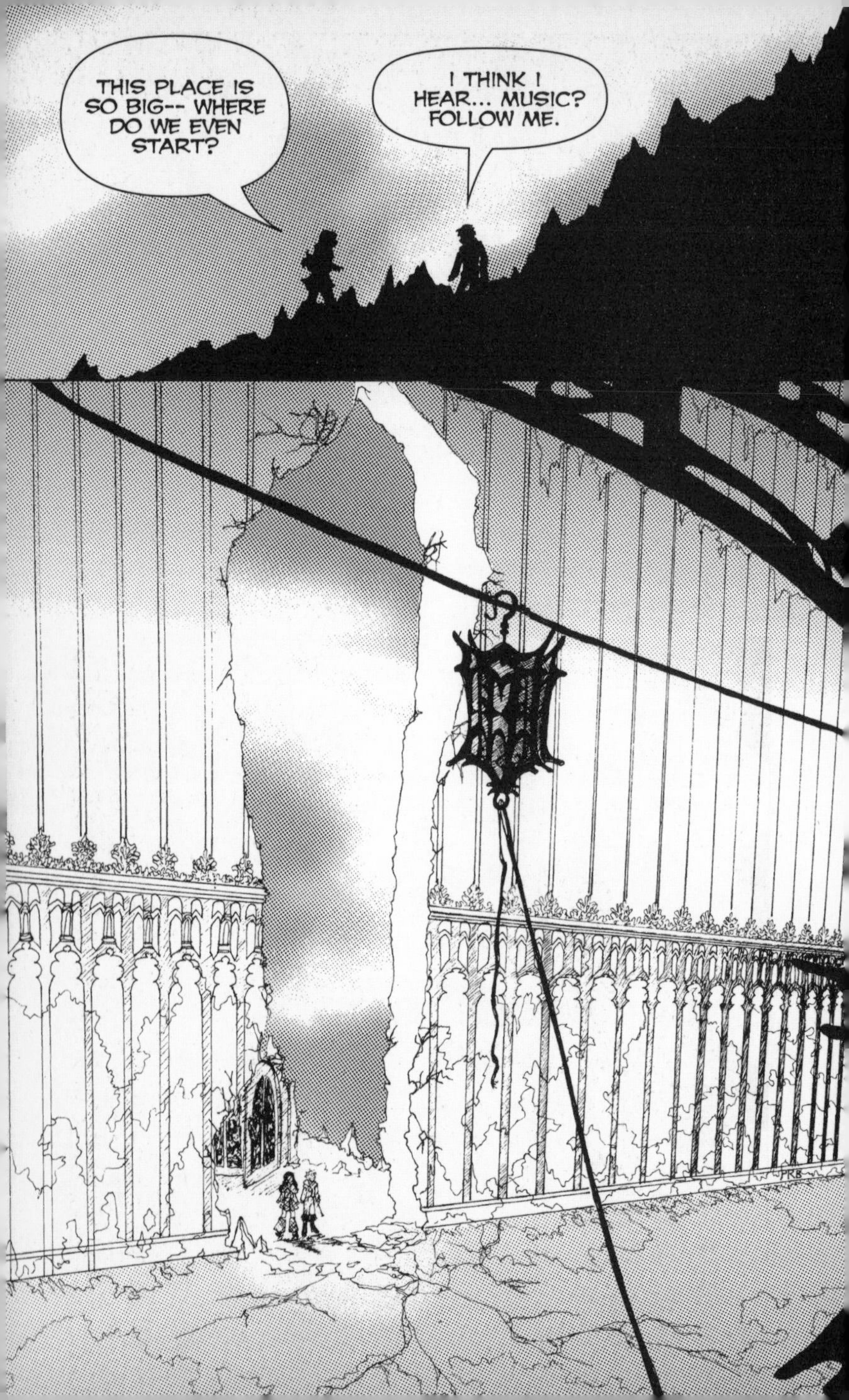
THIS PLACE IS SO BIG-- WHERE DO WE EVEN START?
I THINK I HEAR... MUSIC? FOLLOW ME.
PRB

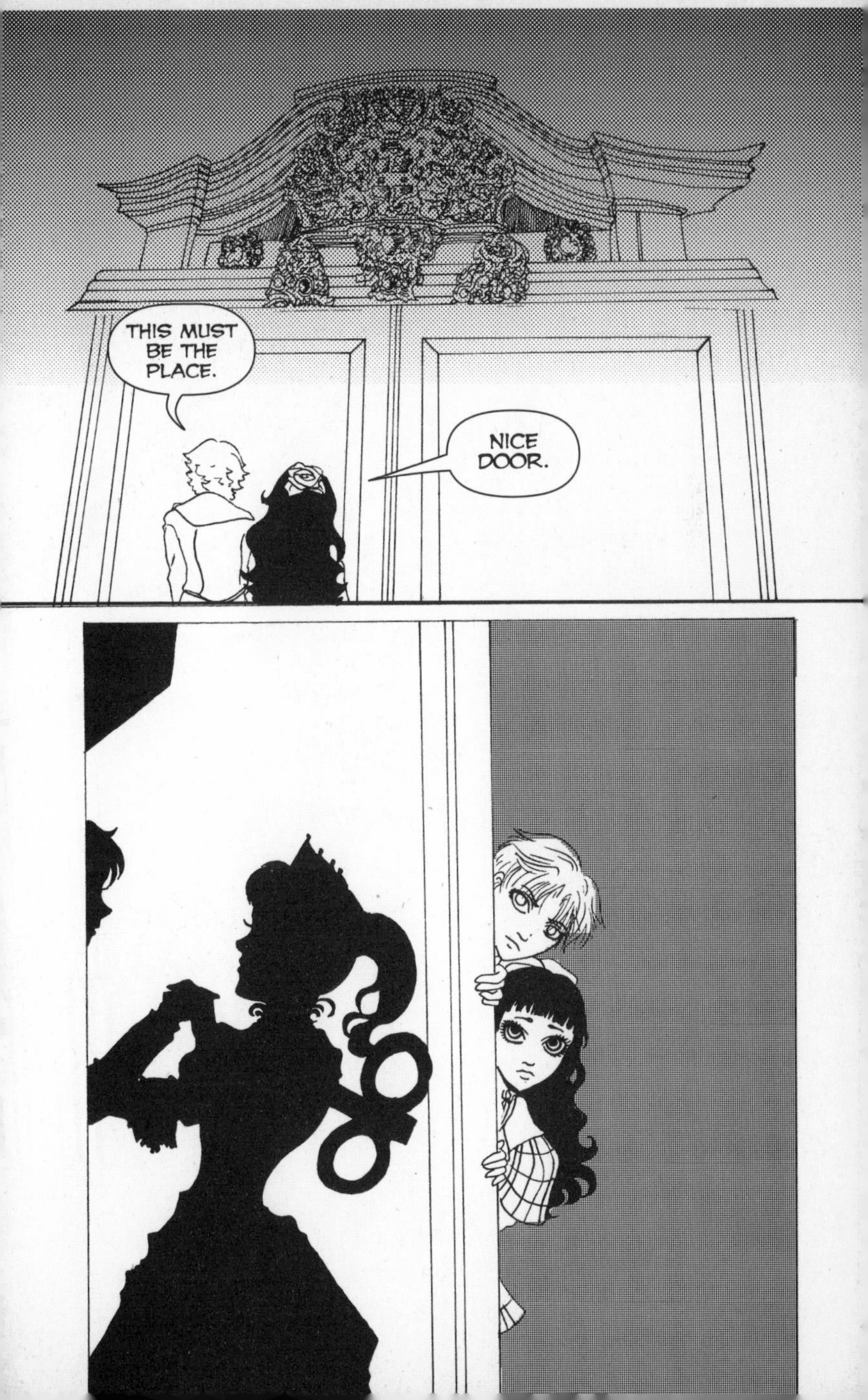
THIS MUST BE THE PLACE.
NICE DOOR.

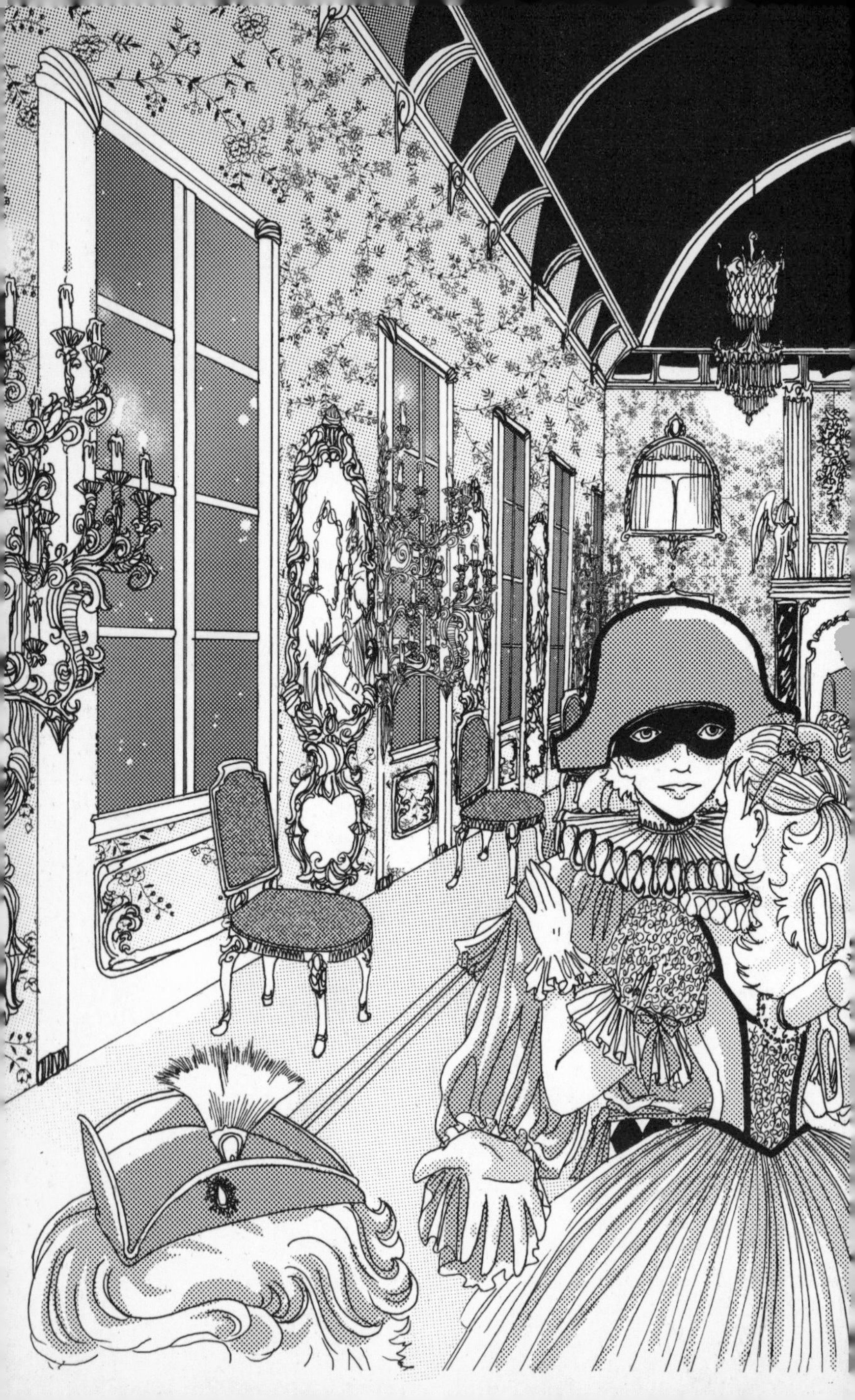

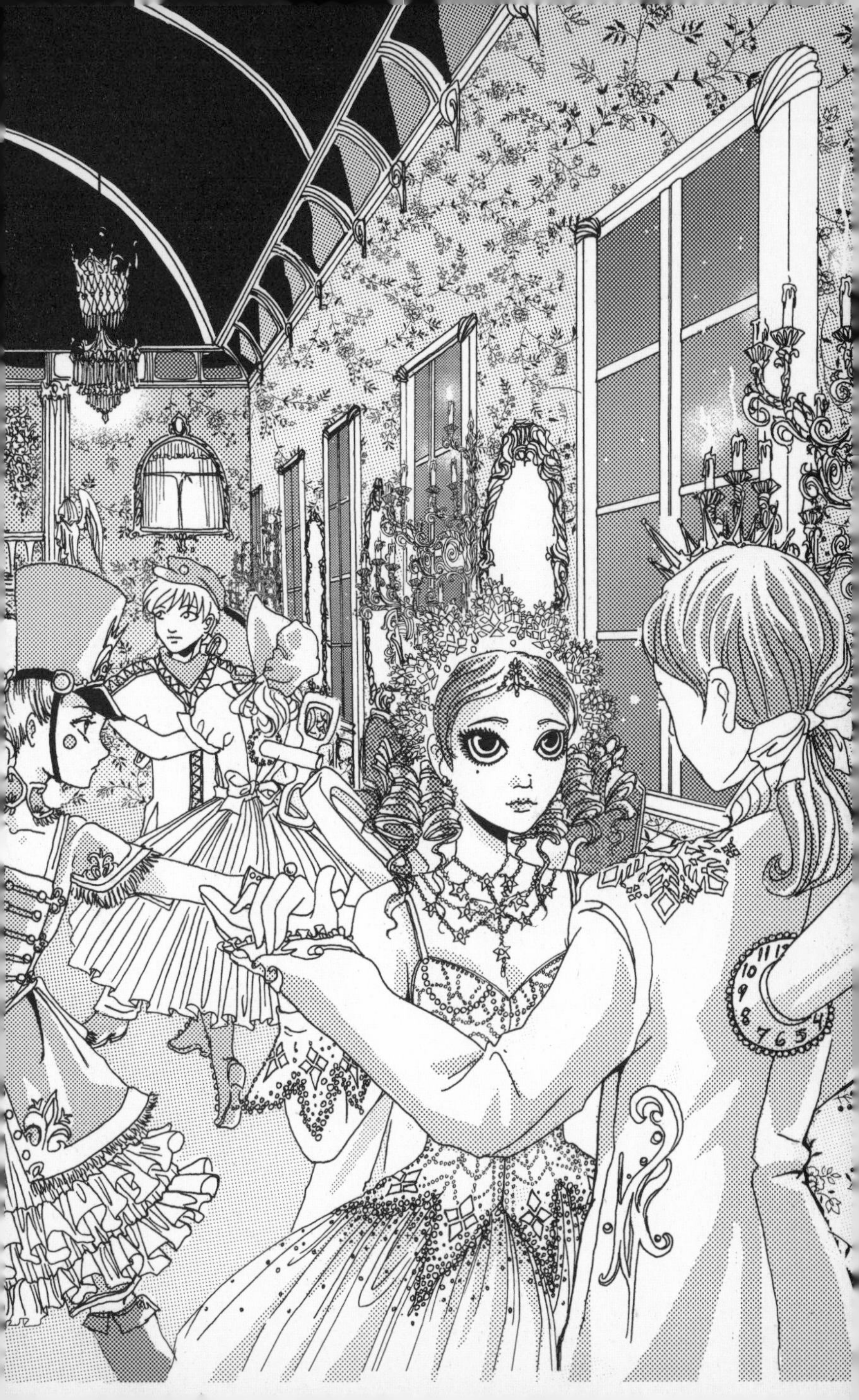

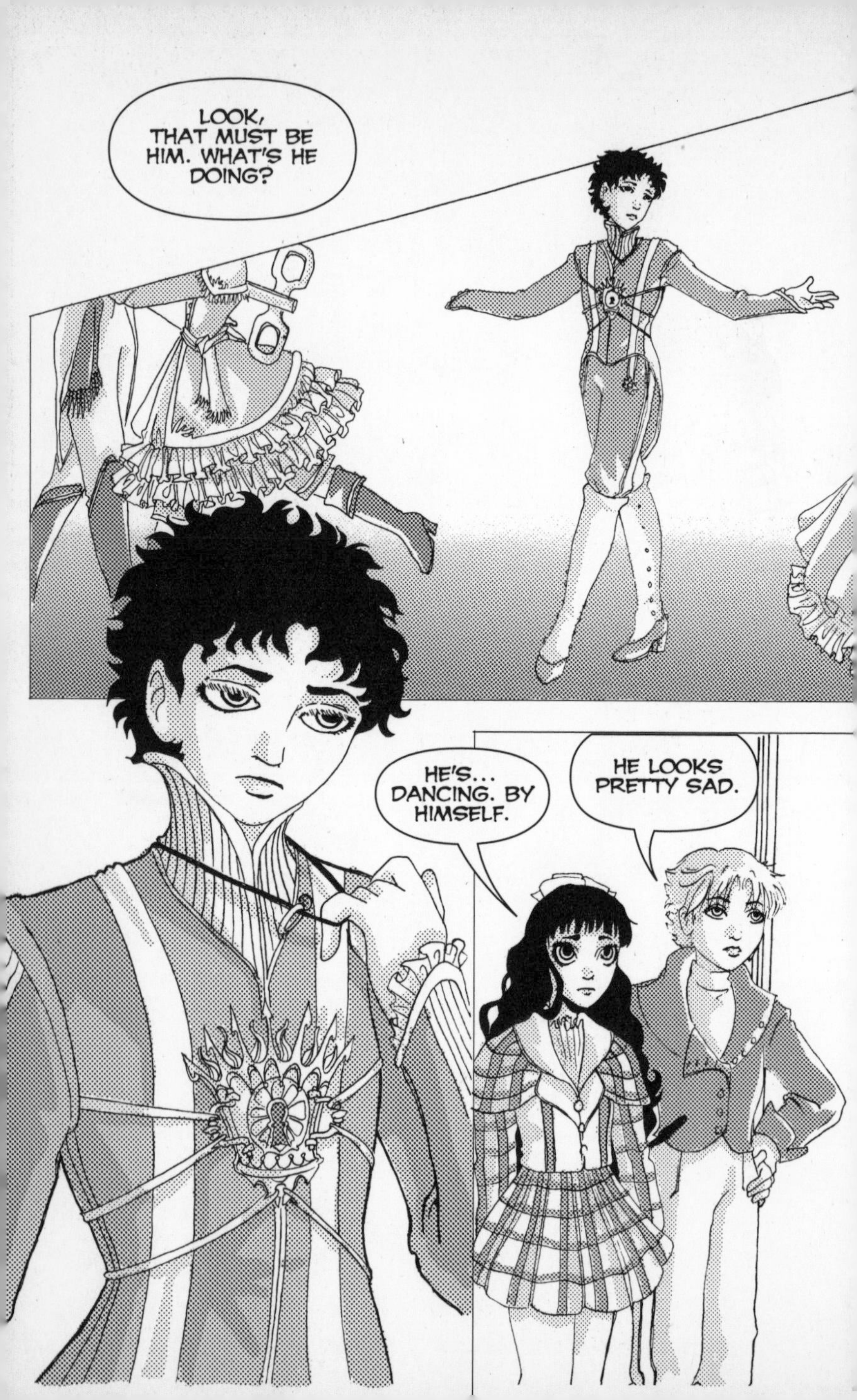
LOOK, THAT MUST BE HIM. WHAT'S HE DOING?
HE'S... DANCING. BY HIMSELF.
HE LOOKS PRETTY SAD.

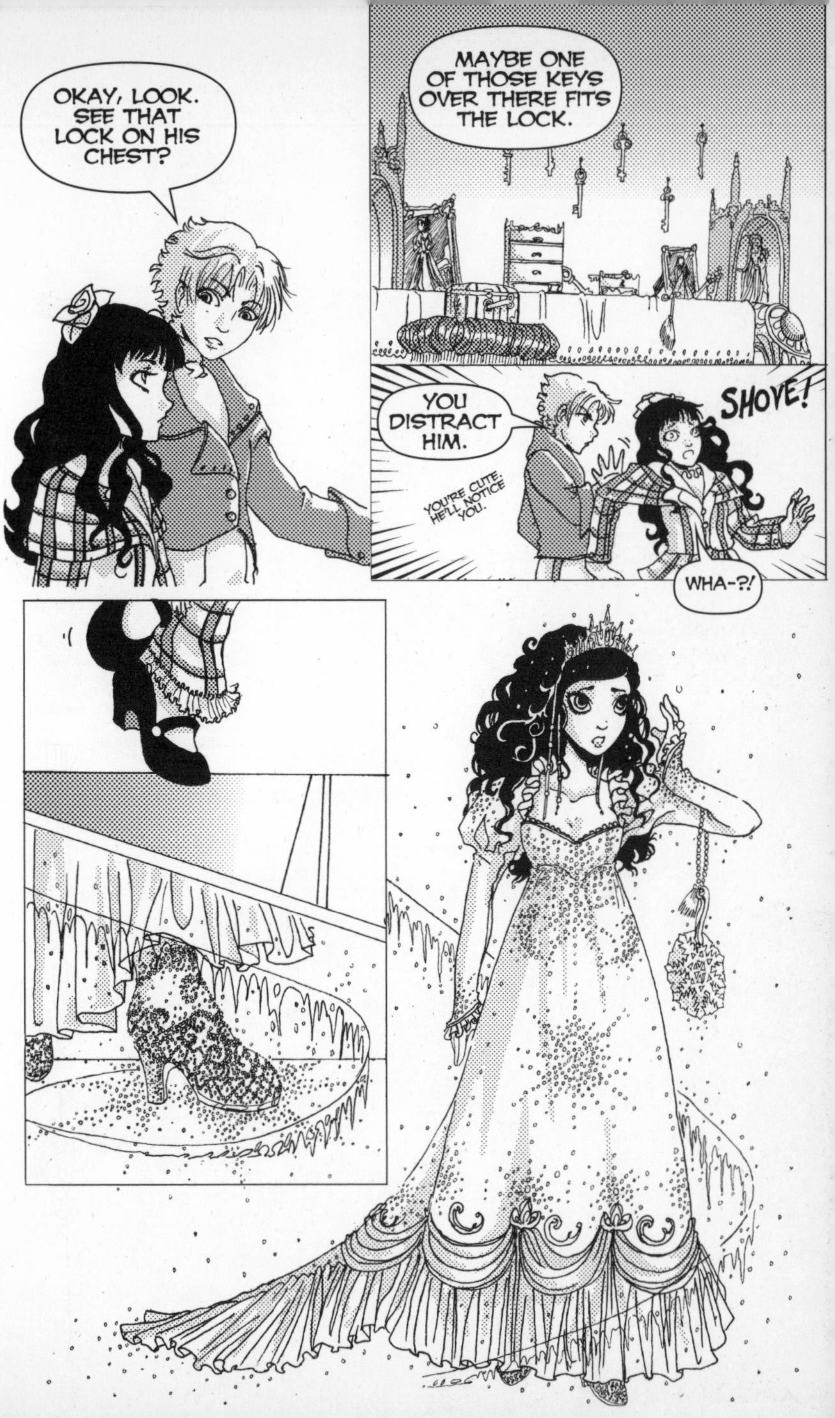
OKAY, LOOK. SEE THAT LOCK ON HIS CHEST?
MAYBE ONE OF THOSE KEYS OVER THERE FITS THE LOCK.
YOU DISTRACT HIM.
YOU'RE CUTE. HE'LL NOTICE YOU.
SHOVE!
WHA-?!

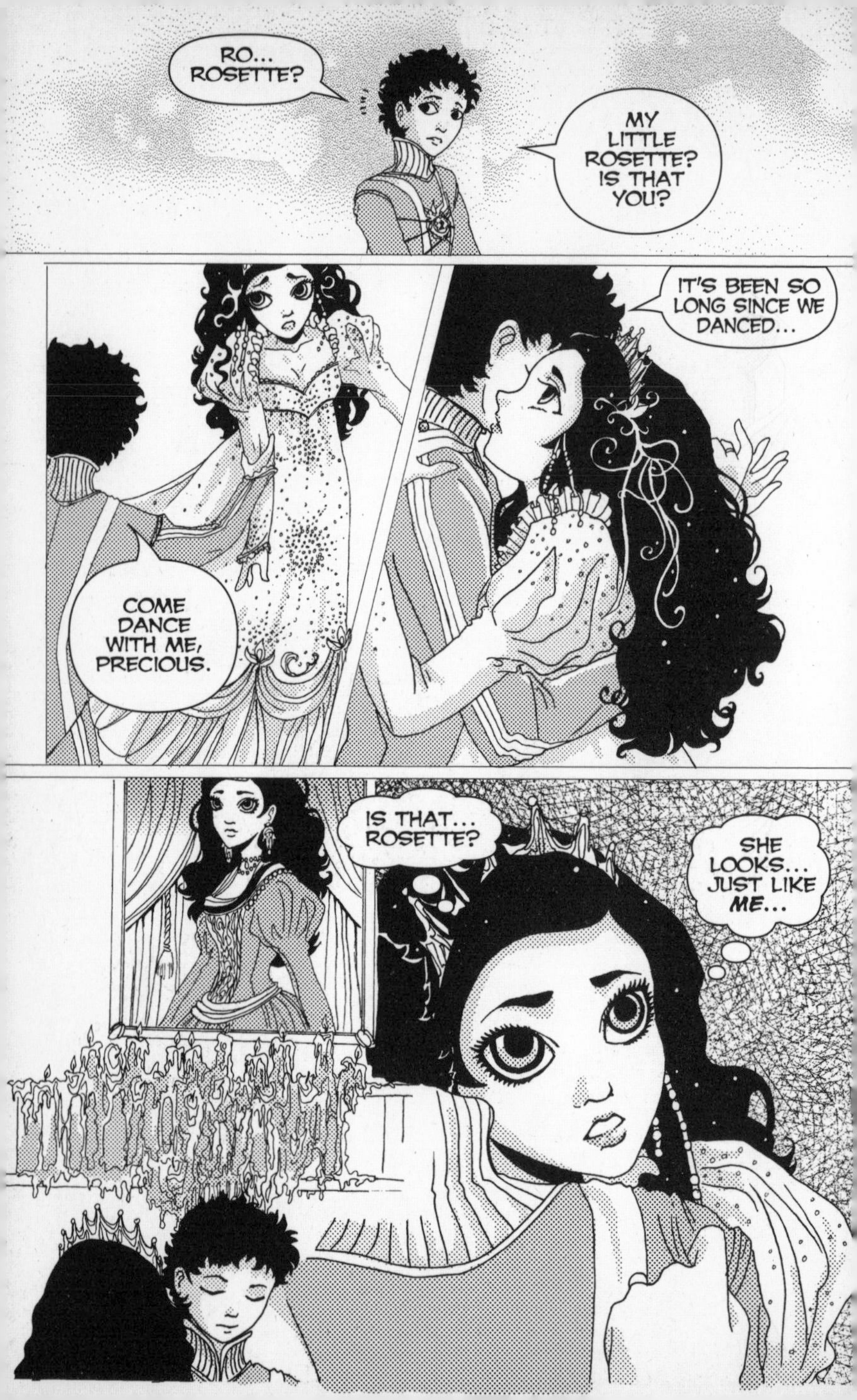
RO... ROSETTE?
MY LITTLE ROSETTE? IS THAT YOU?
COME DANCE WITH ME, PRECIOUS.
IT'S BEEN SO LONG SINCE WE DANCED...
IS THAT... ROSETTE?
SHE LOOKS... JUST LIKE *ME*...

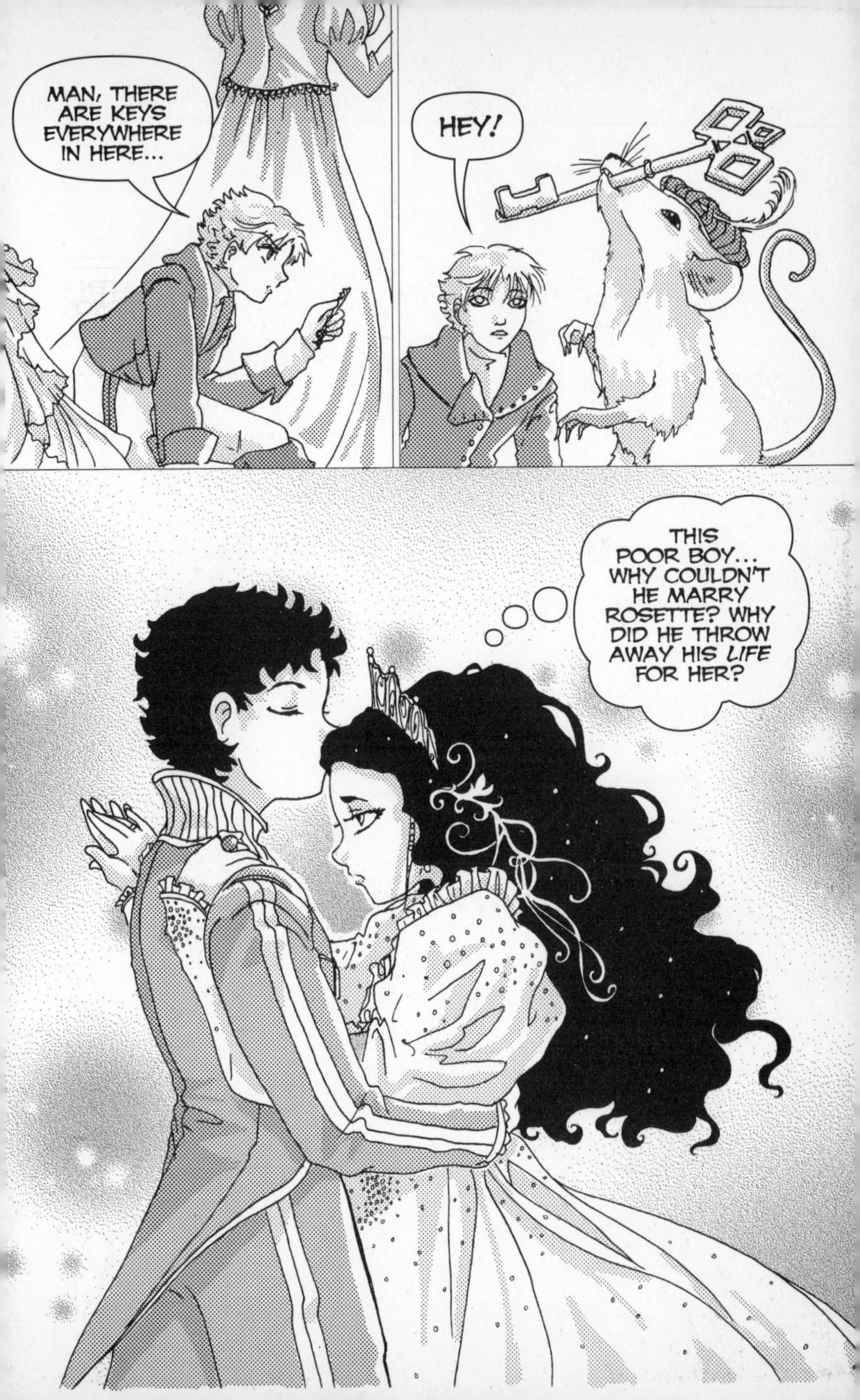
MAN, THERE ARE KEYS EVERYWHERE IN HERE...
HEY!
THIS POOR BOY... WHY COULDN'T HE MARRY ROSETTE? WHY DID HE THROW AWAY HIS *LIFE* FOR HER?

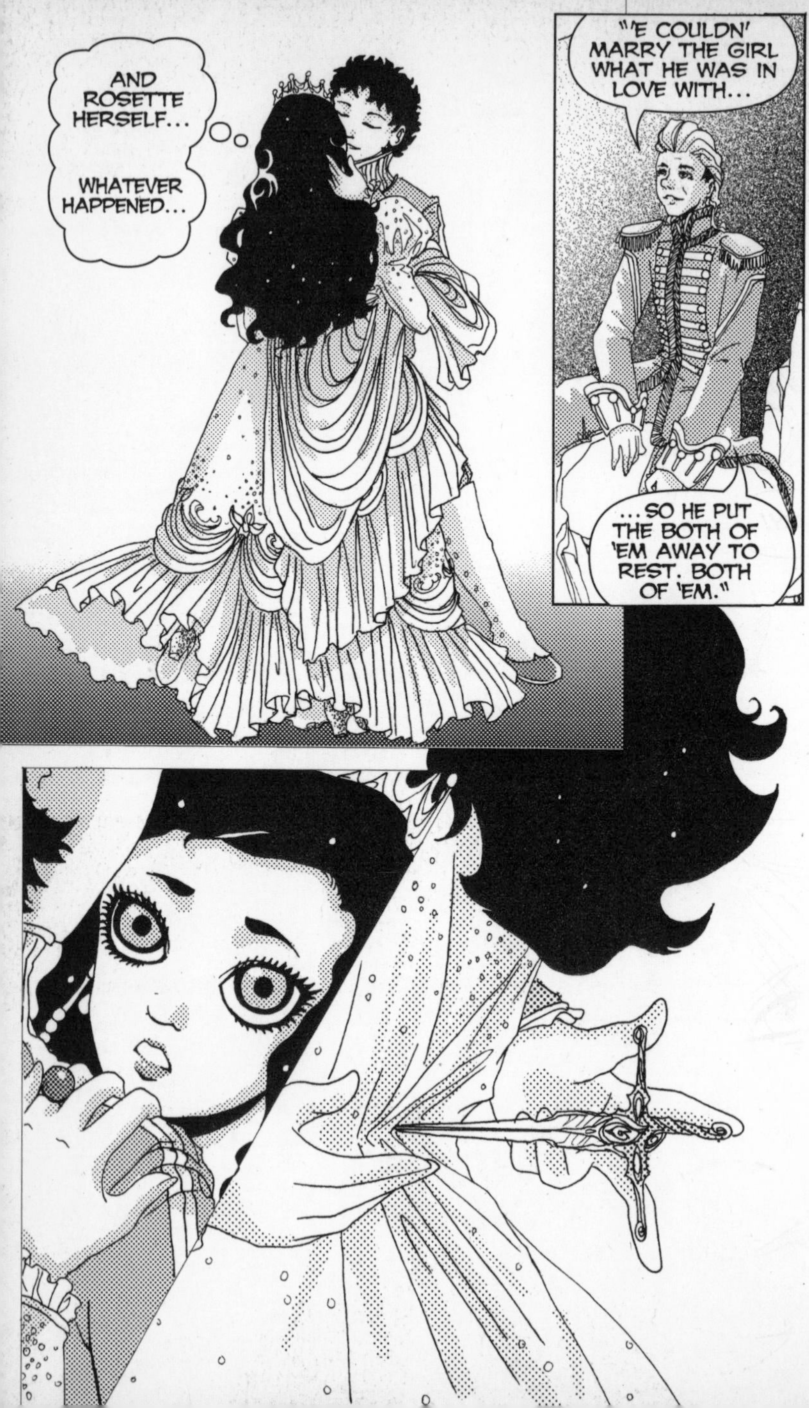
"'E COULDN' MARRY THE GIRL WHAT HE WAS IN LOVE WITH...
...SO HE PUT THE BOTH OF 'EM AWAY TO REST. BOTH OF 'EM."
AND ROSETTE HERSELF...
WHATEVER HAPPENED...

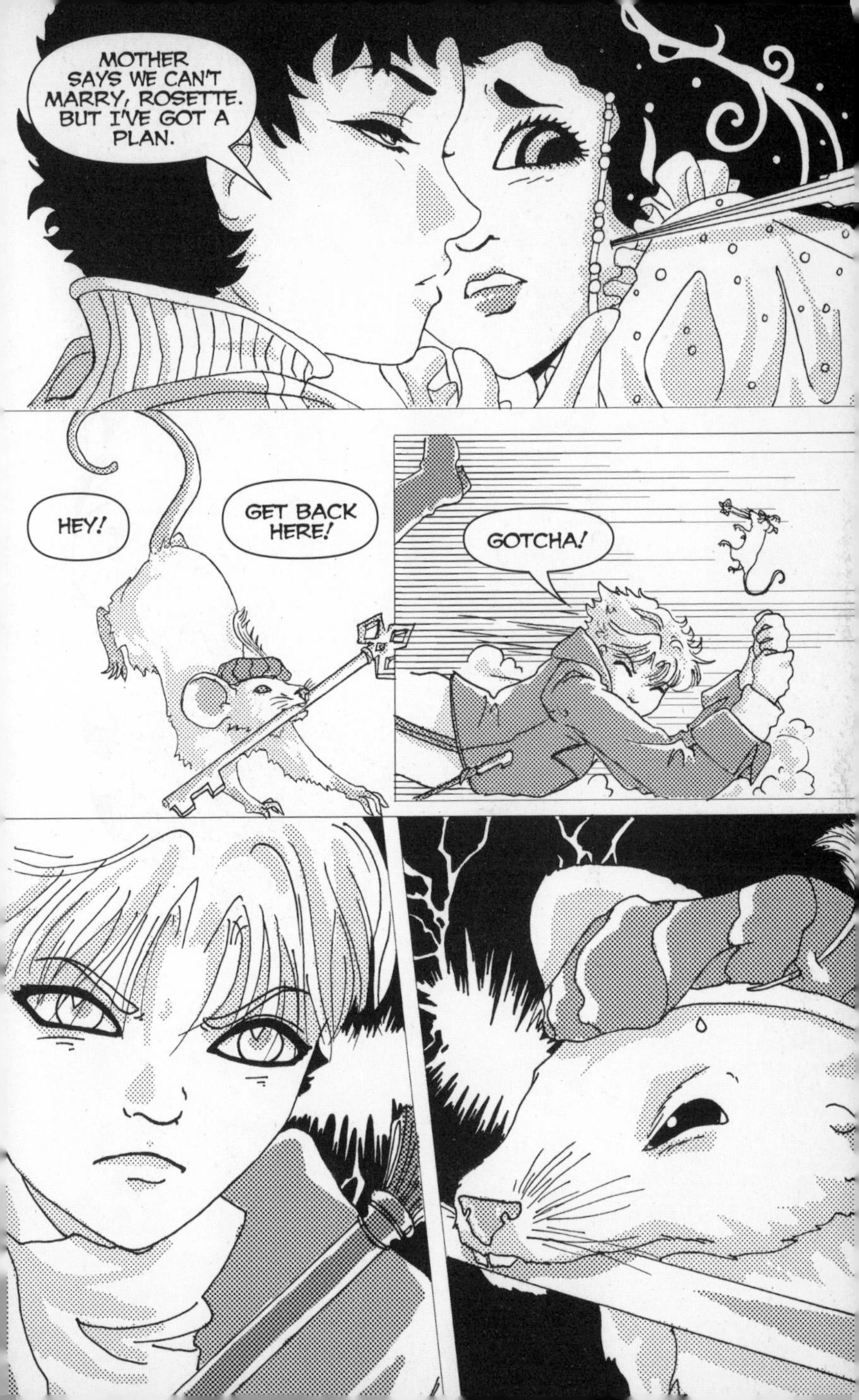
MOTHER SAYS WE CAN'T MARRY, ROSETTE. BUT I'VE GOT A PLAN.
HEY!
GET BACK HERE!
GOTCHA!

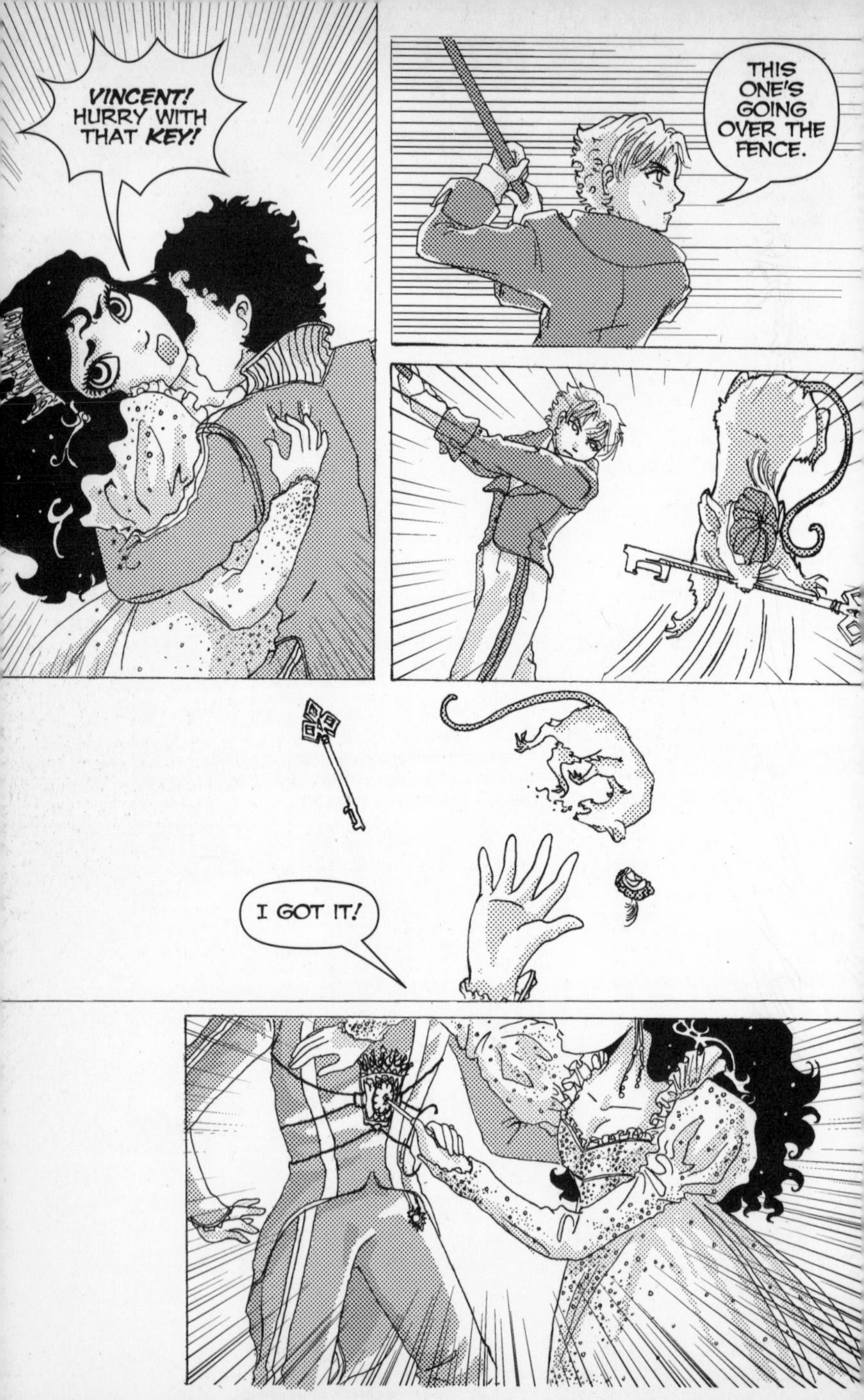
VINCENT! HURRY WITH THAT KEY!
THIS ONE'S GOING OVER THE FENCE.
I GOT IT!

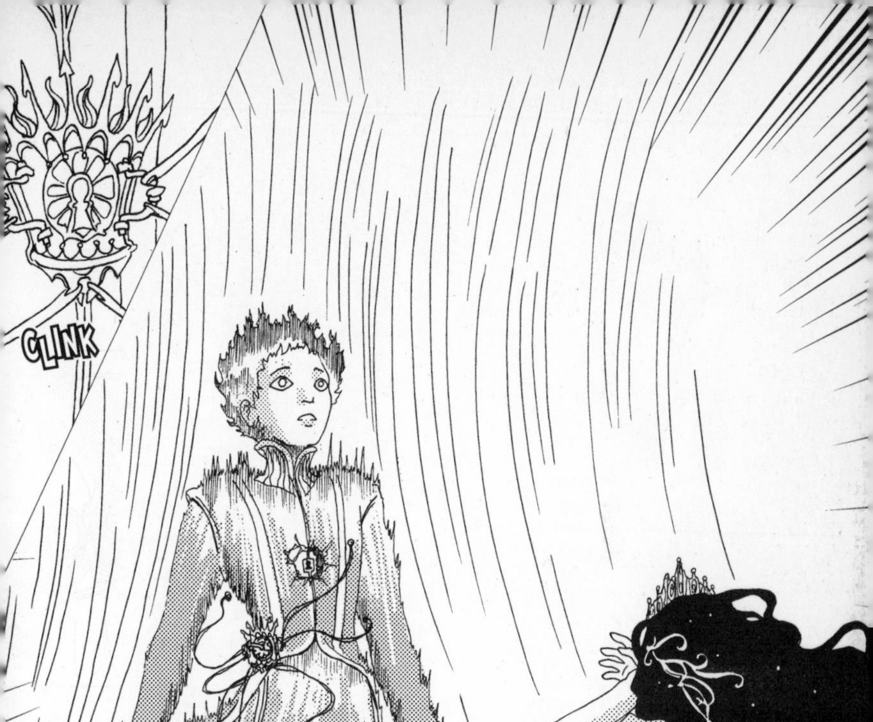
CLINK
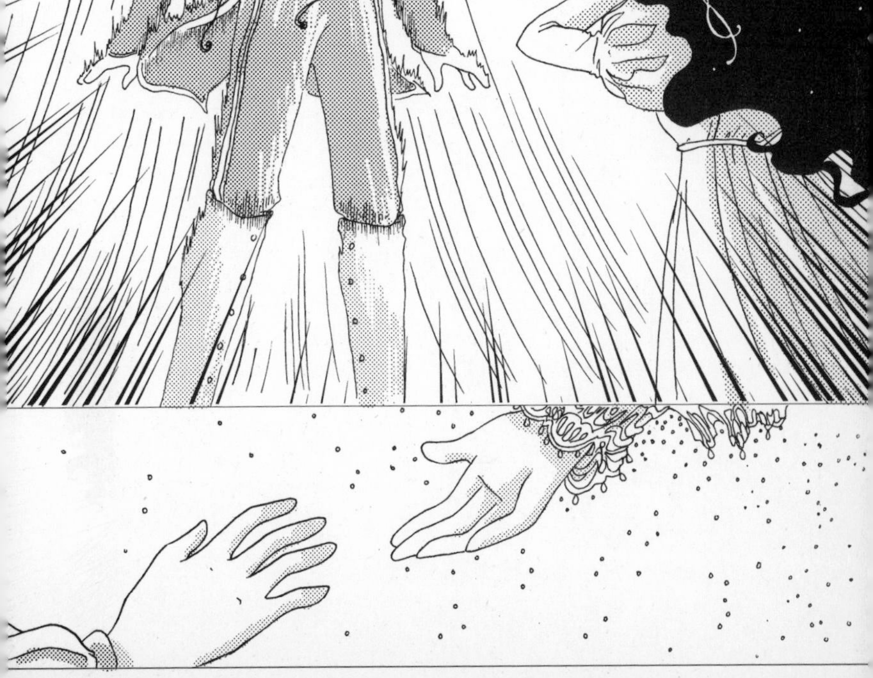

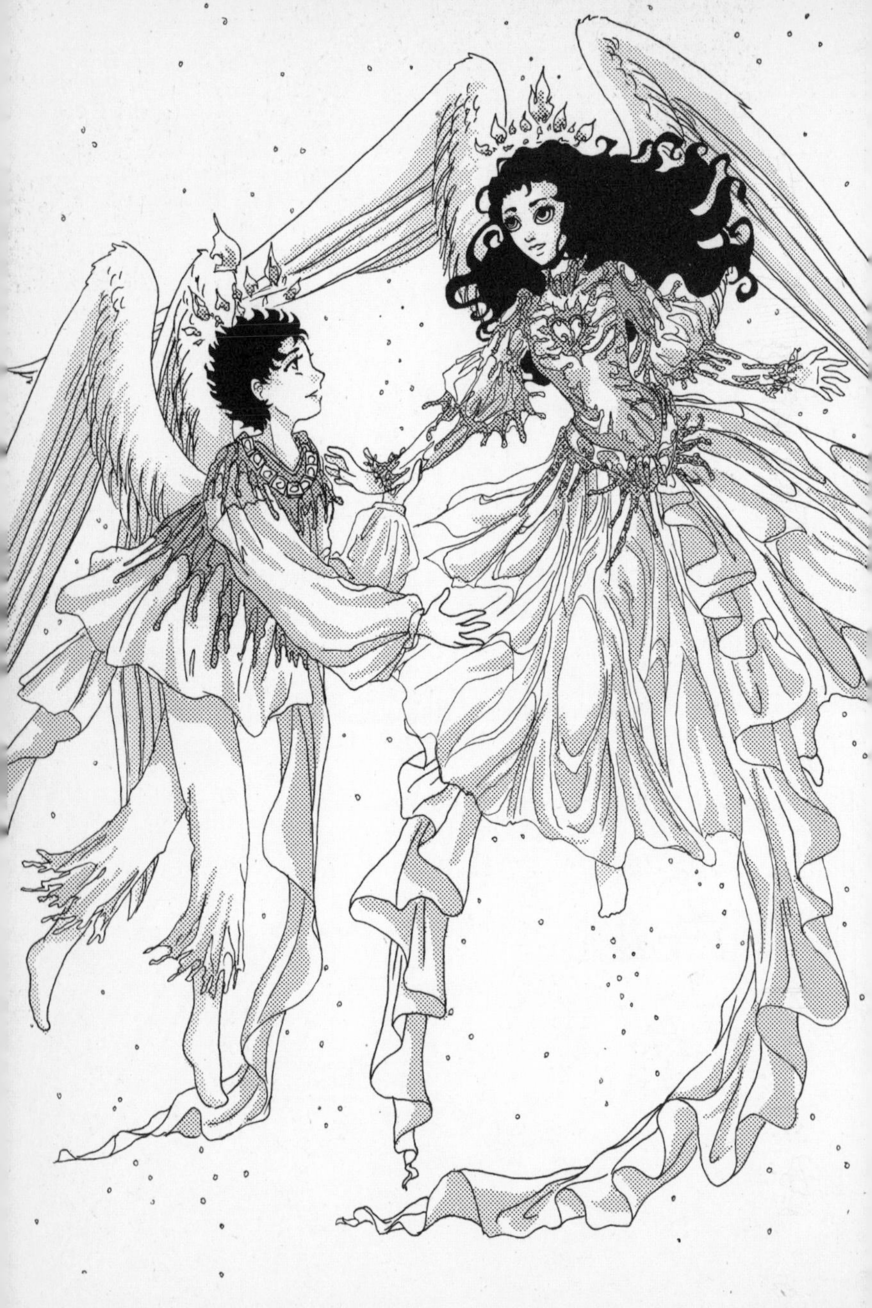

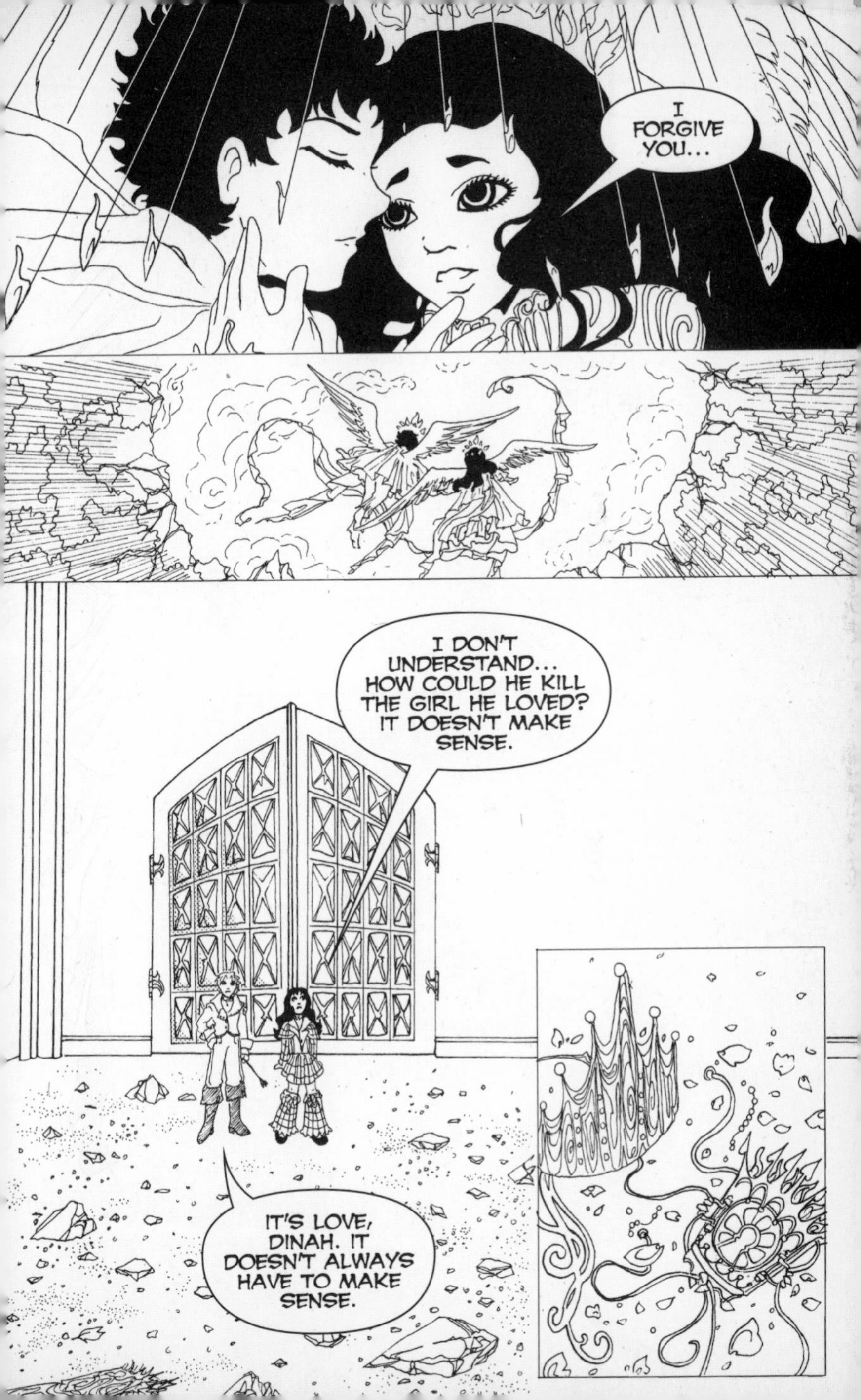
I FORGIVE YOU...
I DON'T UNDERSTAND... HOW COULD HE KILL THE GIRL HE LOVED? IT DOESN'T MAKE SENSE.
IT'S LOVE, DINAH. IT DOESN'T ALWAYS HAVE TO MAKE SENSE.

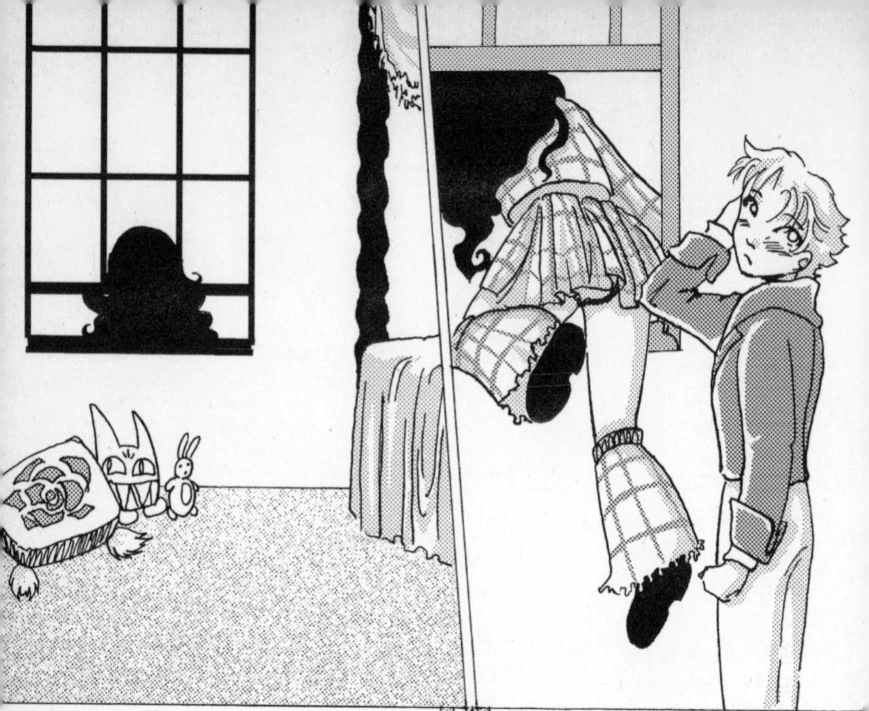

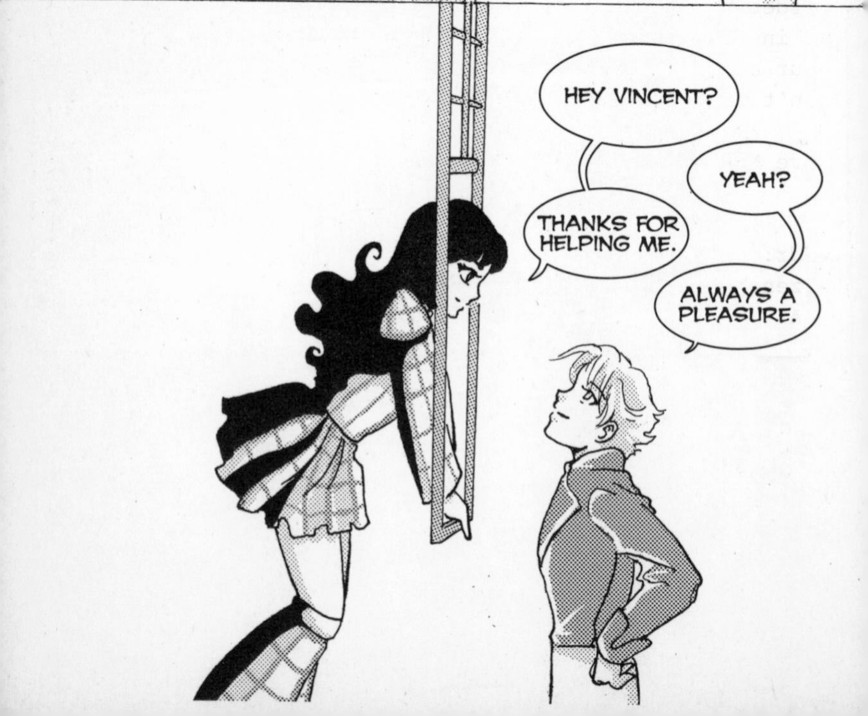
HEY VINCENT?
YEAH?
THANKS FOR HELPING ME.
ALWAYS A PLEASURE.

cn: 168-0229A

dest: 33802   MA

MERCURY
TELEGRAM

582732-348282-009-243
To: V. Monroe
From: V. Monroe Sr.

We're extending our travel plans for a few more months
stop Be sure to water your mother's plants and have the
gardener put the perennials in stop Hope you're keeping
up in your studies stop Wiring money for expenses to
your account tomorrow stop Keep the house clean and
don't make too much work for the housekeeper stop

Love Mom and Dad

Addr: 46 Glass Factory Rd.
Bizenghast, MA 33802
USA

TEAR HERE

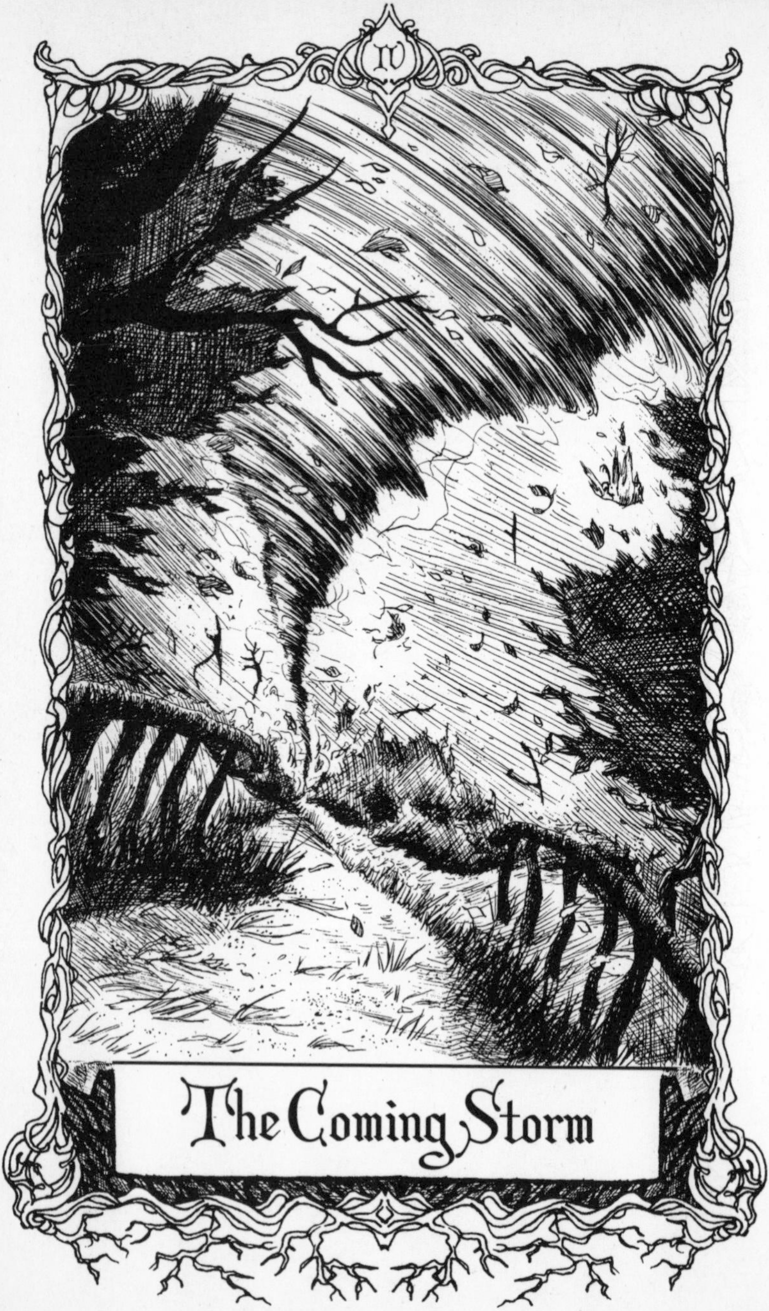
IV
The Coming Storm

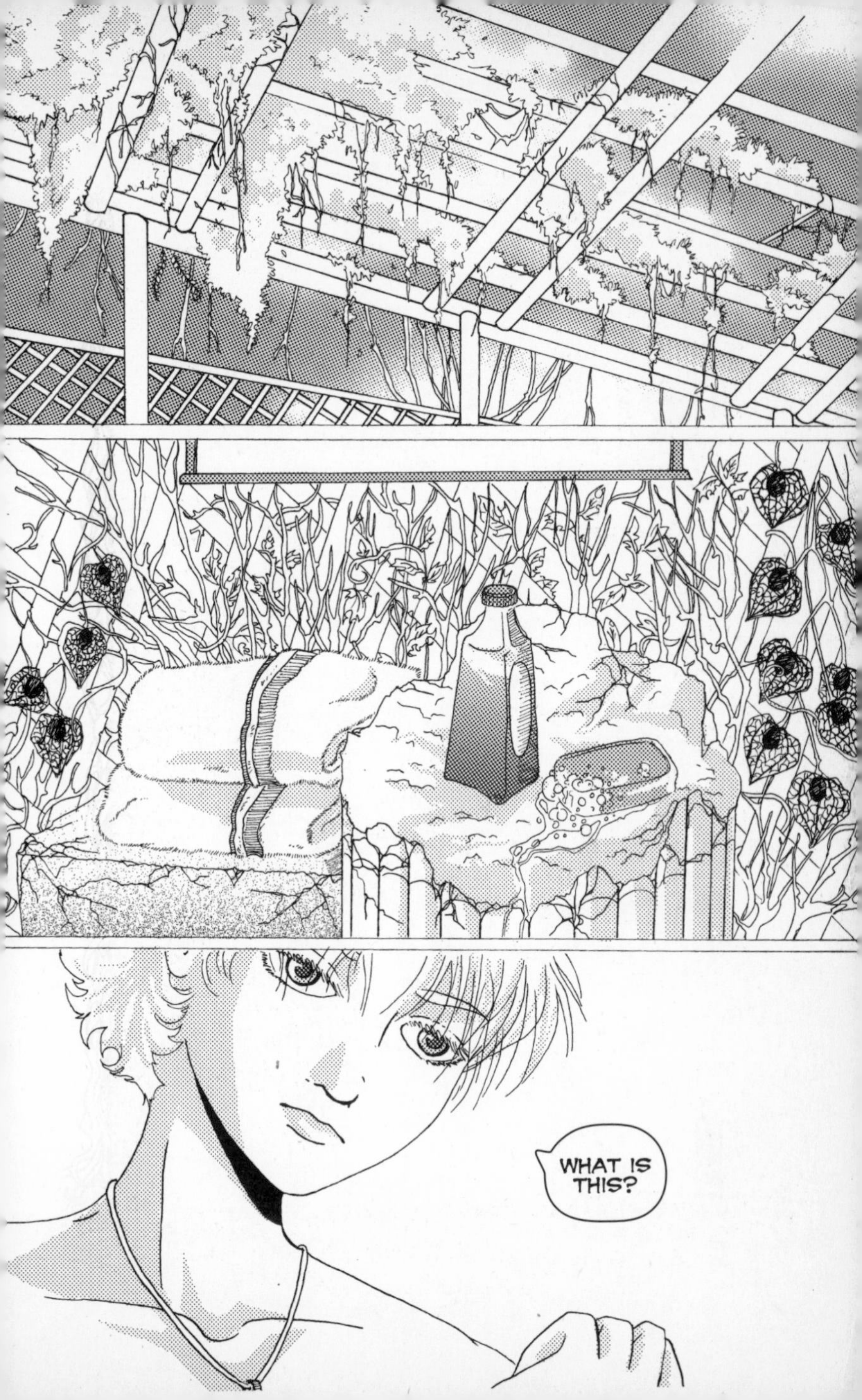
WHAT IS THIS?

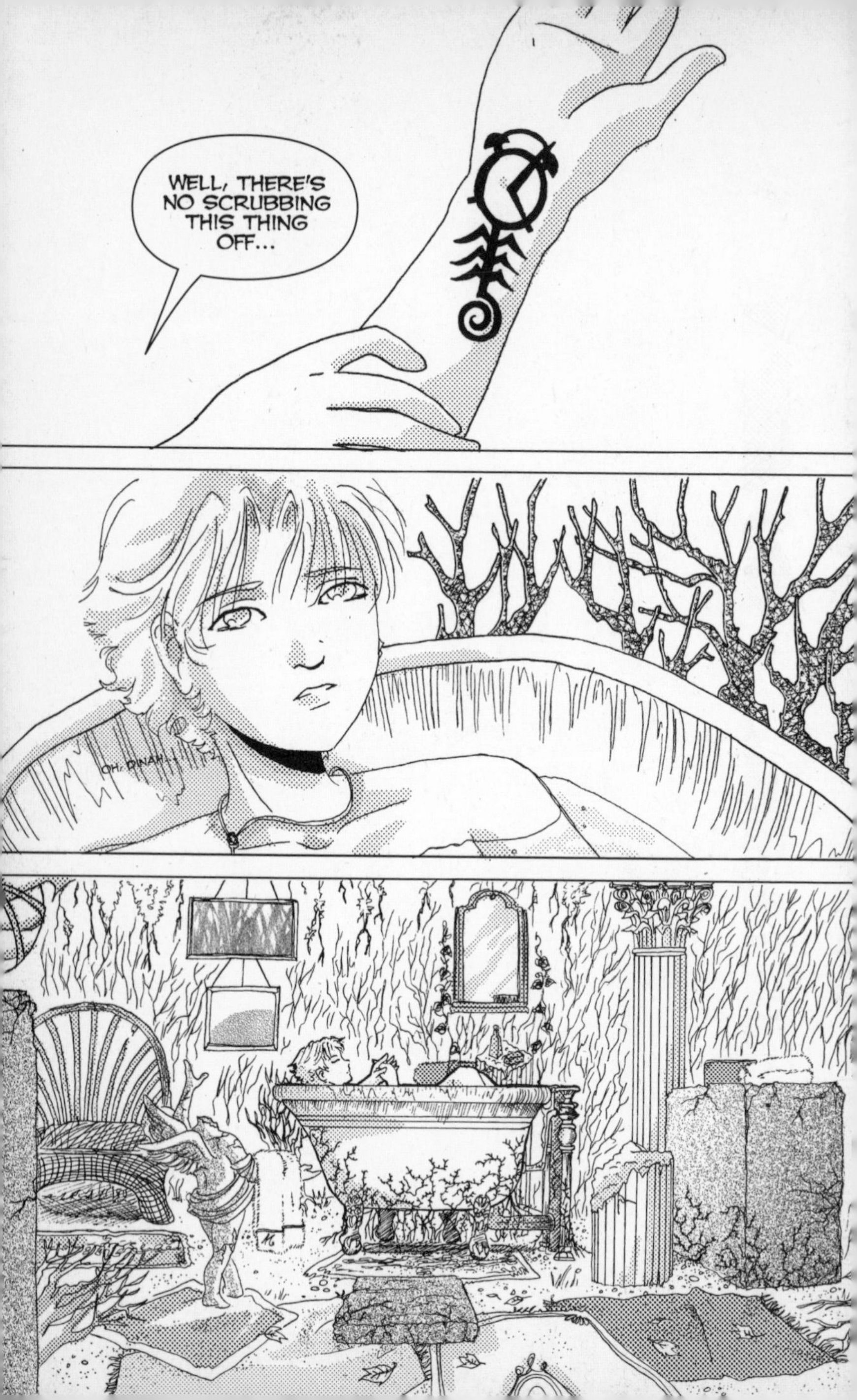
WELL, THERE'S NO SCRUBBING THIS THING OFF...
OH, DINAH...

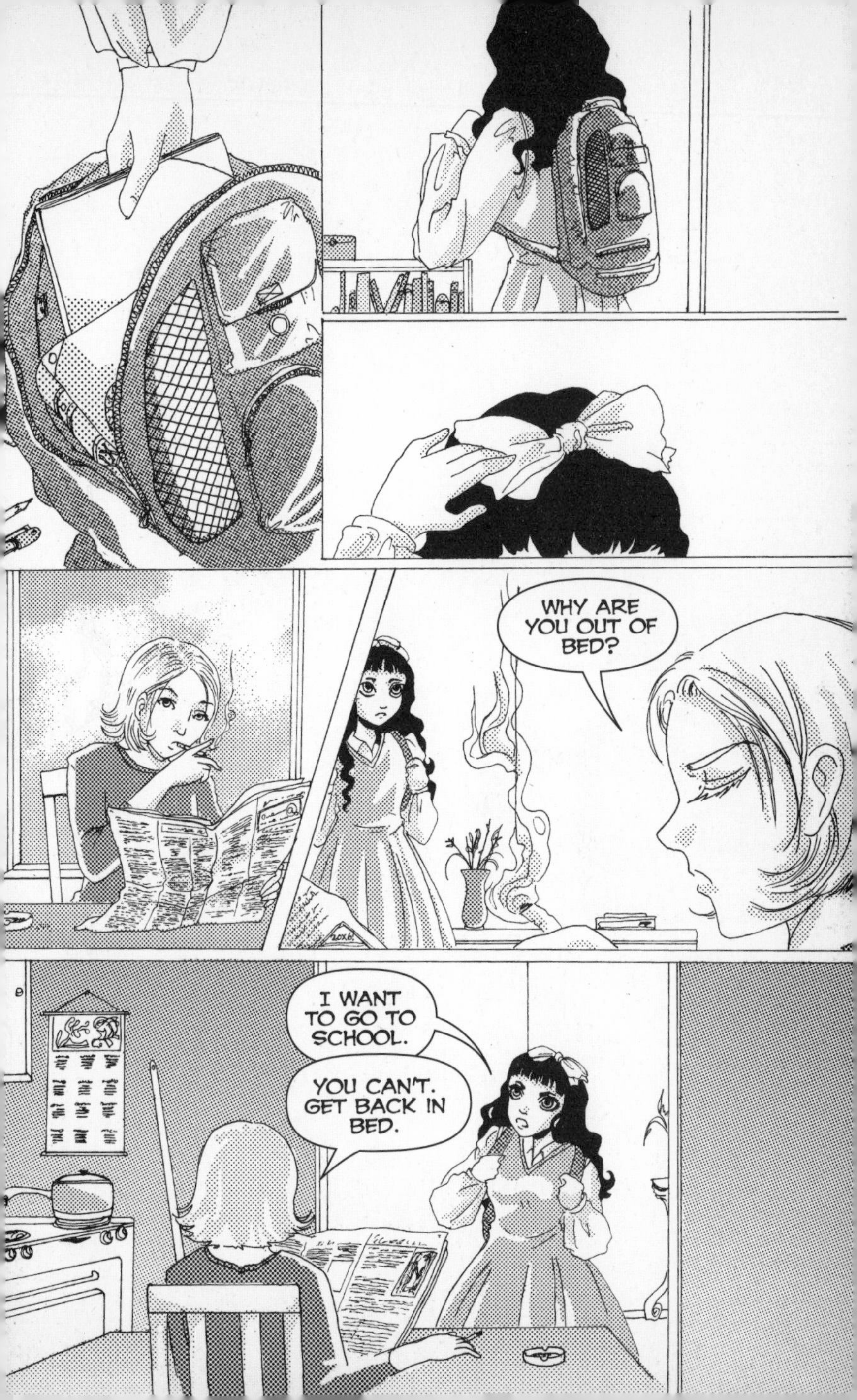
WHY ARE YOU OUT OF BED?
I WANT TO GO TO SCHOOL.
YOU CAN'T. GET BACK IN BED.

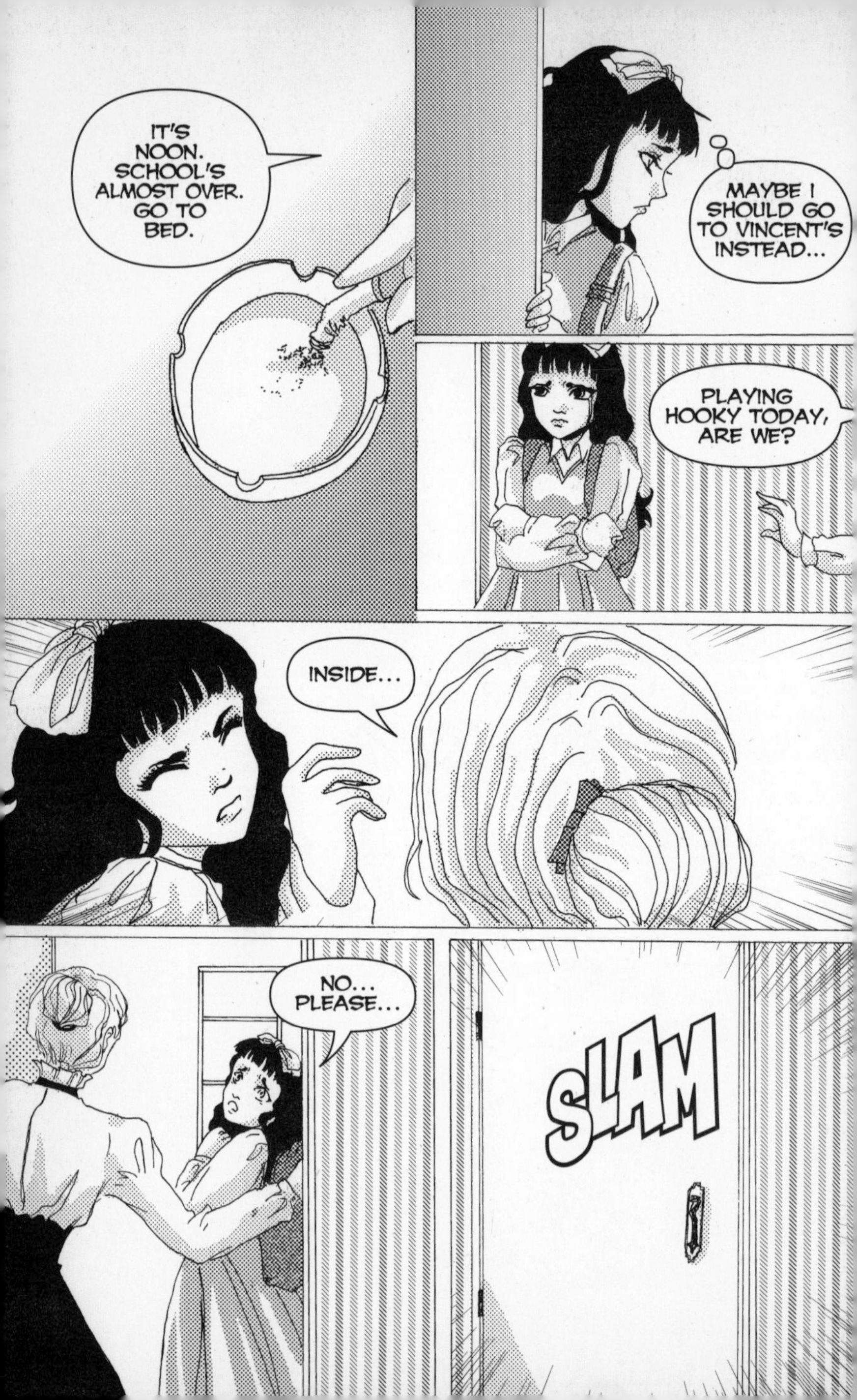
IT'S NOON. SCHOOL'S ALMOST OVER. GO TO BED.
MAYBE I SHOULD GO TO VINCENT'S INSTEAD...
PLAYING HOOKY TODAY, ARE WE?
INSIDE...
NO... PLEASE...
SLAM

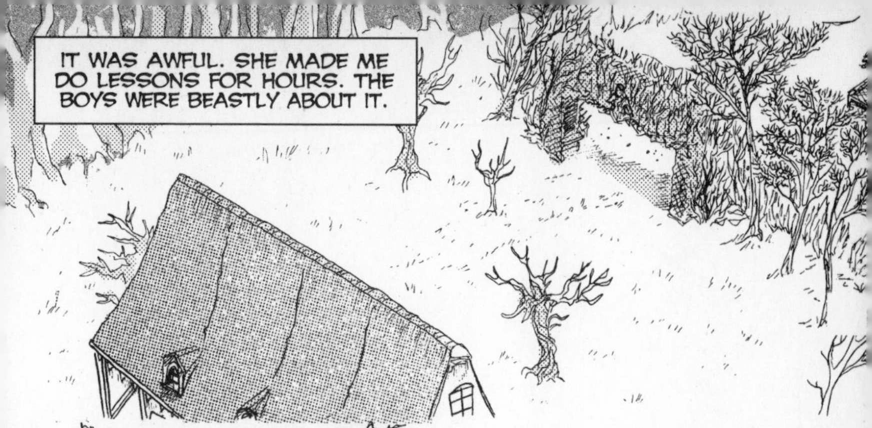
IT WAS AWFUL. SHE MADE ME DO LESSONS FOR HOURS. THE BOYS WERE BEASTLY ABOUT IT.

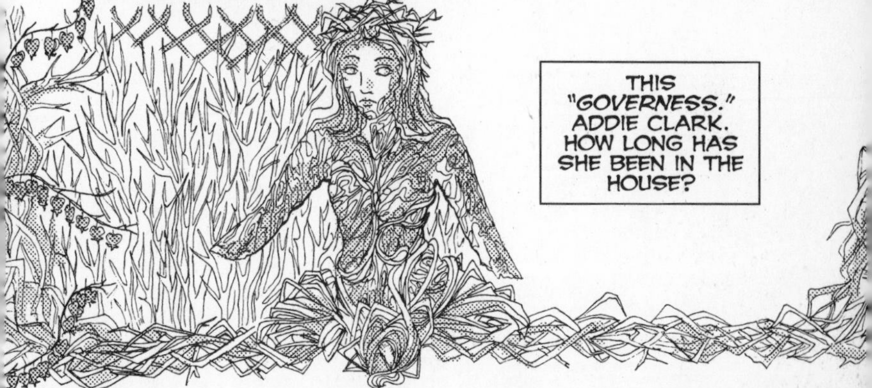
THIS "GOVERNESS." ADDIE CLARK. HOW LONG HAS SHE BEEN IN THE HOUSE?

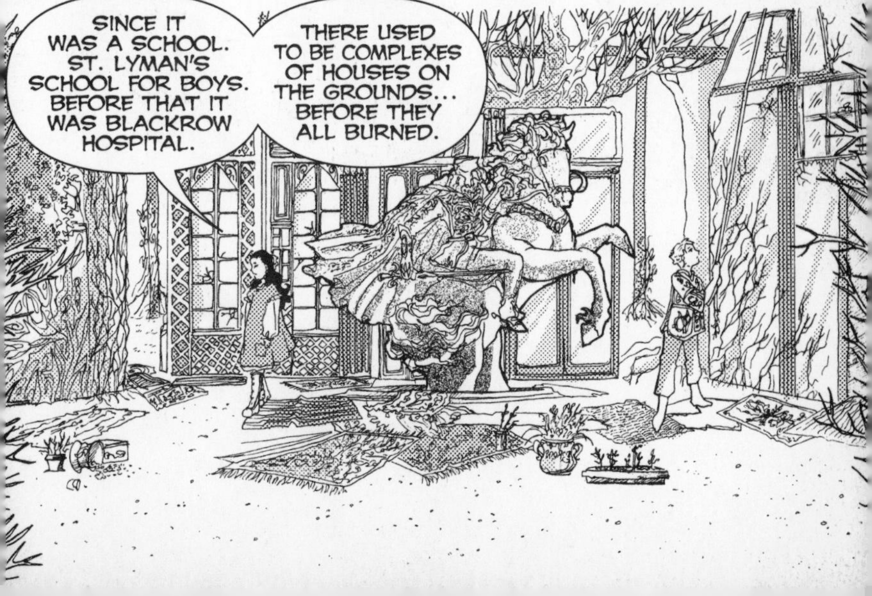
SINCE IT WAS A SCHOOL. ST. LYMAN'S SCHOOL FOR BOYS. BEFORE THAT IT WAS BLACKROW HOSPITAL.
THERE USED TO BE COMPLEXES OF HOUSES ON THE GROUNDS... BEFORE THEY ALL BURNED.

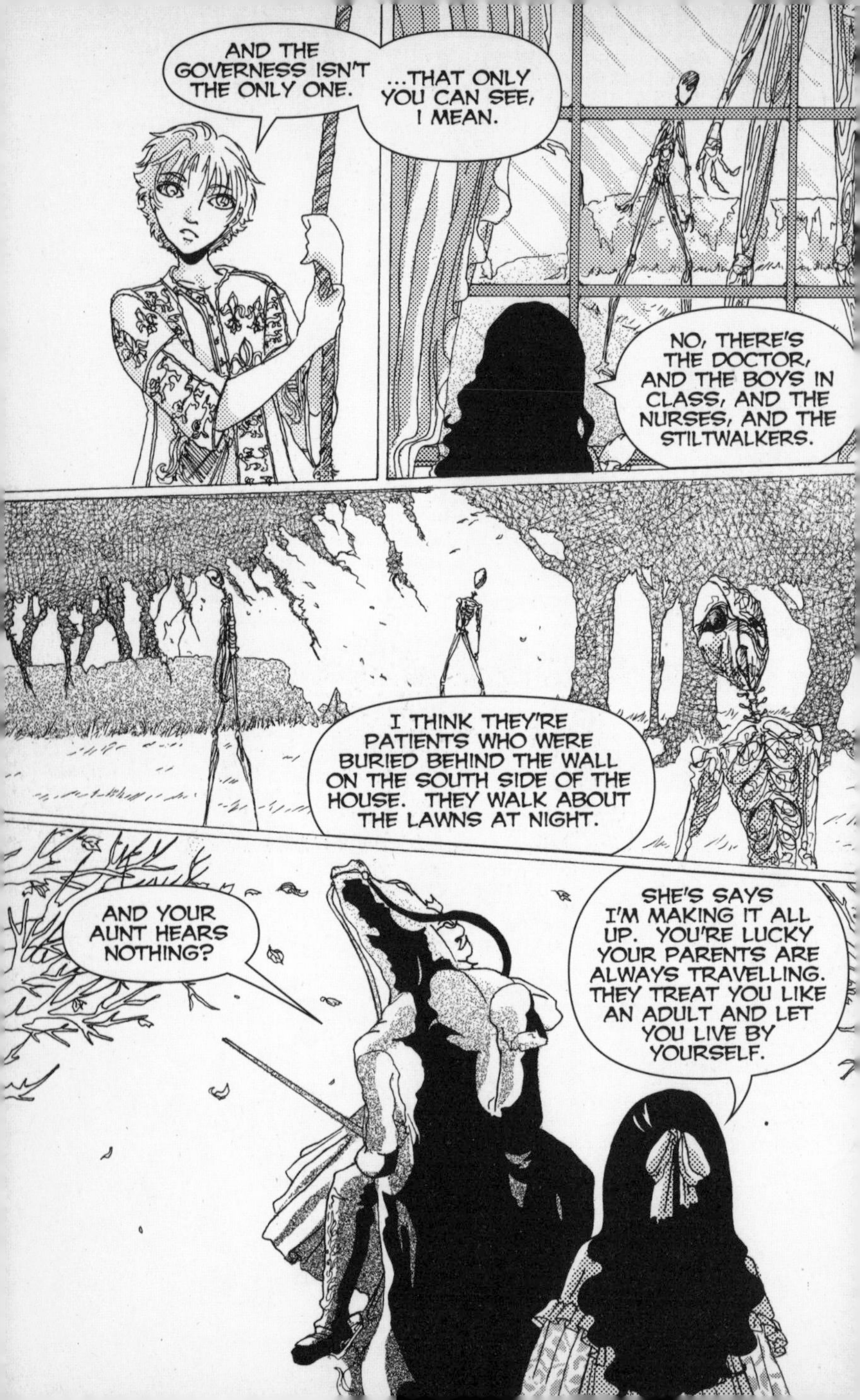
AND THE GOVERNESS ISN'T THE ONLY ONE.
...THAT ONLY YOU CAN SEE, I MEAN.
NO, THERE'S THE DOCTOR, AND THE BOYS IN CLASS, AND THE NURSES, AND THE STILTWALKERS.
I THINK THEY'RE PATIENTS WHO WERE BURIED BEHIND THE WALL ON THE SOUTH SIDE OF THE HOUSE. THEY WALK ABOUT THE LAWNS AT NIGHT.
AND YOUR AUNT HEARS NOTHING?
SHE'S SAYS I'M MAKING IT ALL UP. YOU'RE LUCKY YOUR PARENTS ARE ALWAYS TRAVELLING. THEY TREAT YOU LIKE AN ADULT AND LET YOU LIVE BY YOURSELF.

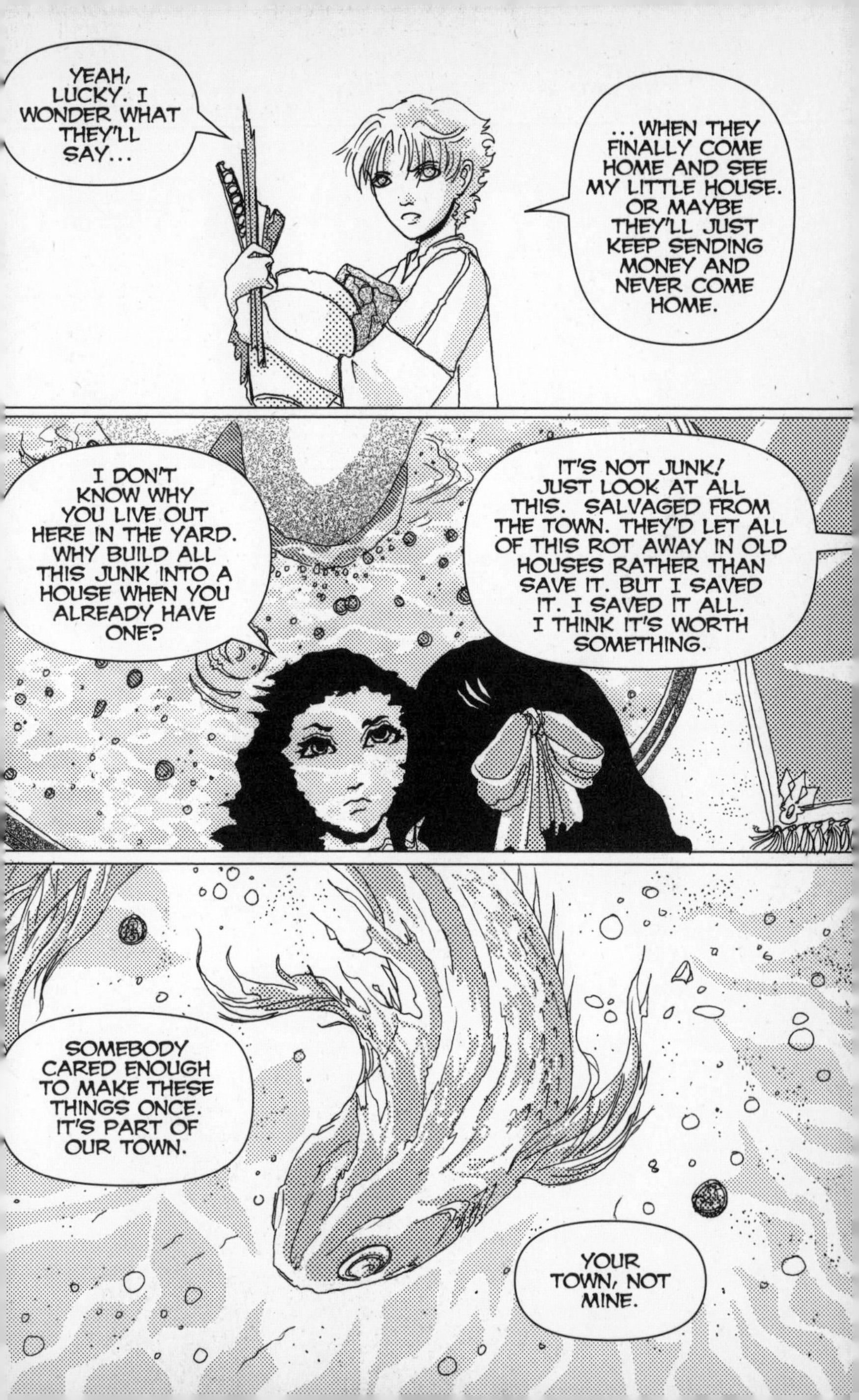
YEAH, LUCKY. I WONDER WHAT THEY'LL SAY...
...WHEN THEY FINALLY COME HOME AND SEE MY LITTLE HOUSE. OR MAYBE THEY'LL JUST KEEP SENDING MONEY AND NEVER COME HOME.
I DON'T KNOW WHY YOU LIVE OUT HERE IN THE YARD. WHY BUILD ALL THIS JUNK INTO A HOUSE WHEN YOU ALREADY HAVE ONE?
IT'S NOT JUNK! JUST LOOK AT ALL THIS. SALVAGED FROM THE TOWN. THEY'D LET ALL OF THIS ROT AWAY IN OLD HOUSES RATHER THAN SAVE IT. BUT I SAVED IT. I SAVED IT ALL. I THINK IT'S WORTH SOMETHING.
SOMEBODY CARED ENOUGH TO MAKE THESE THINGS ONCE. IT'S PART OF OUR TOWN.
YOUR TOWN, NOT MINE.

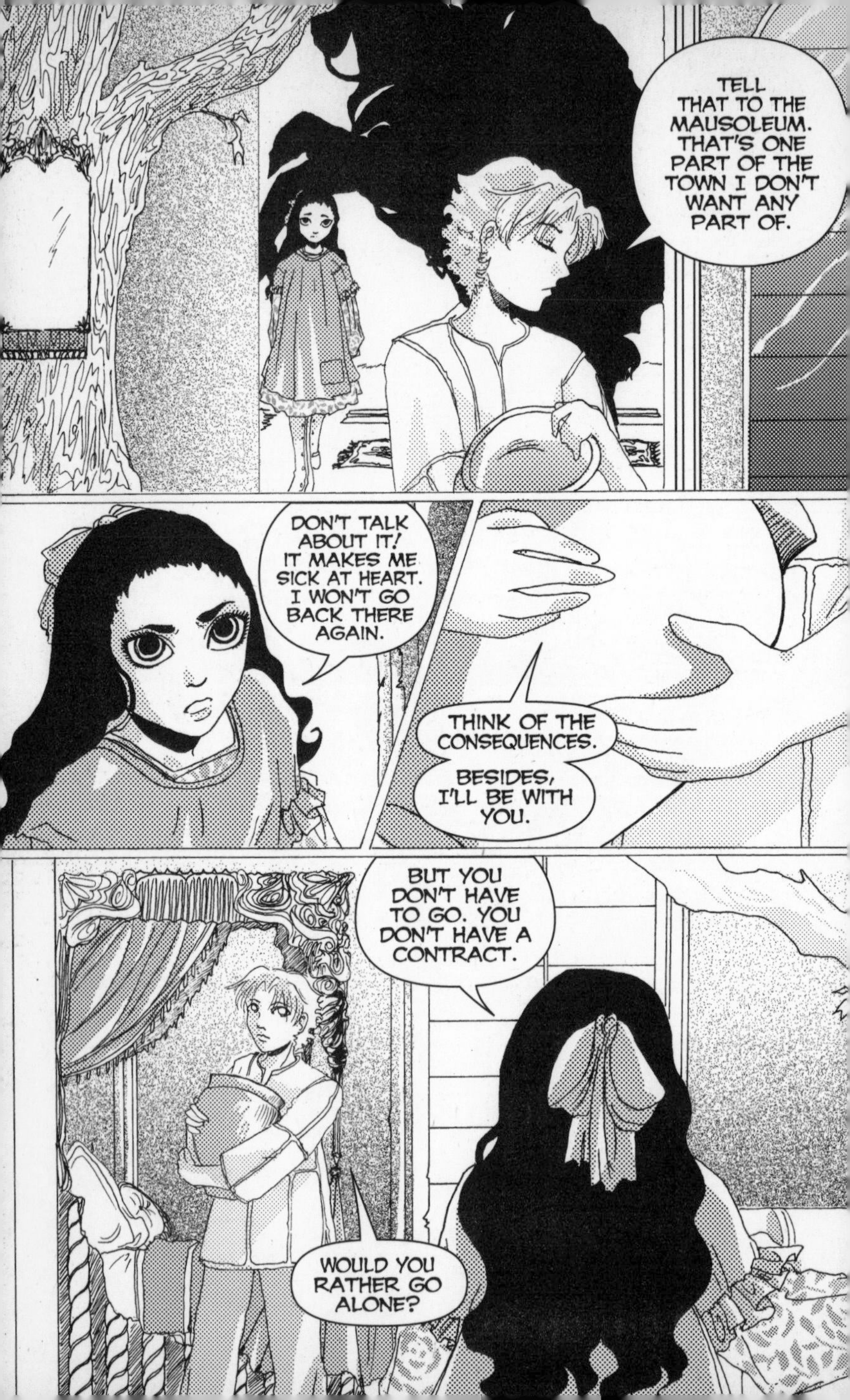
TELL THAT TO THE MAUSOLEUM. THAT'S ONE PART OF THE TOWN I DON'T WANT ANY PART OF.
DON'T TALK ABOUT IT! IT MAKES ME SICK AT HEART. I WON'T GO BACK THERE AGAIN.
THINK OF THE CONSEQUENCES.
BESIDES, I'LL BE WITH YOU.
BUT YOU DON'T HAVE TO GO. YOU DON'T HAVE A CONTRACT.
WOULD YOU RATHER GO ALONE?

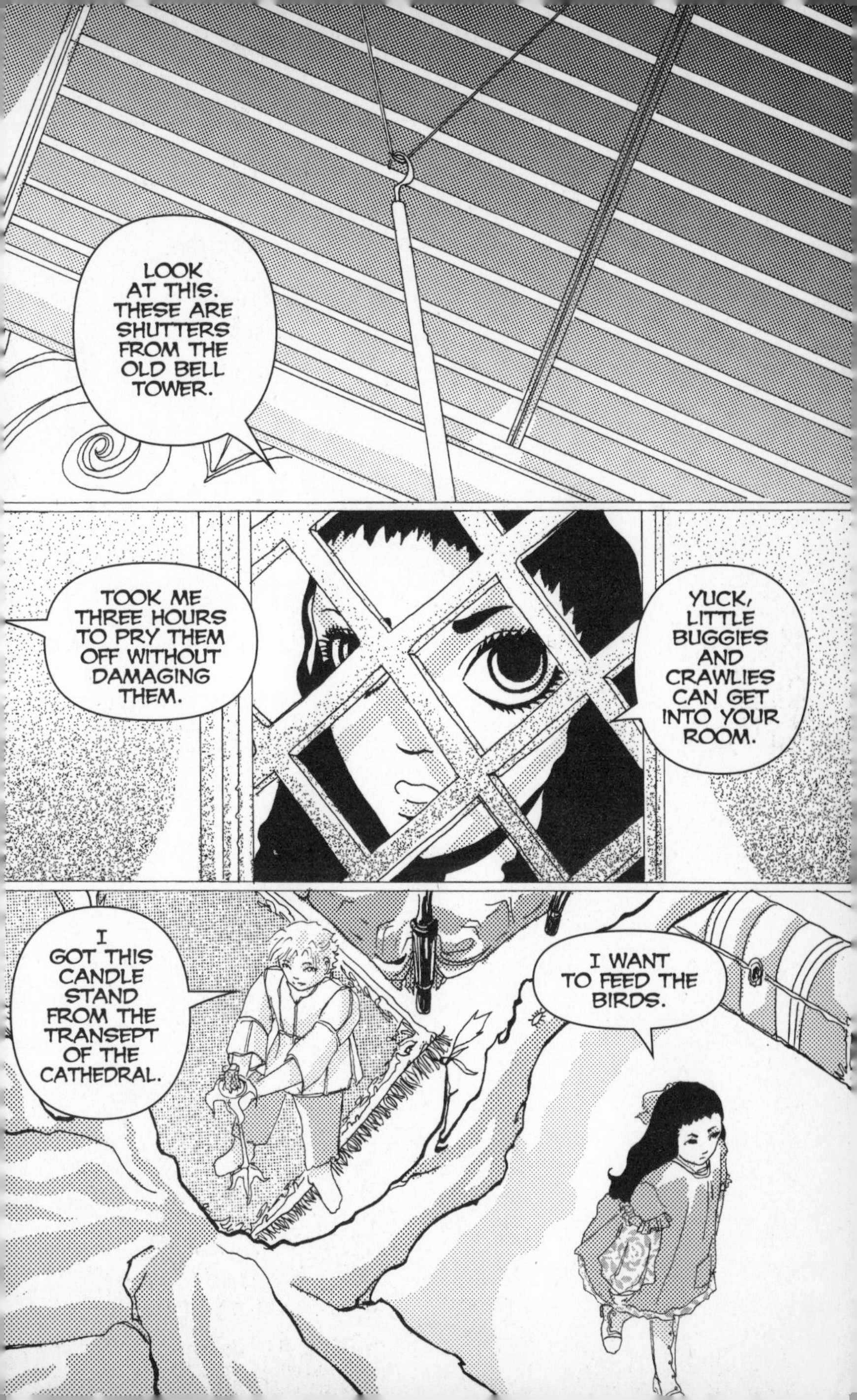
LOOK AT THIS. THESE ARE SHUTTERS FROM THE OLD BELL TOWER.
TOOK ME THREE HOURS TO PRY THEM OFF WITHOUT DAMAGING THEM.
YUCK, LITTLE BUGGIES AND CRAWLIES CAN GET INTO YOUR ROOM.
I GOT THIS CANDLE STAND FROM THE TRANSEPT OF THE CATHEDRAL.
I WANT TO FEED THE BIRDS.

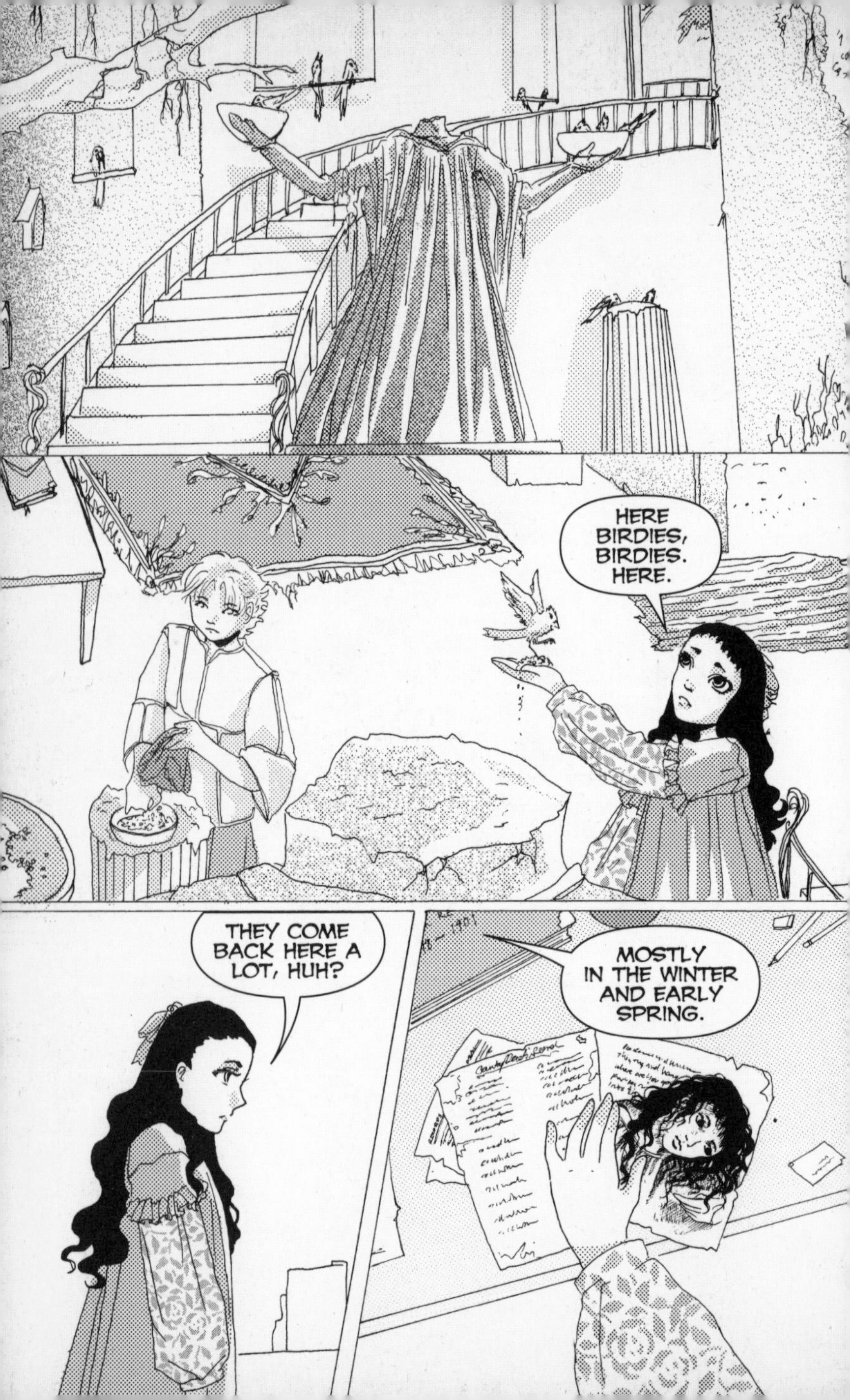
HERE BIRDIES, BIRDIES. HERE.
THEY COME BACK HERE A LOT, HUH?
MOSTLY IN THE WINTER AND EARLY SPRING.

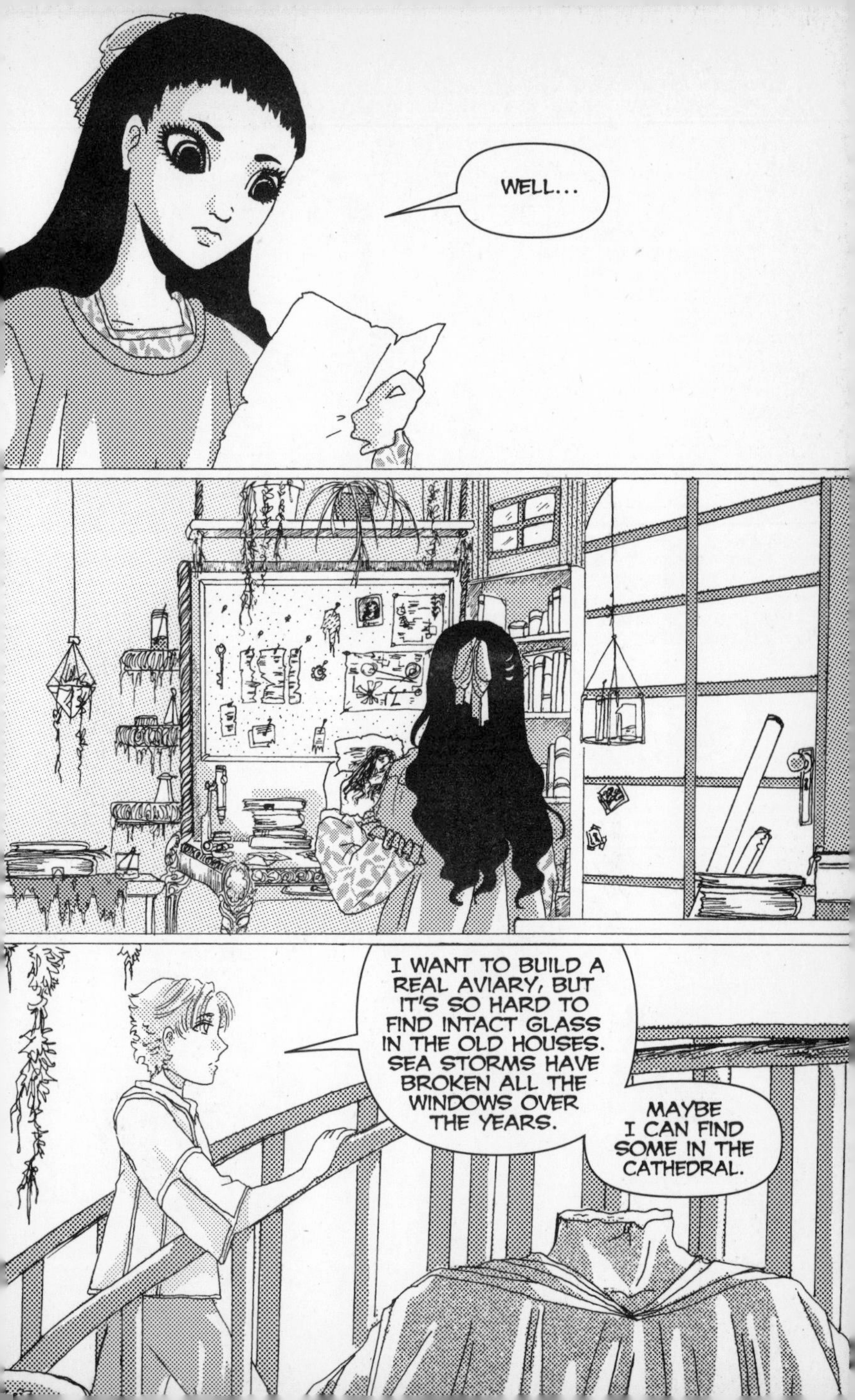
WELL...
I WANT TO BUILD A REAL AVIARY, BUT IT'S SO HARD TO FIND INTACT GLASS IN THE OLD HOUSES. SEA STORMS HAVE BROKEN ALL THE WINDOWS OVER THE YEARS.
MAYBE I CAN FIND SOME IN THE CATHEDRAL.

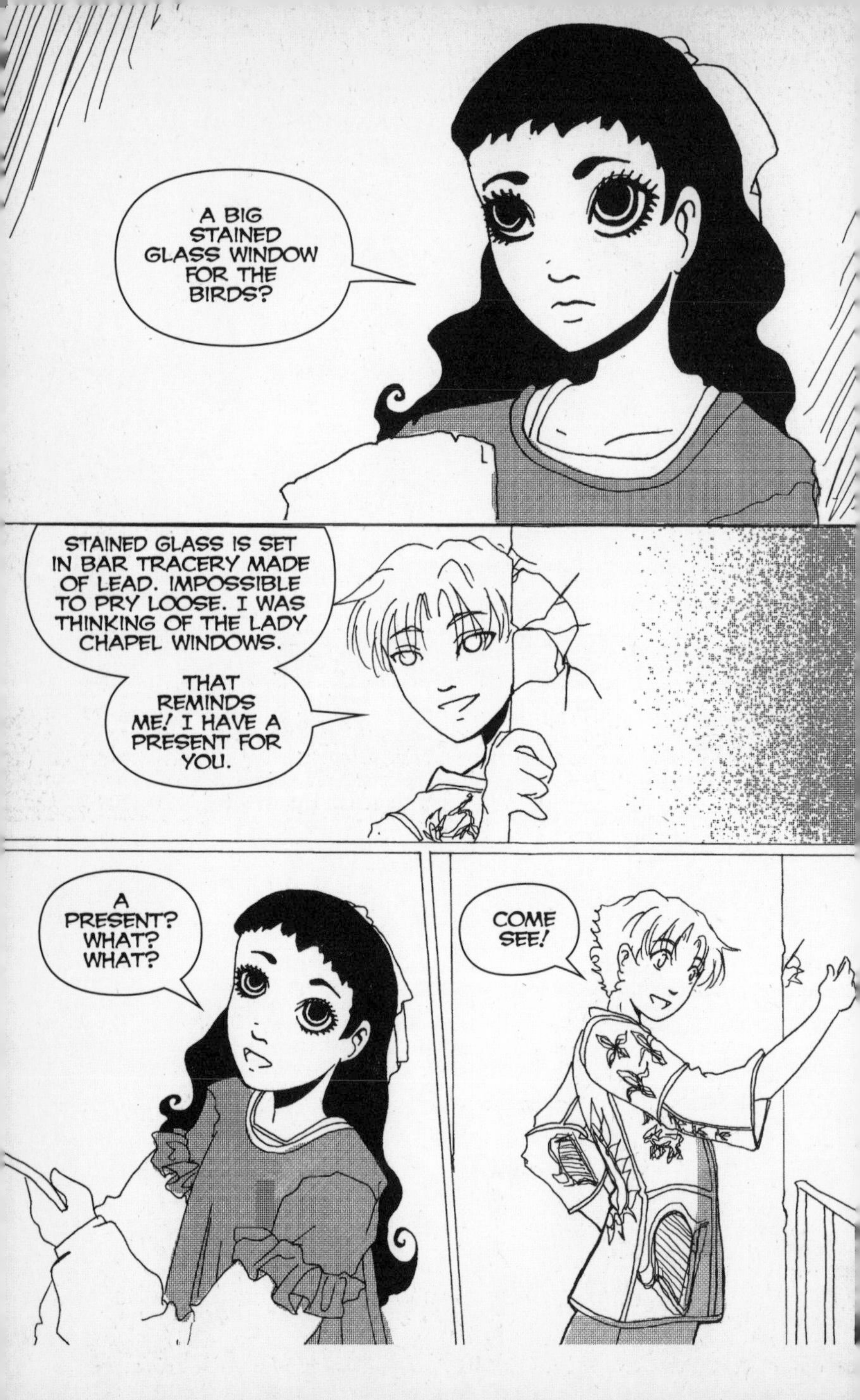
A BIG STAINED GLASS WINDOW FOR THE BIRDS?
STAINED GLASS IS SET IN BAR TRACERY MADE OF LEAD. IMPOSSIBLE TO PRY LOOSE. I WAS THINKING OF THE LADY CHAPEL WINDOWS.
THAT REMINDS ME! I HAVE A PRESENT FOR YOU.
A PRESENT? WHAT? WHAT?
COME SEE!

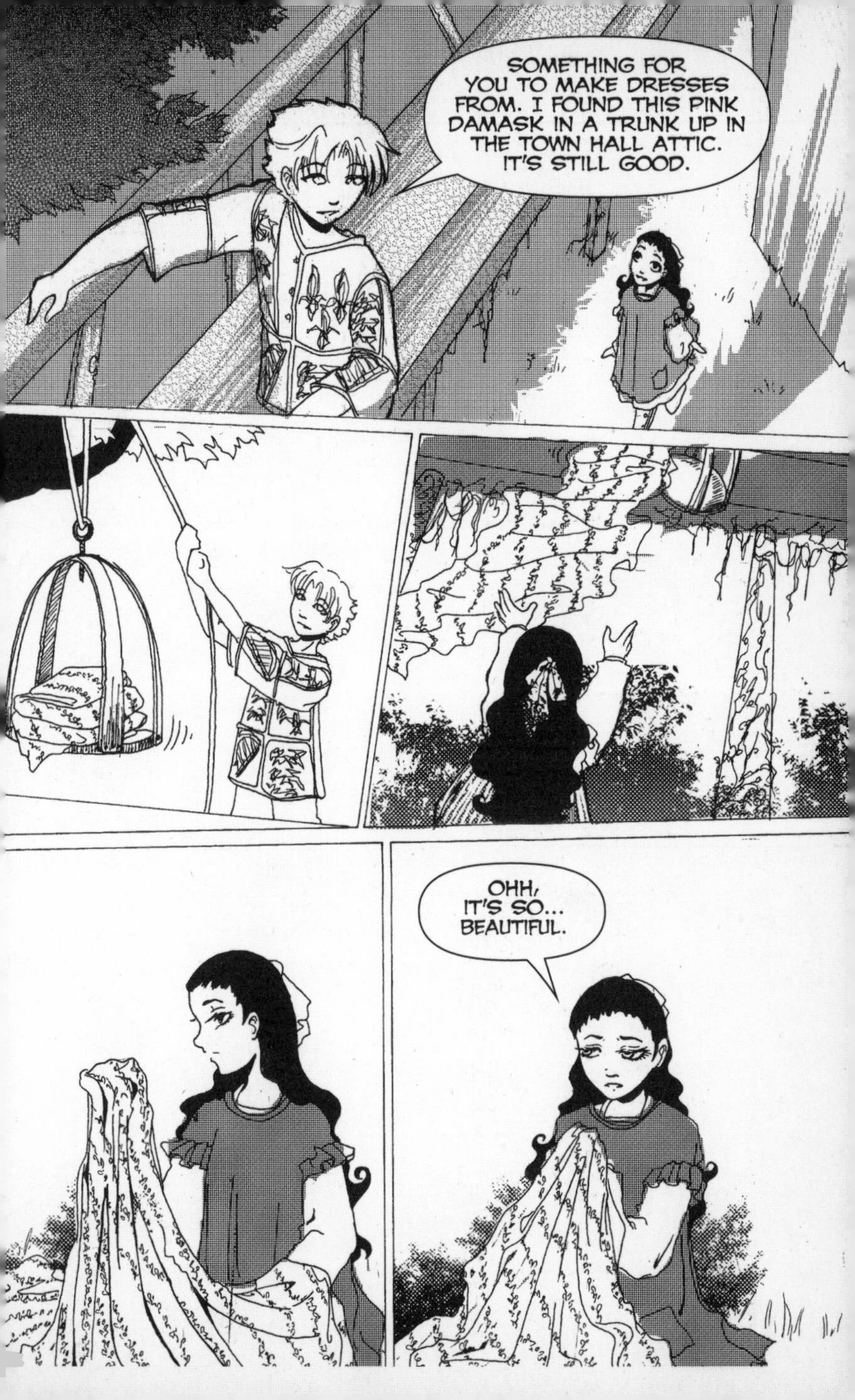
SOMETHING FOR YOU TO MAKE DRESSES FROM. I FOUND THIS PINK DAMASK IN A TRUNK UP IN THE TOWN HALL ATTIC. IT'S STILL GOOD.
OHH, IT'S SO... BEAUTIFUL.

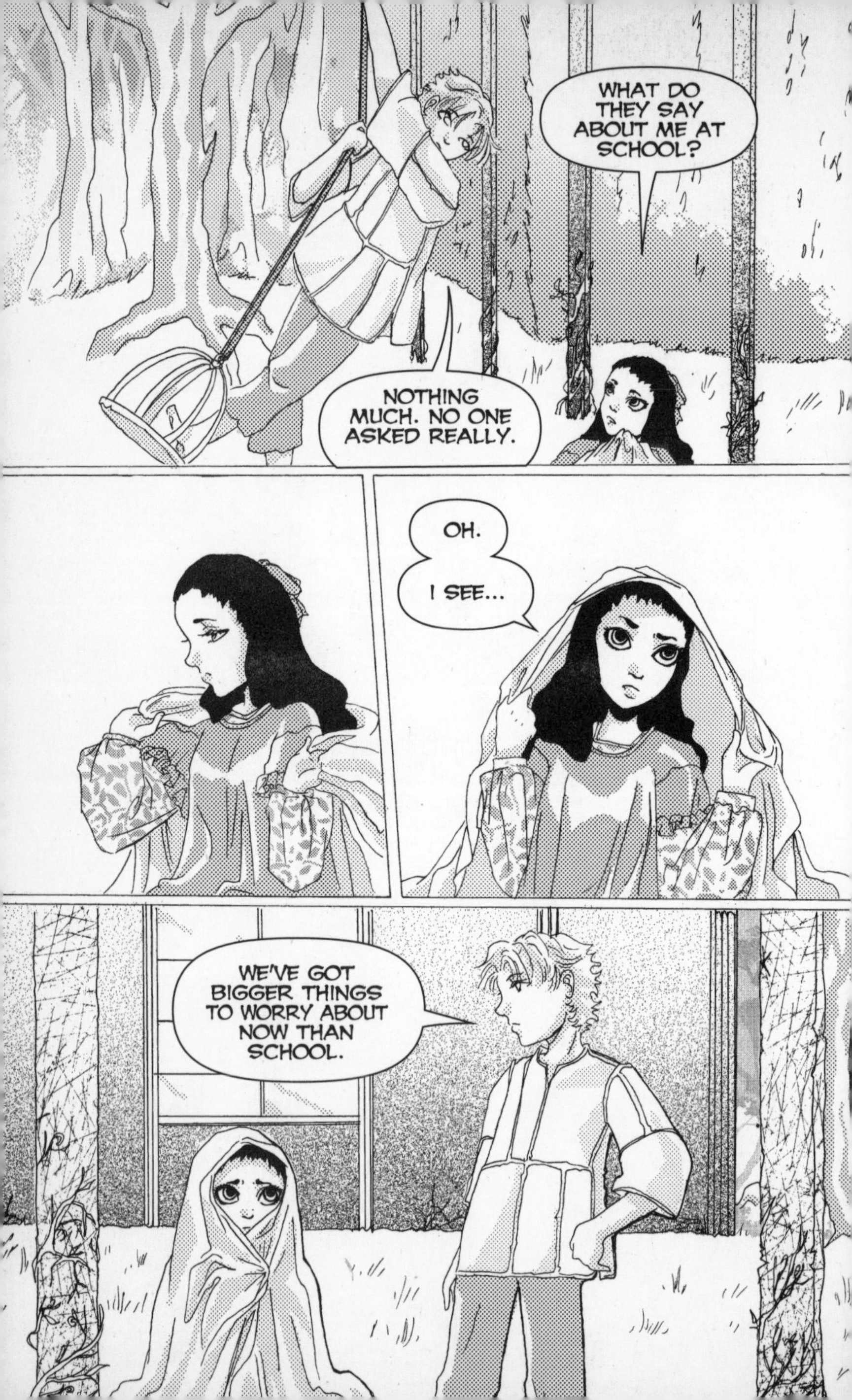
WHAT DO THEY SAY ABOUT ME AT SCHOOL?
NOTHING MUCH. NO ONE ASKED REALLY.
OH.
I SEE...
WE'VE GOT BIGGER THINGS TO WORRY ABOUT NOW THAN SCHOOL.

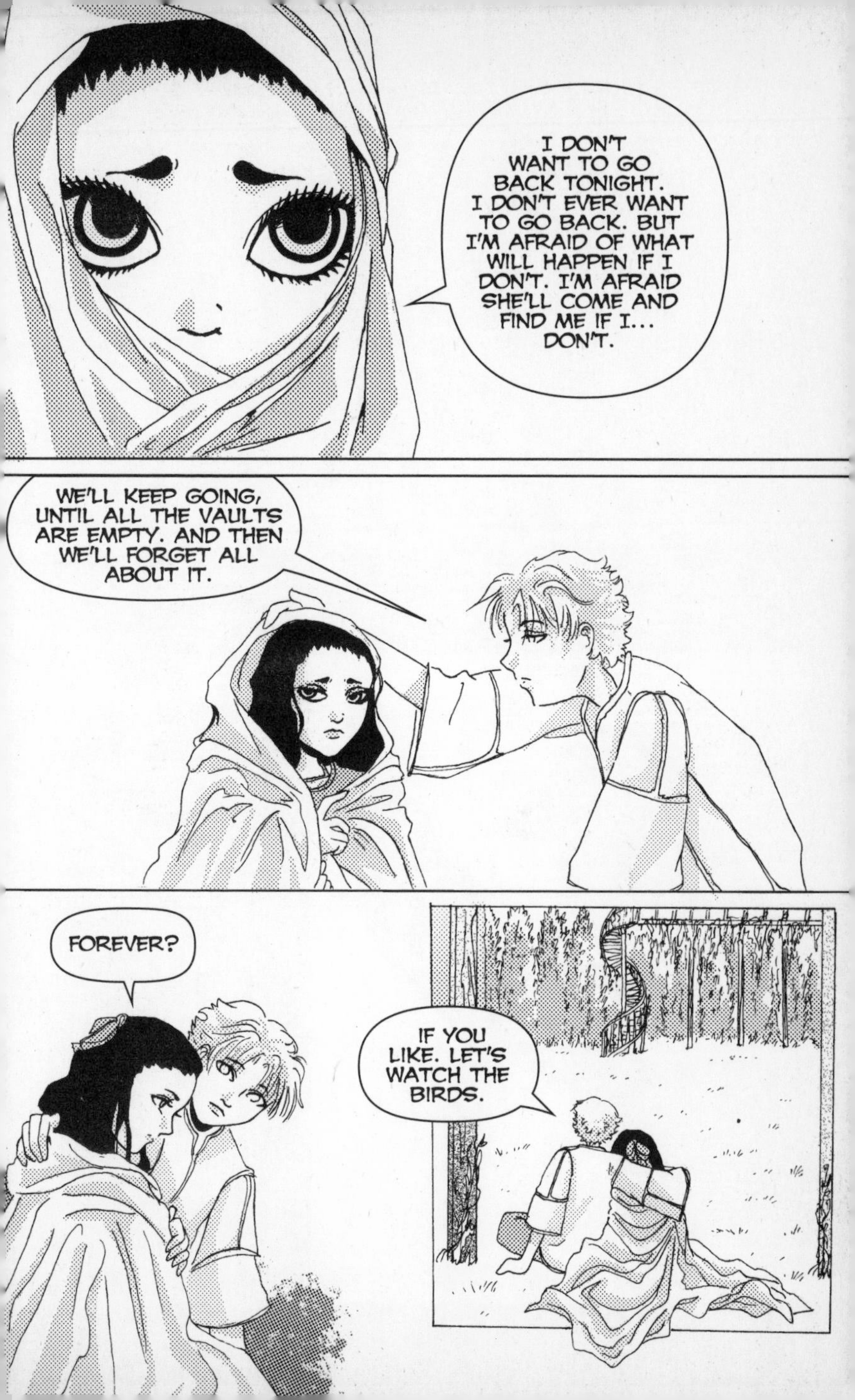
I DON'T WANT TO GO BACK TONIGHT. I DON'T EVER WANT TO GO BACK. BUT I'M AFRAID OF WHAT WILL HAPPEN IF I DON'T. I'M AFRAID SHE'LL COME AND FIND ME IF I... DON'T.
WE'LL KEEP GOING, UNTIL ALL THE VAULTS ARE EMPTY. AND THEN WE'LL FORGET ALL ABOUT IT.
FOREVER?
IF YOU LIKE. LET'S WATCH THE BIRDS.

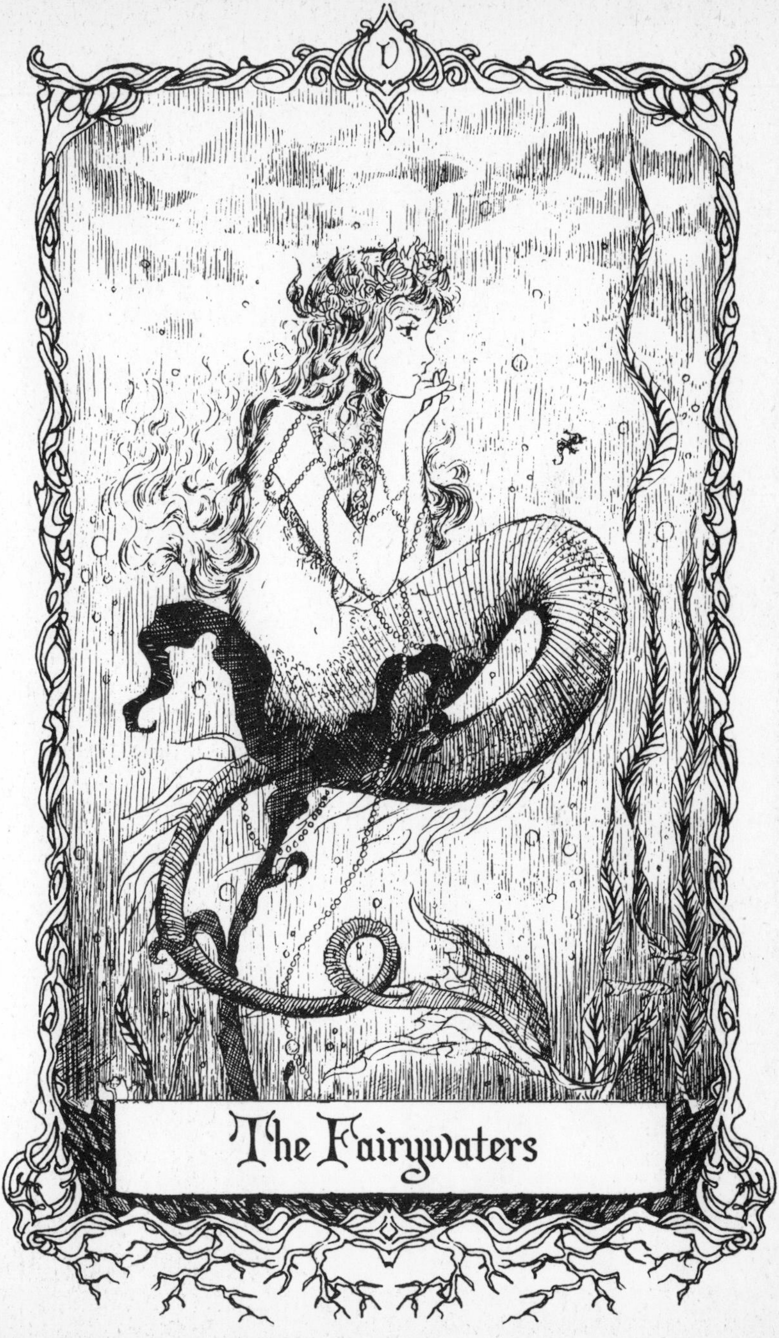
V
The Fairywaters

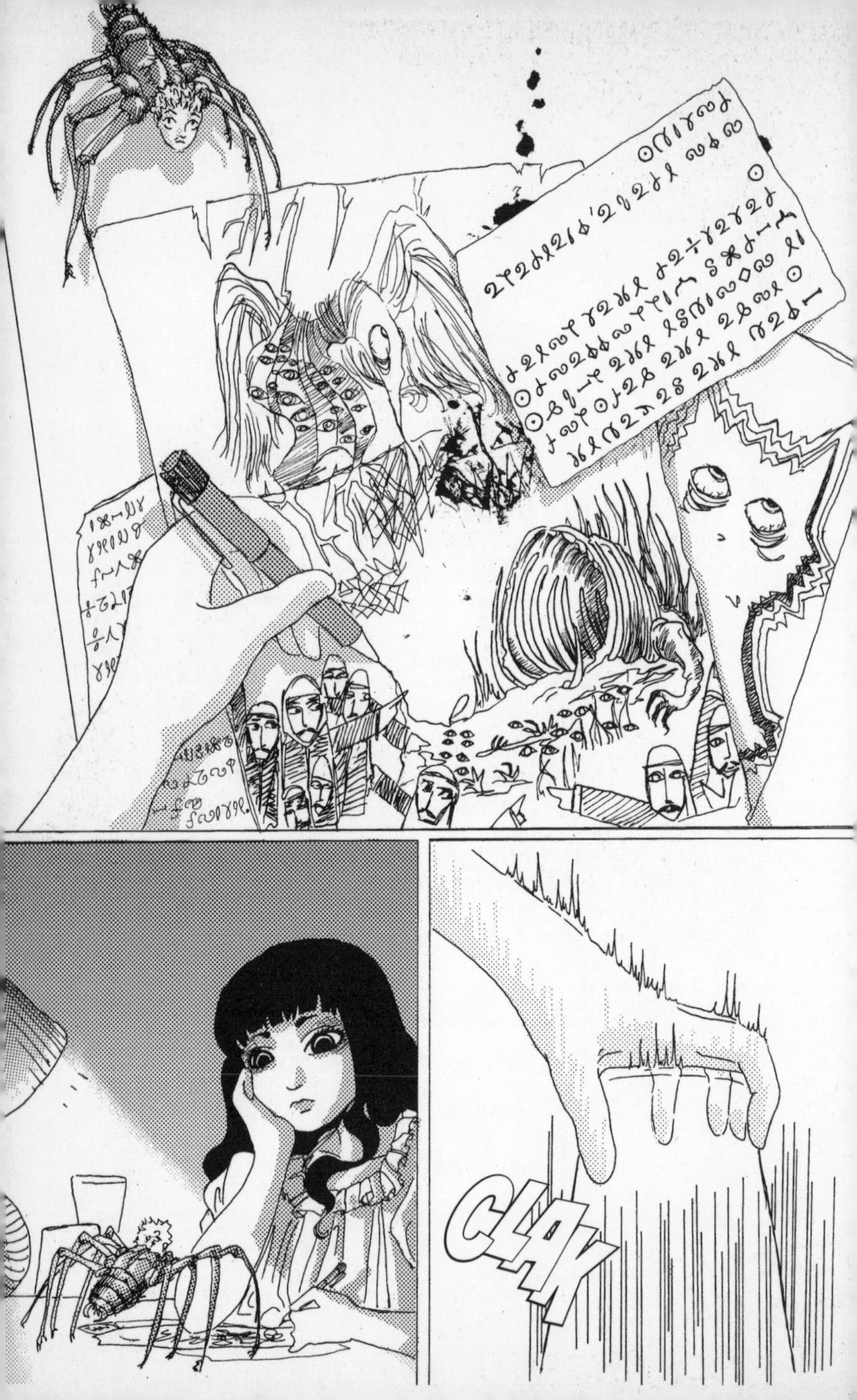
CLAK

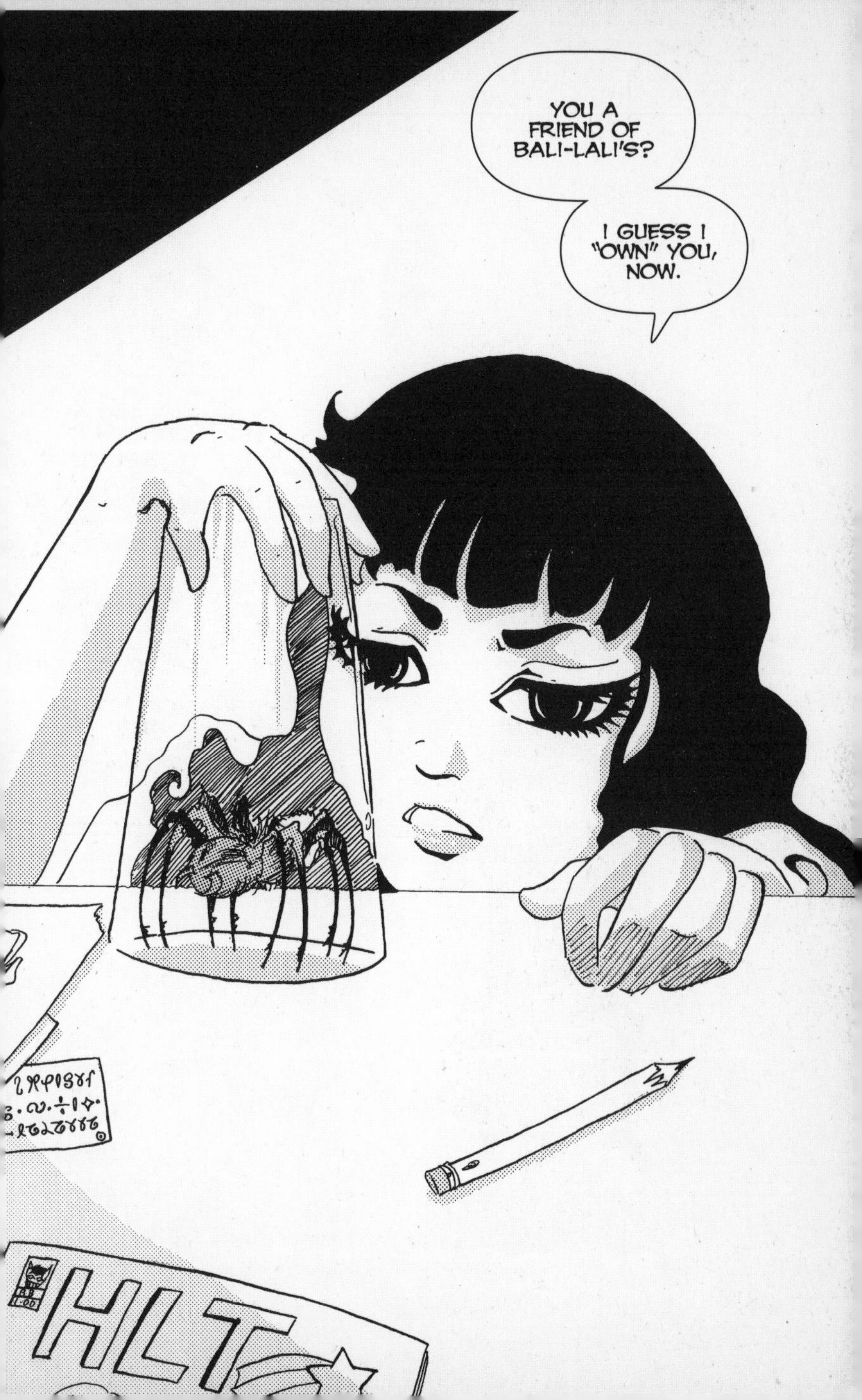
YOU A FRIEND OF BALI-LALI'S?
I GUESS I "OWN" YOU, NOW.
HLT

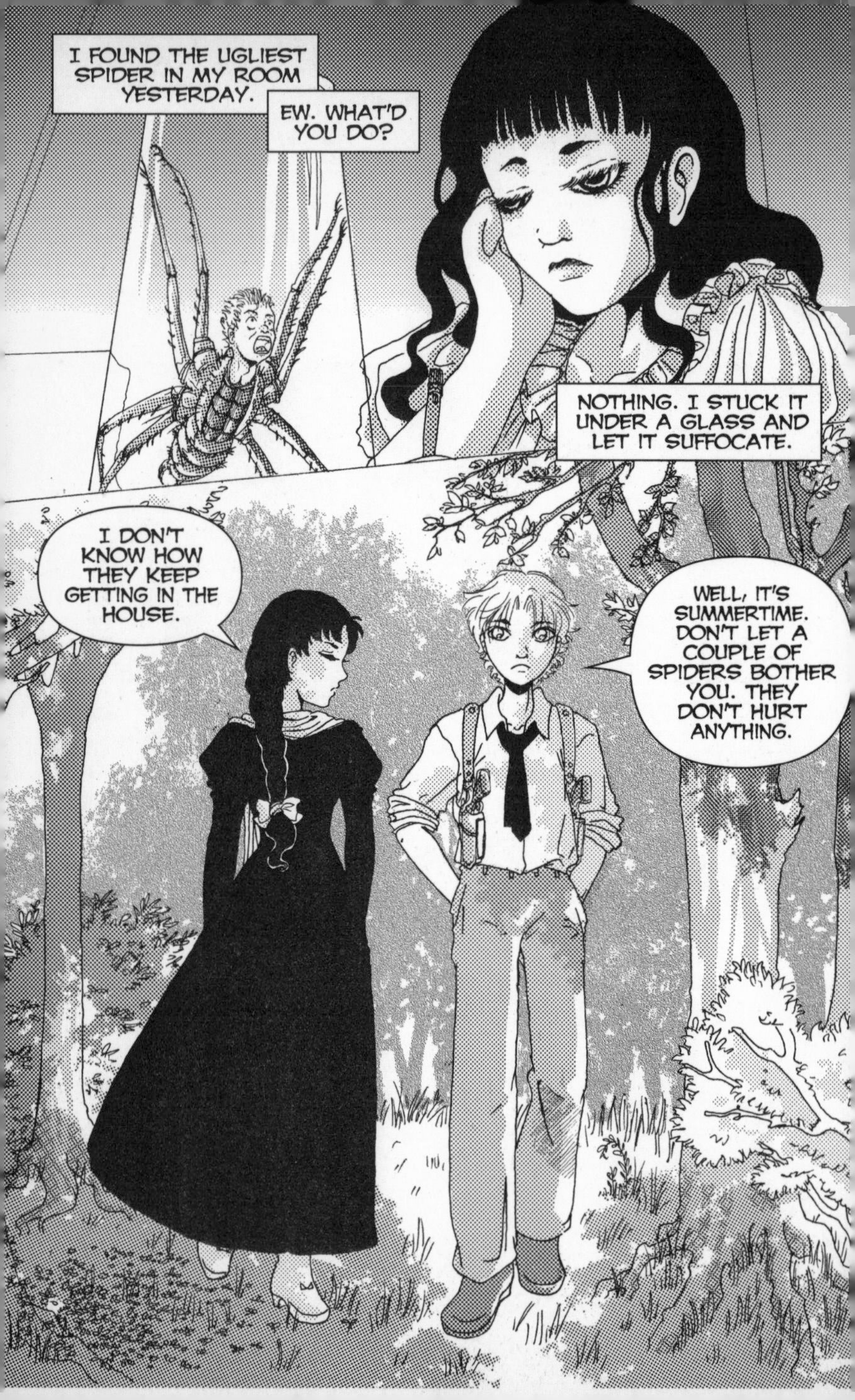
I FOUND THE UGLIEST SPIDER IN MY ROOM YESTERDAY.
EW. WHAT'D YOU DO?
NOTHING. I STUCK IT UNDER A GLASS AND LET IT SUFFOCATE.
I DON'T KNOW HOW THEY KEEP GETTING IN THE HOUSE.
WELL, IT'S SUMMERTIME. DON'T LET A COUPLE OF SPIDERS BOTHER YOU. THEY DON'T HURT ANYTHING.

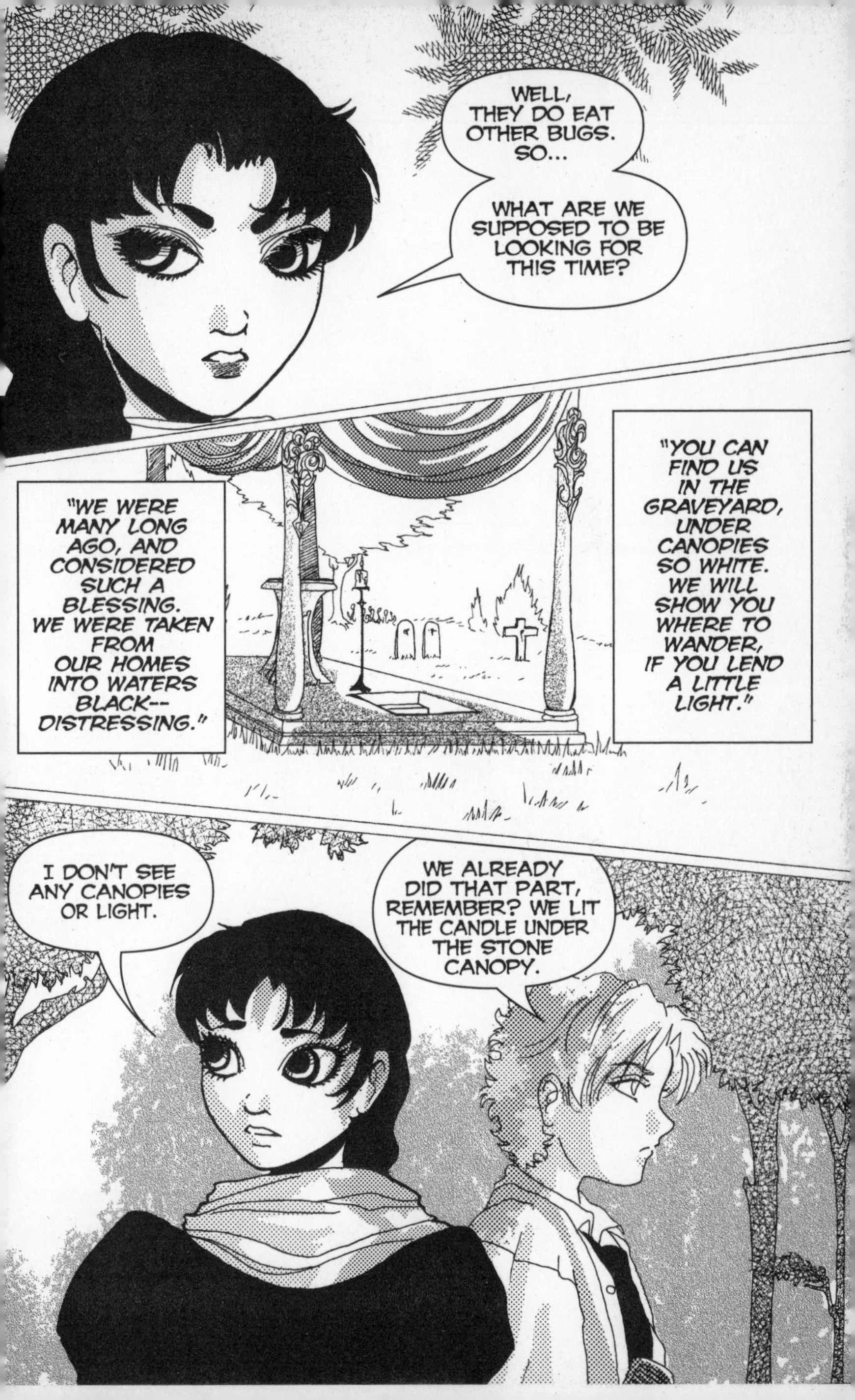
WELL, THEY DO EAT OTHER BUGS. SO...
WHAT ARE WE SUPPOSED TO BE LOOKING FOR THIS TIME?
"WE WERE MANY LONG AGO, AND CONSIDERED SUCH A BLESSING. WE WERE TAKEN FROM OUR HOMES INTO WATERS BLACK--DISTRESSING."
"YOU CAN FIND US IN THE GRAVEYARD, UNDER CANOPIES SO WHITE. WE WILL SHOW YOU WHERE TO WANDER, IF YOU LEND A LITTLE LIGHT."
I DON'T SEE ANY CANOPIES OR LIGHT.
WE ALREADY DID THAT PART, REMEMBER? WE LIT THE CANDLE UNDER THE STONE CANOPY.

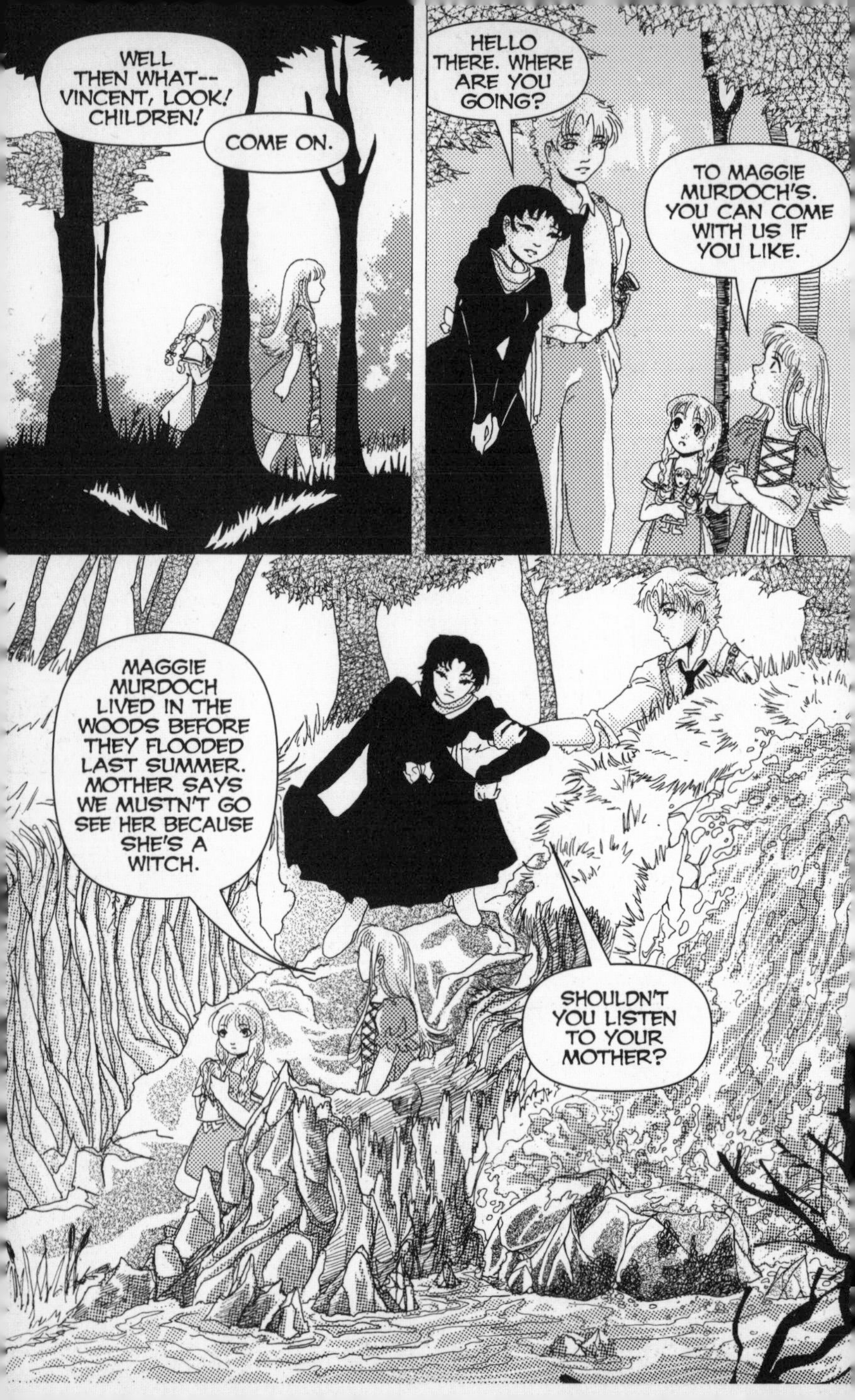
WELL THEN WHAT-- VINCENT, LOOK! CHILDREN!
COME ON.
HELLO THERE. WHERE ARE YOU GOING?
TO MAGGIE MURDOCH'S. YOU CAN COME WITH US IF YOU LIKE.
MAGGIE MURDOCH LIVED IN THE WOODS BEFORE THEY FLOODED LAST SUMMER. MOTHER SAYS WE MUSTN'T GO SEE HER BECAUSE SHE'S A WITCH.
SHOULDN'T YOU LISTEN TO YOUR MOTHER?

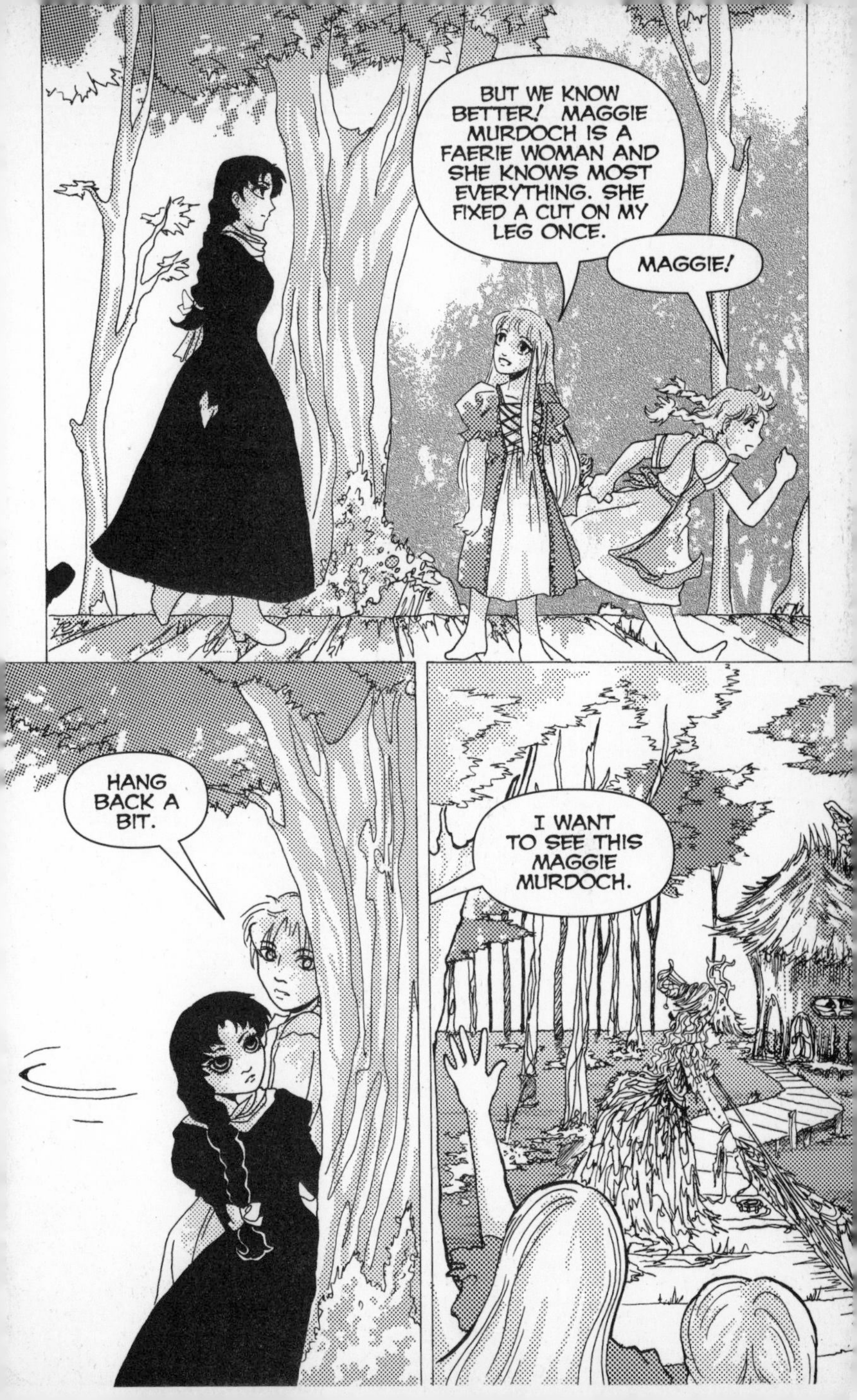
BUT WE KNOW BETTER! MAGGIE MURDOCH IS A FAERIE WOMAN AND SHE KNOWS MOST EVERYTHING. SHE FIXED A CUT ON MY LEG ONCE.
MAGGIE!
HANG BACK A BIT.
I WANT TO SEE THIS MAGGIE MURDOCH.

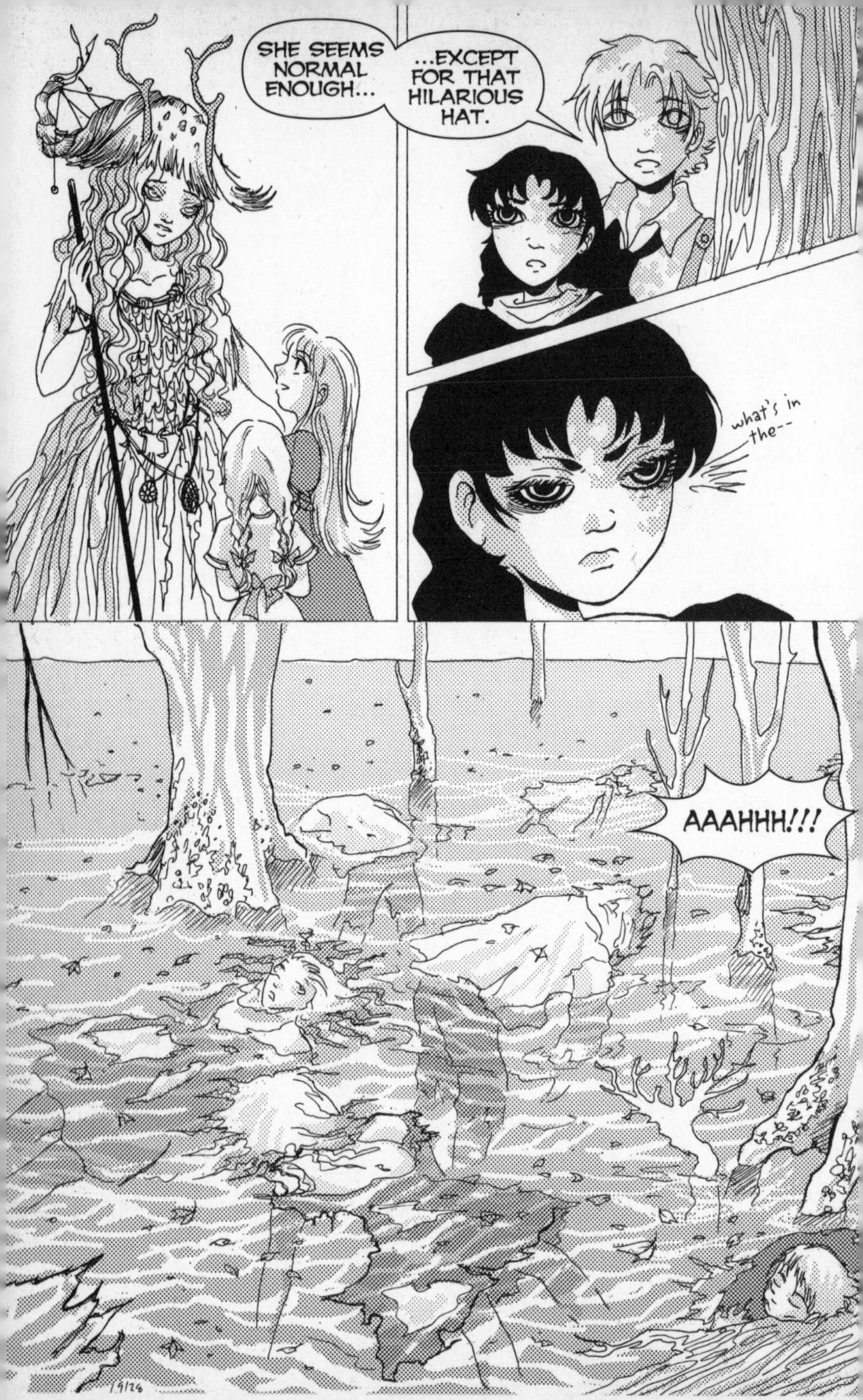
SHE SEEMS NORMAL ENOUGH...
...EXCEPT FOR THAT HILARIOUS HAT.
what's in the--
AAAHHH!!!

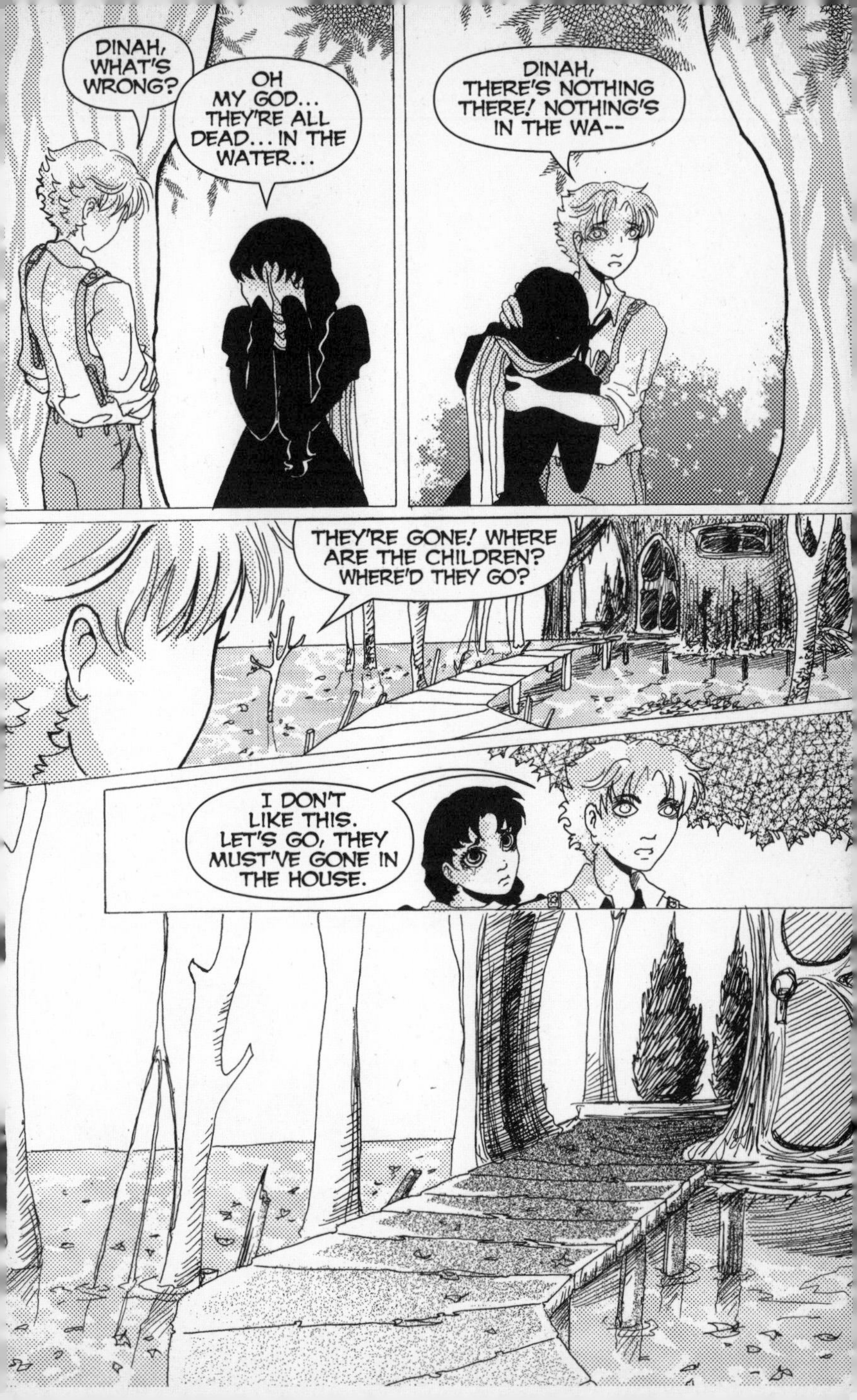
DINAH, WHAT'S WRONG?
OH MY GOD... THEY'RE ALL DEAD... IN THE WATER...
DINAH, THERE'S NOTHING THERE! NOTHING'S IN THE WA--
THEY'RE GONE! WHERE ARE THE CHILDREN? WHERE'D THEY GO?
I DON'T LIKE THIS. LET'S GO, THEY MUST'VE GONE IN THE HOUSE.

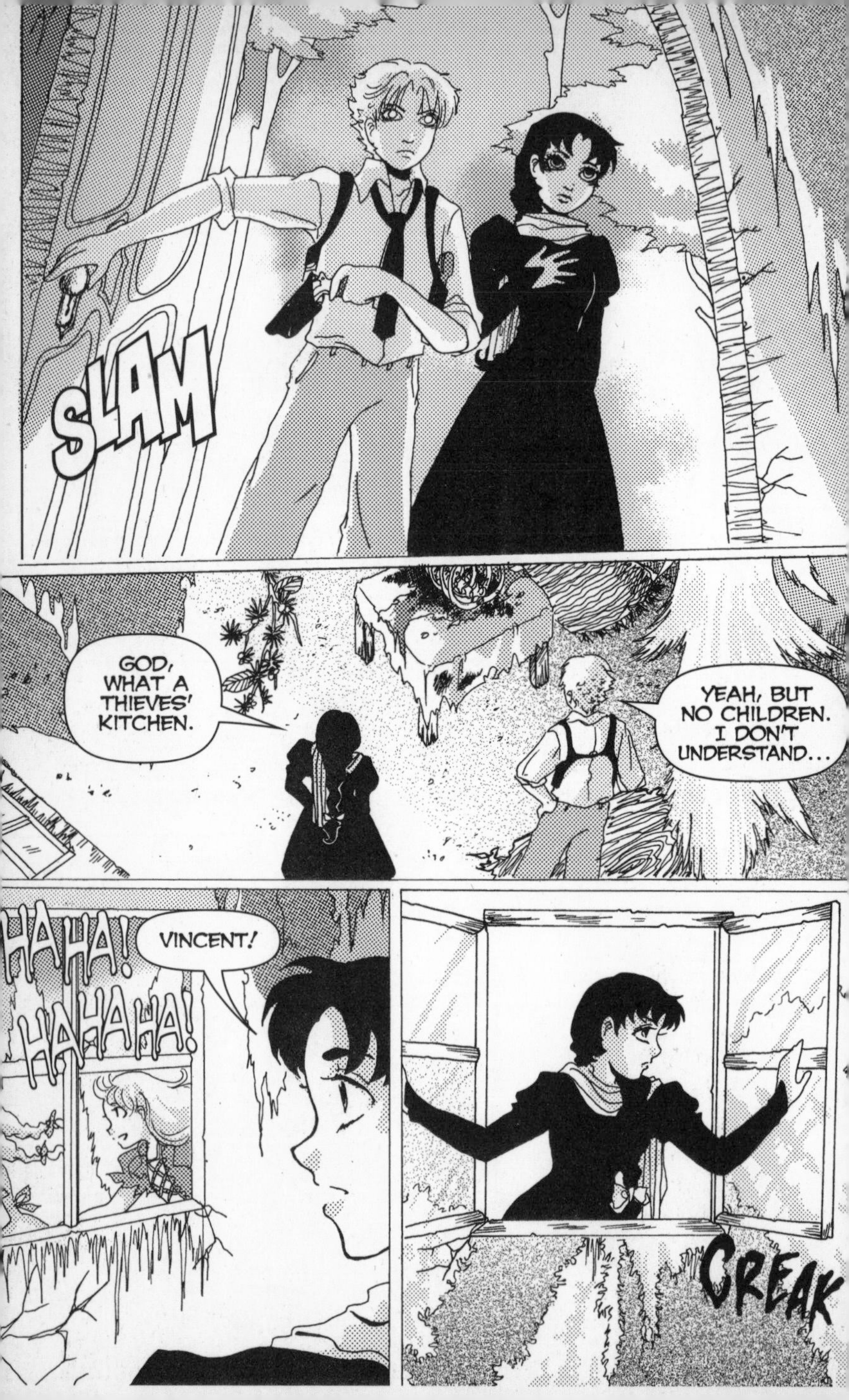
SLAM
GOD, WHAT A THIEVES' KITCHEN.
YEAH, BUT NO CHILDREN. I DON'T UNDERSTAND...
HAHA! HAHAHA!
VINCENT!
CREAK

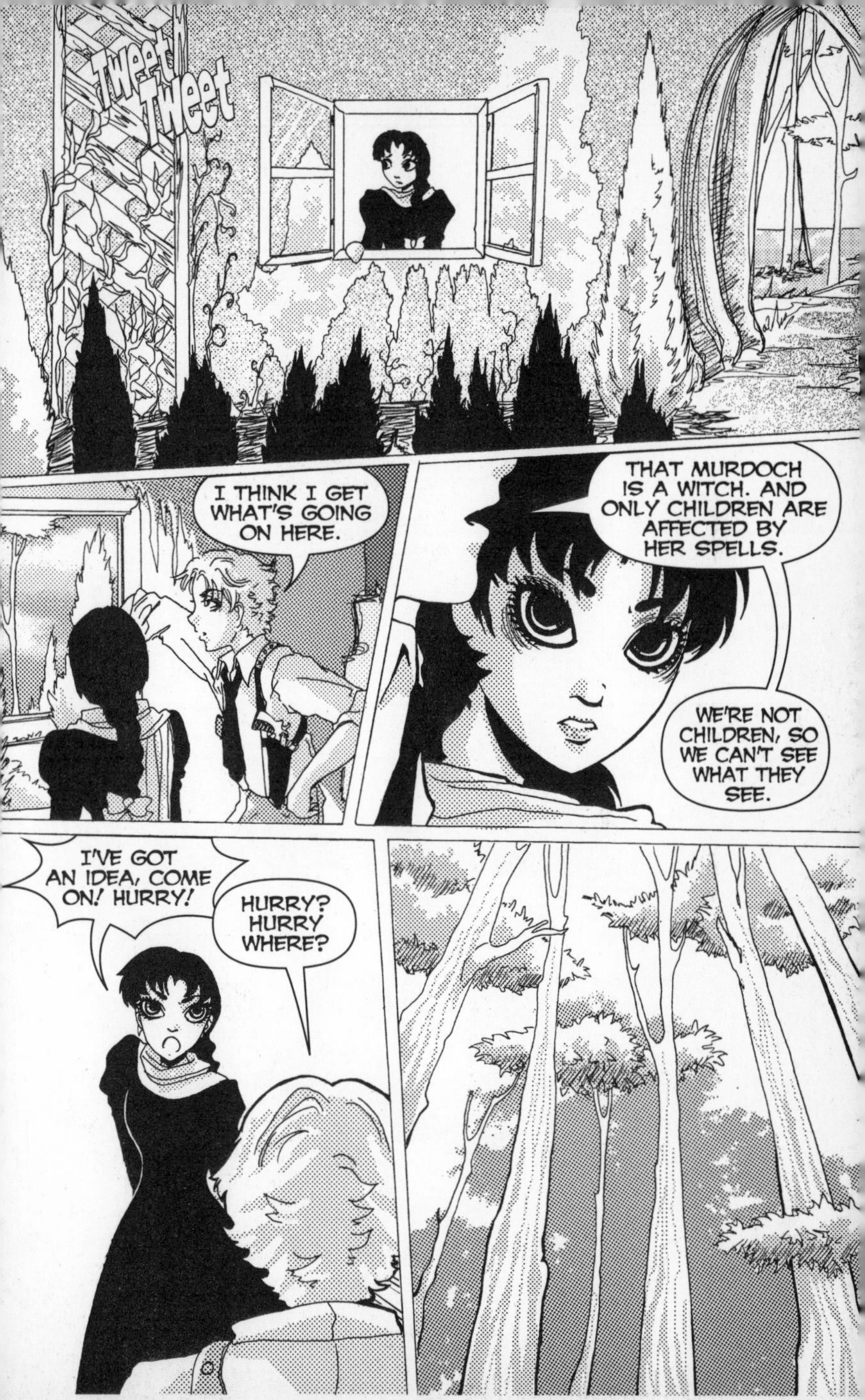
TWEET TWEET
I THINK I GET WHAT'S GOING ON HERE.
THAT MURDOCH IS A WITCH. AND ONLY CHILDREN ARE AFFECTED BY HER SPELLS.
WE'RE NOT CHILDREN, SO WE CAN'T SEE WHAT THEY SEE.
I'VE GOT AN IDEA, COME ON! HURRY!
HURRY? HURRY WHERE?

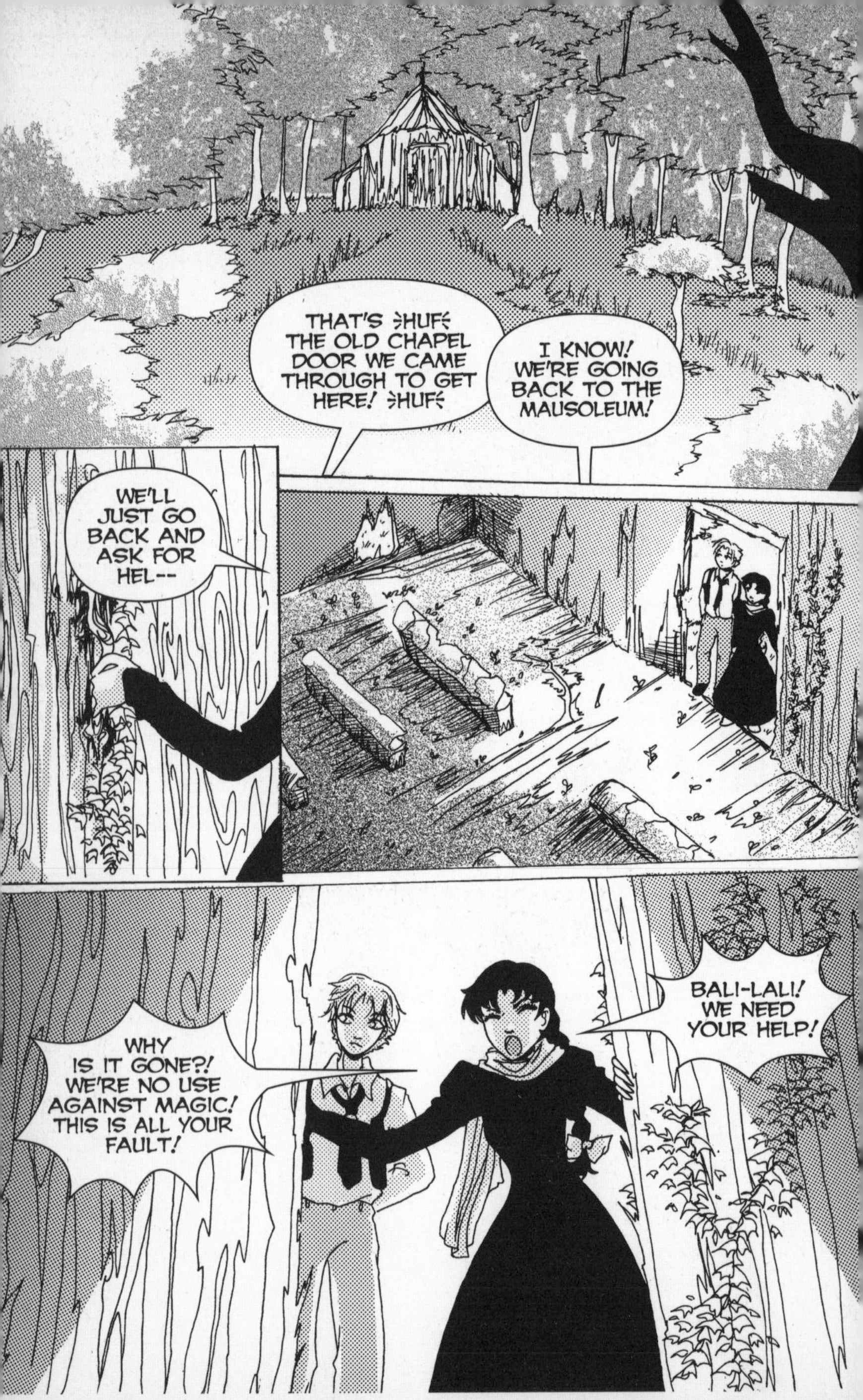
THAT'S ⪢HUF⪡ THE OLD CHAPEL DOOR WE CAME THROUGH TO GET HERE! ⪢HUF⪡
I KNOW! WE'RE GOING BACK TO THE MAUSOLEUM!
WE'LL JUST GO BACK AND ASK FOR HEL--
WHY IS IT GONE?! WE'RE NO USE AGAINST MAGIC! THIS IS ALL YOUR FAULT!
BALI-LALI! WE NEED YOUR HELP!

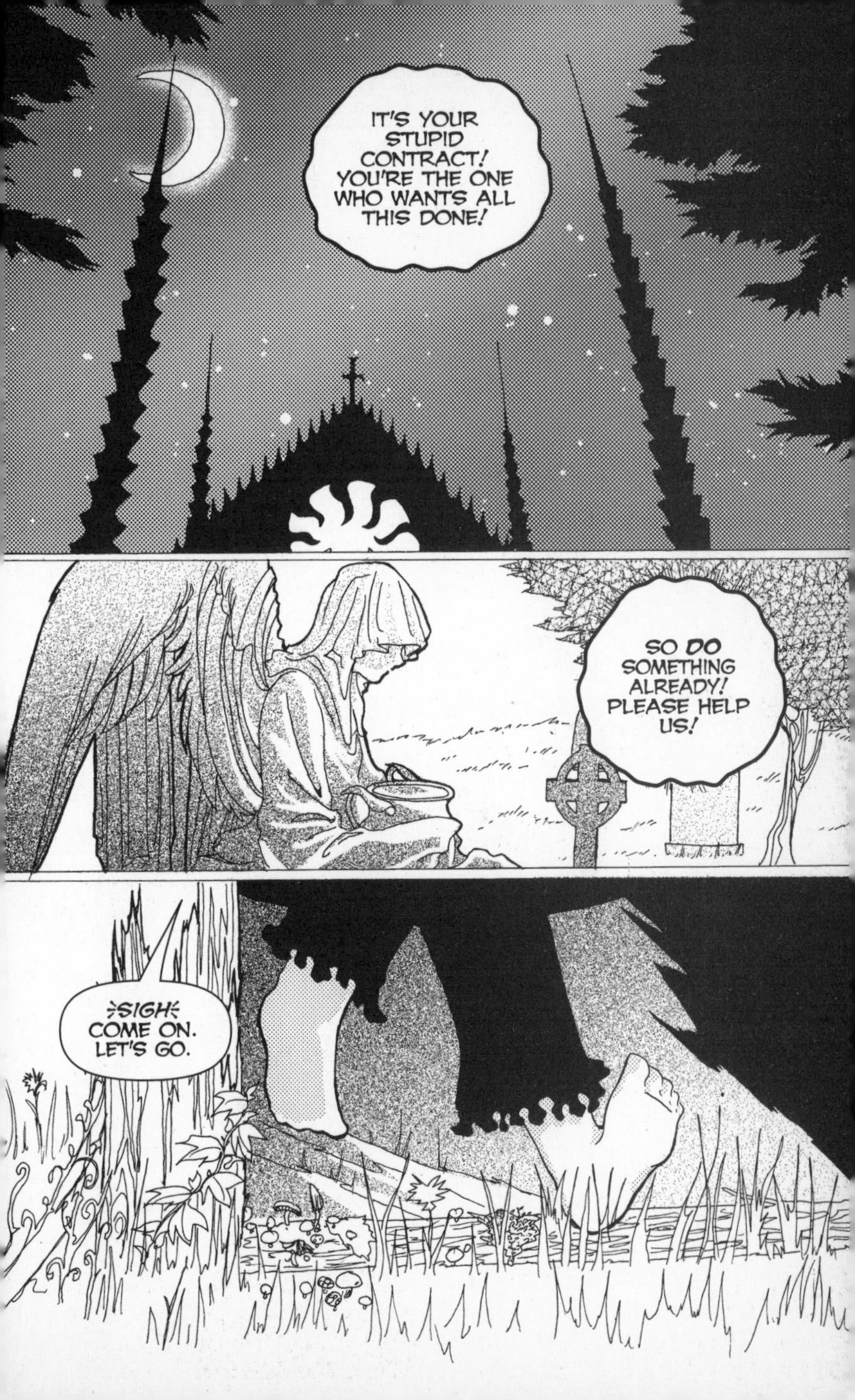
IT'S YOUR STUPID CONTRACT! YOU'RE THE ONE WHO WANTS ALL THIS DONE!
SO DO SOMETHING ALREADY! PLEASE HELP US!
SIGH COME ON. LET'S GO.

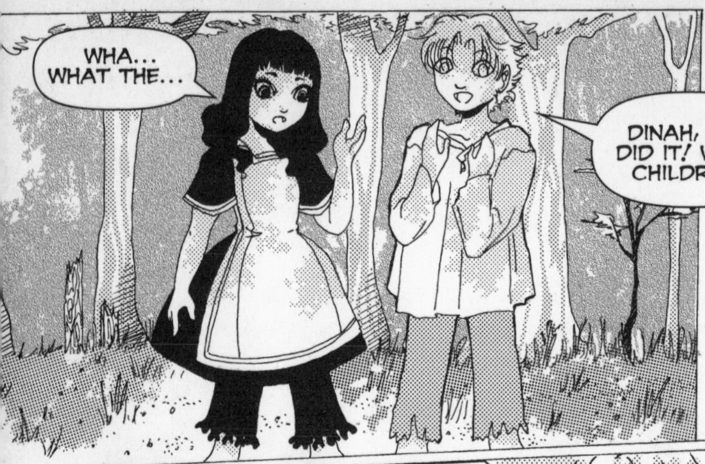
WHA... WHAT THE...
DINAH, YOU DID IT! WE'RE CHILDREN!

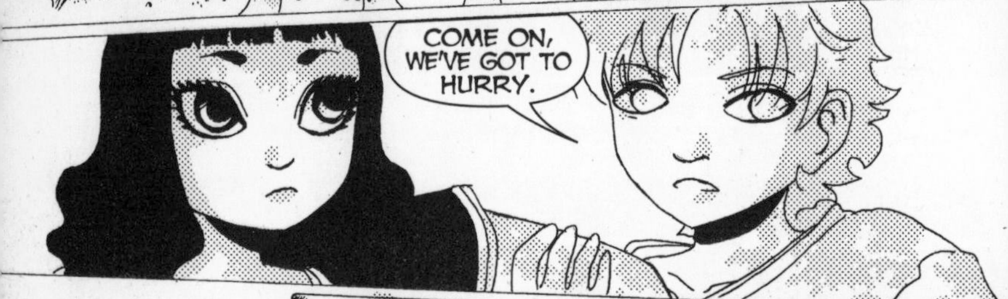
COME ON, WE'VE GOT TO HURRY.

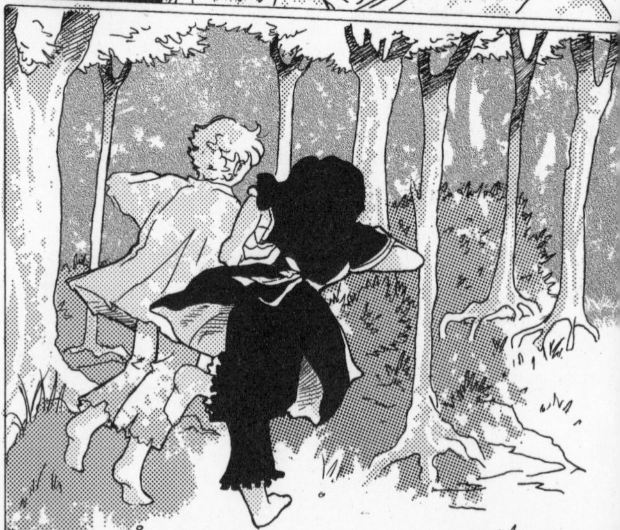

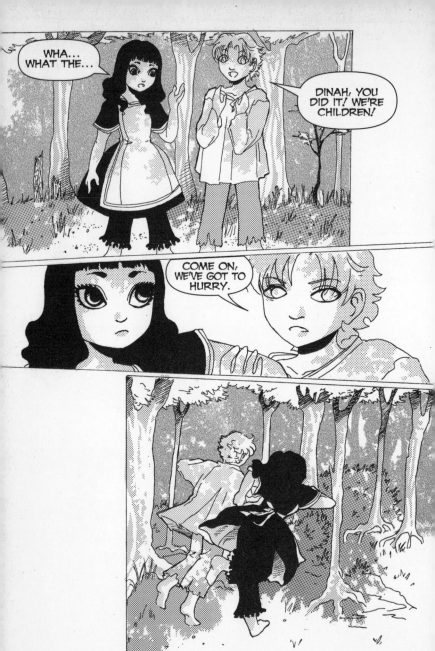

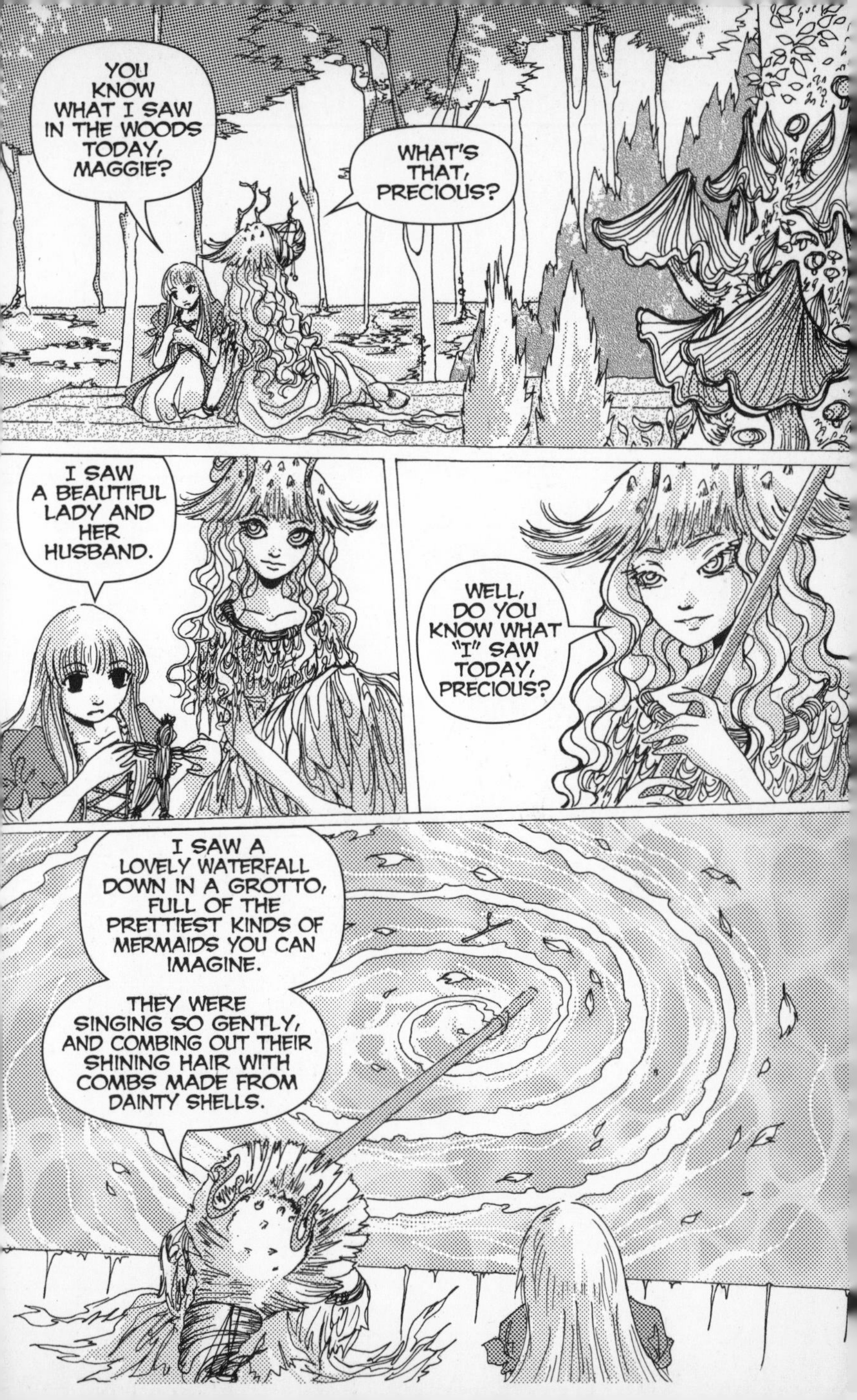
YOU KNOW WHAT I SAW IN THE WOODS TODAY, MAGGIE?
WHAT'S THAT, PRECIOUS?
I SAW A BEAUTIFUL LADY AND HER HUSBAND.
WELL, DO YOU KNOW WHAT "I" SAW TODAY, PRECIOUS?
I SAW A LOVELY WATERFALL DOWN IN A GROTTO, FULL OF THE PRETTIEST KINDS OF MERMAIDS YOU CAN IMAGINE.
THEY WERE SINGING SO GENTLY, AND COMBING OUT THEIR SHINING HAIR WITH COMBS MADE FROM DAINTY SHELLS.

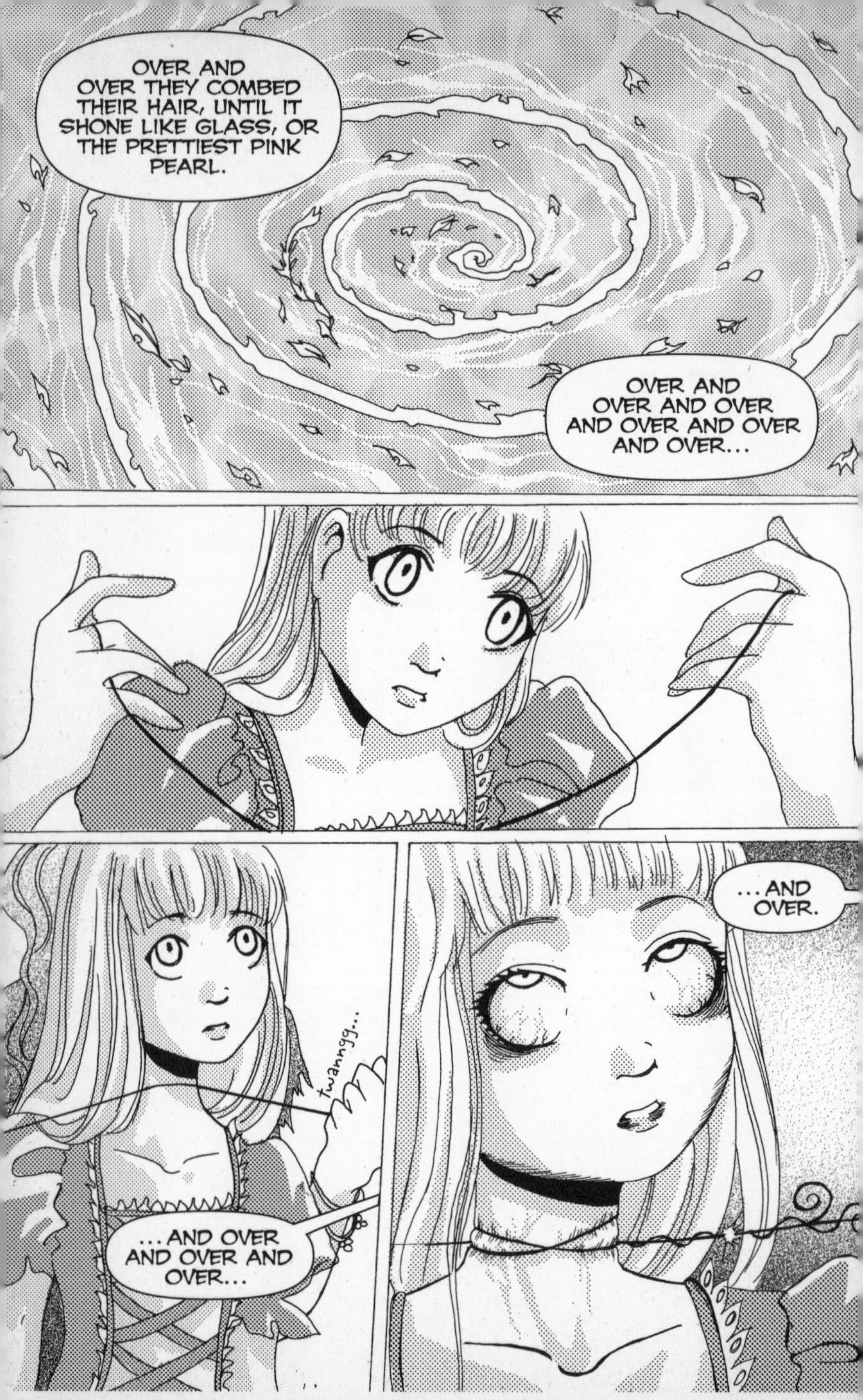
OVER AND OVER THEY COMBED THEIR HAIR, UNTIL IT SHONE LIKE GLASS, OR THE PRETTIEST PINK PEARL.
OVER AND OVER AND OVER AND OVER AND OVER AND OVER...
twanngg...
...AND OVER AND OVER AND OVER...
...AND OVER.

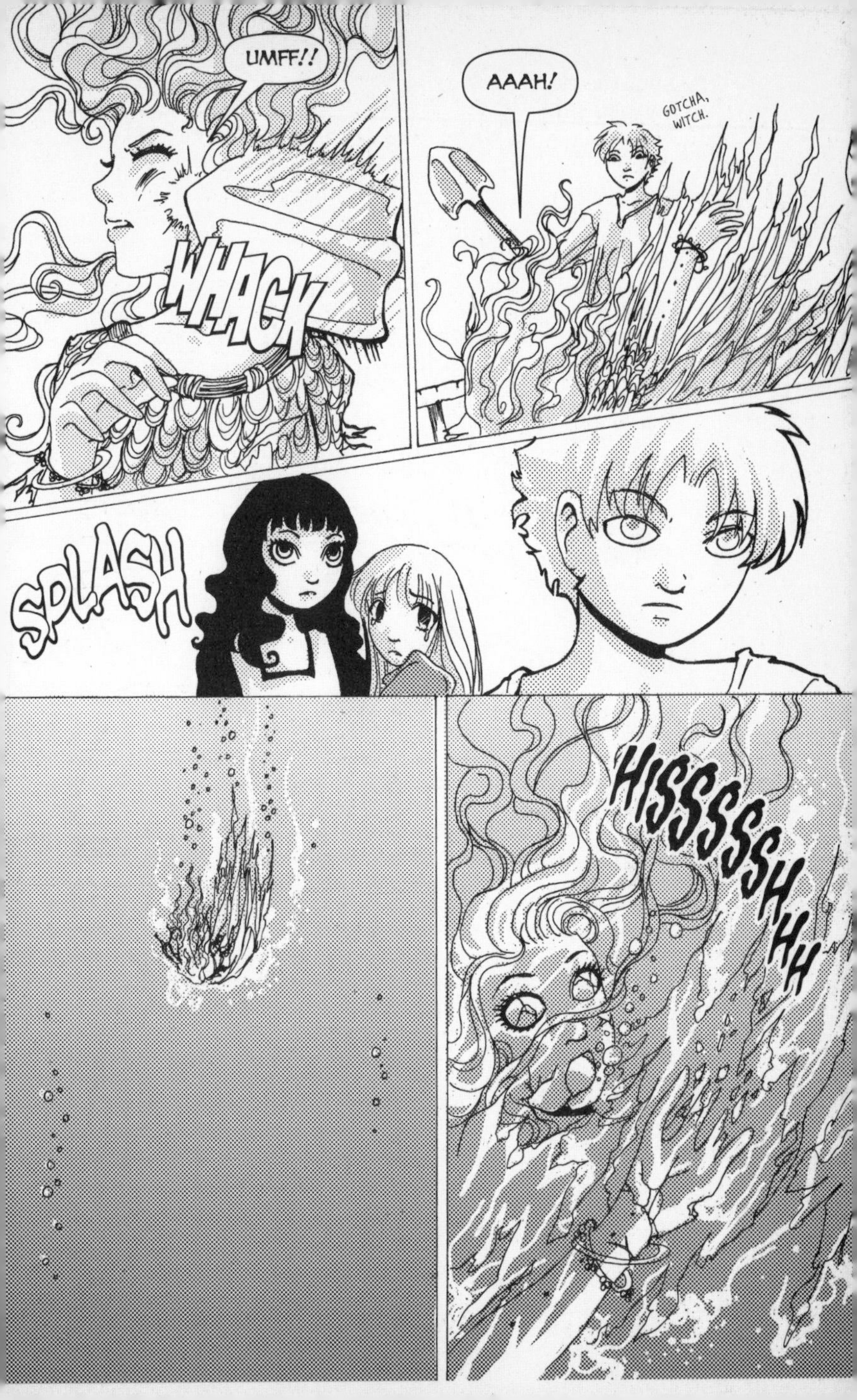
AAAH!
GOTCHA, WITCH.
UMFF!!
WHACK
SPLASH
HISSSSSHHH

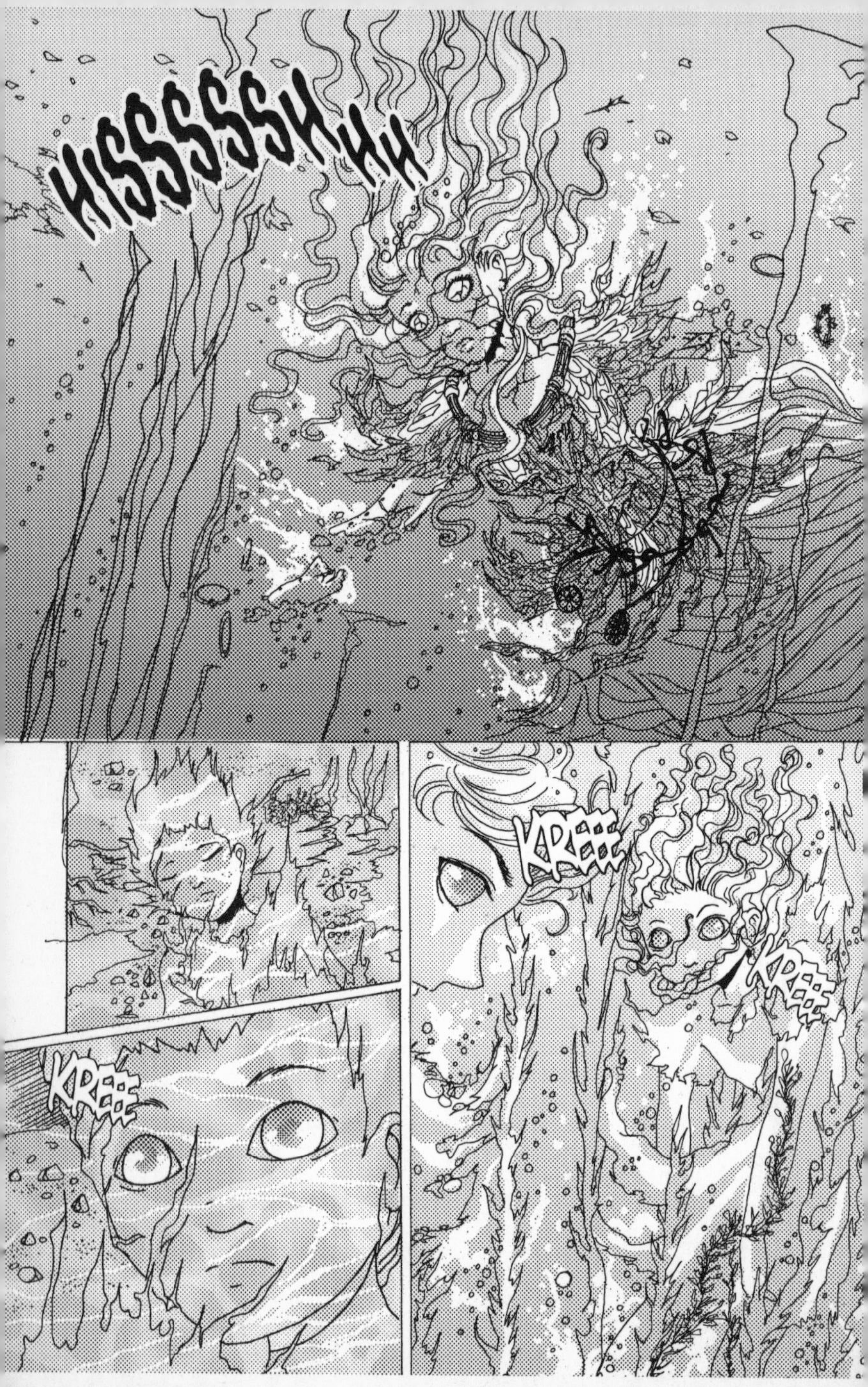
HISSSSSHHH
KREEE
KREEE
KREEE

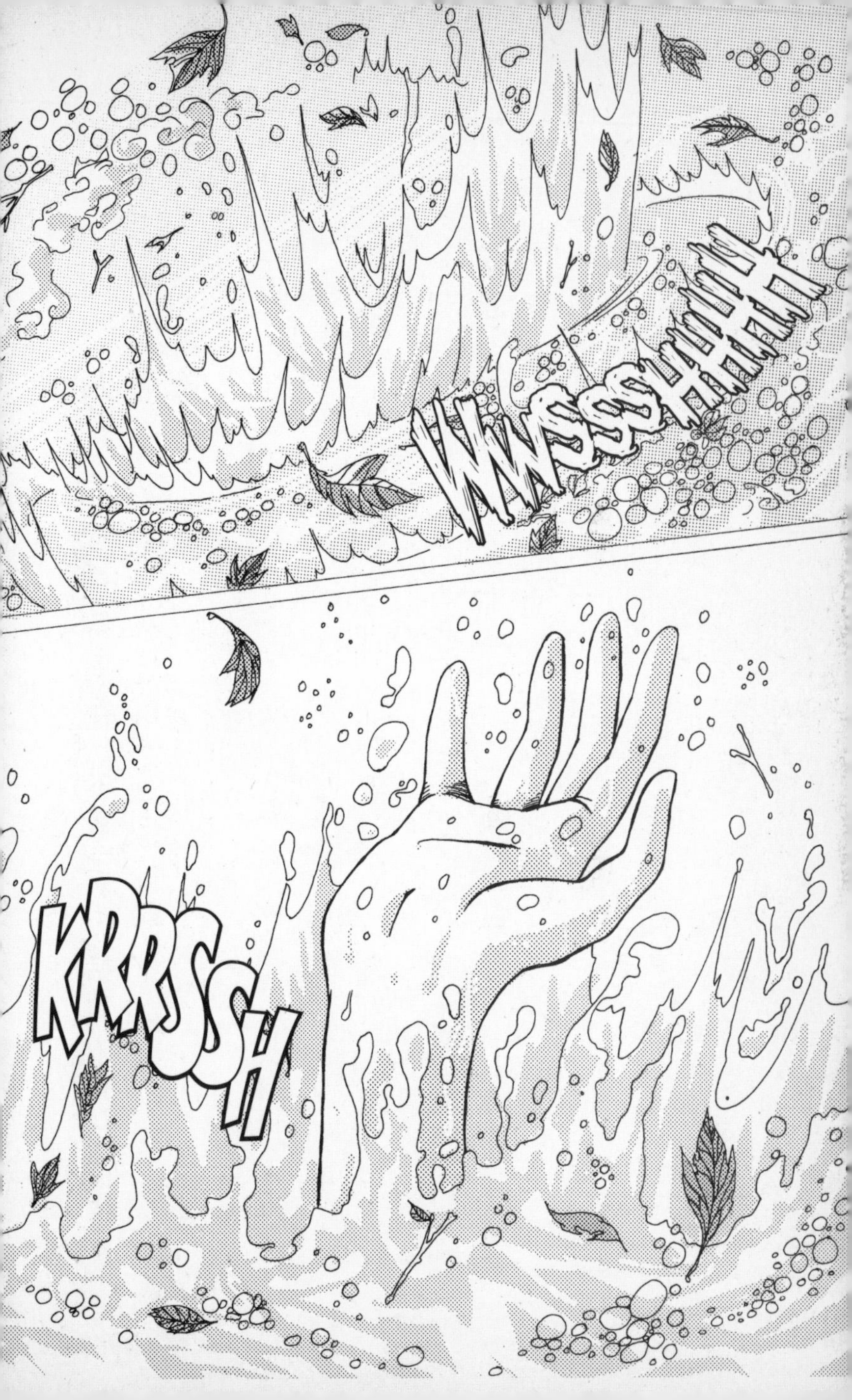
WWSSHHHH
KRRSSH

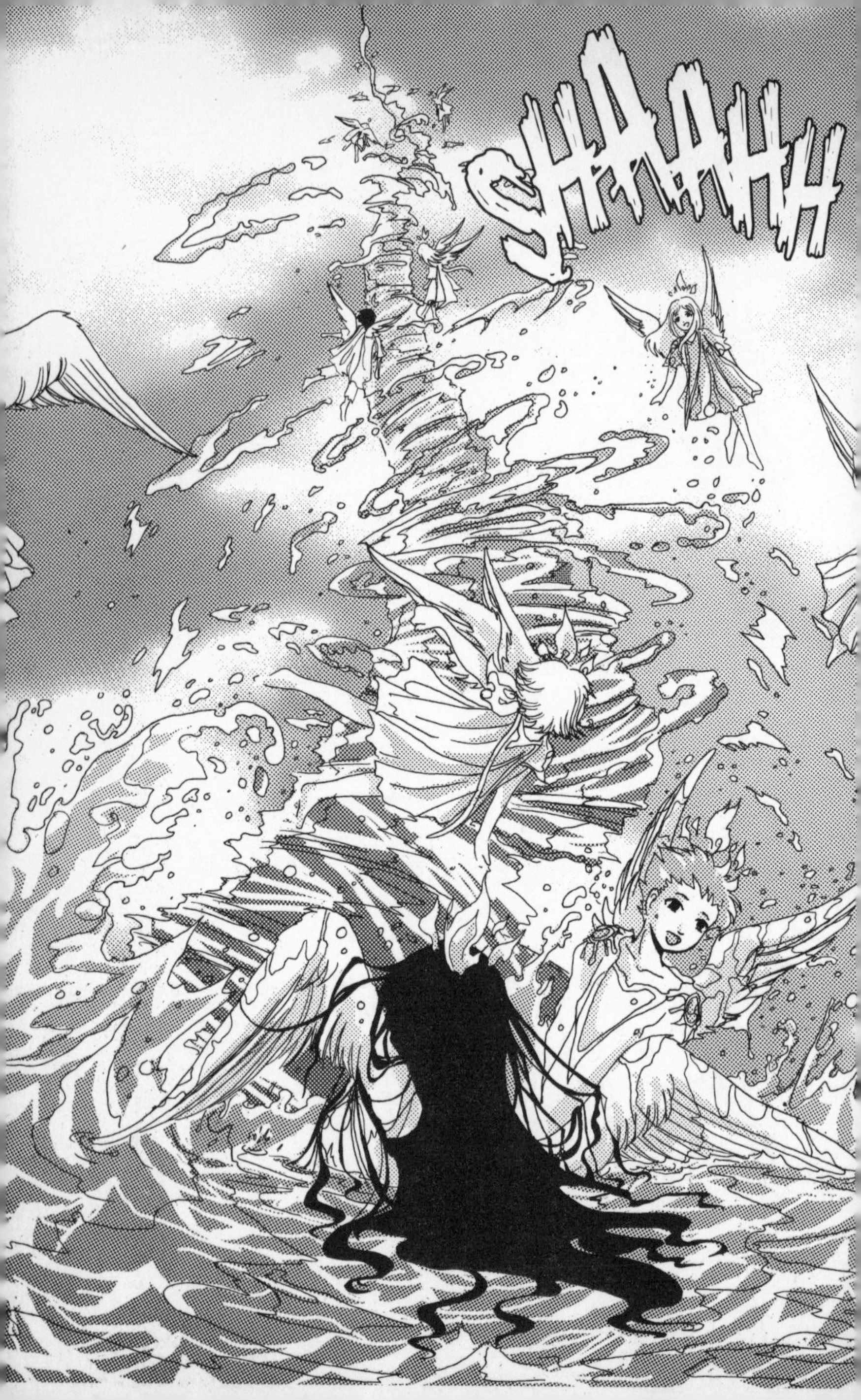
SHAAHH

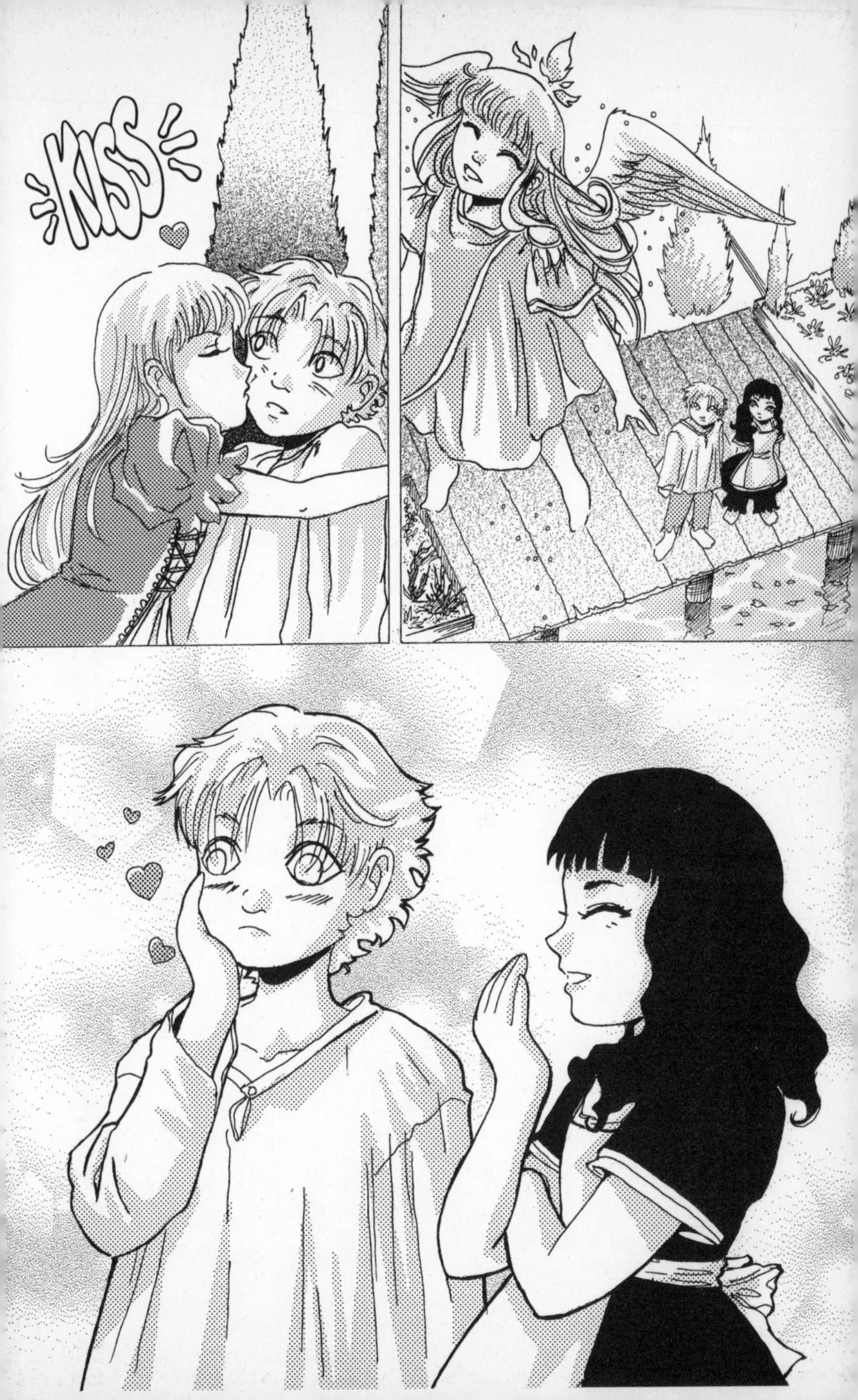
KISS

DR. RICHARD MORSTAN, M.D.
129 SOUTH STREET
WATERTOWN, MA 33607

Dear Ms. Jane Audrey,

After much deliberation, I contacted Dr. Weller at the Row Sanitarium in Watertown to schedule an evaluation for Dinah on the 26th. I regret that the situation is such that I feel she would do better with 24-hour professional help, in an environment most condusive to mental healing. She cannot be allowed to remain at home by herself for most of the day.

The cost of admitting Dinah to the sanitarium on a full-time basis is rather steep, but we can arrange for most of the expenses to be absorbed by your insurance. I will schedule a separate appointment for you and I to meet with Dr. Weller and go over the necessary paperwork.

Regards,

R. Morstan

Dr. R. Morstan, M.D.

cc. Elijah Weller, RS

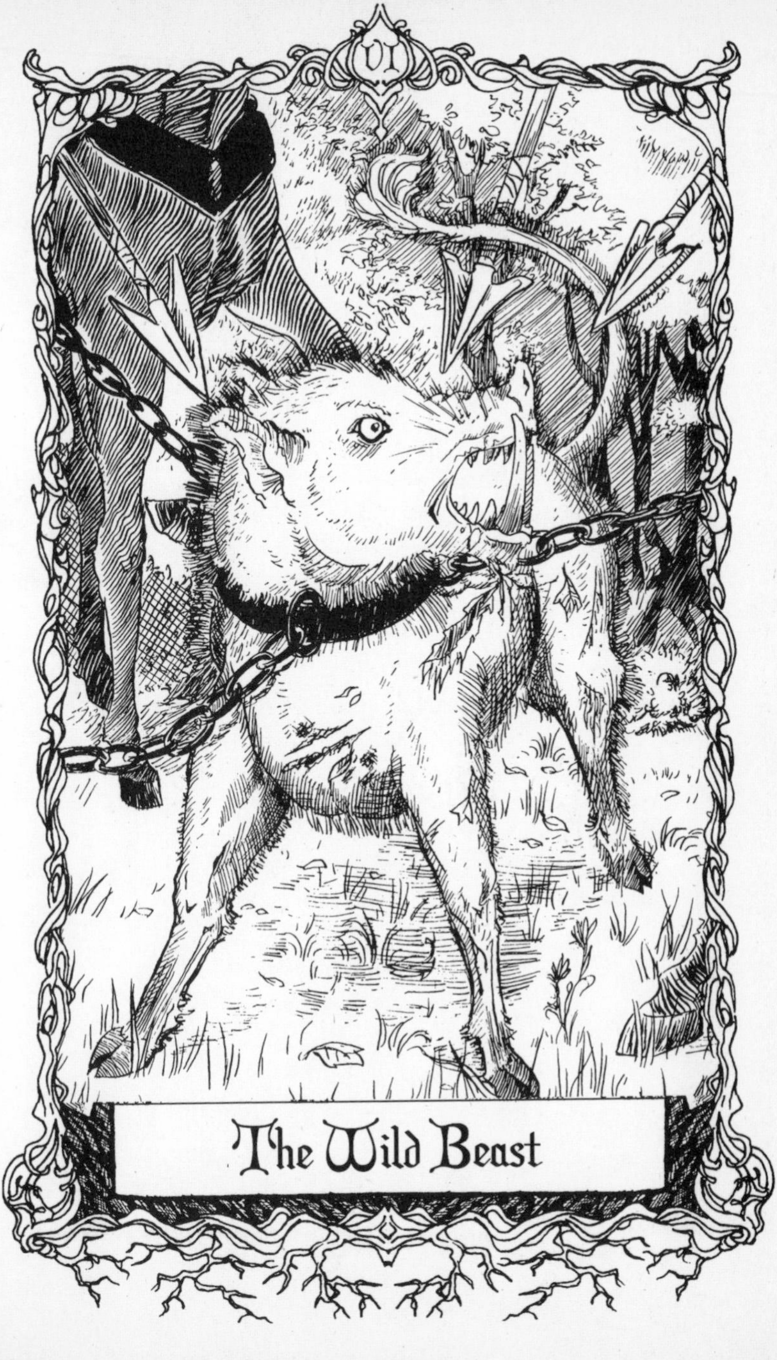
VI
The Wild Beast

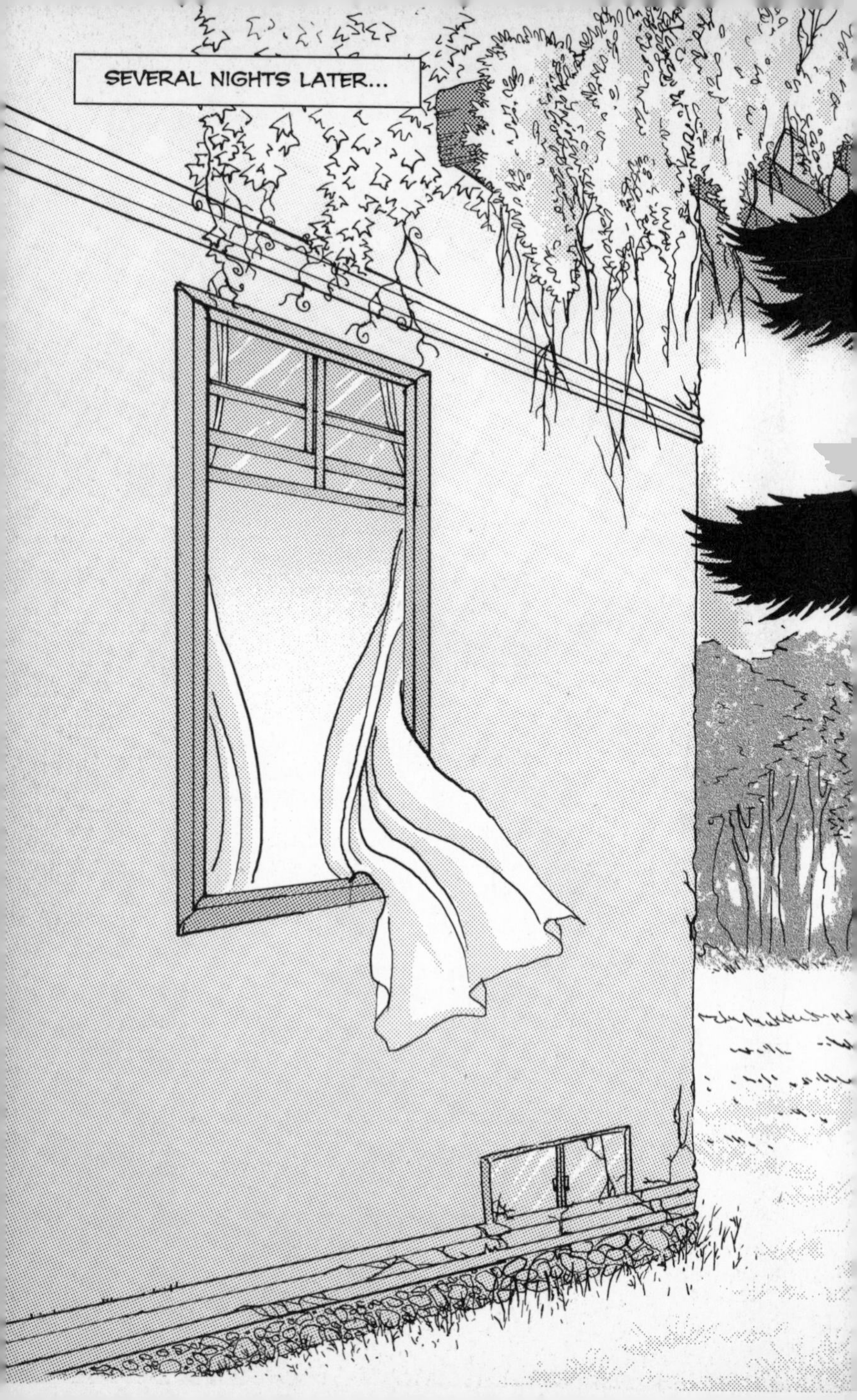
SEVERAL NIGHTS LATER...

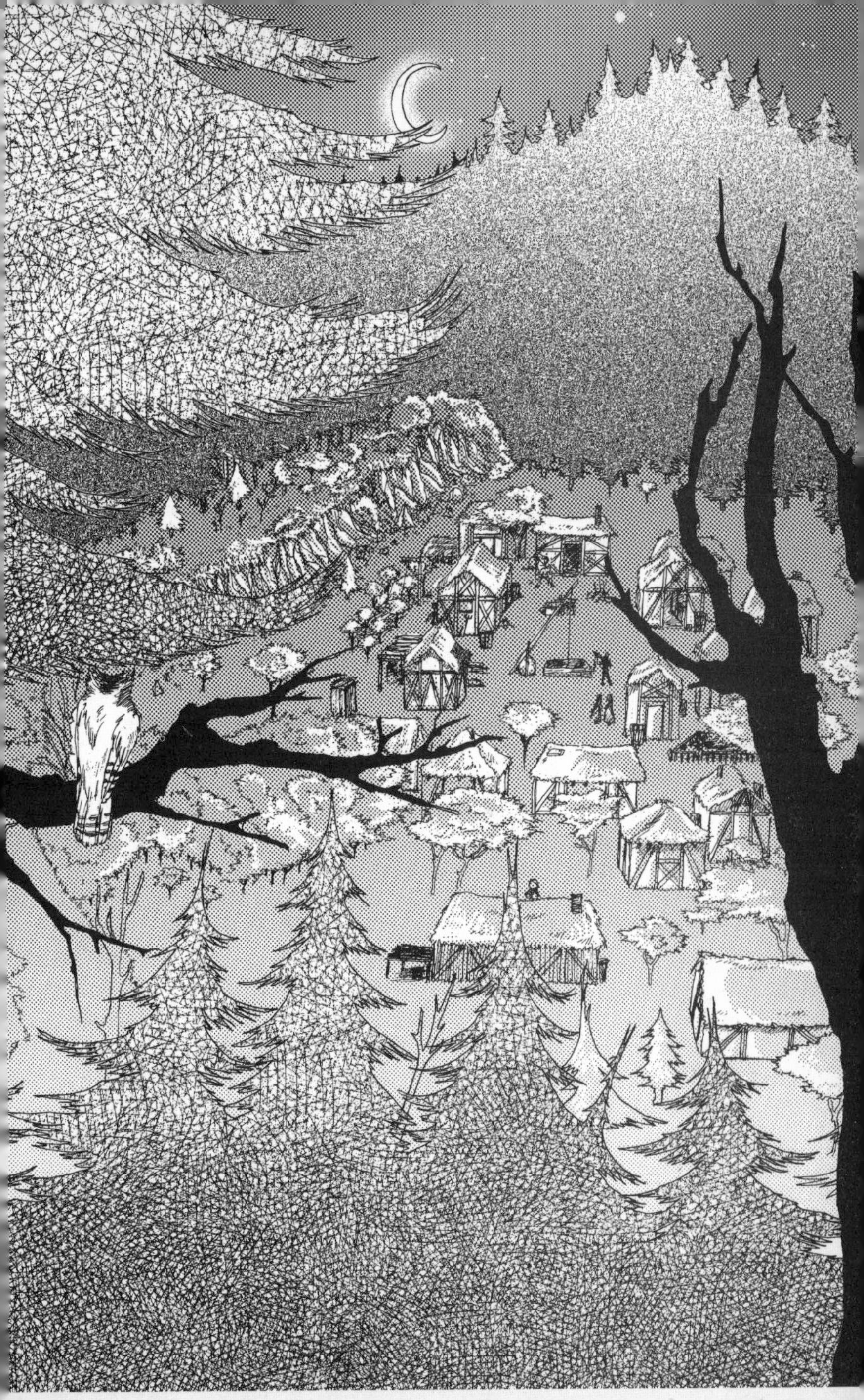

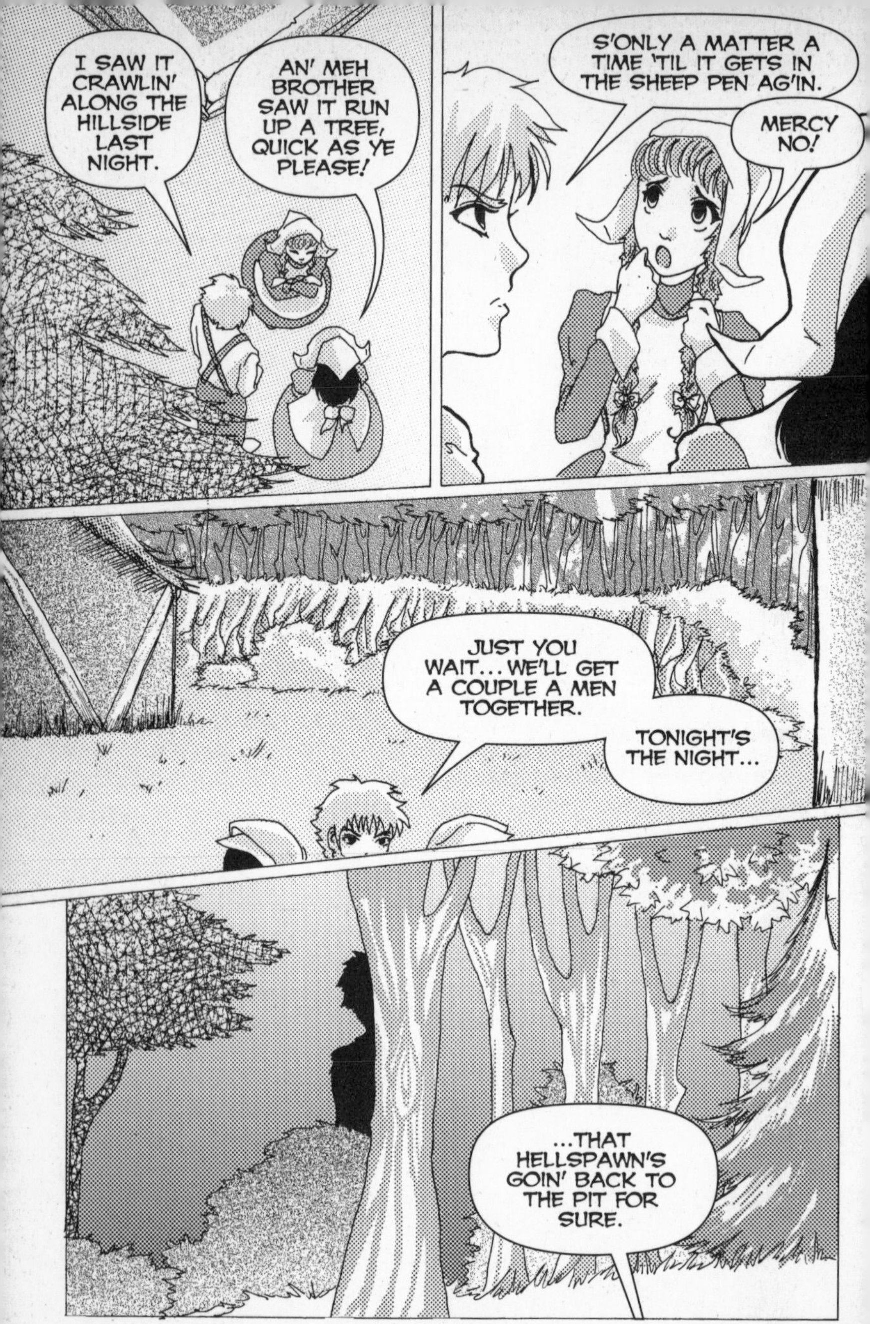
I SAW IT CRAWLIN' ALONG THE HILLSIDE LAST NIGHT.
AN' MEH BROTHER SAW IT RUN UP A TREE, QUICK AS YE PLEASE!
S'ONLY A MATTER A TIME 'TIL IT GETS IN THE SHEEP PEN AG'IN.
MERCY NO!
JUST YOU WAIT... WE'LL GET A COUPLE A MEN TOGETHER.
TONIGHT'S THE NIGHT...
...THAT HELLSPAWN'S GOIN' BACK TO THE PIT FOR SURE.

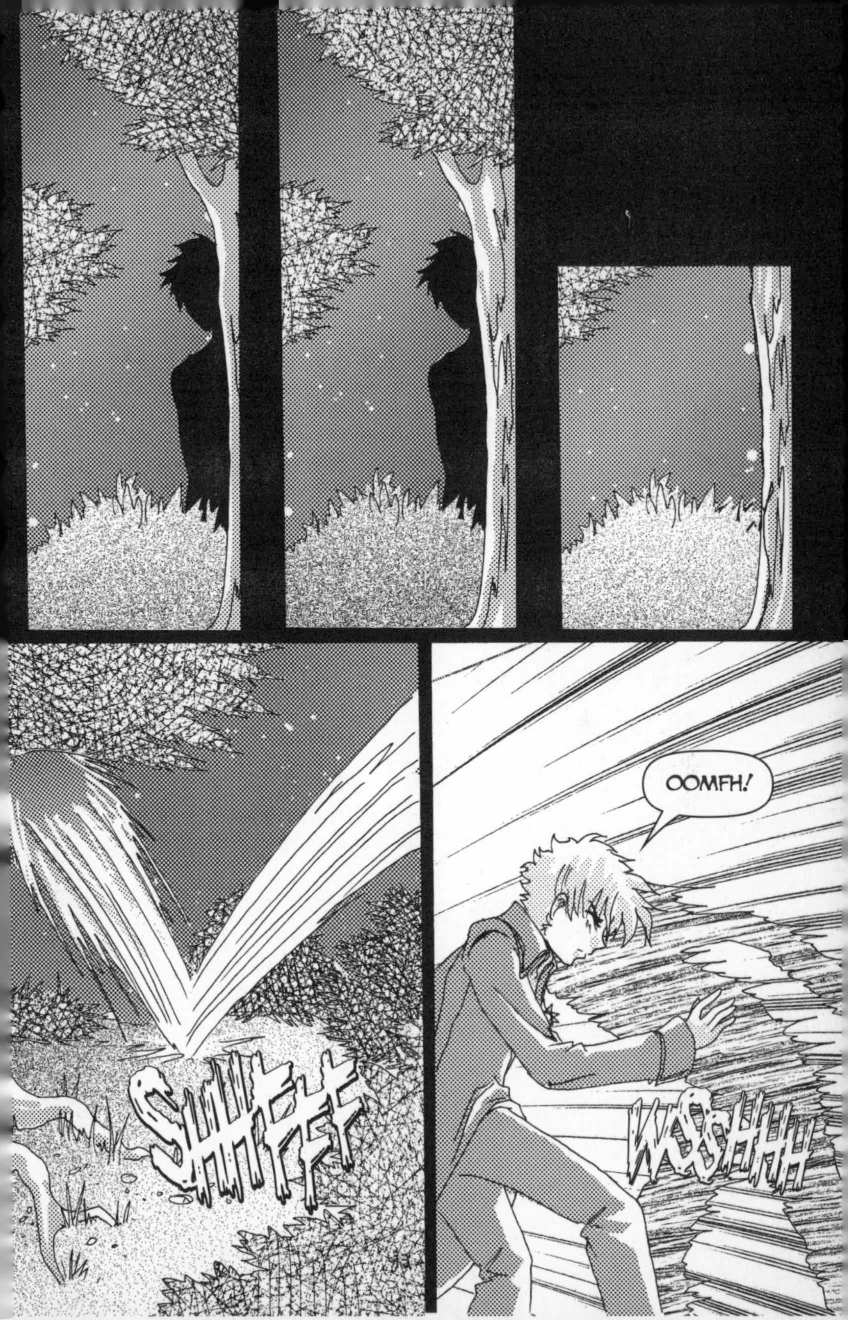
OOMFH!
WOSHHH
SHHFFF

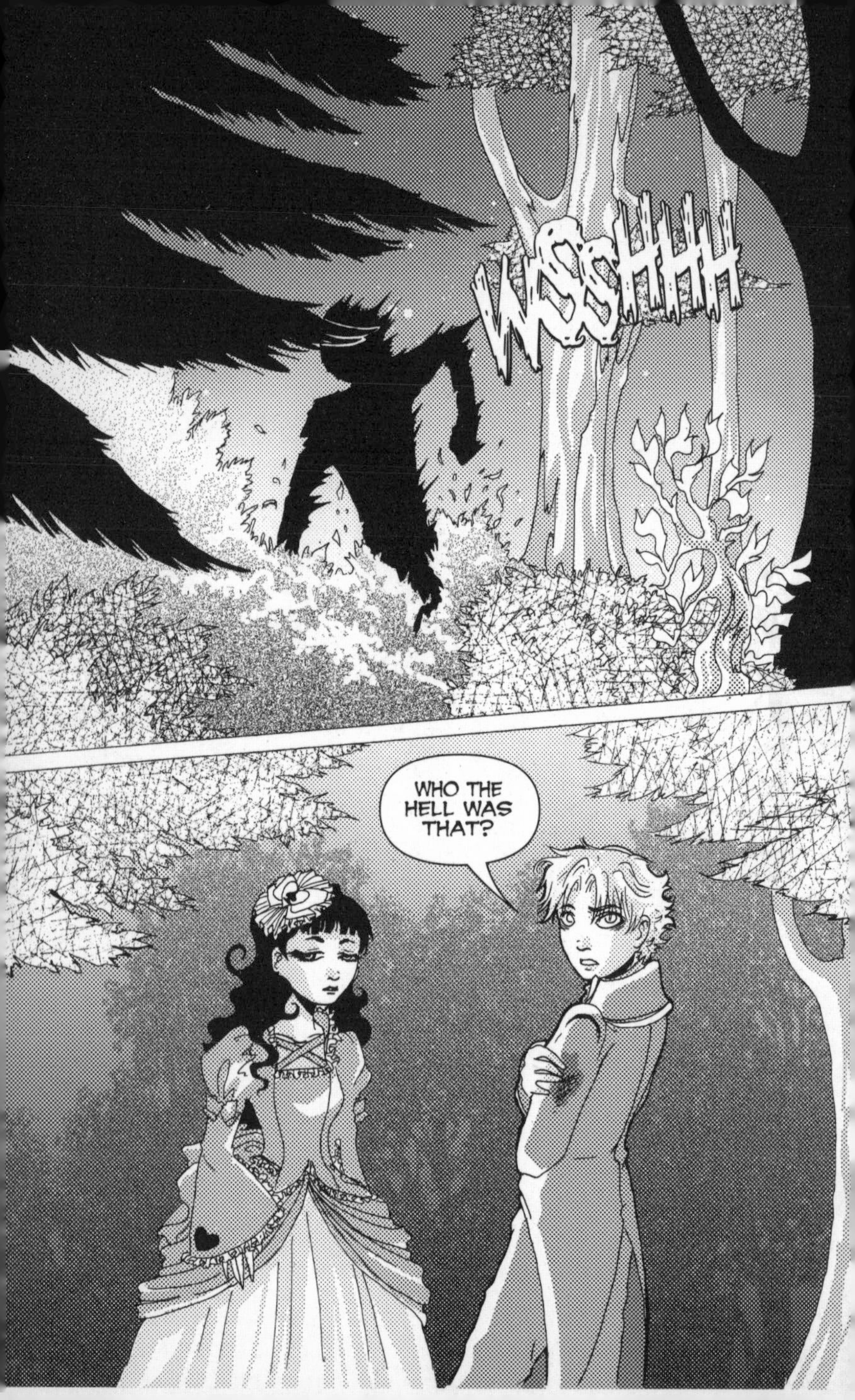
WSSHHH
WHO THE HELL WAS THAT?

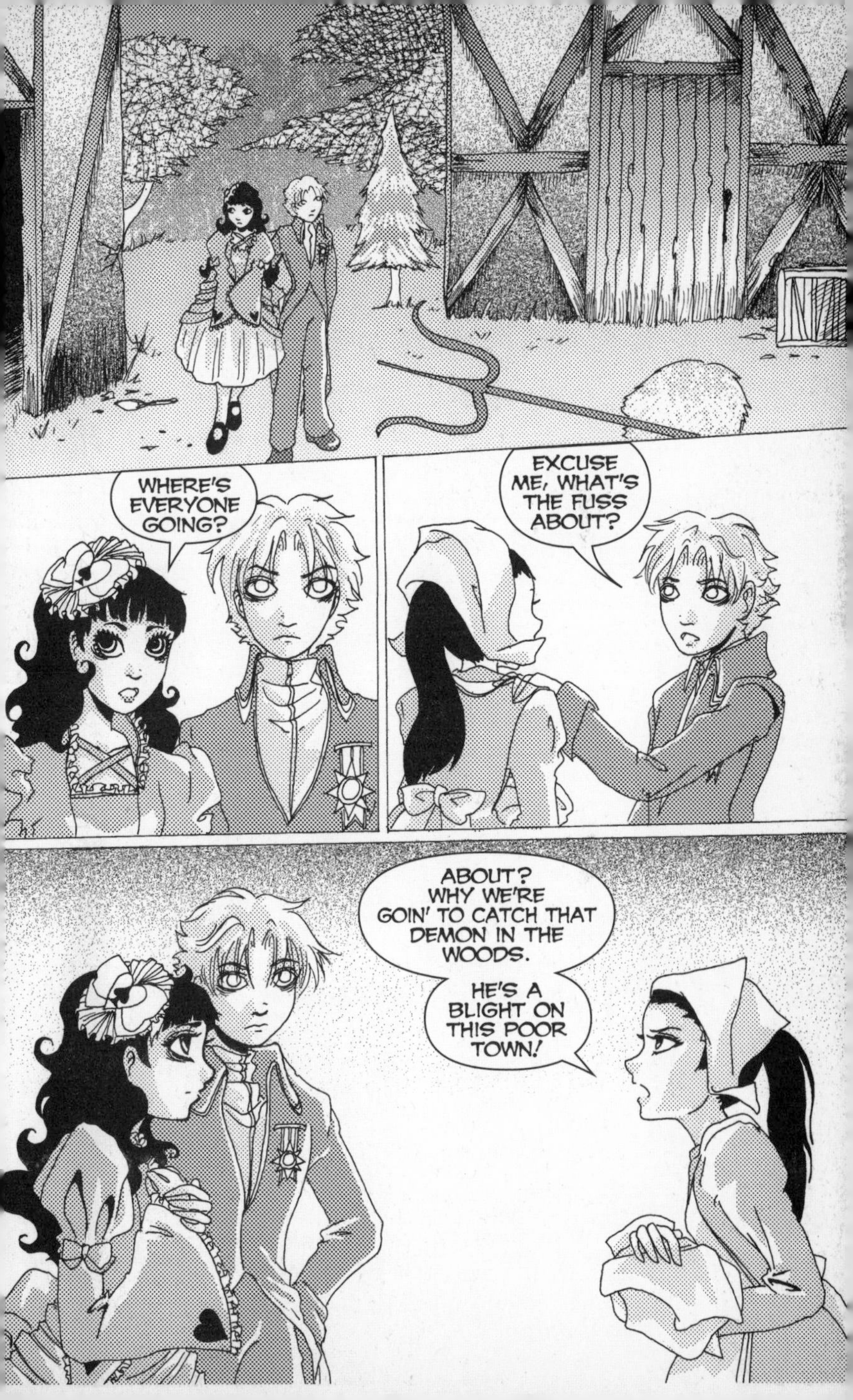
WHERE'S EVERYONE GOING?
EXCUSE ME, WHAT'S THE FUSS ABOUT?
ABOUT? WHY WE'RE GOIN' TO CATCH THAT DEMON IN THE WOODS.
HE'S A BLIGHT ON THIS POOR TOWN!

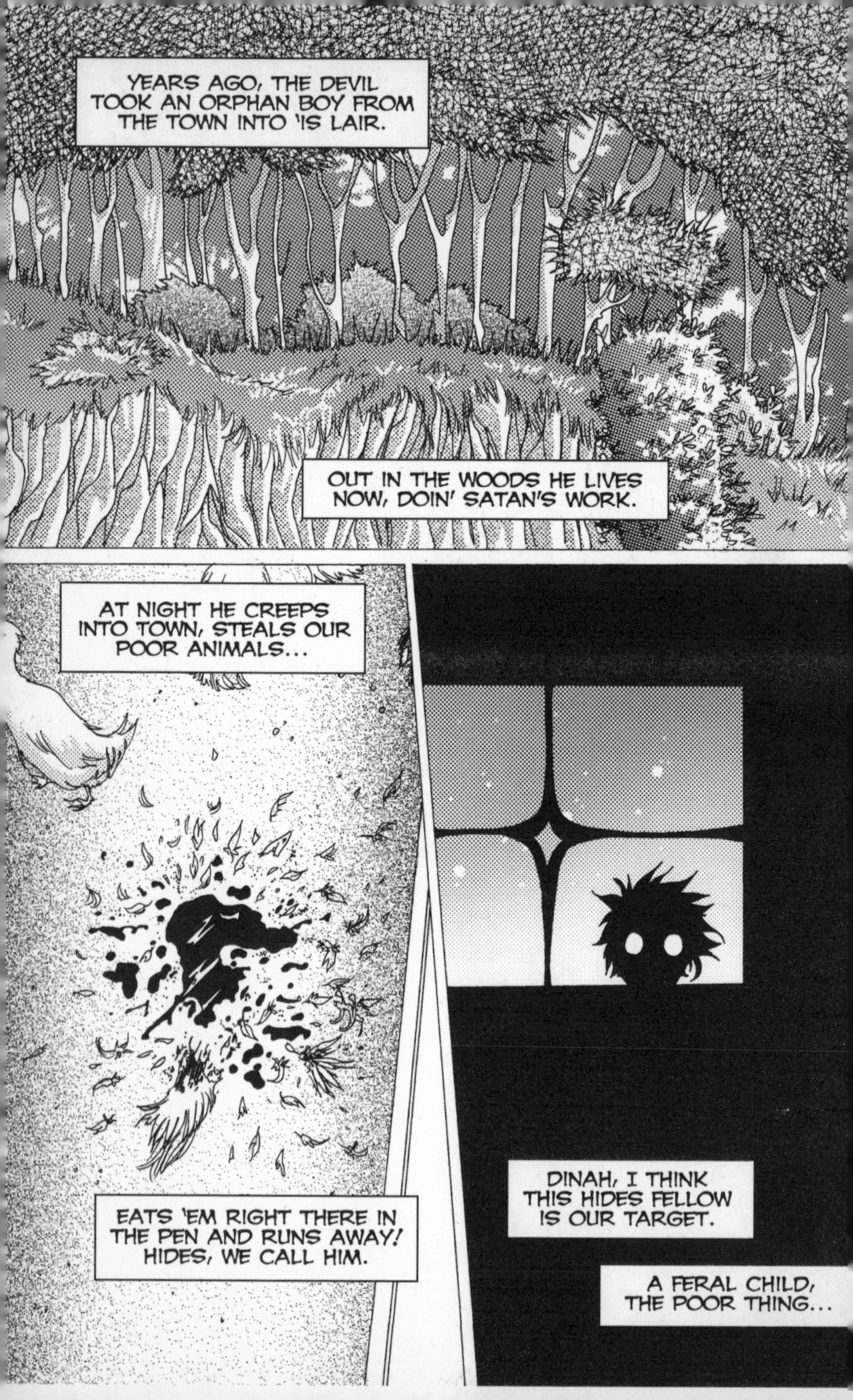
YEARS AGO, THE DEVIL TOOK AN ORPHAN BOY FROM THE TOWN INTO 'IS LAIR.
OUT IN THE WOODS HE LIVES NOW, DOIN' SATAN'S WORK.
AT NIGHT HE CREEPS INTO TOWN, STEALS OUR POOR ANIMALS...
EATS 'EM RIGHT THERE IN THE PEN AND RUNS AWAY! HIDES, WE CALL HIM.
DINAH, I THINK THIS HIDES FELLOW IS OUR TARGET.
A FERAL CHILD, THE POOR THING...

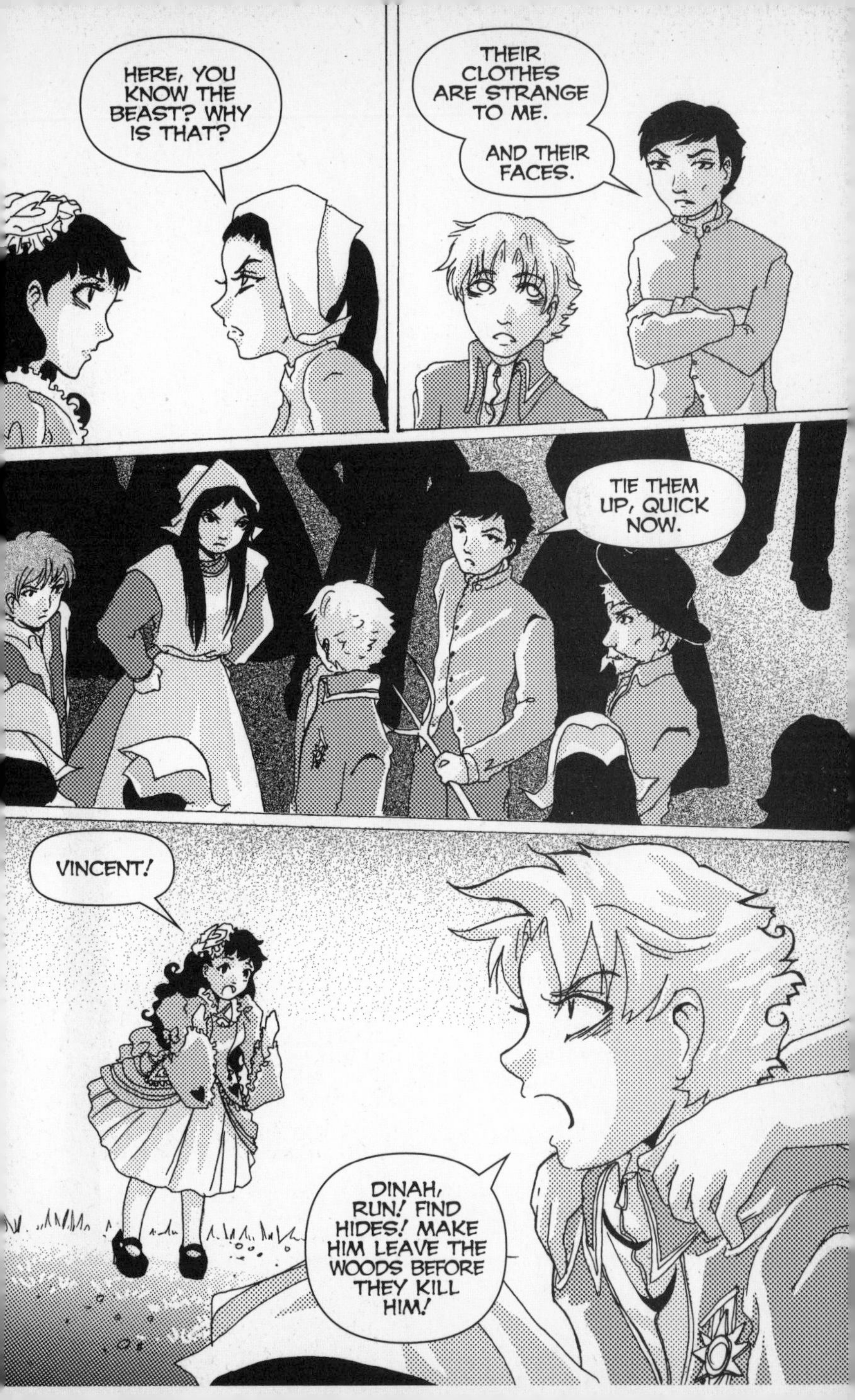
HERE, YOU KNOW THE BEAST? WHY IS THAT?
THEIR CLOTHES ARE STRANGE TO ME.
AND THEIR FACES.
TIE THEM UP, QUICK NOW.
VINCENT!
DINAH, RUN! FIND HIDES! MAKE HIM LEAVE THE WOODS BEFORE THEY KILL HIM!

STOP HER!

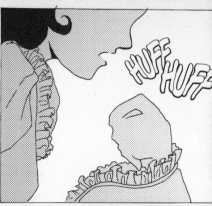

HUFF HUFF

HWOOOOOO

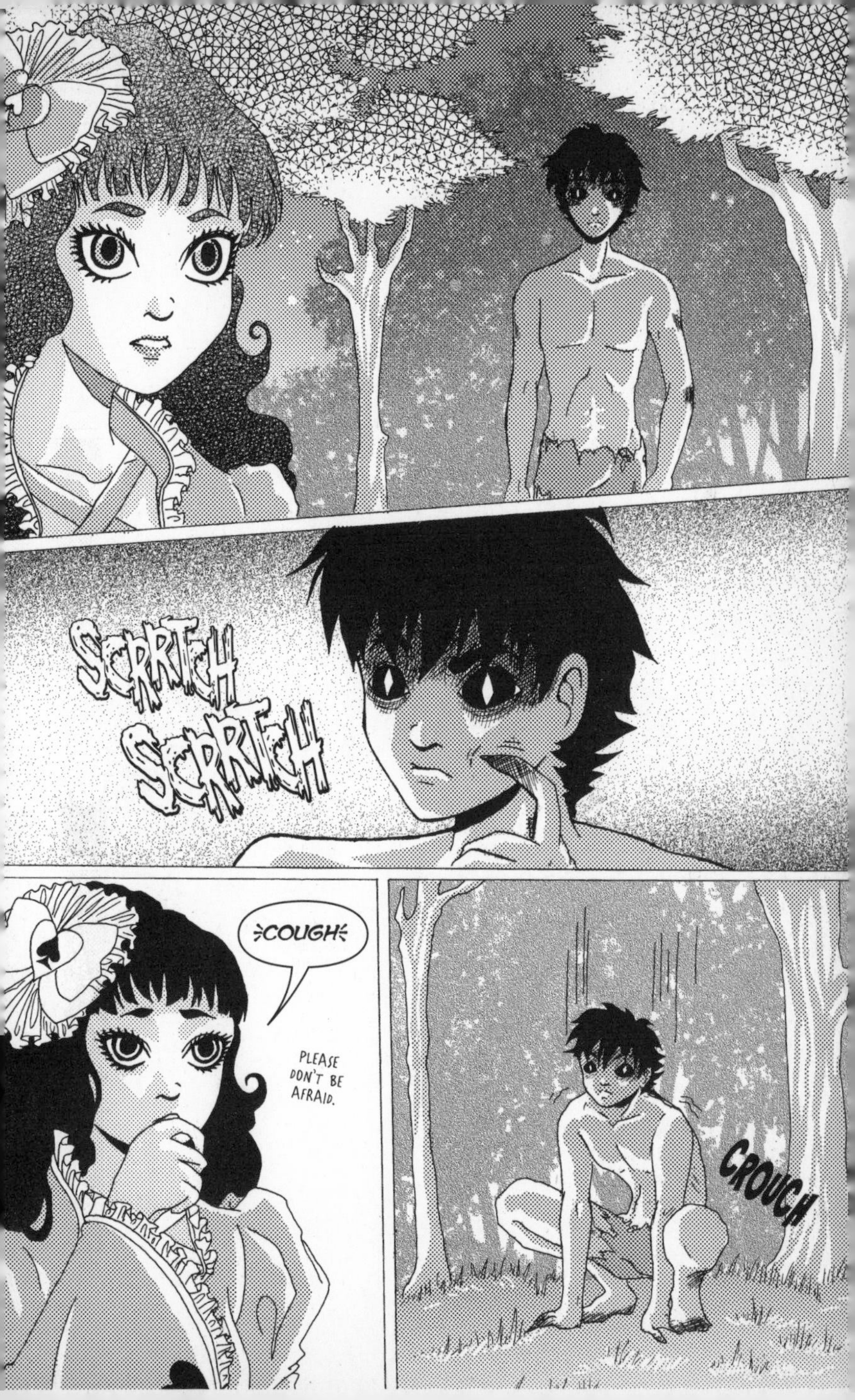
SCRATCH SCRATCH
CROUCH
COUGH
PLEASE DON'T BE AFRAID.

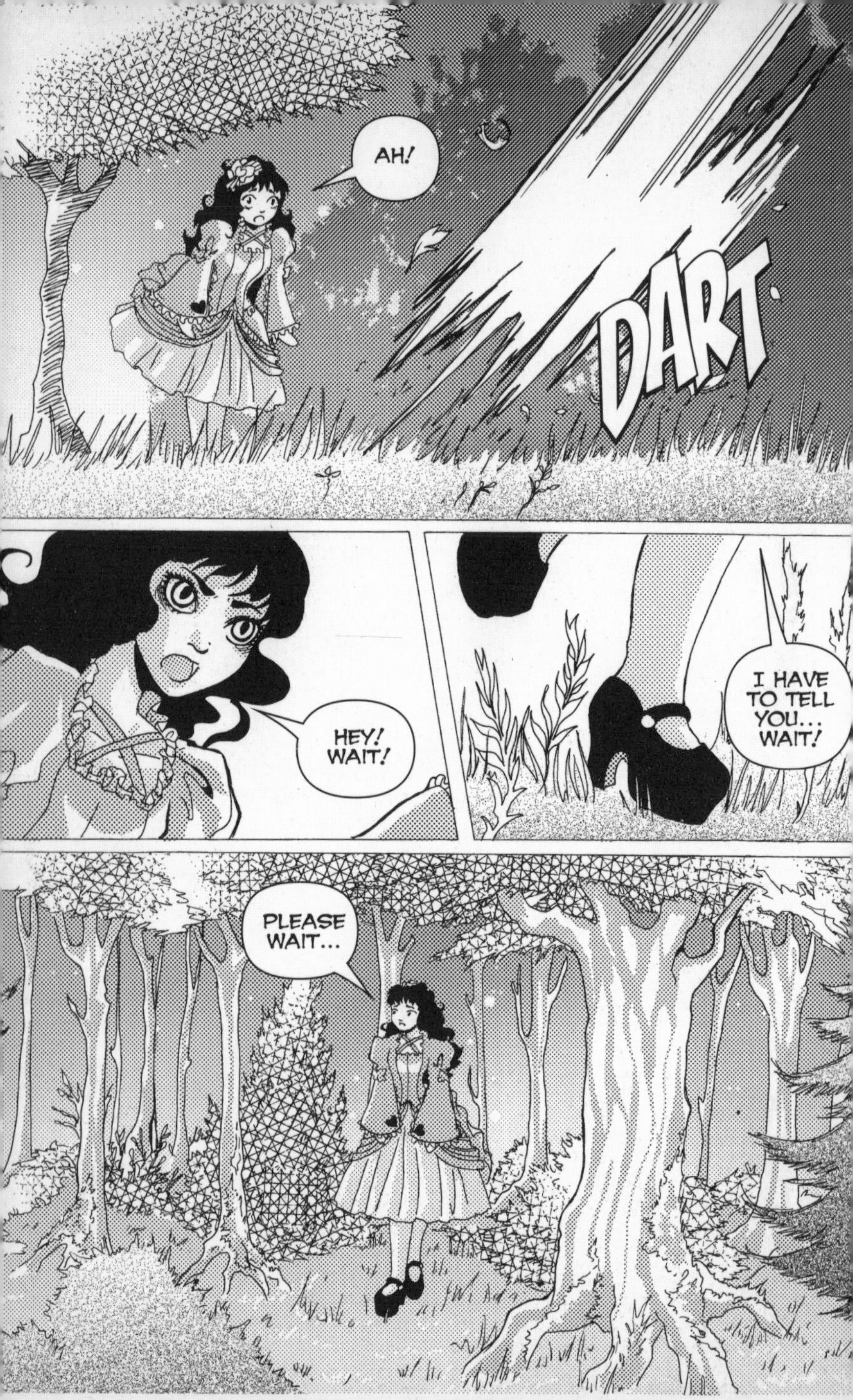
AH!
DART
I HAVE TO TELL YOU... WAIT!
HEY! WAIT!
PLEASE WAIT...

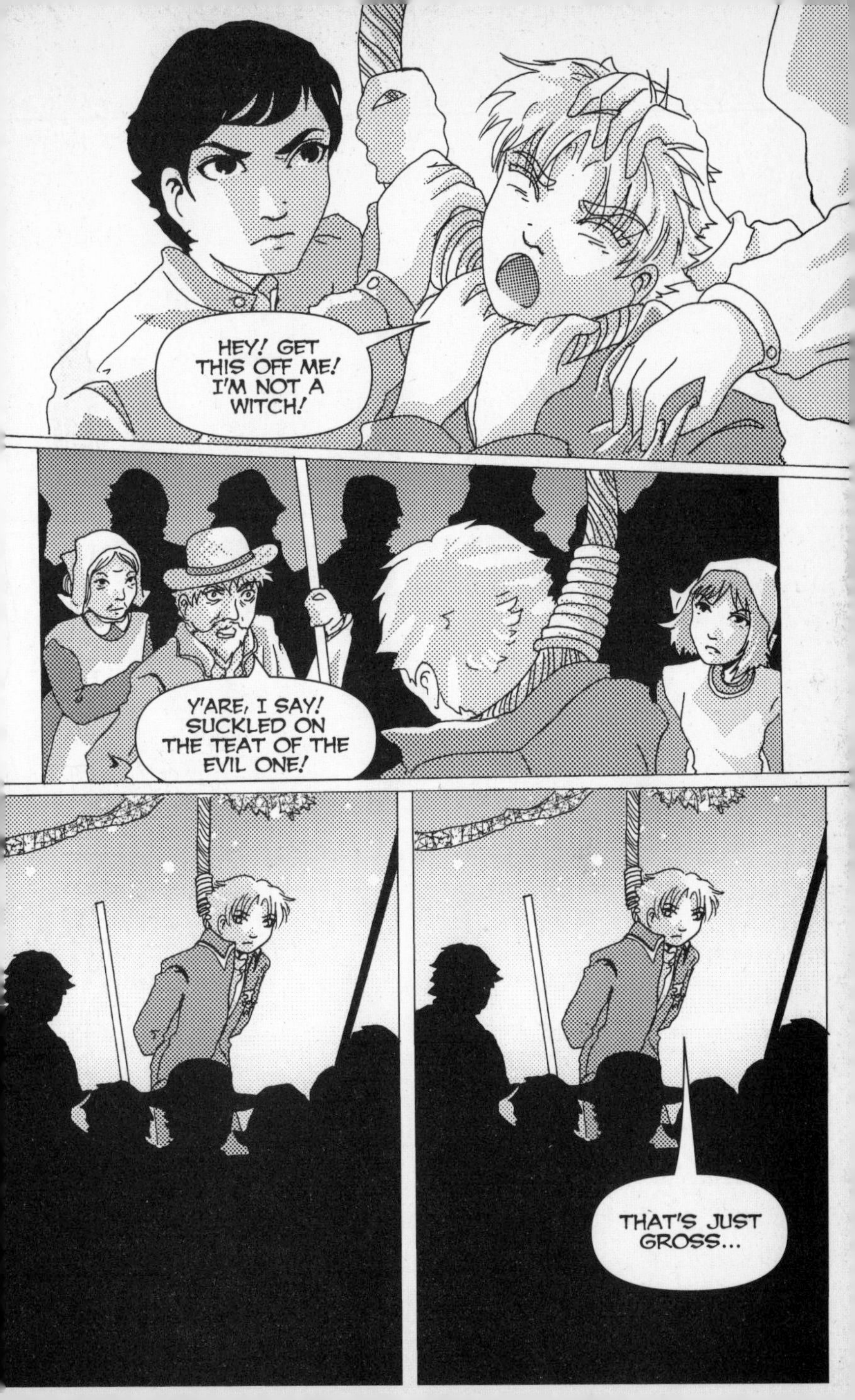
HEY! GET THIS OFF ME! I'M NOT A WITCH!
Y'ARE, I SAY! SUCKLED ON THE TEAT OF THE EVIL ONE!
THAT'S JUST GROSS...

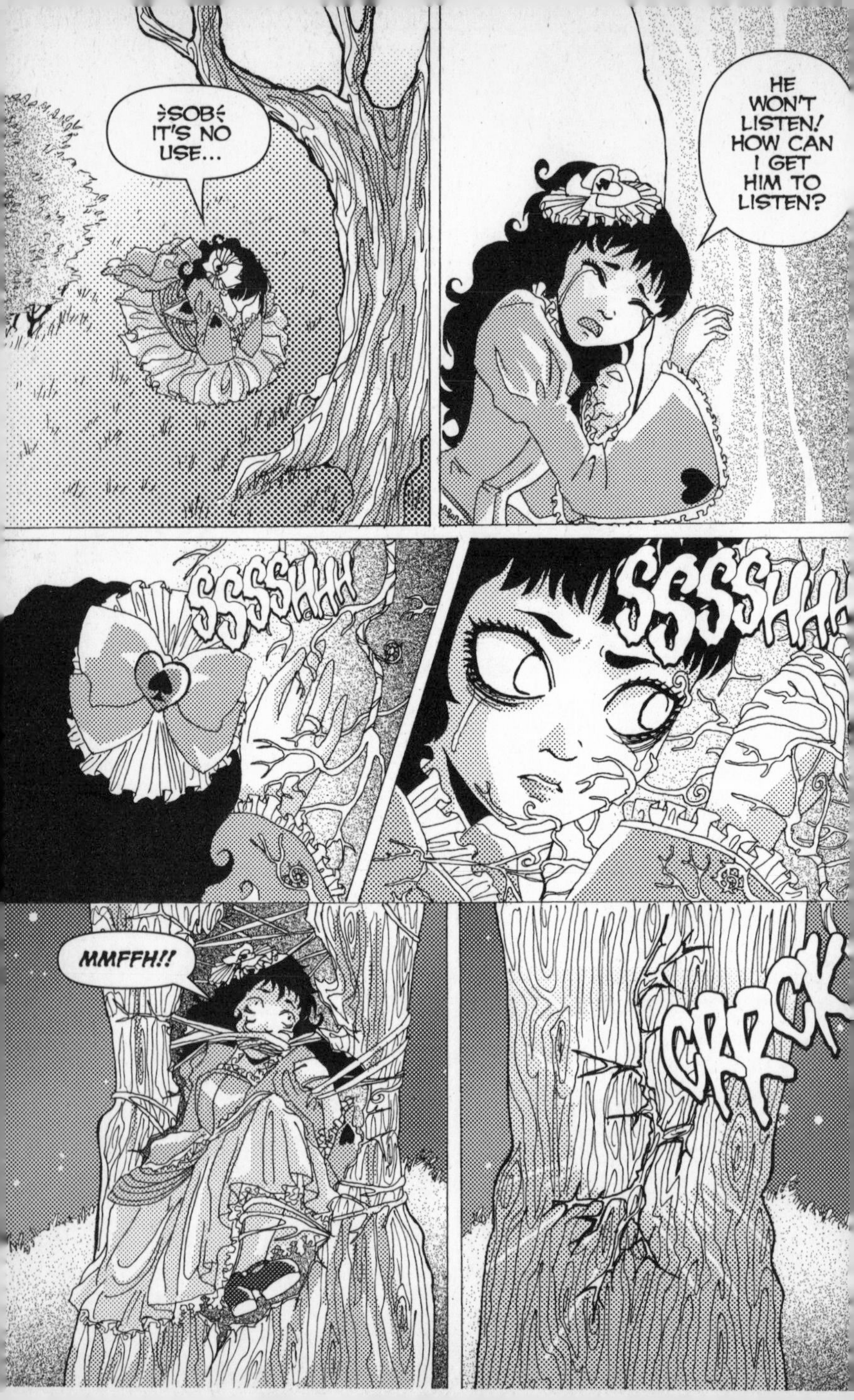

SOB IT'S NO USE...
HE WON'T LISTEN! HOW CAN I GET HIM TO LISTEN?
SSSSHH
SSSSHH
MMFFH!!
CRRCK

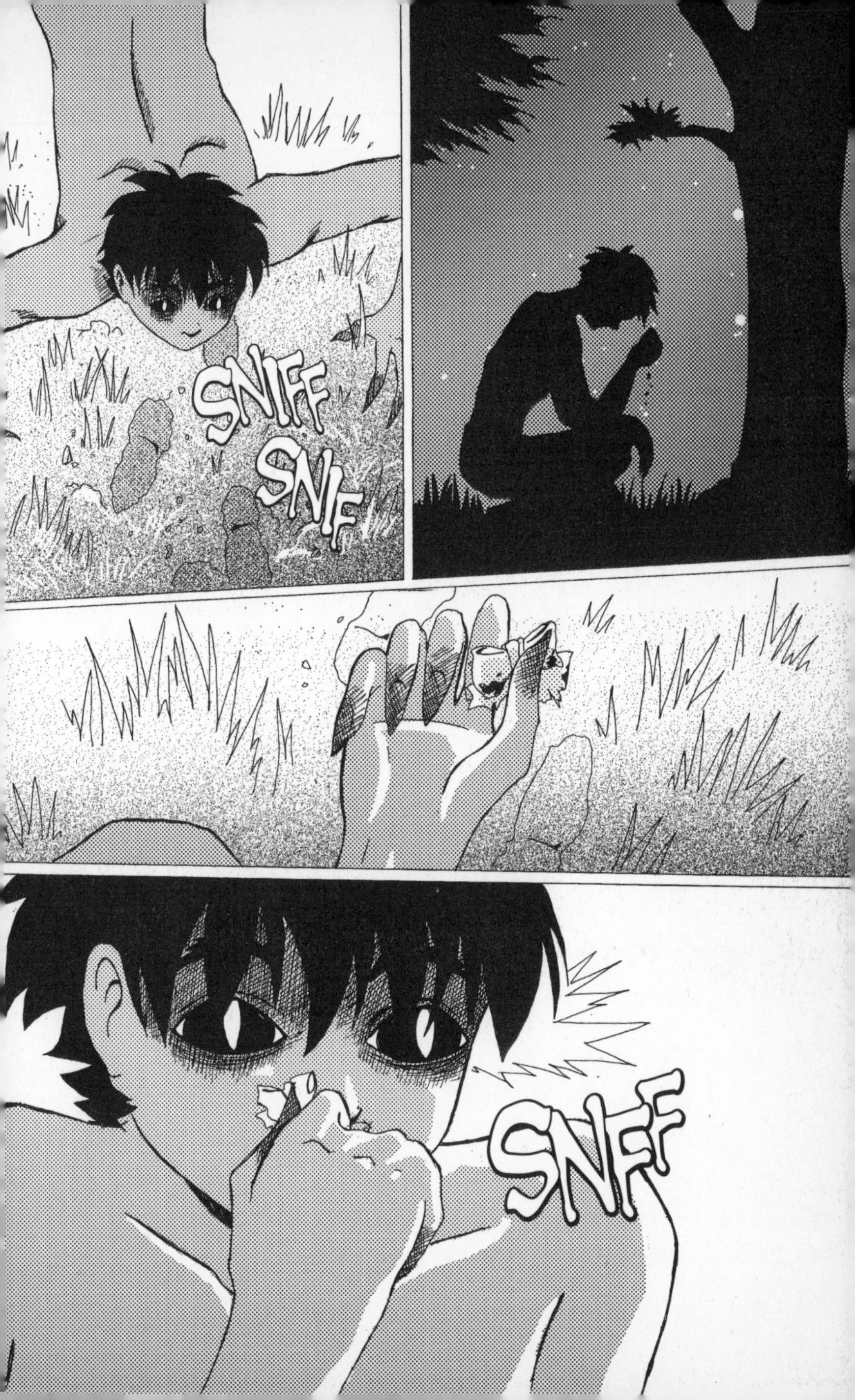
SNIFF
SNIF
SNFF

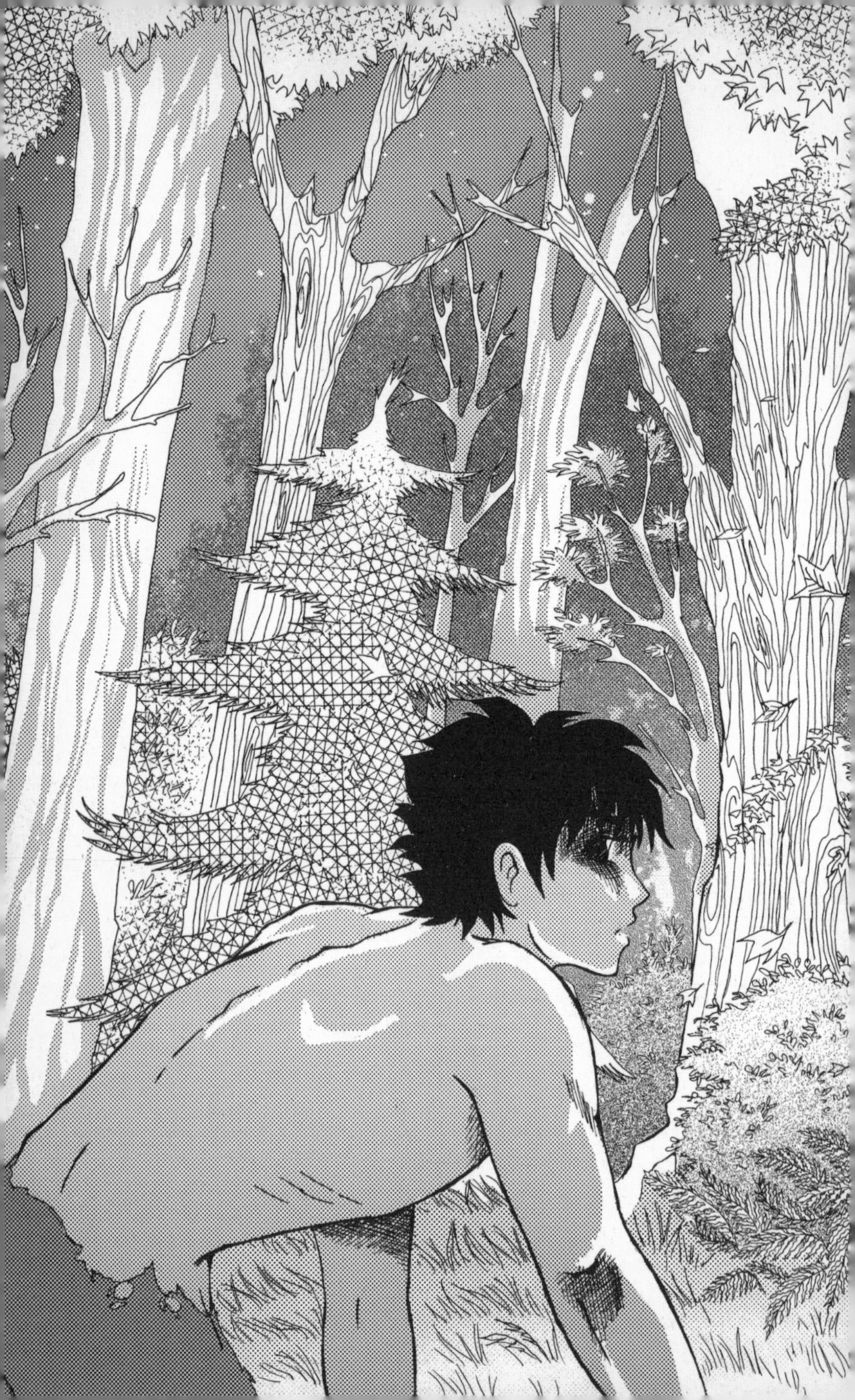

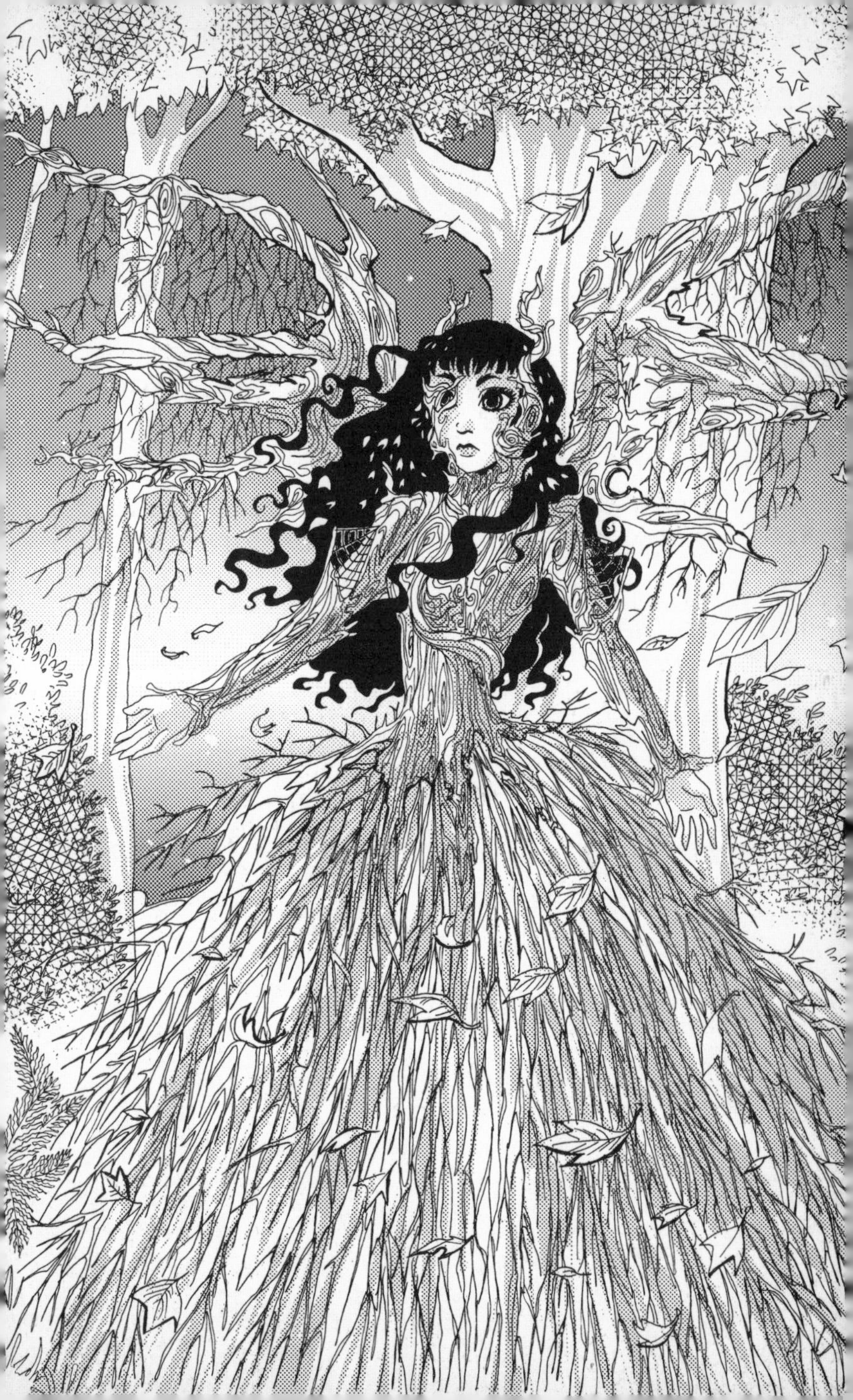

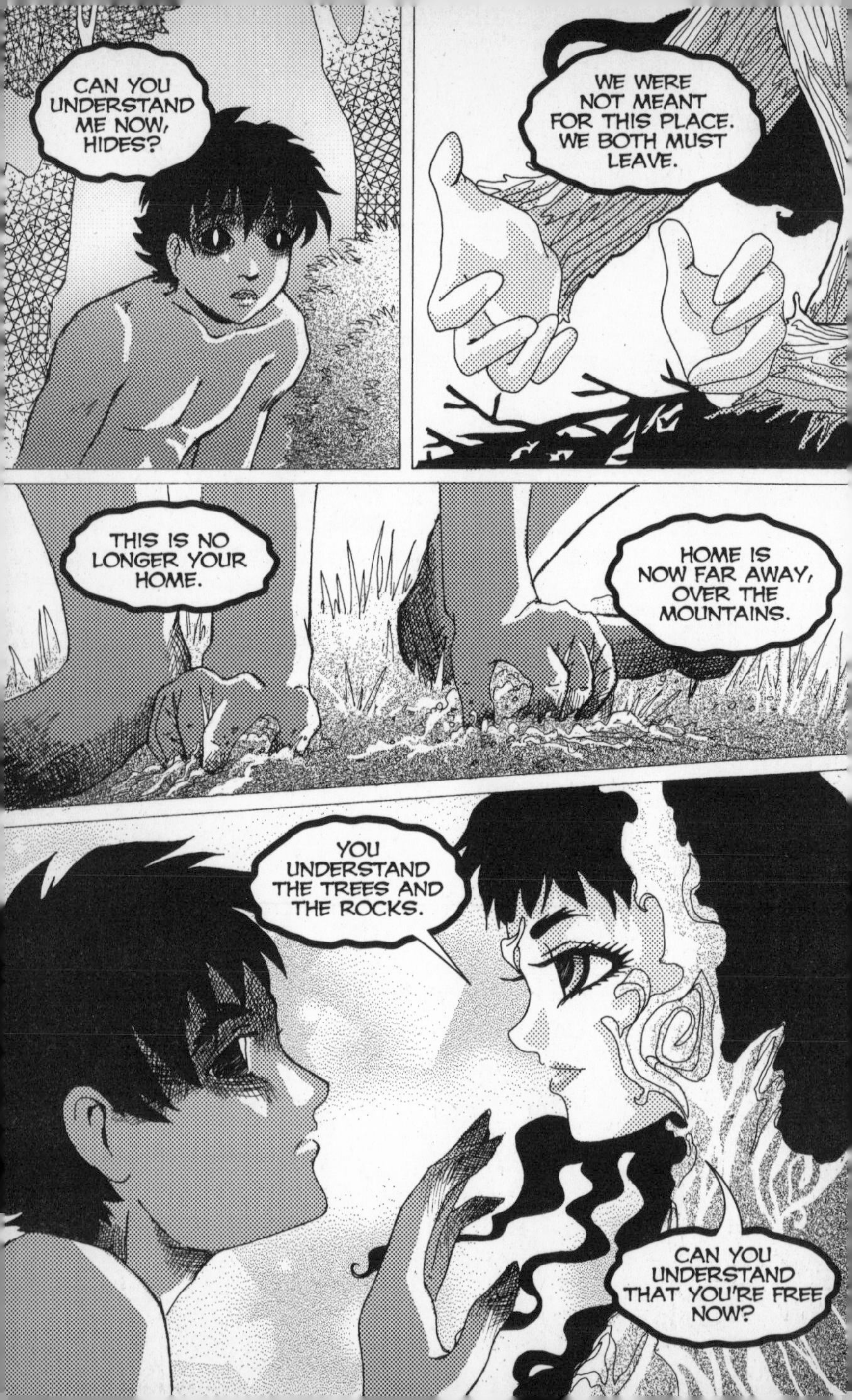
CAN YOU UNDERSTAND ME NOW, HIDES?
WE WERE NOT MEANT FOR THIS PLACE. WE BOTH MUST LEAVE.
THIS IS NO LONGER YOUR HOME.
HOME IS NOW FAR AWAY, OVER THE MOUNTAINS.
YOU UNDERSTAND THE TREES AND THE ROCKS.
CAN YOU UNDERSTAND THAT YOU'RE FREE NOW?

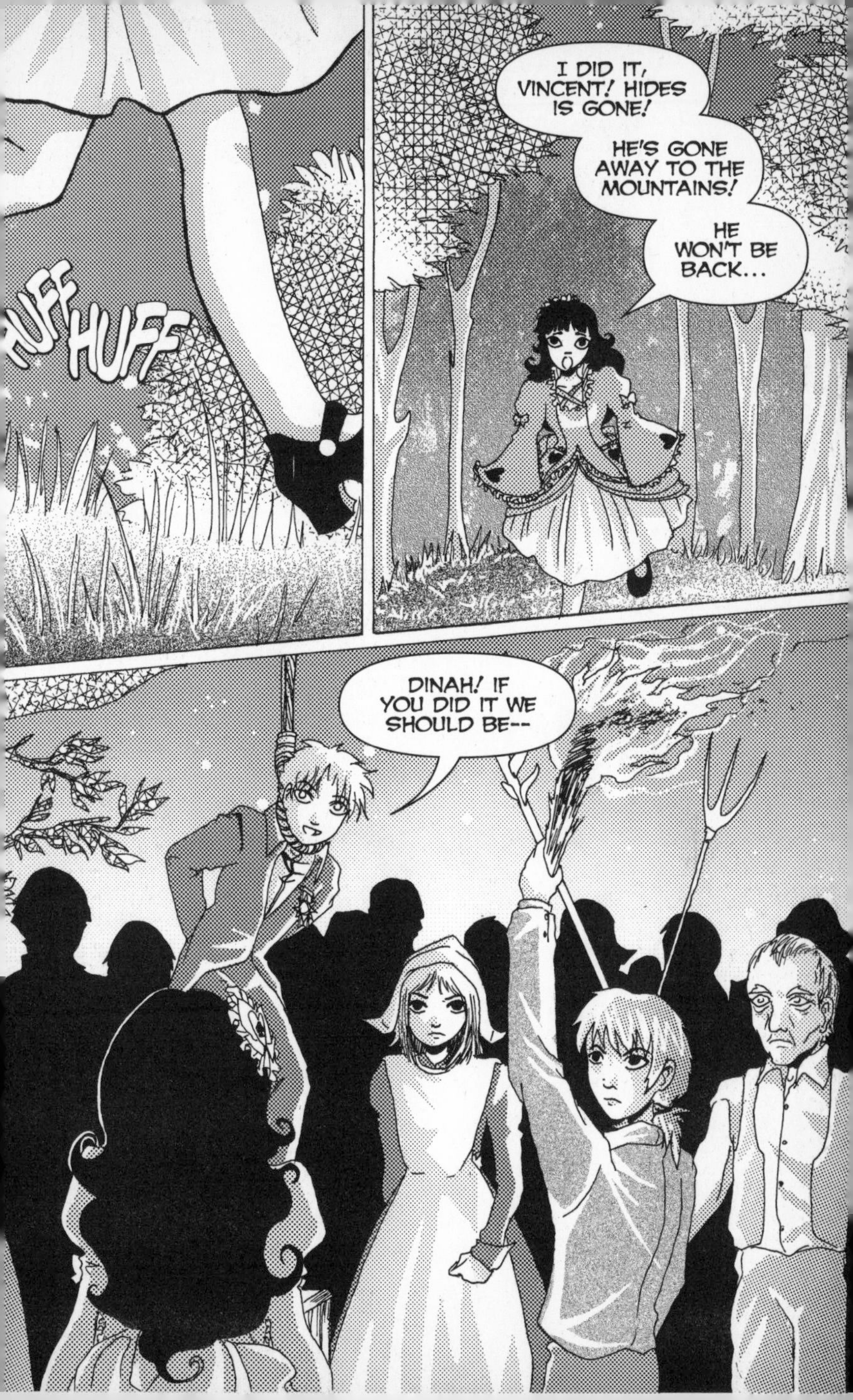
HUFF HUFF
I DID IT, VINCENT! HIDES IS GONE!
HE'S GONE AWAY TO THE MOUNTAINS!
HE WON'T BE BACK...
DINAH! IF YOU DID IT WE SHOULD BE--

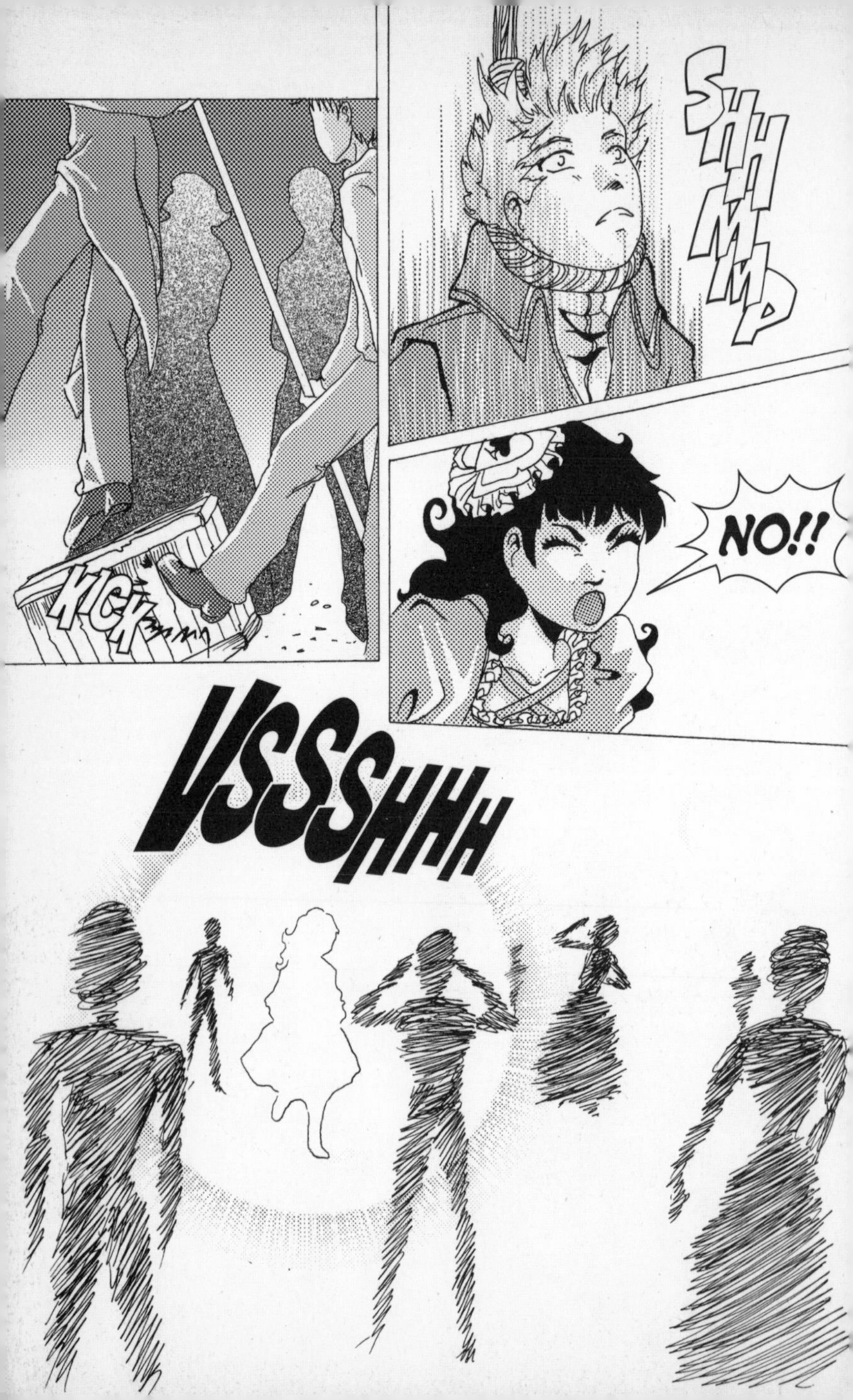
SHHMMP
NO!!
KICK
VSSSHHH

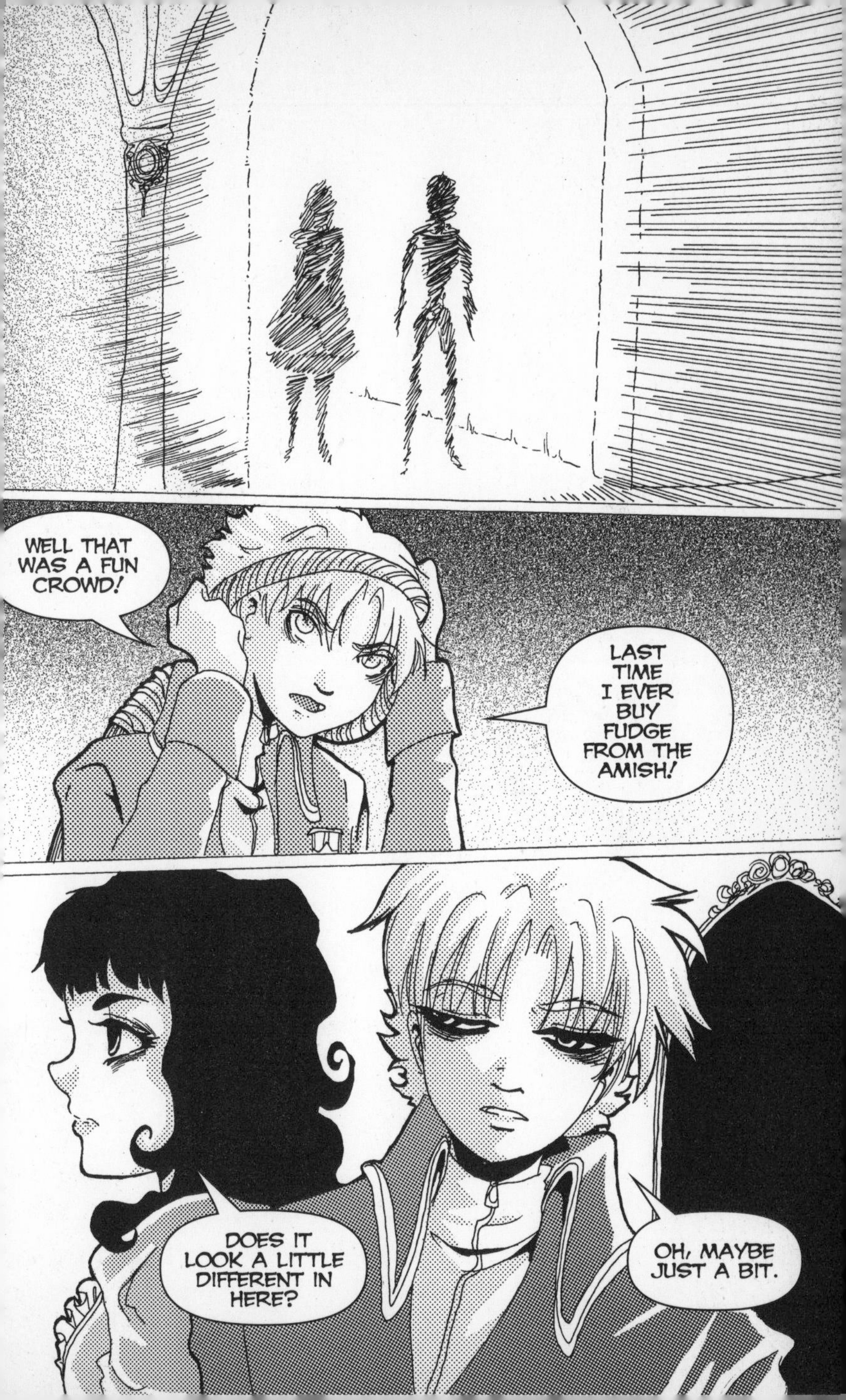
WELL THAT WAS A FUN CROWD!
LAST TIME I EVER BUY FUDGE FROM THE AMISH!
DOES IT LOOK A LITTLE DIFFERENT IN HERE?
OH, MAYBE JUST A BIT.

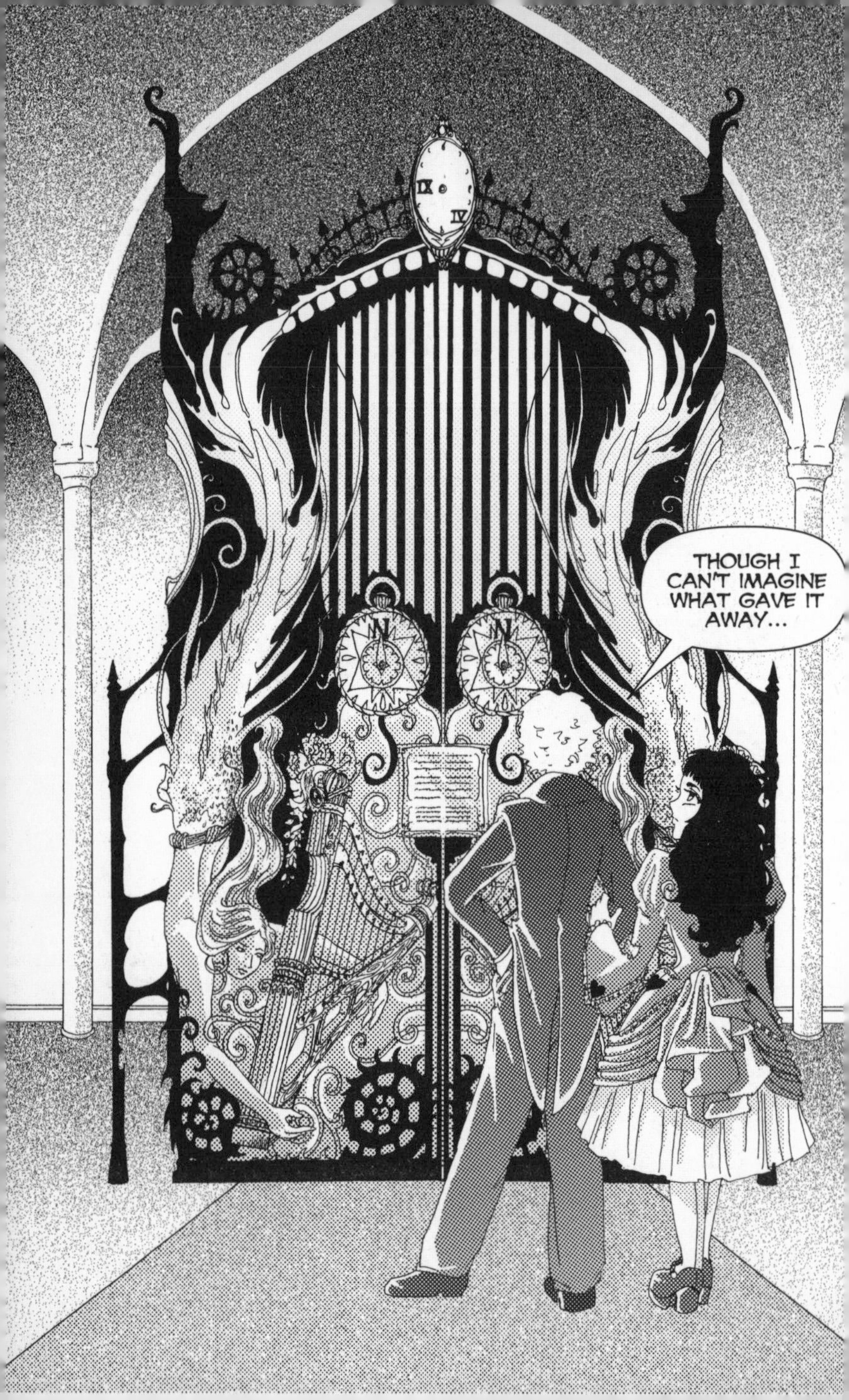
THOUGH I CAN'T IMAGINE WHAT GAVE IT AWAY...

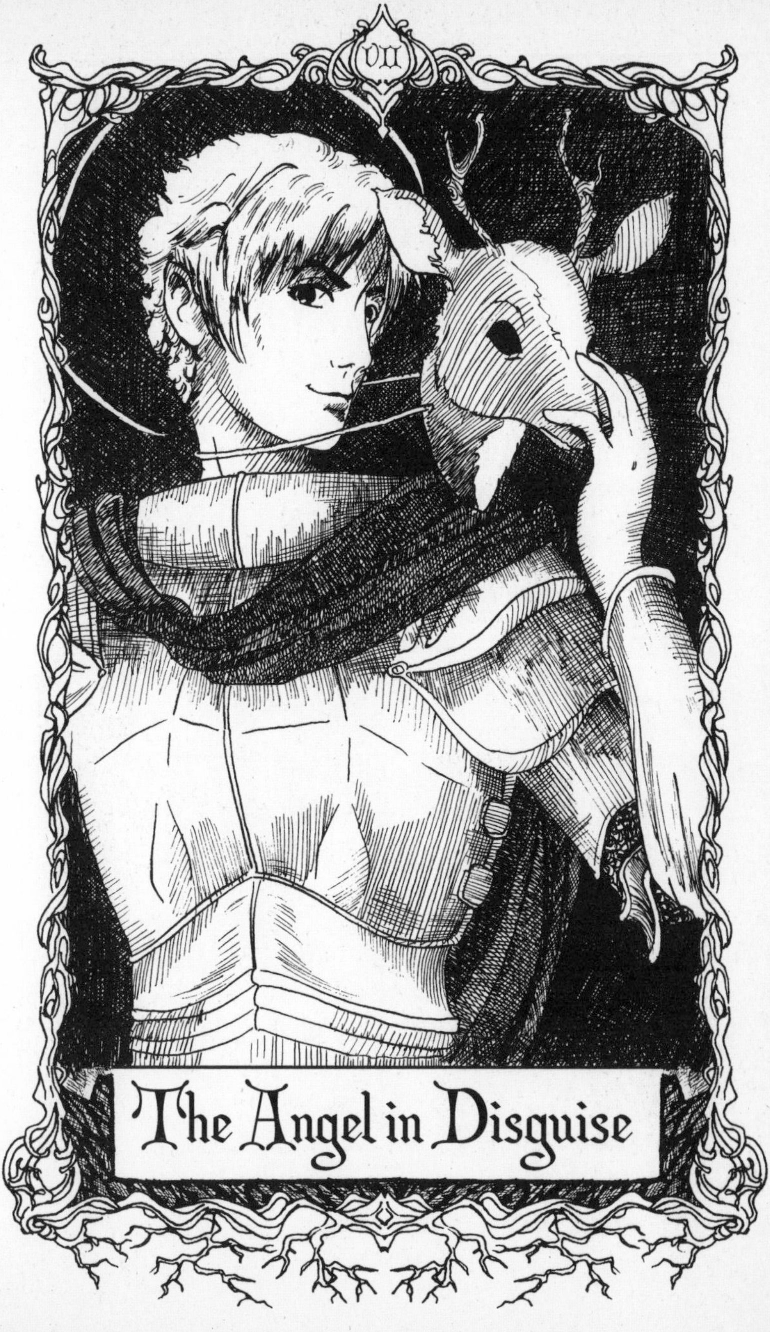
VII
The Angel in Disguise

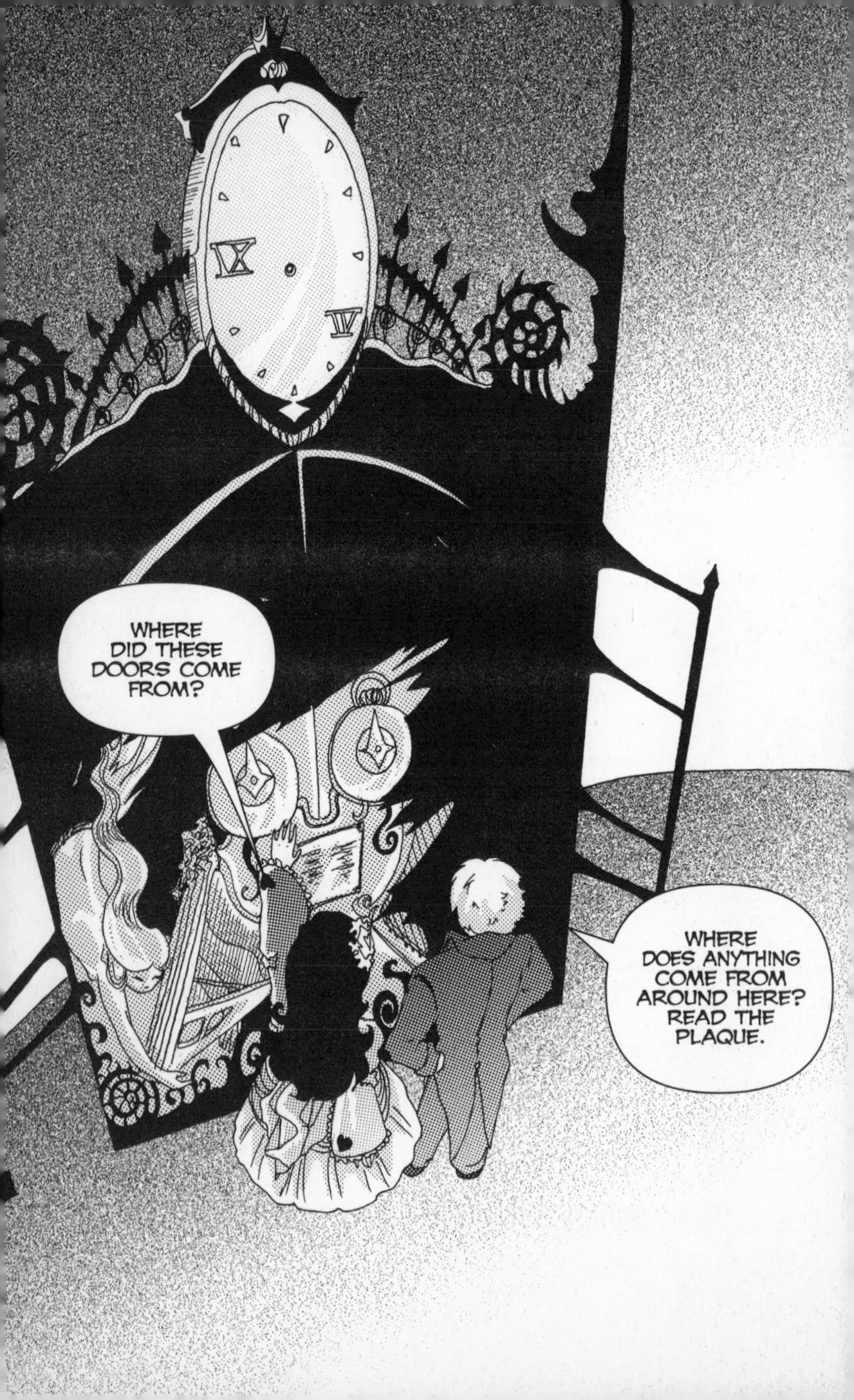
WHERE DID THESE DOORS COME FROM?
WHERE DOES ANYTHING COME FROM AROUND HERE? READ THE PLAQUE.

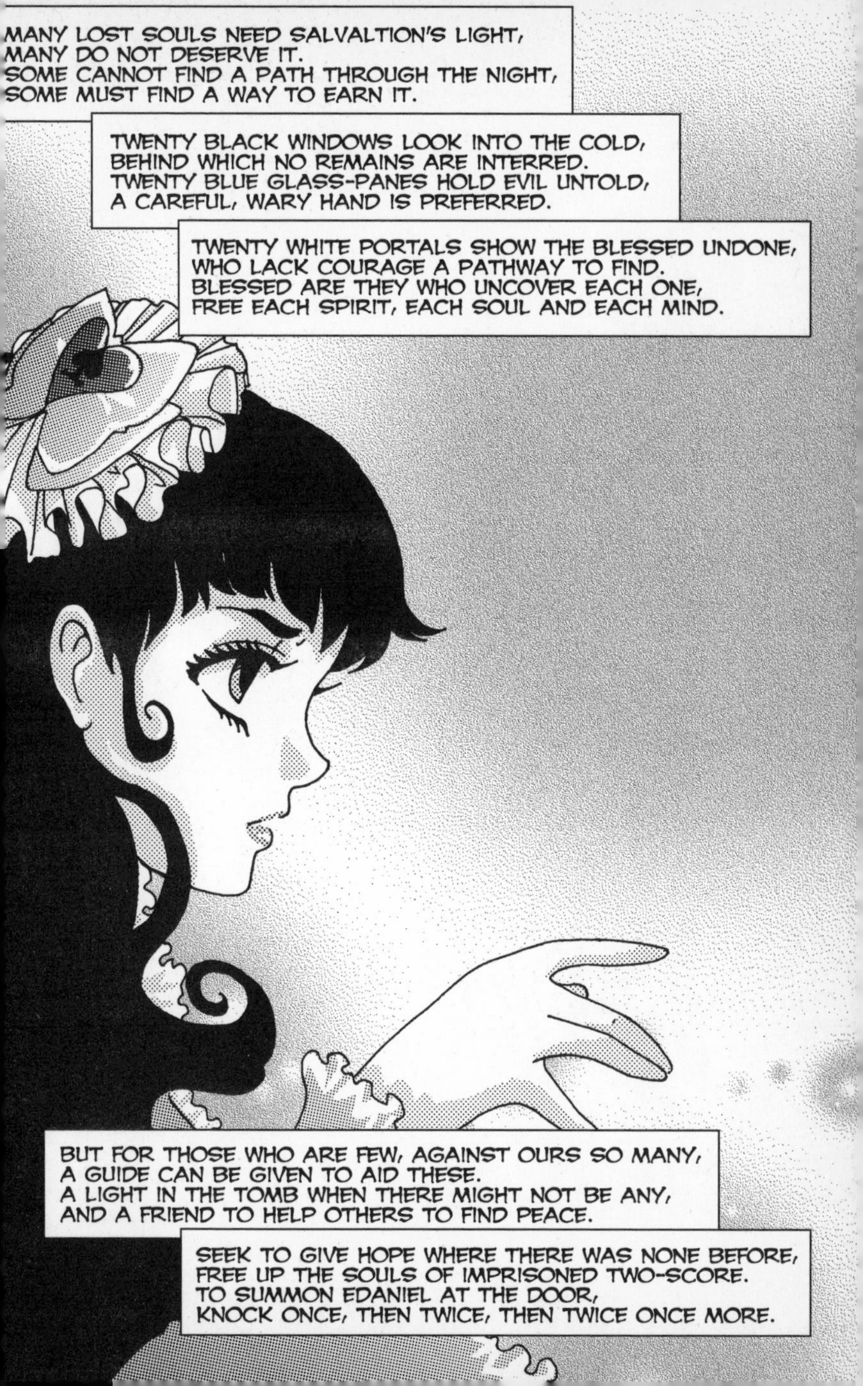
MANY LOST SOULS NEED SALVALTION'S LIGHT,
MANY DO NOT DESERVE IT.
SOME CANNOT FIND A PATH THROUGH THE NIGHT,
SOME MUST FIND A WAY TO EARN IT.
TWENTY BLACK WINDOWS LOOK INTO THE COLD,
BEHIND WHICH NO REMAINS ARE INTERRED.
TWENTY BLUE GLASS-PANES HOLD EVIL UNTOLD,
A CAREFUL, WARY HAND IS PREFERRED.
TWENTY WHITE PORTALS SHOW THE BLESSED UNDONE,
WHO LACK COURAGE A PATHWAY TO FIND.
BLESSED ARE THEY WHO UNCOVER EACH ONE,
FREE EACH SPIRIT, EACH SOUL AND EACH MIND.
BUT FOR THOSE WHO ARE FEW, AGAINST OURS SO MANY,
A GUIDE CAN BE GIVEN TO AID THESE.
A LIGHT IN THE TOMB WHEN THERE MIGHT NOT BE ANY,
AND A FRIEND TO HELP OTHERS TO FIND PEACE.
SEEK TO GIVE HOPE WHERE THERE WAS NONE BEFORE,
FREE UP THE SOULS OF IMPRISONED TWO-SCORE.
TO SUMMON EDANIEL AT THE DOOR,
KNOCK ONCE, THEN TWICE, THEN TWICE ONCE MORE.

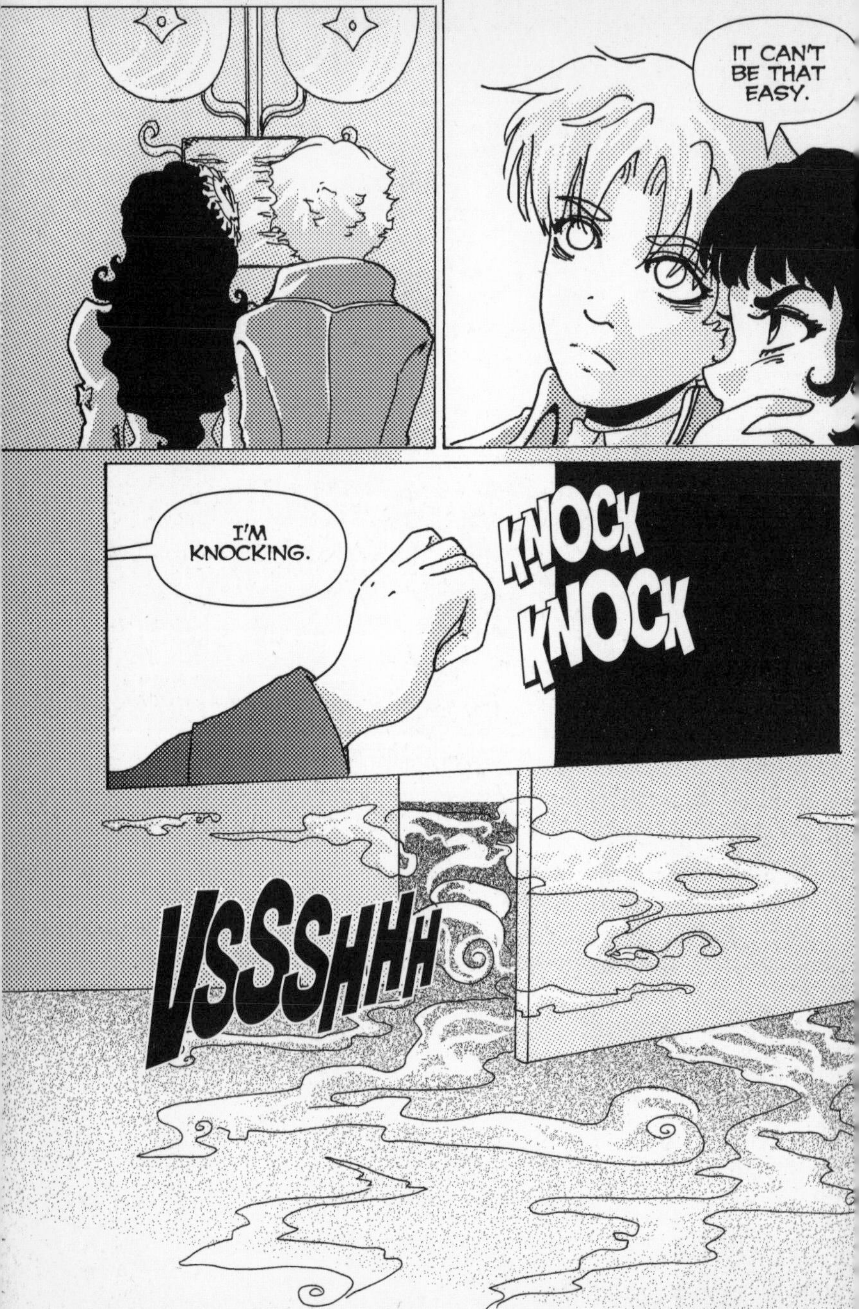
IT CAN'T BE THAT EASY.
I'M KNOCKING.
KNOCK KNOCK
VSSSHHH

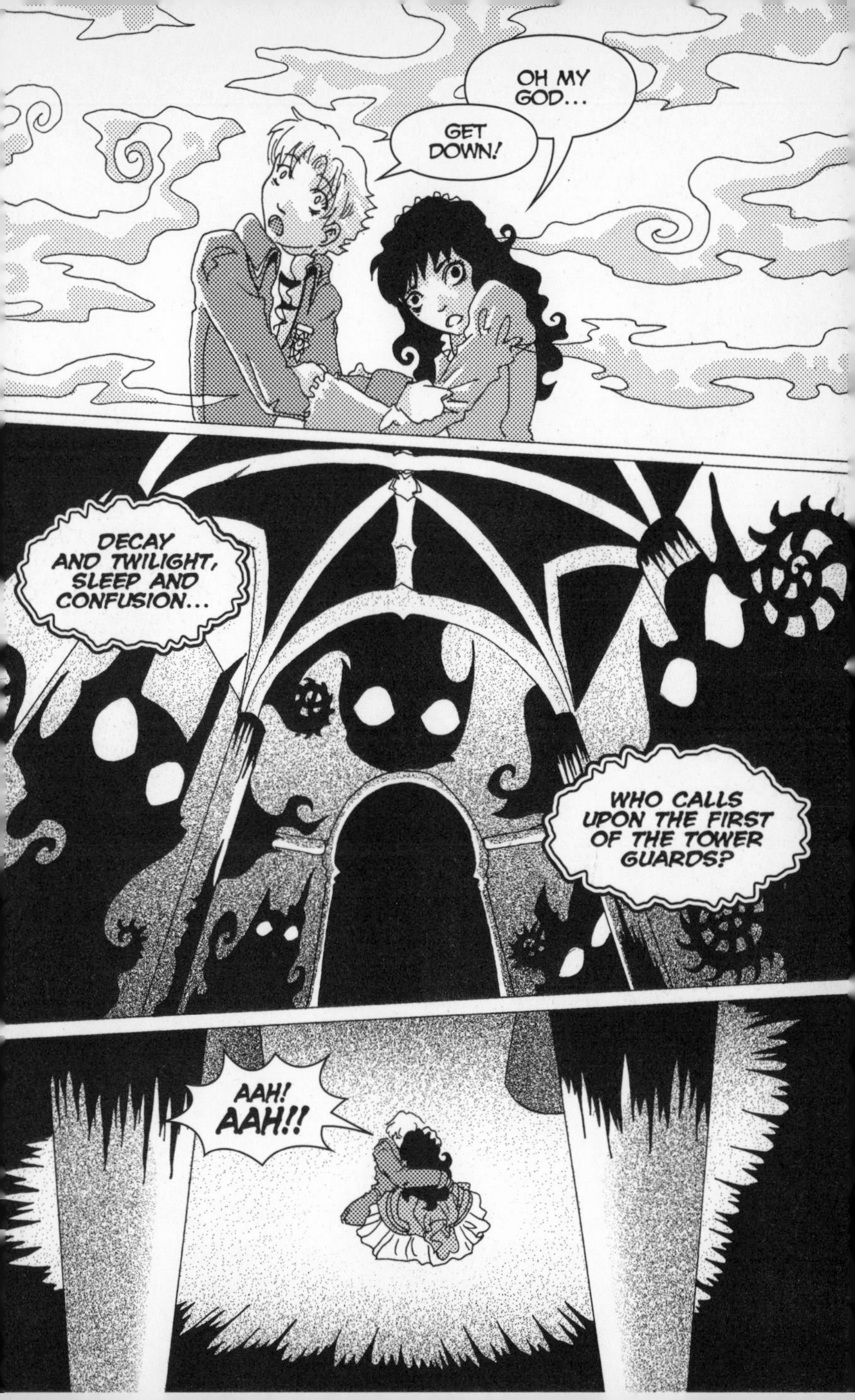
OH MY GOD...
GET DOWN!
DECAY AND TWILIGHT, SLEEP AND CONFUSION...
WHO CALLS UPON THE FIRST OF THE TOWER GUARDS?
AAH! AAH!!

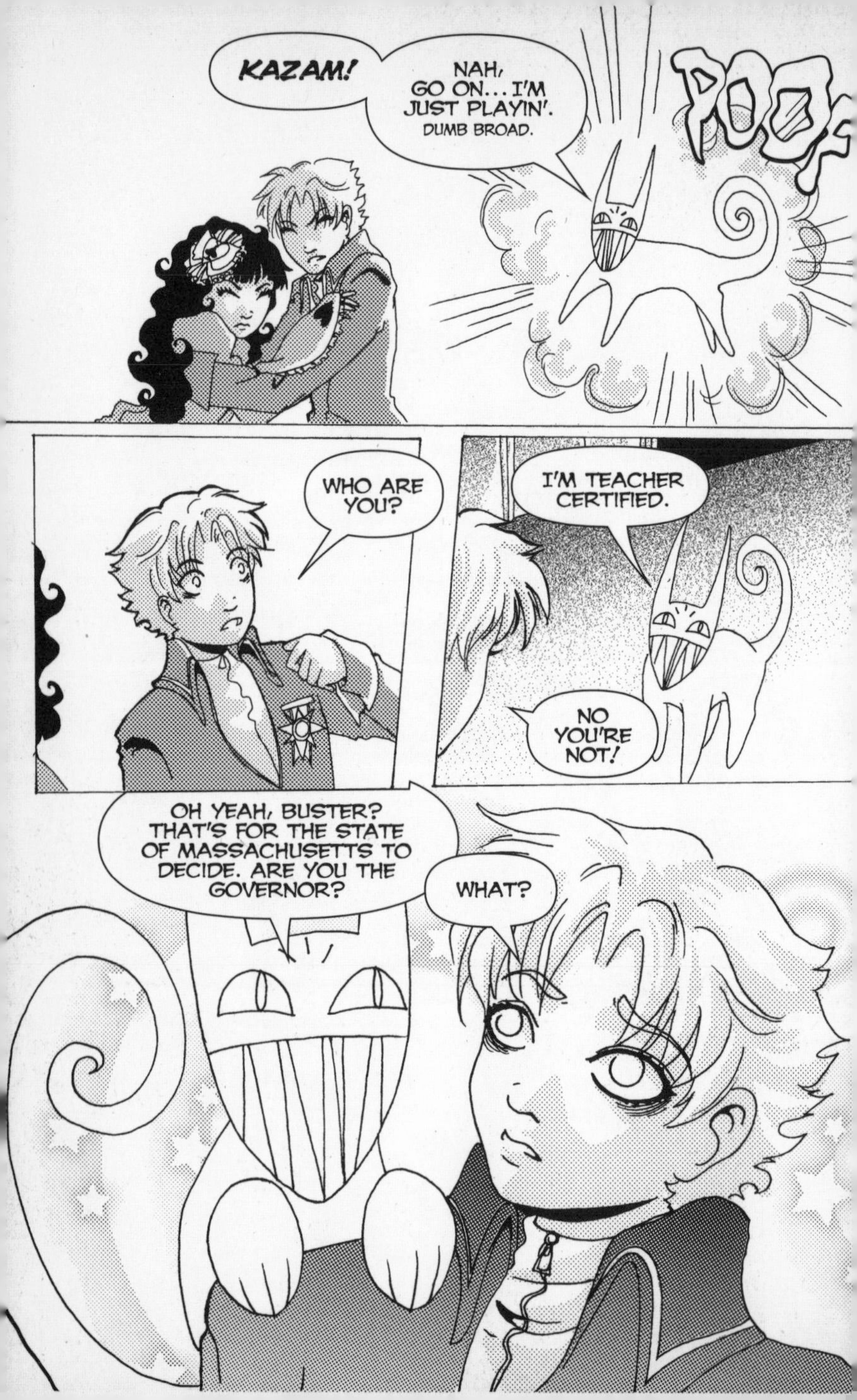
KAZAM!
NAH, GO ON... I'M JUST PLAYIN'. DUMB BROAD.
POOF
WHO ARE YOU?
I'M TEACHER CERTIFIED.
NO YOU'RE NOT!
OH YEAH, BUSTER? THAT'S FOR THE STATE OF MASSACHUSETTS TO DECIDE. ARE YOU THE GOVERNOR?
WHAT?

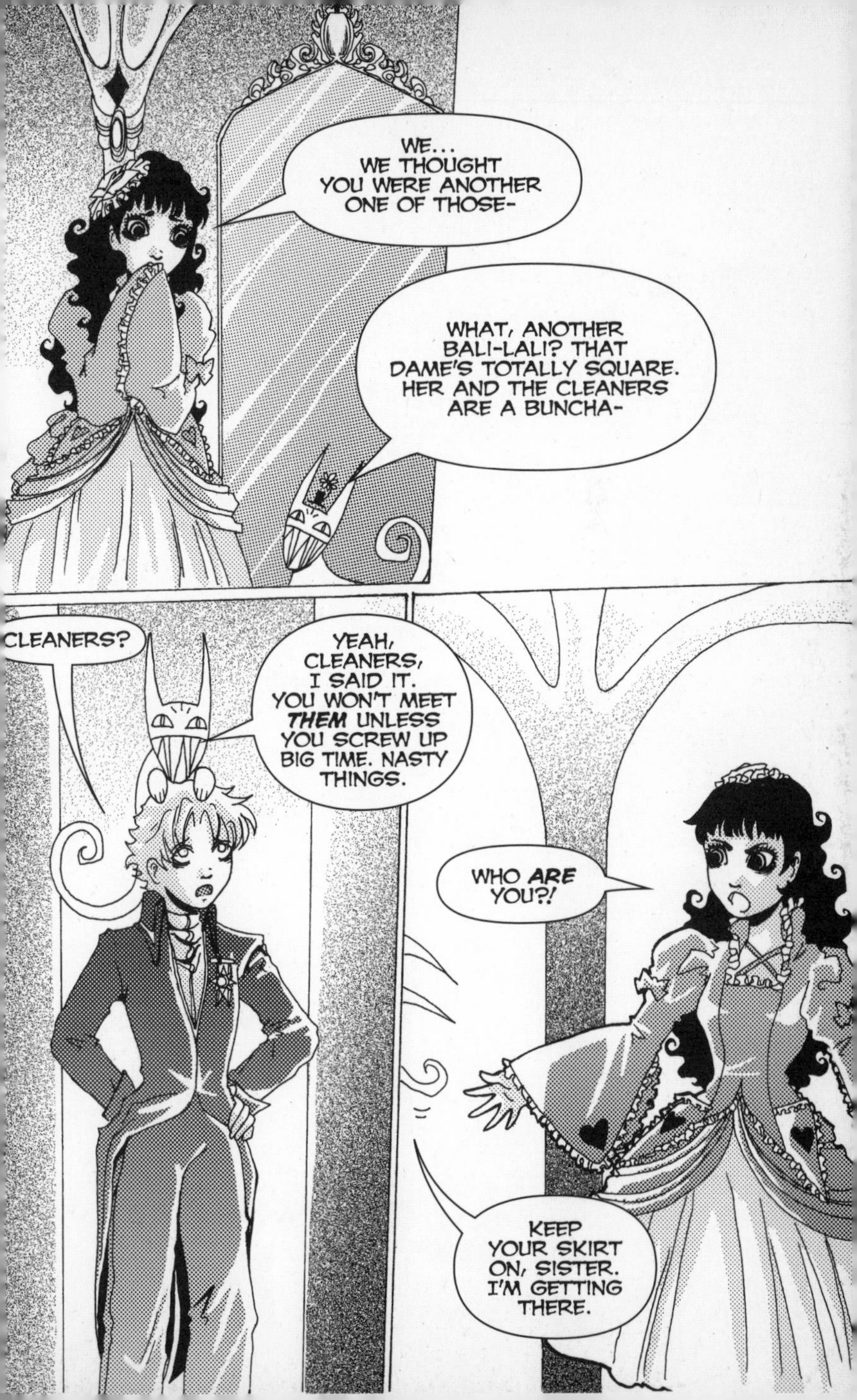
WE... WE THOUGHT YOU WERE ANOTHER ONE OF THOSE-
WHAT, ANOTHER BALI-LALI? THAT DAME'S TOTALLY SQUARE. HER AND THE CLEANERS ARE A BUNCHA-
CLEANERS?
YEAH, CLEANERS, I SAID IT. YOU WON'T MEET *THEM* UNLESS YOU SCREW UP BIG TIME. NASTY THINGS.
WHO *ARE* YOU?!
KEEP YOUR SKIRT ON, SISTER. I'M GETTING THERE.

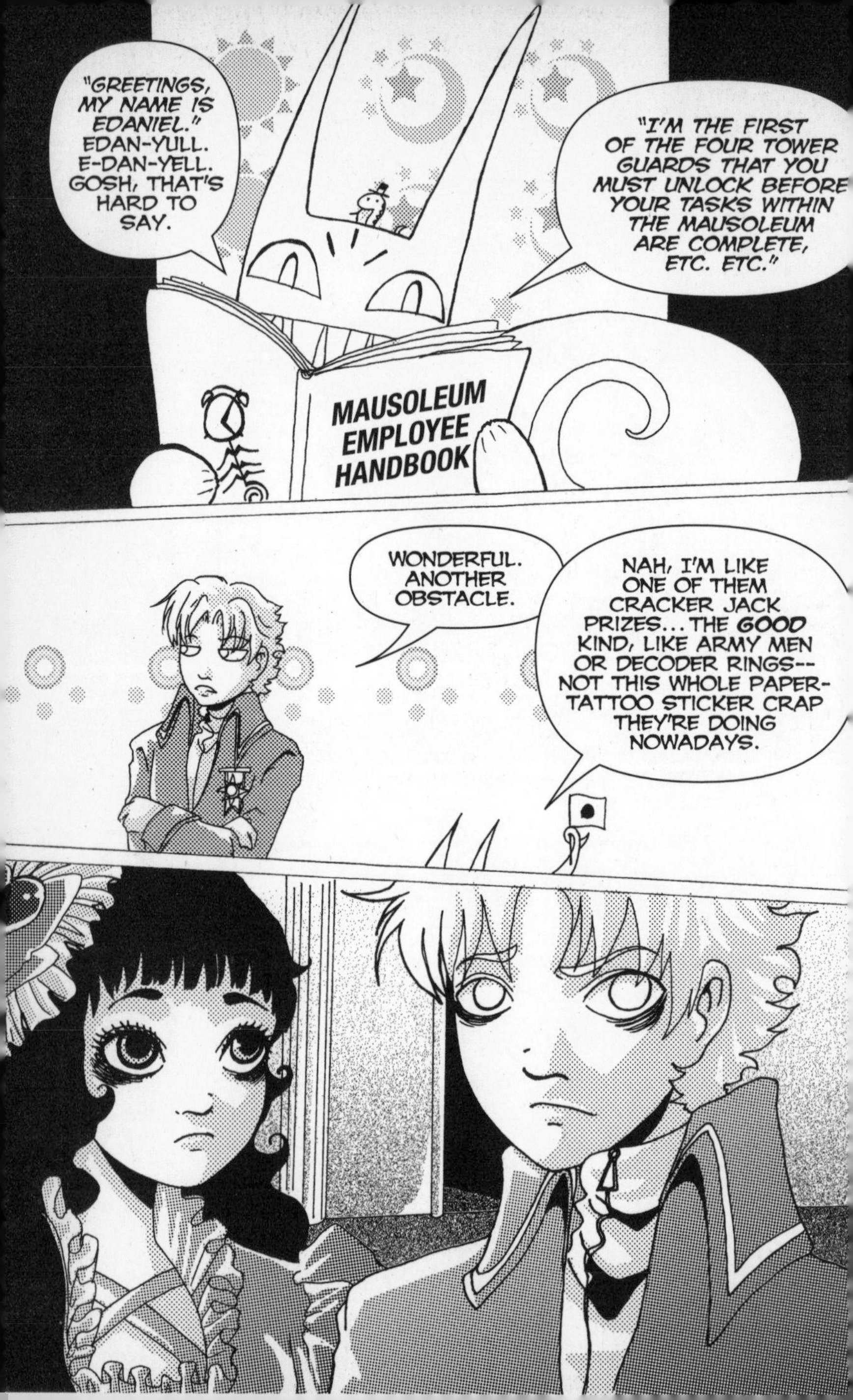
"GREETINGS, MY NAME IS EDANIEL." EDAN-YULL. E-DAN-YELL. GOSH, THAT'S HARD TO SAY.
"I'M THE FIRST OF THE FOUR TOWER GUARDS THAT YOU MUST UNLOCK BEFORE YOUR TASKS WITHIN THE MAUSOLEUM ARE COMPLETE, ETC. ETC."
MAUSOLEUM EMPLOYEE HANDBOOK
WONDERFUL. ANOTHER OBSTACLE.
NAH, I'M LIKE ONE OF THEM CRACKER JACK PRIZES... THE GOOD KIND, LIKE ARMY MEN OR DECODER RINGS-- NOT THIS WHOLE PAPER-TATTOO STICKER CRAP THEY'RE DOING NOWADAYS.

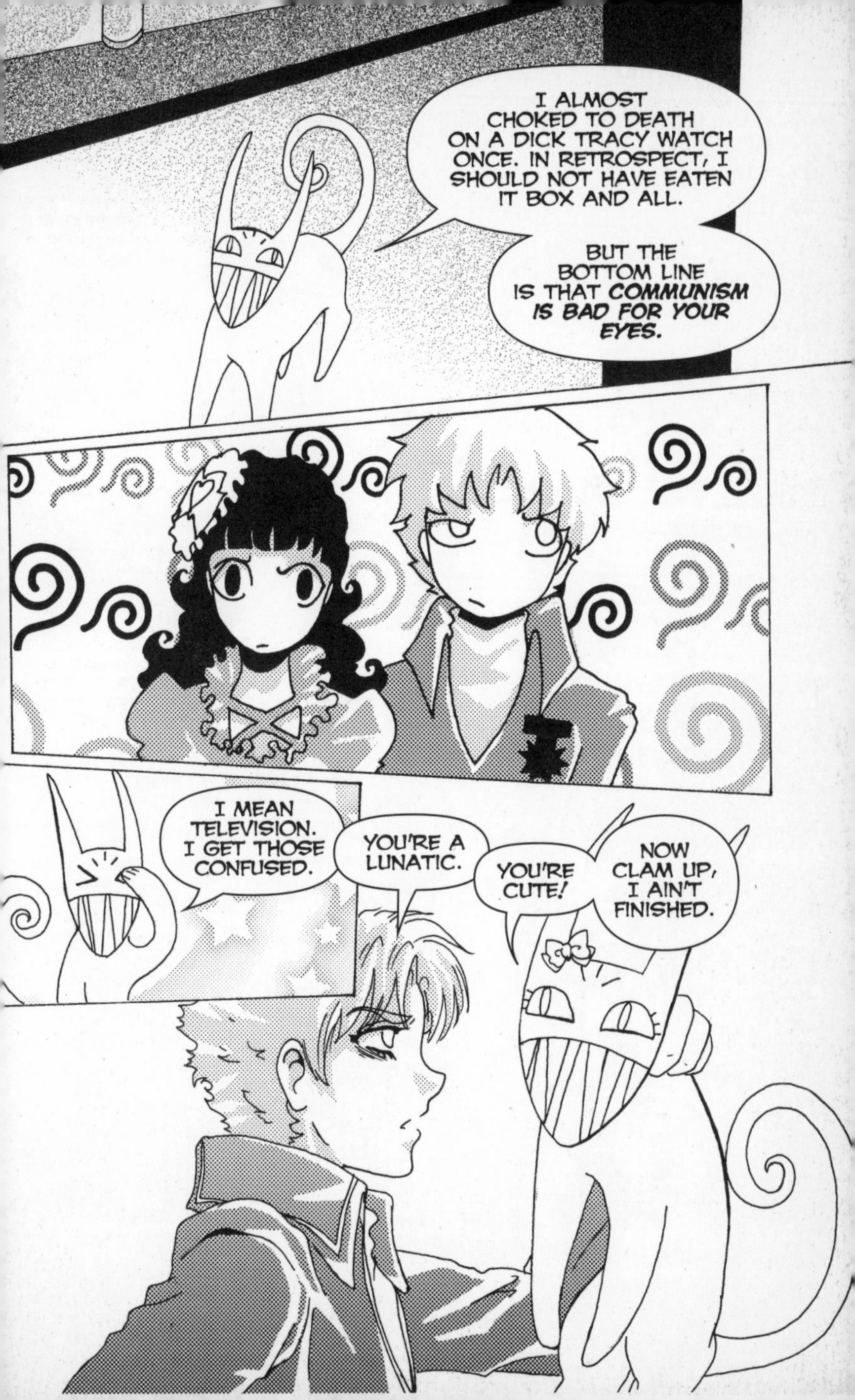
I ALMOST CHOKED TO DEATH ON A DICK TRACY WATCH ONCE. IN RETROSPECT, I SHOULD NOT HAVE EATEN IT BOX AND ALL.
BUT THE BOTTOM LINE IS THAT *COMMUNISM IS BAD FOR YOUR EYES.*
I MEAN TELEVISION. I GET THOSE CONFUSED.
YOU'RE A LUNATIC.
YOU'RE CUTE!
NOW CLAM UP, I AIN'T FINISHED.

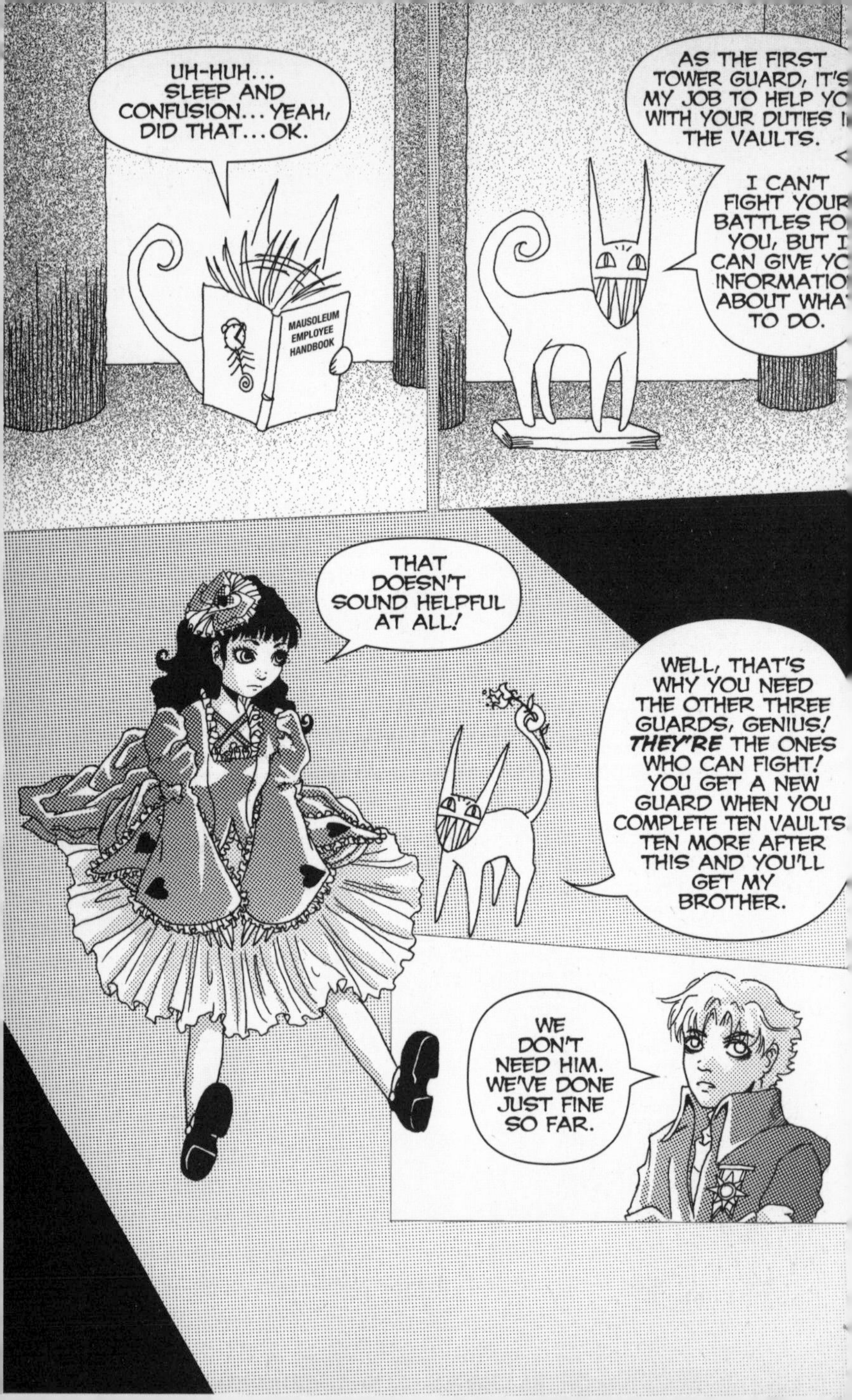
UH-HUH... SLEEP AND CONFUSION... YEAH, DID THAT...OK.
MAUSOLEUM EMPLOYEE HANDBOOK
AS THE FIRST TOWER GUARD, IT'S MY JOB TO HELP YO WITH YOUR DUTIES I THE VAULTS.
I CAN'T FIGHT YOUR BATTLES FO YOU, BUT I CAN GIVE YO INFORMATIO ABOUT WHA TO DO.
THAT DOESN'T SOUND HELPFUL AT ALL!
WELL, THAT'S WHY YOU NEED THE OTHER THREE GUARDS, GENIUS! *THEY'RE* THE ONES WHO CAN FIGHT! YOU GET A NEW GUARD WHEN YOU COMPLETE TEN VAULTS. TEN MORE AFTER THIS AND YOU'LL GET MY BROTHER.
WE DON'T NEED HIM. WE'VE DONE JUST FINE SO FAR.

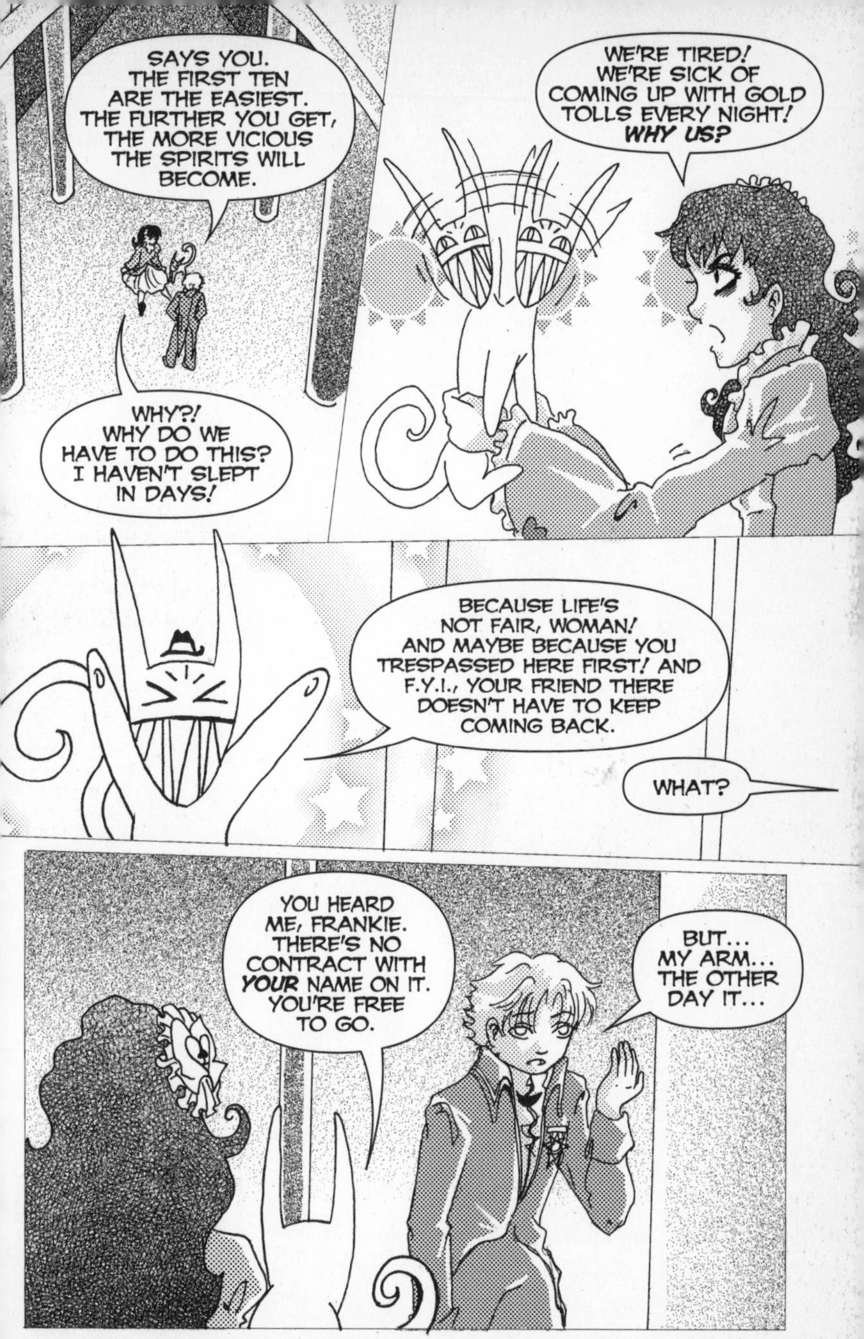
SAYS YOU. THE FIRST TEN ARE THE EASIEST. THE FURTHER YOU GET, THE MORE VICIOUS THE SPIRITS WILL BECOME.
WHY?! WHY DO WE HAVE TO DO THIS? I HAVEN'T SLEPT IN DAYS!
WE'RE TIRED! WE'RE SICK OF COMING UP WITH GOLD TOLLS EVERY NIGHT! *WHY US?*
BECAUSE LIFE'S NOT FAIR, WOMAN! AND MAYBE BECAUSE YOU TRESPASSED HERE FIRST! AND F.Y.I., YOUR FRIEND THERE DOESN'T HAVE TO KEEP COMING BACK.
WHAT?
YOU HEARD ME, FRANKIE. THERE'S NO CONTRACT WITH *YOUR* NAME ON IT. YOU'RE FREE TO GO.
BUT... MY ARM... THE OTHER DAY IT...

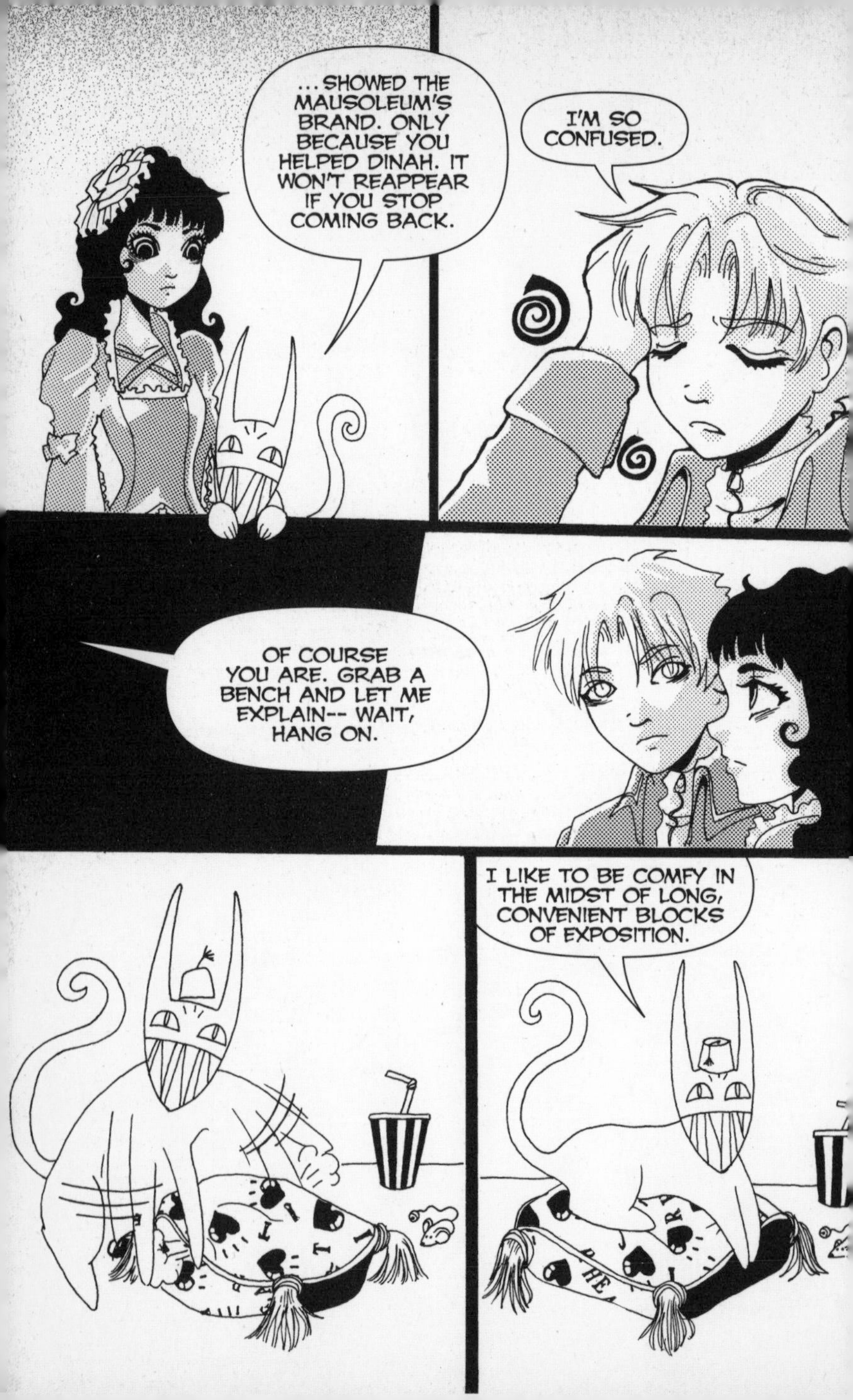
...SHOWED THE MAUSOLEUM'S BRAND. ONLY BECAUSE YOU HELPED DINAH. IT WON'T REAPPEAR IF YOU STOP COMING BACK.
I'M SO CONFUSED.
OF COURSE YOU ARE. GRAB A BENCH AND LET ME EXPLAIN-- WAIT, HANG ON.
I LIKE TO BE COMFY IN THE MIDST OF LONG, CONVENIENT BLOCKS OF EXPOSITION.

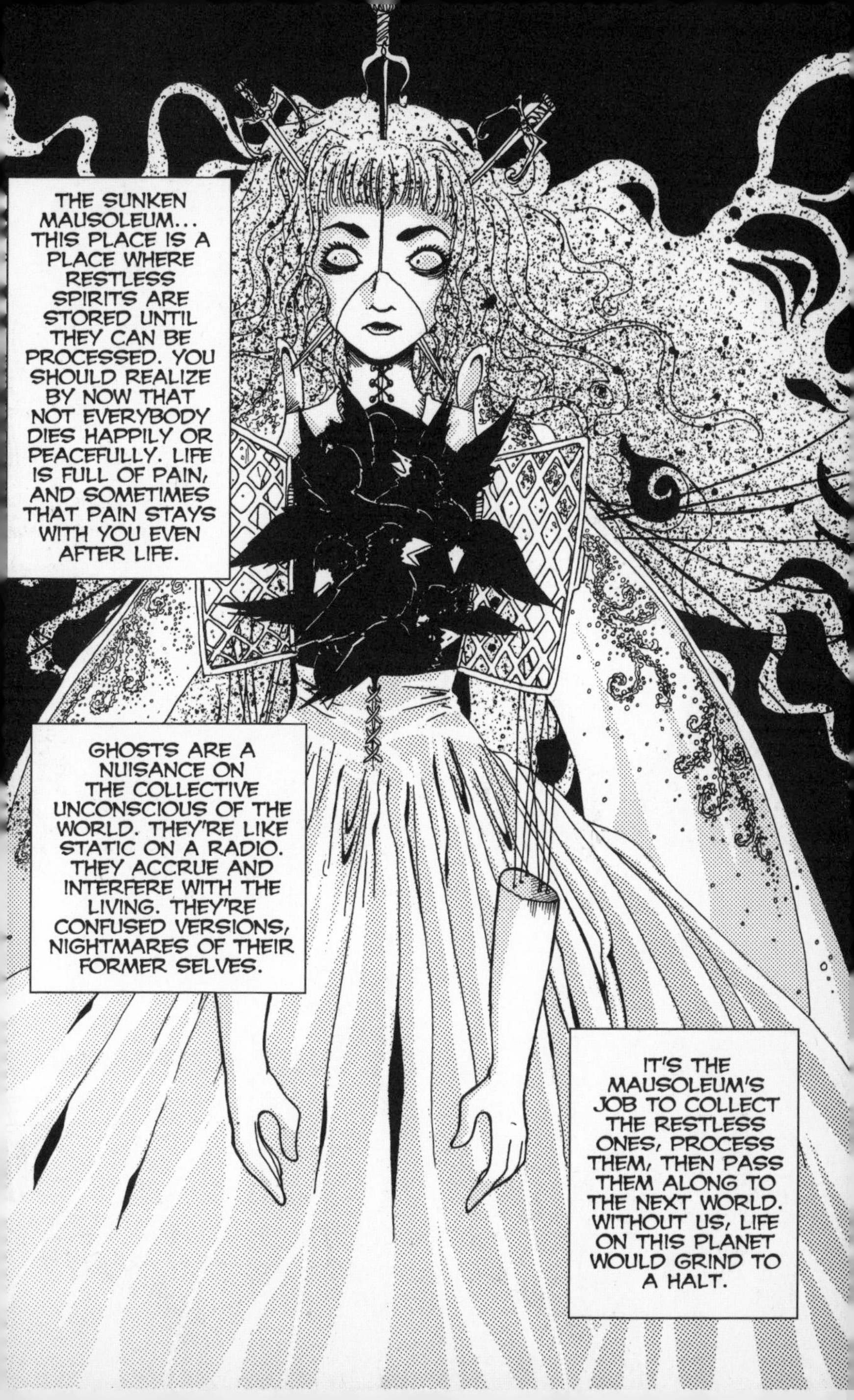
THE SUNKEN MAUSOLEUM... THIS PLACE IS A PLACE WHERE RESTLESS SPIRITS ARE STORED UNTIL THEY CAN BE PROCESSED. YOU SHOULD REALIZE BY NOW THAT NOT EVERYBODY DIES HAPPILY OR PEACEFULLY. LIFE IS FULL OF PAIN, AND SOMETIMES THAT PAIN STAYS WITH YOU EVEN AFTER LIFE.
GHOSTS ARE A NUISANCE ON THE COLLECTIVE UNCONSCIOUS OF THE WORLD. THEY'RE LIKE STATIC ON A RADIO. THEY ACCRUE AND INTERFERE WITH THE LIVING. THEY'RE CONFUSED VERSIONS, NIGHTMARES OF THEIR FORMER SELVES.
IT'S THE MAUSOLEUM'S JOB TO COLLECT THE RESTLESS ONES, PROCESS THEM, THEN PASS THEM ALONG TO THE NEXT WORLD. WITHOUT US, LIFE ON THIS PLANET WOULD GRIND TO A HALT.

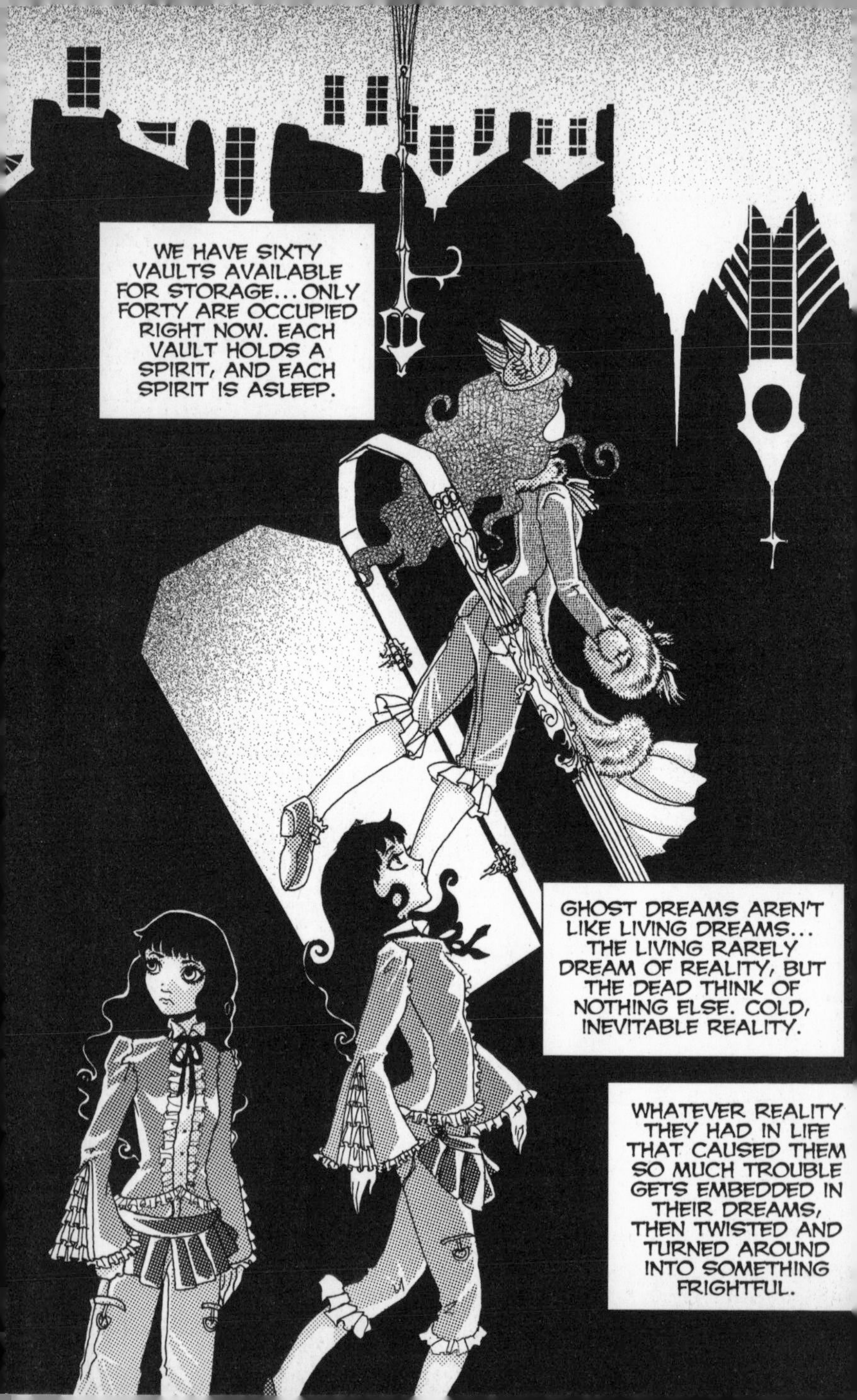
WE HAVE SIXTY VAULTS AVAILABLE FOR STORAGE...ONLY FORTY ARE OCCUPIED RIGHT NOW. EACH VAULT HOLDS A SPIRIT, AND EACH SPIRIT IS ASLEEP.
GHOST DREAMS AREN'T LIKE LIVING DREAMS... THE LIVING RARELY DREAM OF REALITY, BUT THE DEAD THINK OF NOTHING ELSE. COLD, INEVITABLE REALITY.
WHATEVER REALITY THEY HAD IN LIFE THAT CAUSED THEM SO MUCH TROUBLE GETS EMBEDDED IN THEIR DREAMS, THEN TWISTED AND TURNED AROUND INTO SOMETHING FRIGHTFUL.

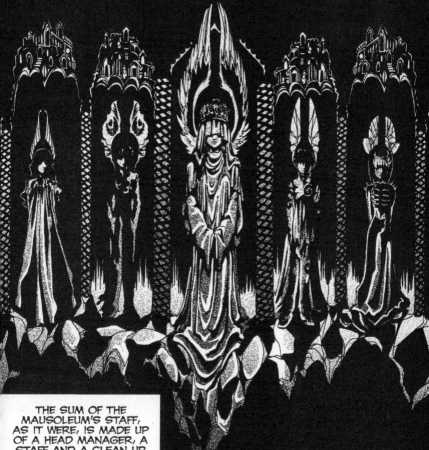

THE SUM OF THE MAUSOLEUM'S STAFF, AS IT WERE, IS MADE UP OF A HEAD MANAGER, A STAFF AND A CLEAN UP CREW. THE HOODED ANGEL IS THE MANAGER, THE TOWER GUARDS ARE THE STAFF AND BALI-LALI AND HER CREW OF CLEANERS ARE CARETAKERS. BUT WE'RE ALL SPIRITS, EVERY ONE OF US, MADE FROM REMNANTS OF OTHER PEOPLE'S SOULS. YOU'LL MEET MY BROTHER EDREAR NEXT, THEN MY TWO SISTERS.

WE CAN'T INTERFERE WITH THE DREAMS OF OTHER SPIRITS WITHOUT THE HELP OF THE LIVING. THAT'S WHY WE EMPLOY HUMAN AGENTS TO DO SOME OF THE WORK.

THAT'S WHERE YOU COME IN.

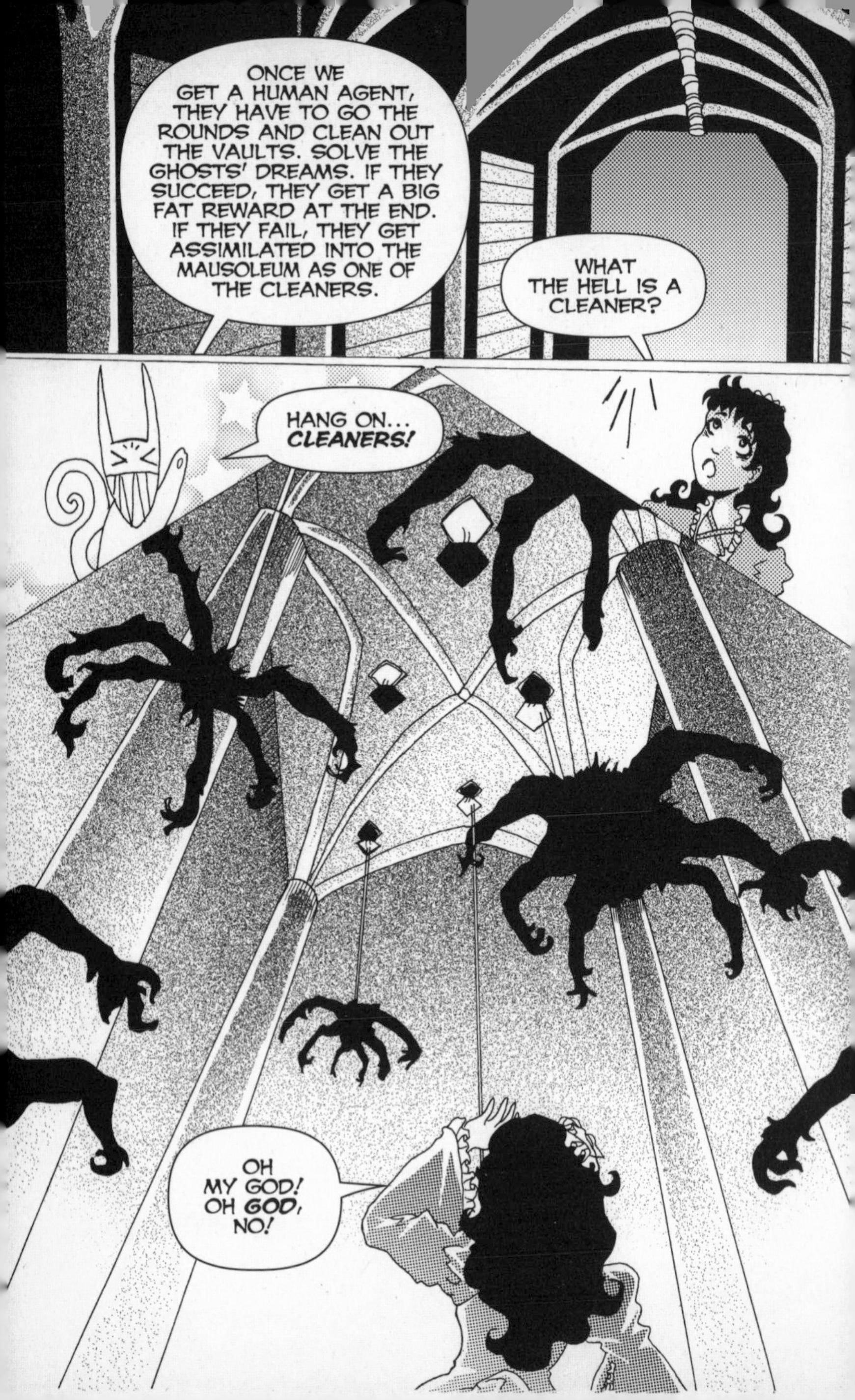
ONCE WE GET A HUMAN AGENT, THEY HAVE TO GO THE ROUNDS AND CLEAN OUT THE VAULTS. SOLVE THE GHOSTS' DREAMS. IF THEY SUCCEED, THEY GET A BIG FAT REWARD AT THE END. IF THEY FAIL, THEY GET ASSIMILATED INTO THE MAUSOLEUM AS ONE OF THE CLEANERS.
WHAT THE HELL IS A CLEANER?
HANG ON... *CLEANERS!*
OH MY GOD! OH *GOD*, NO!

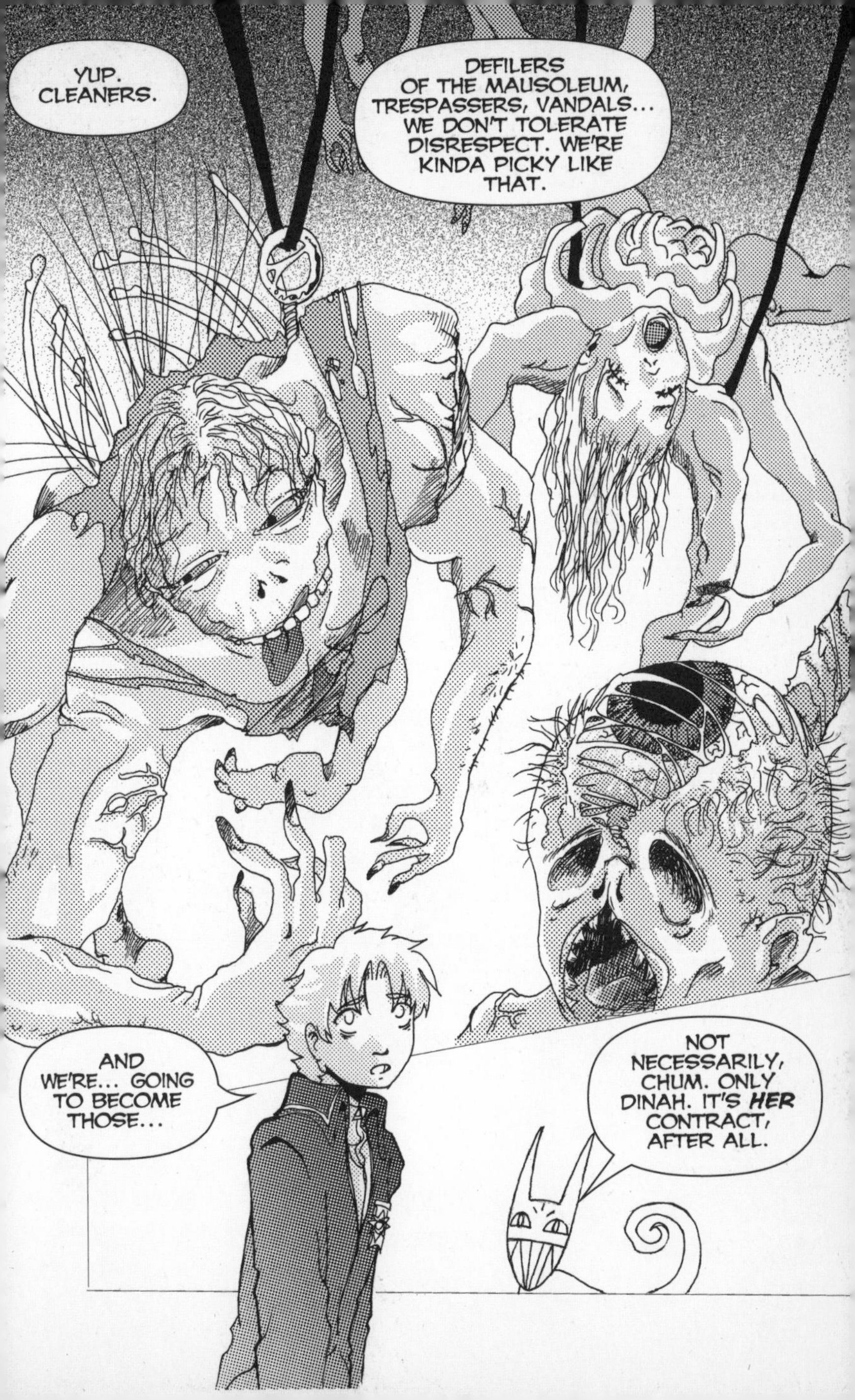
YUP. CLEANERS.
DEFILERS OF THE MAUSOLEUM, TRESPASSERS, VANDALS... WE DON'T TOLERATE DISRESPECT. WE'RE KINDA PICKY LIKE THAT.
AND WE'RE... GOING TO BECOME THOSE...
NOT NECESSARILY, CHUM. ONLY DINAH. IT'S **HER** CONTRACT, AFTER ALL.

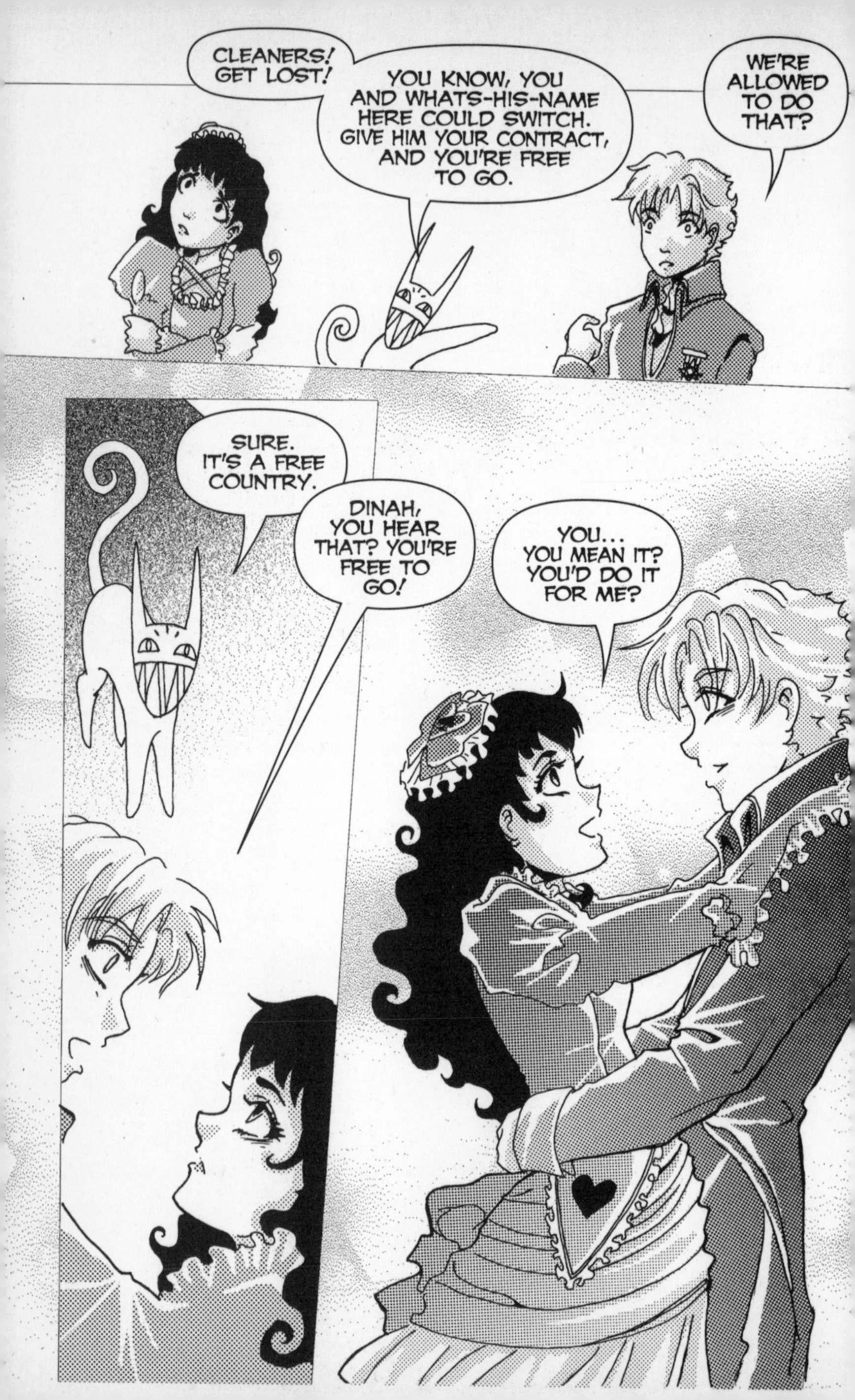
CLEANERS! GET LOST!
YOU KNOW, YOU AND WHATS-HIS-NAME HERE COULD SWITCH. GIVE HIM YOUR CONTRACT, AND YOU'RE FREE TO GO.
WE'RE ALLOWED TO DO THAT?
SURE. IT'S A FREE COUNTRY.
DINAH, YOU HEAR THAT? YOU'RE FREE TO GO!
YOU... YOU MEAN IT? YOU'D DO IT FOR ME?

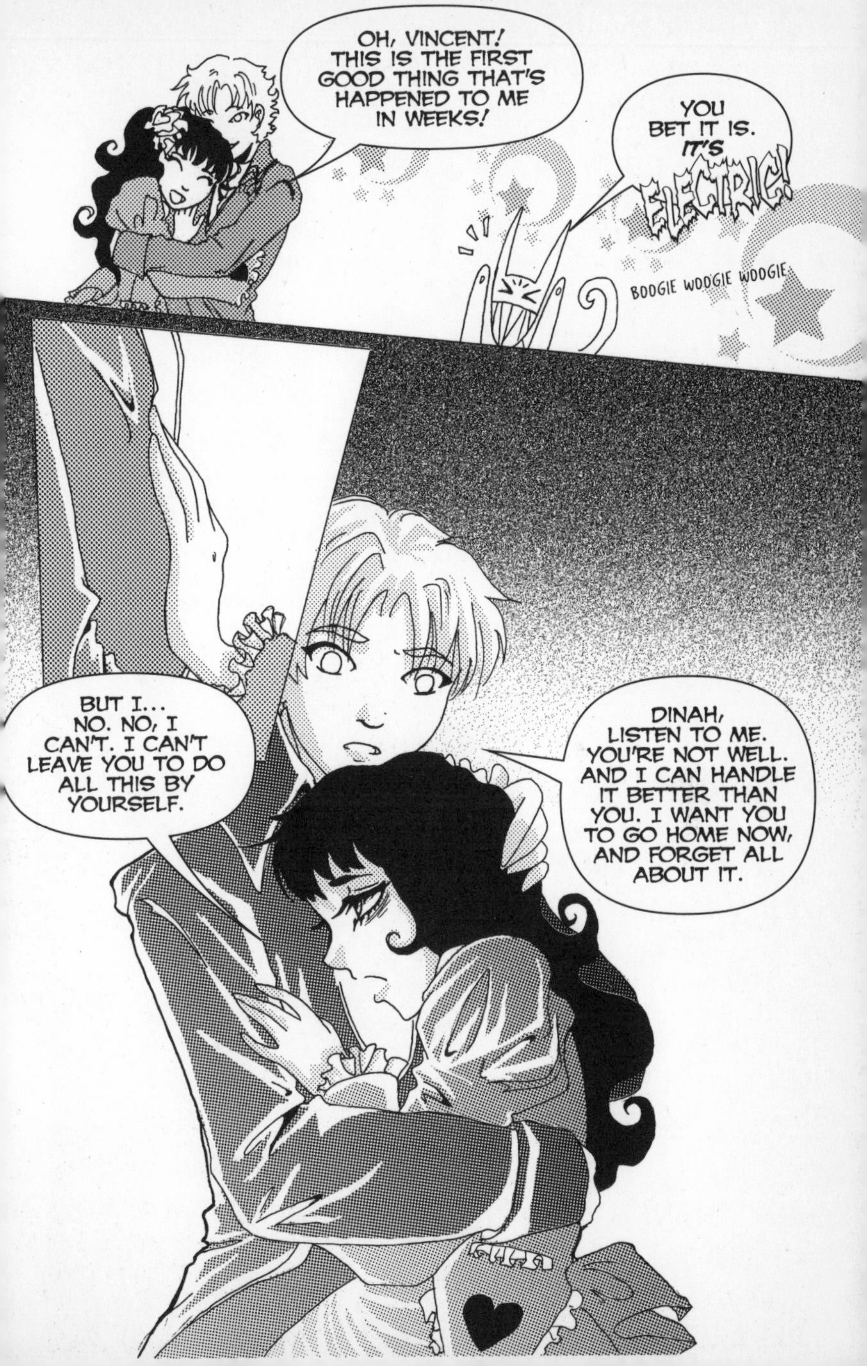
OH, VINCENT! THIS IS THE FIRST GOOD THING THAT'S HAPPENED TO ME IN WEEKS!
YOU BET IT IS. IT'S ELECTRIC!
BOOGIE WOOGIE WOOGIE
DINAH, LISTEN TO ME. YOU'RE NOT WELL. AND I CAN HANDLE IT BETTER THAN YOU. I WANT YOU TO GO HOME NOW, AND FORGET ALL ABOUT IT.
BUT I... NO. NO, I CAN'T. I CAN'T LEAVE YOU TO DO ALL THIS BY YOURSELF.

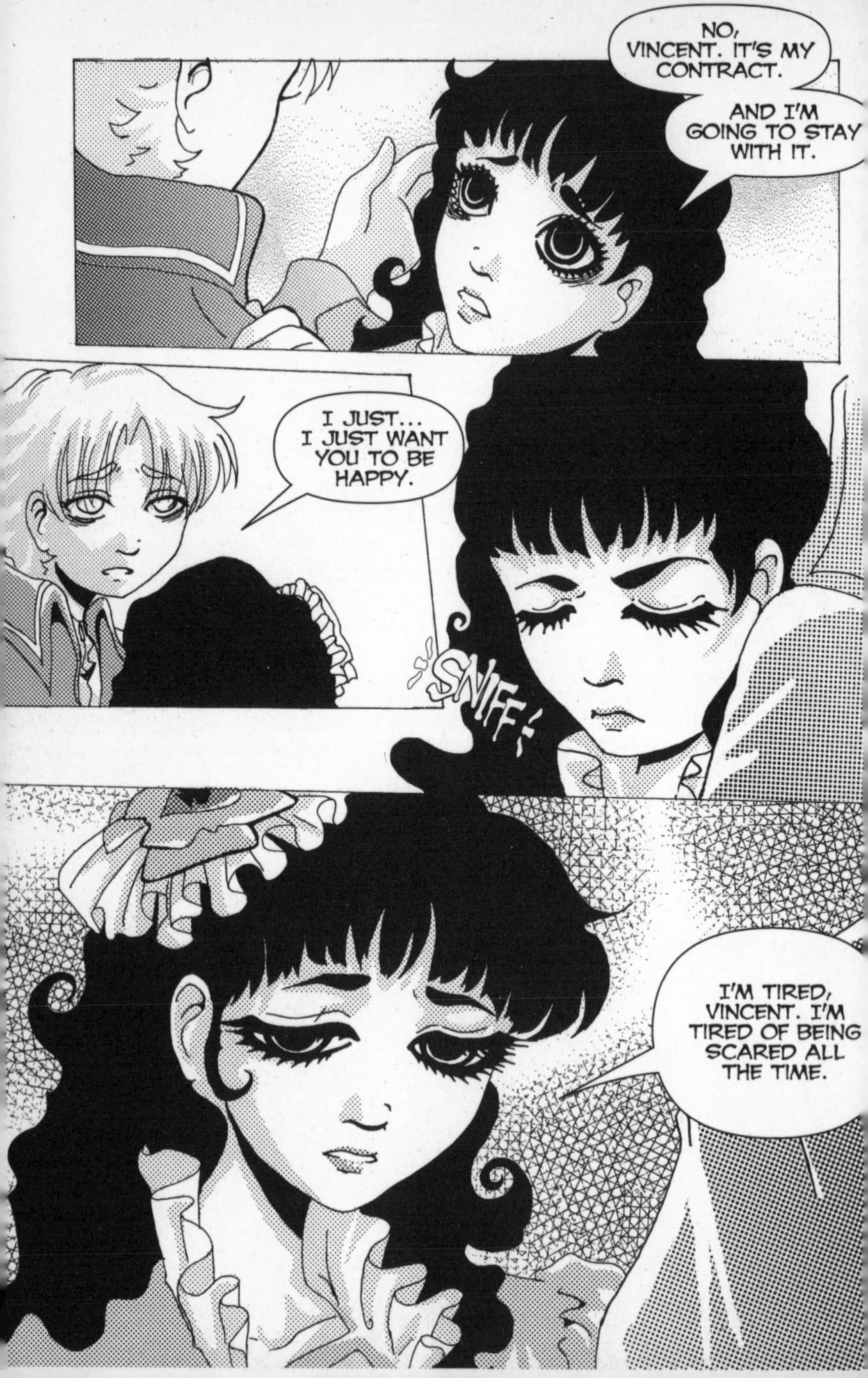
NO, VINCENT. IT'S MY CONTRACT.
AND I'M GOING TO STAY WITH IT.
I JUST... I JUST WANT YOU TO BE HAPPY.
SNIFF
I'M TIRED, VINCENT. I'M TIRED OF BEING SCARED ALL THE TIME.

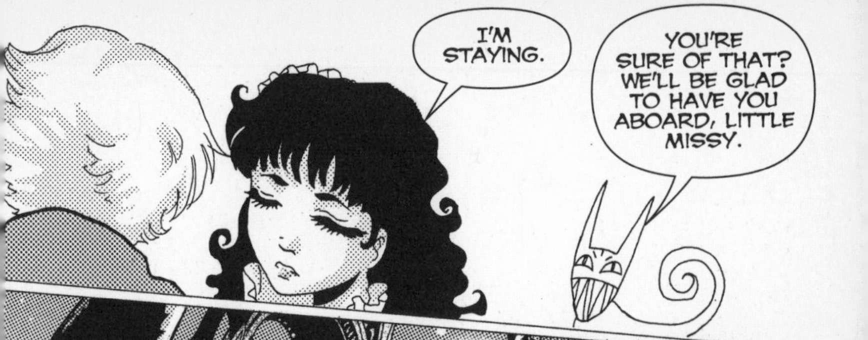
I'M STAYING.
YOU'RE SURE OF THAT? WE'LL BE GLAD TO HAVE YOU ABOARD, LITTLE MISSY.

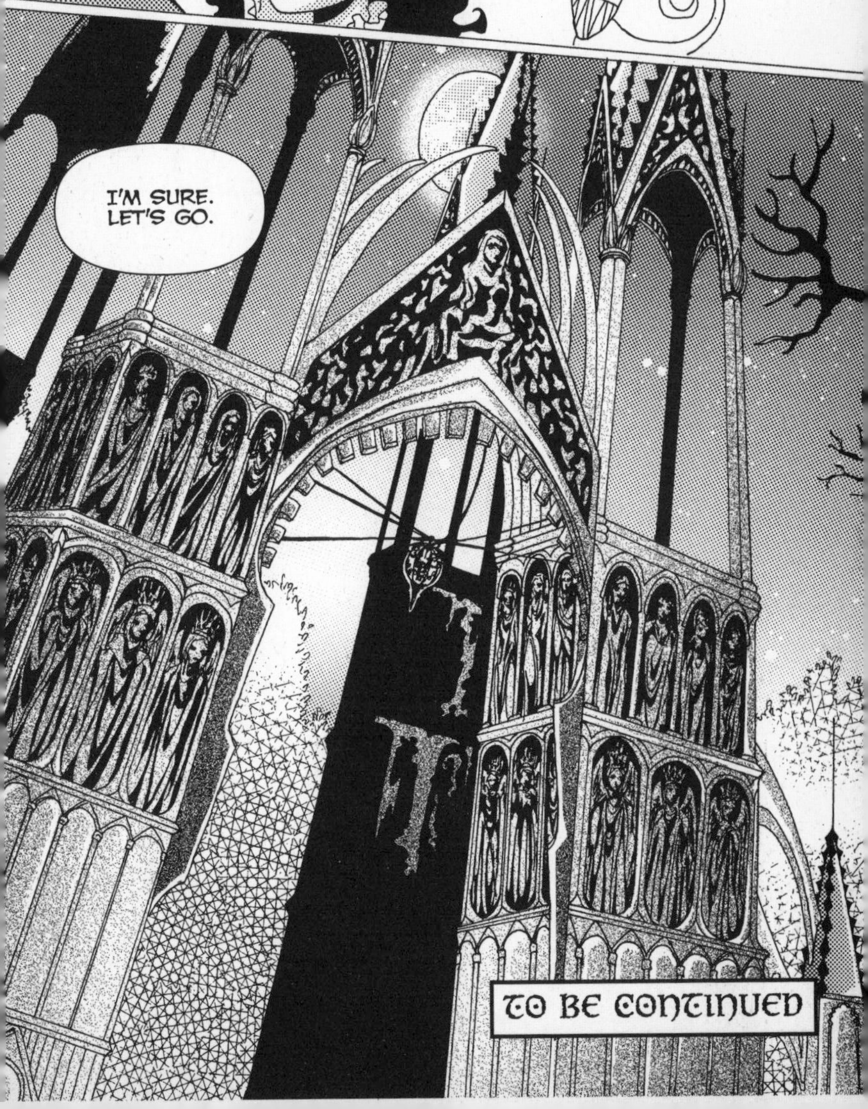
I'M SURE. LET'S GO.
TO BE CONTINUED

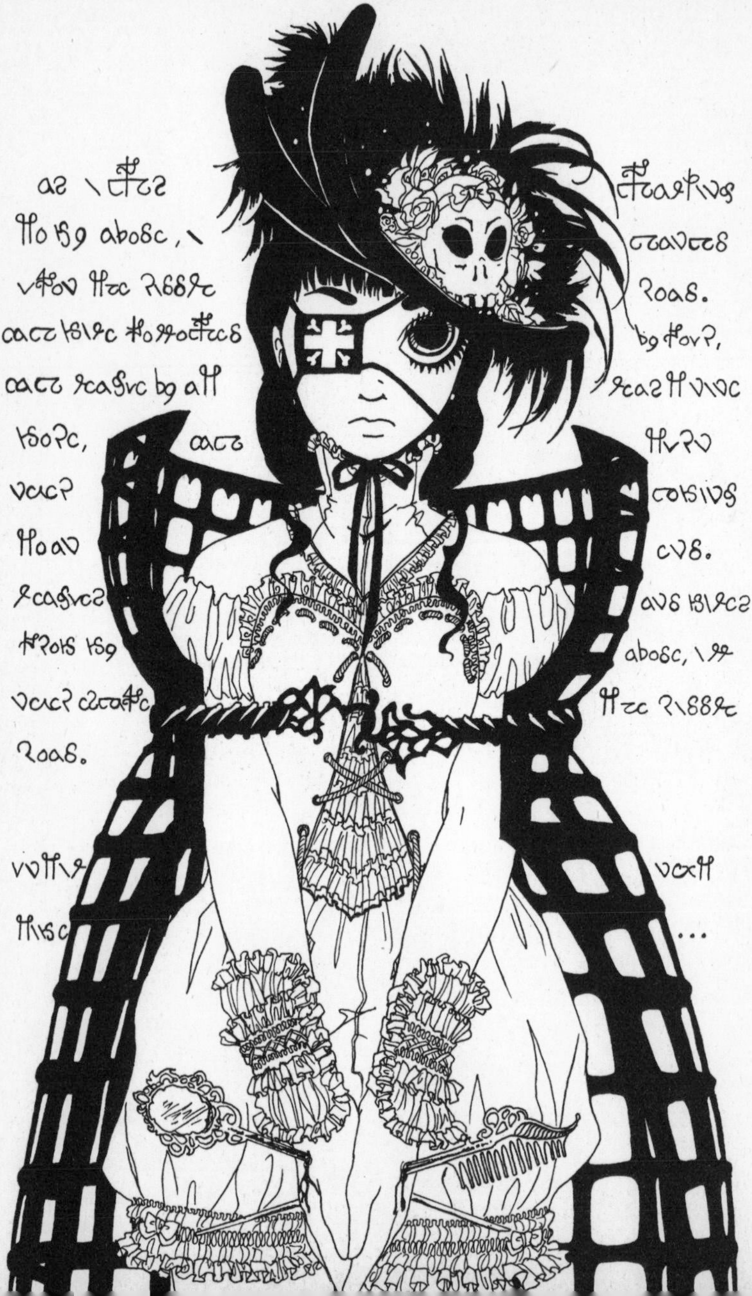

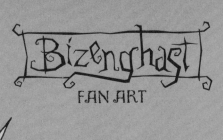

Bizenghast
FAN ART

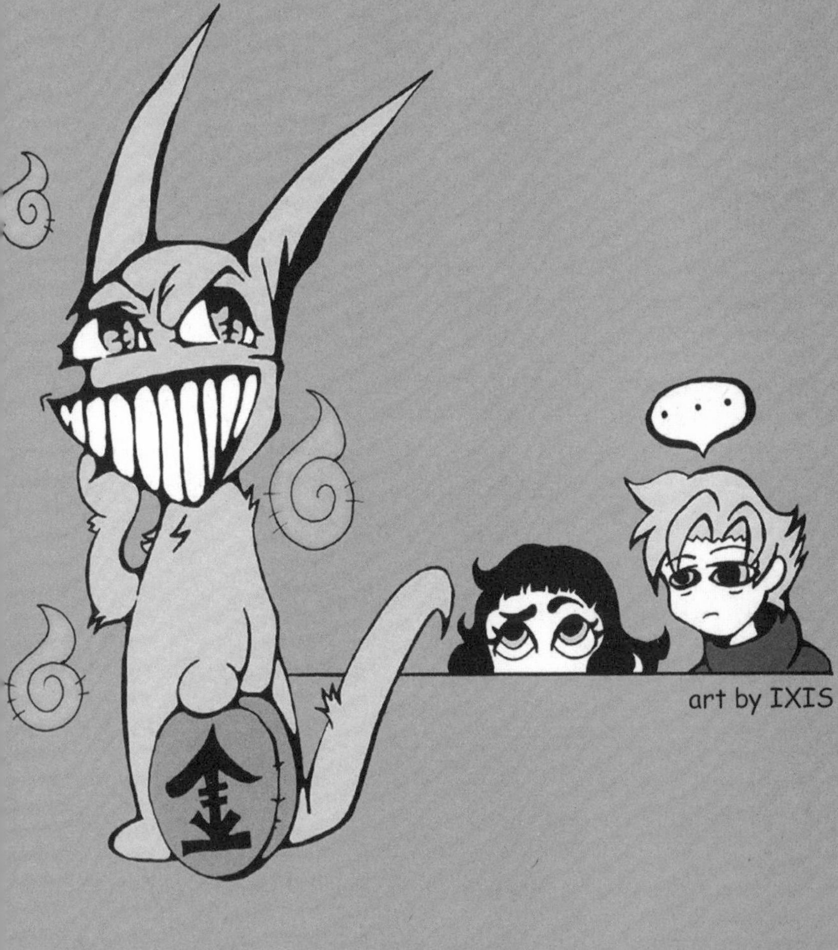
...

art by IXIS

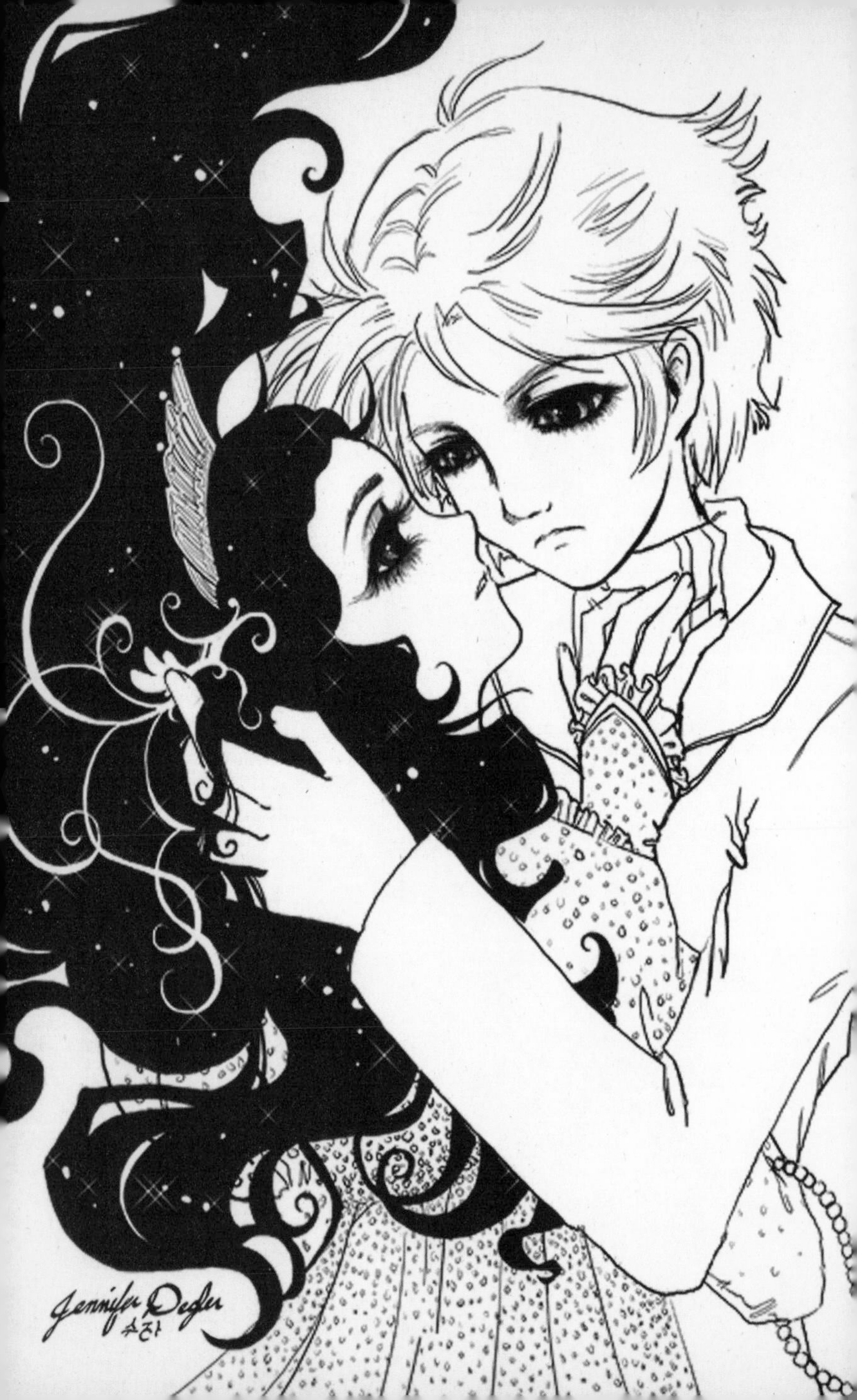
Jennifer Degler

Bizengha

art by Connor Carrot

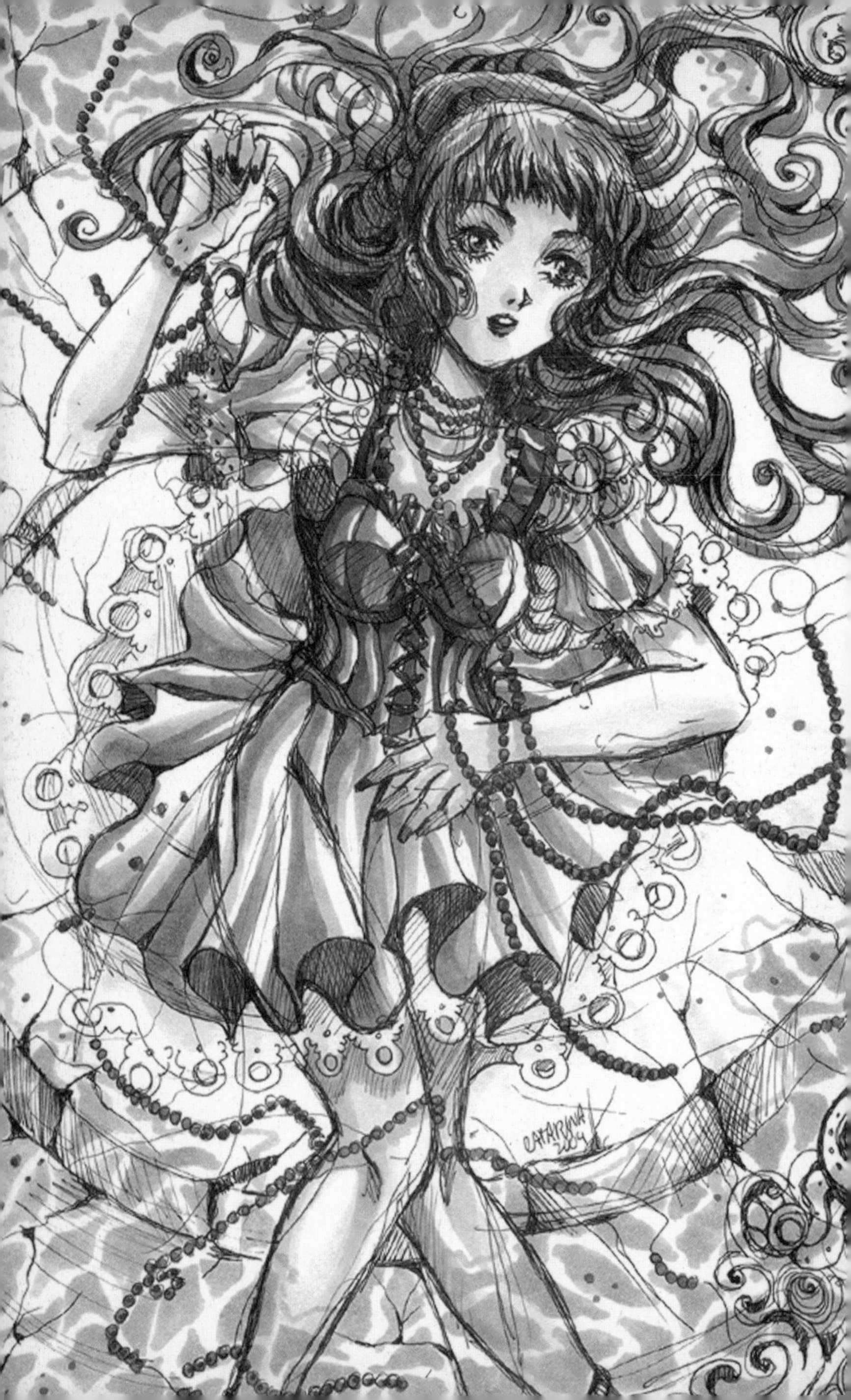
CATARINA
2004

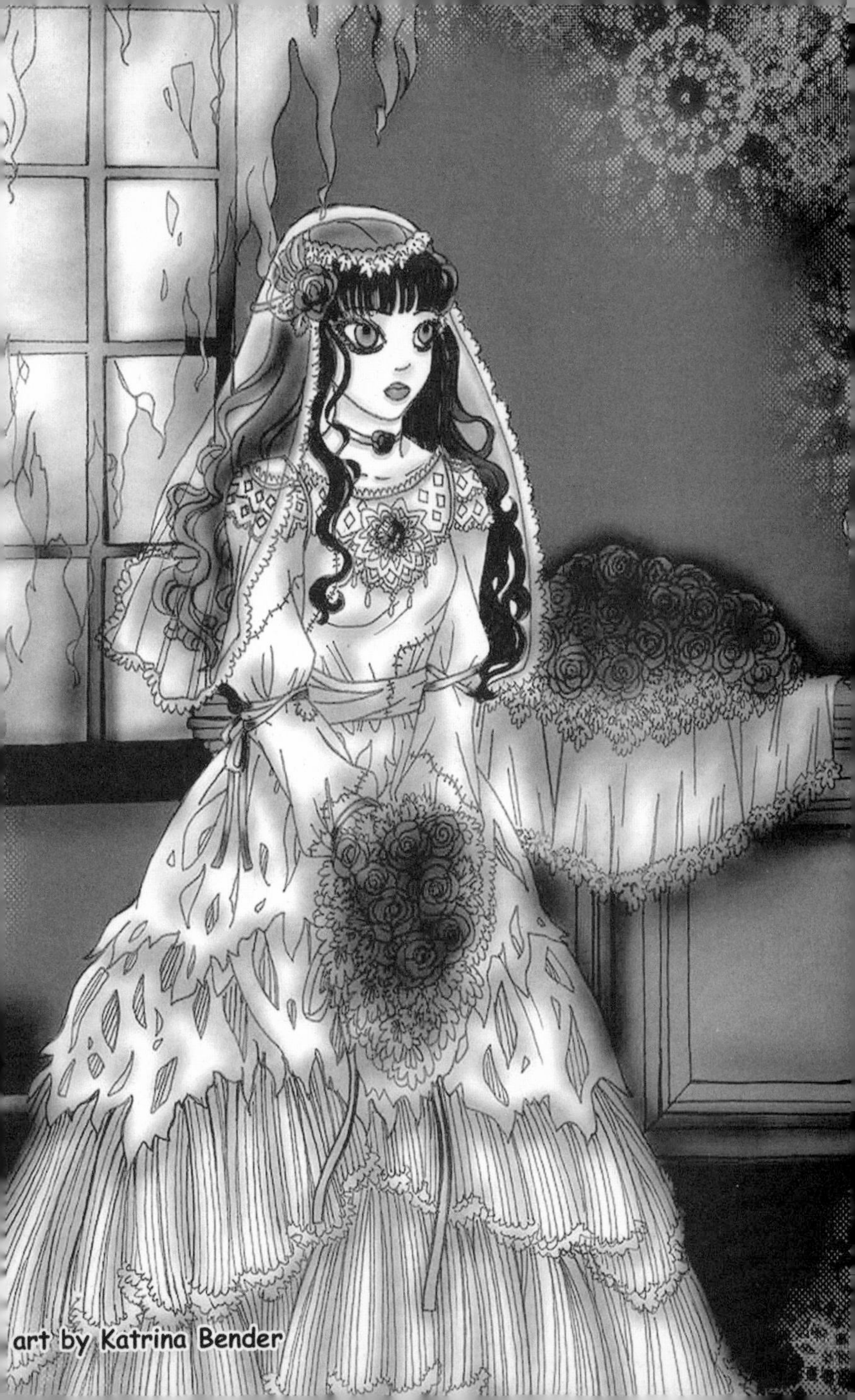
art by Katrina Bender

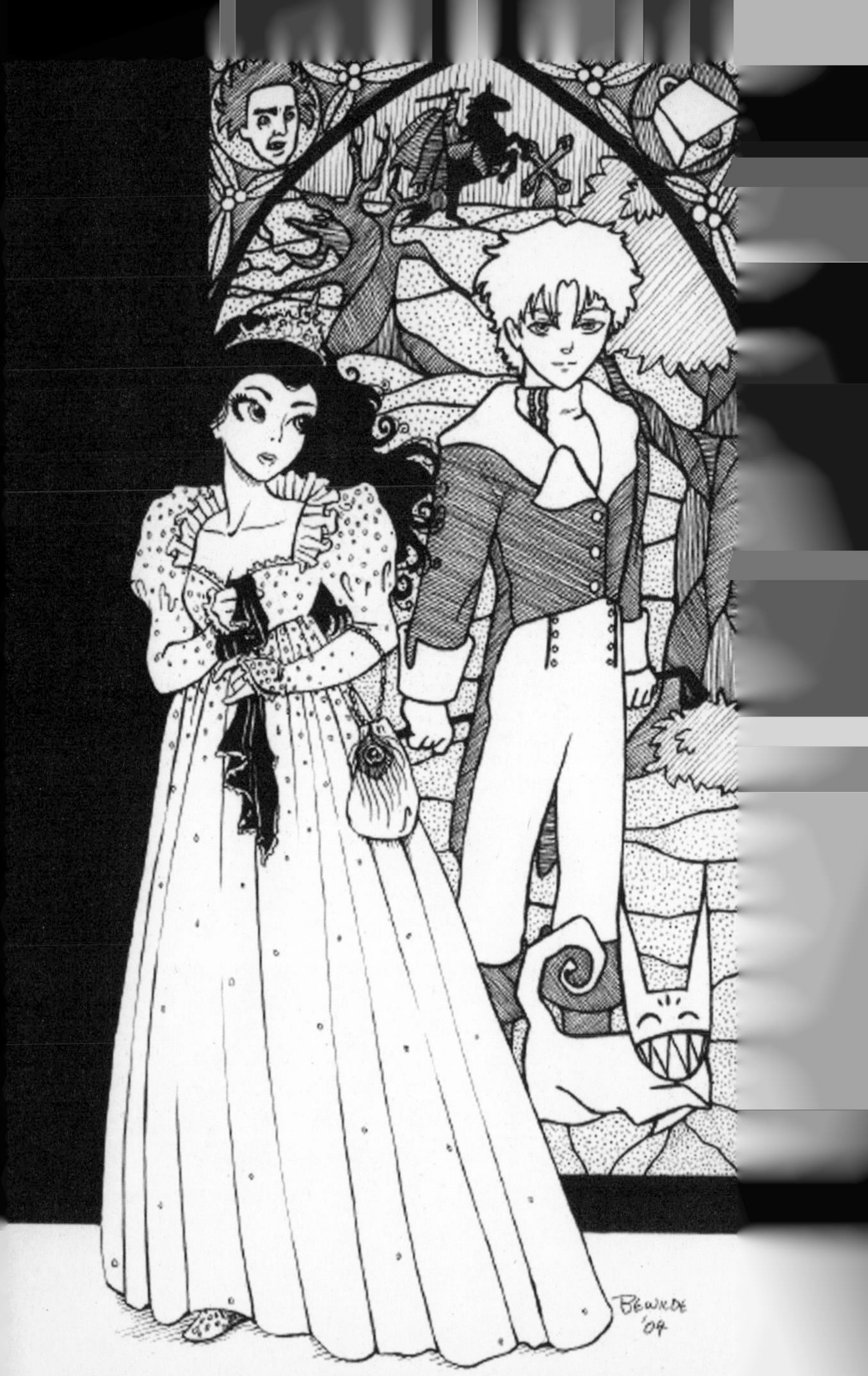

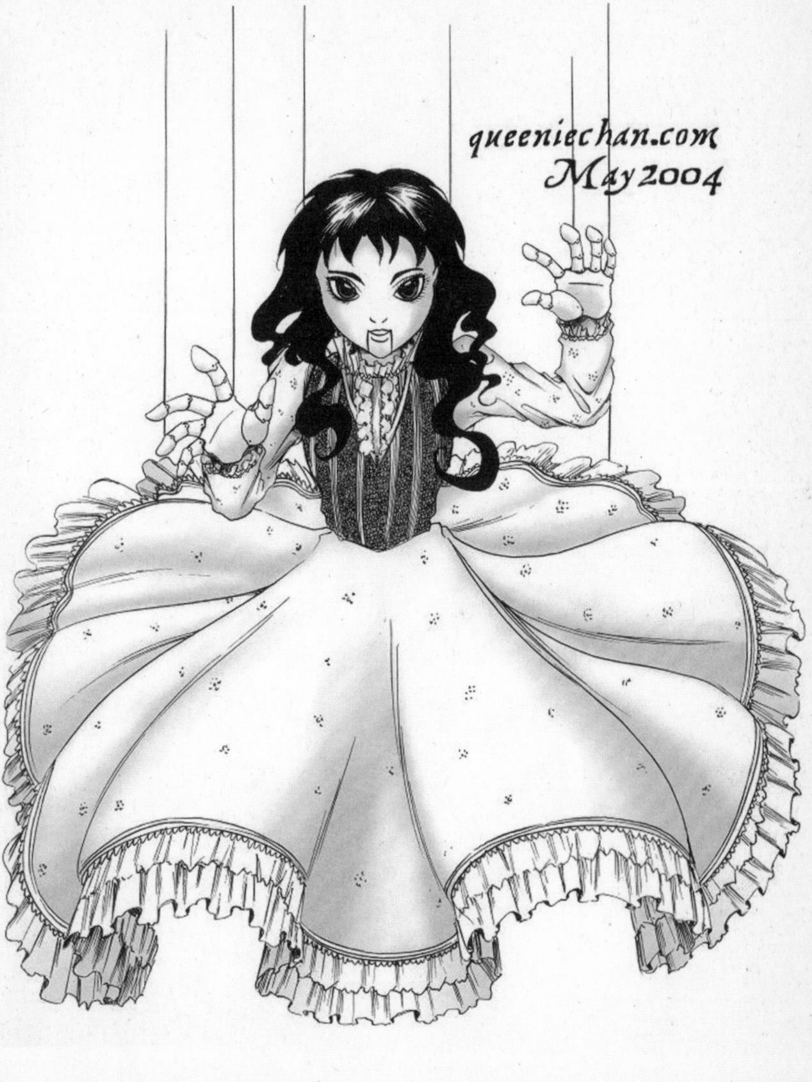
queeniechan.com
May 2004

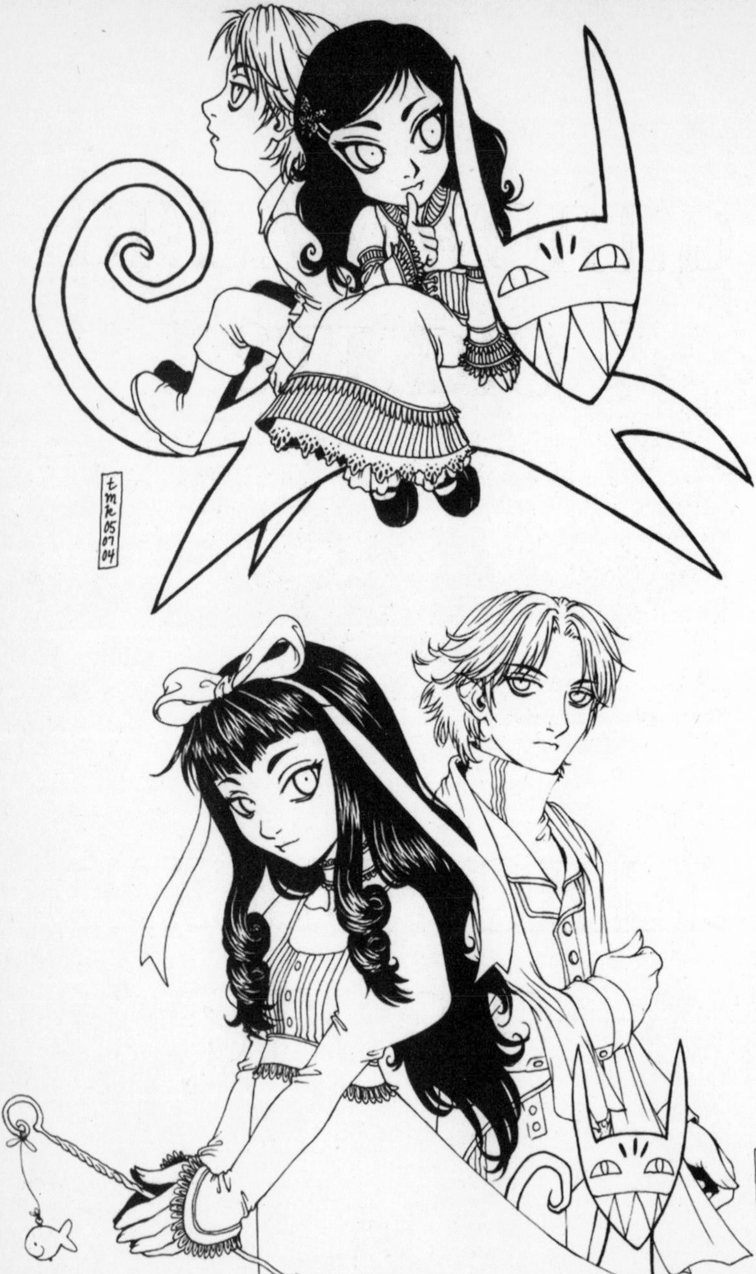
tmk 05 07 04
tmk 05 07 04

art by Bettina

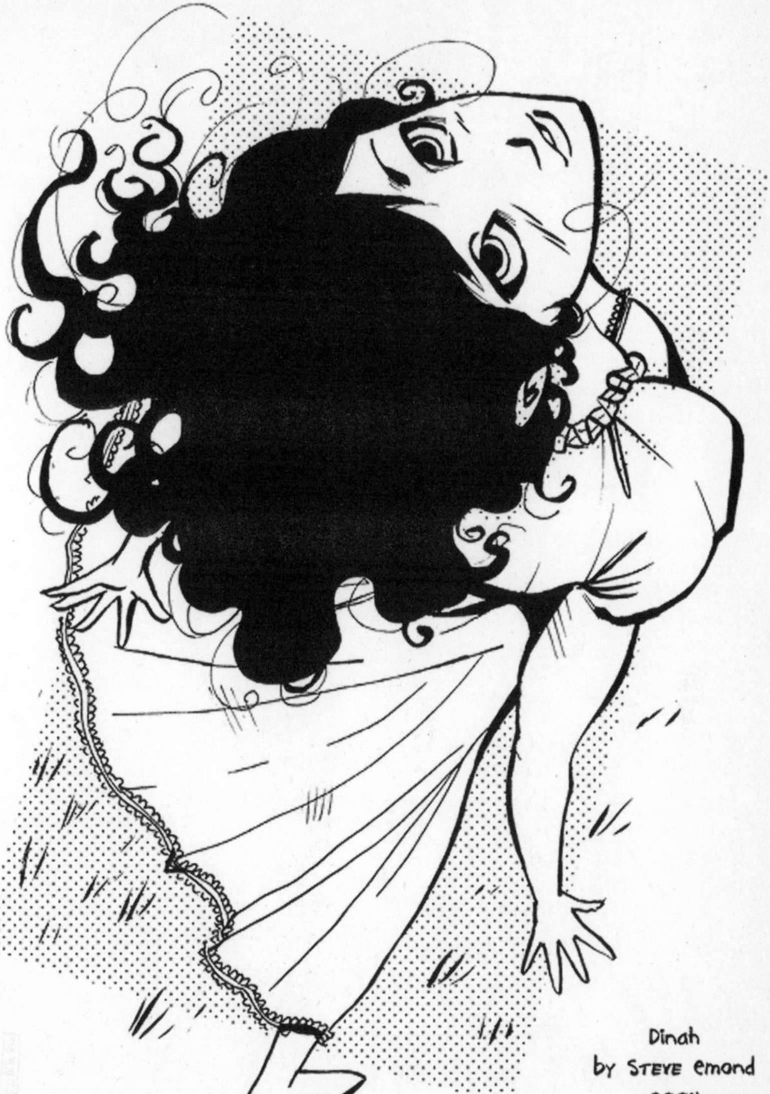
Dinah
by STEVE emond
2004

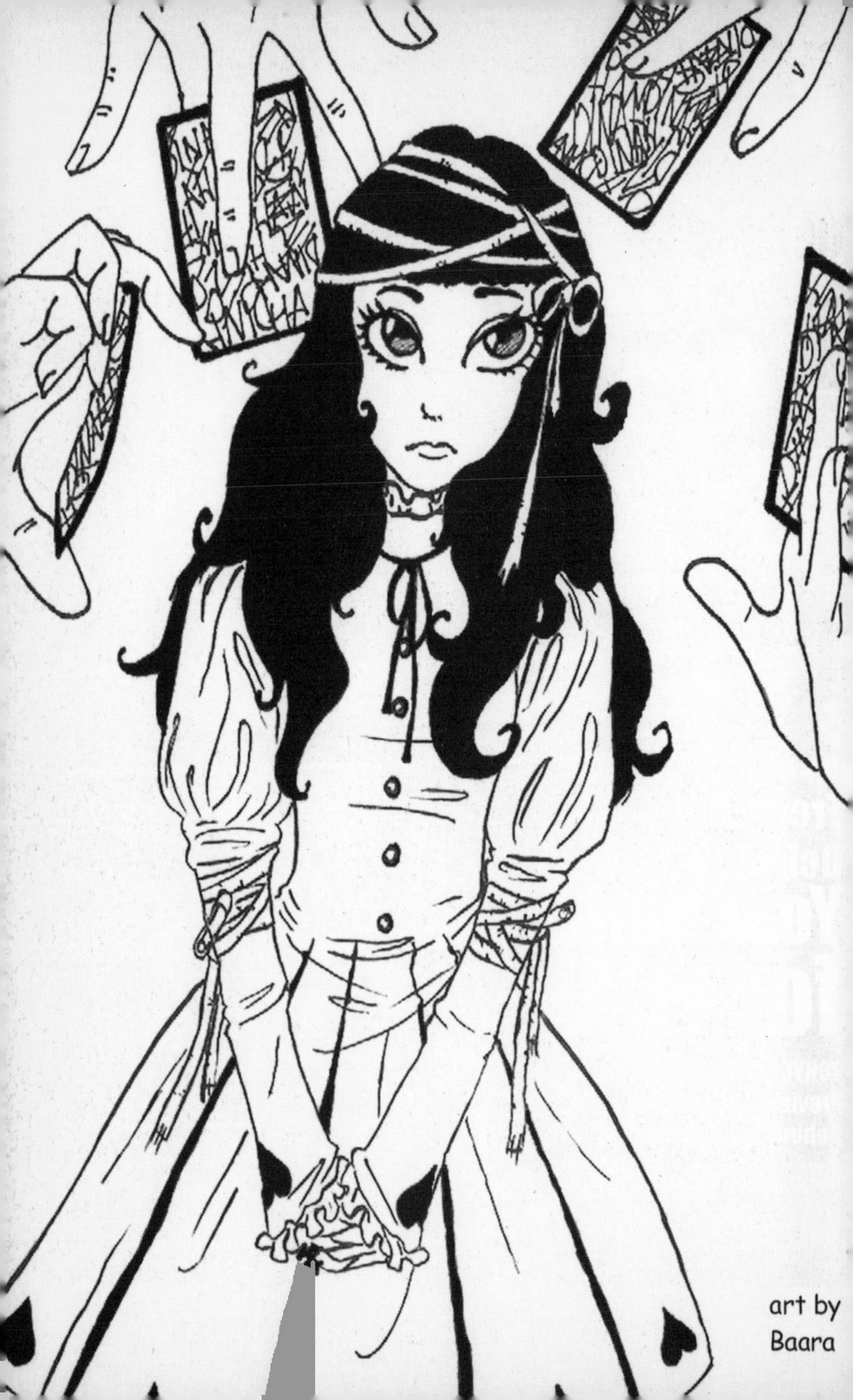

art by
Baara

TOKYOPOP SHOP

SPOTLIGHT TOKYOPOP MANGA SUPPLEMENT

GIRLS BRAVO
BY MARIO KANEDA

T
TEEN
AGE 13+

BOY MEETS GIRL. BOY BREAKS OUT IN HIVES.
BOY STUMBLES ONTO ALIEN PLANET FULL OF GIRLS...

Meet Yukinari Sasaki, an average high school boy who has extreme girl phobia—and an allergic reaction when girls touch him. One day, he befriends an alien named Miharu, who comes from a planet that is inhabited by only women. Remarkably, Yukinari is able to touch Miharu, without breaking out. He returns to his own world accompanied by Miharu, but shortly thereafter, other girls follow them to his world...and his life turns into one big mess!

THE LAUGH-OUT-LOUD MANGA THAT INSPIRED THE POPULAR ANIME ADAPTATION!

© MARIO KANEDA

WAR ON FLESH

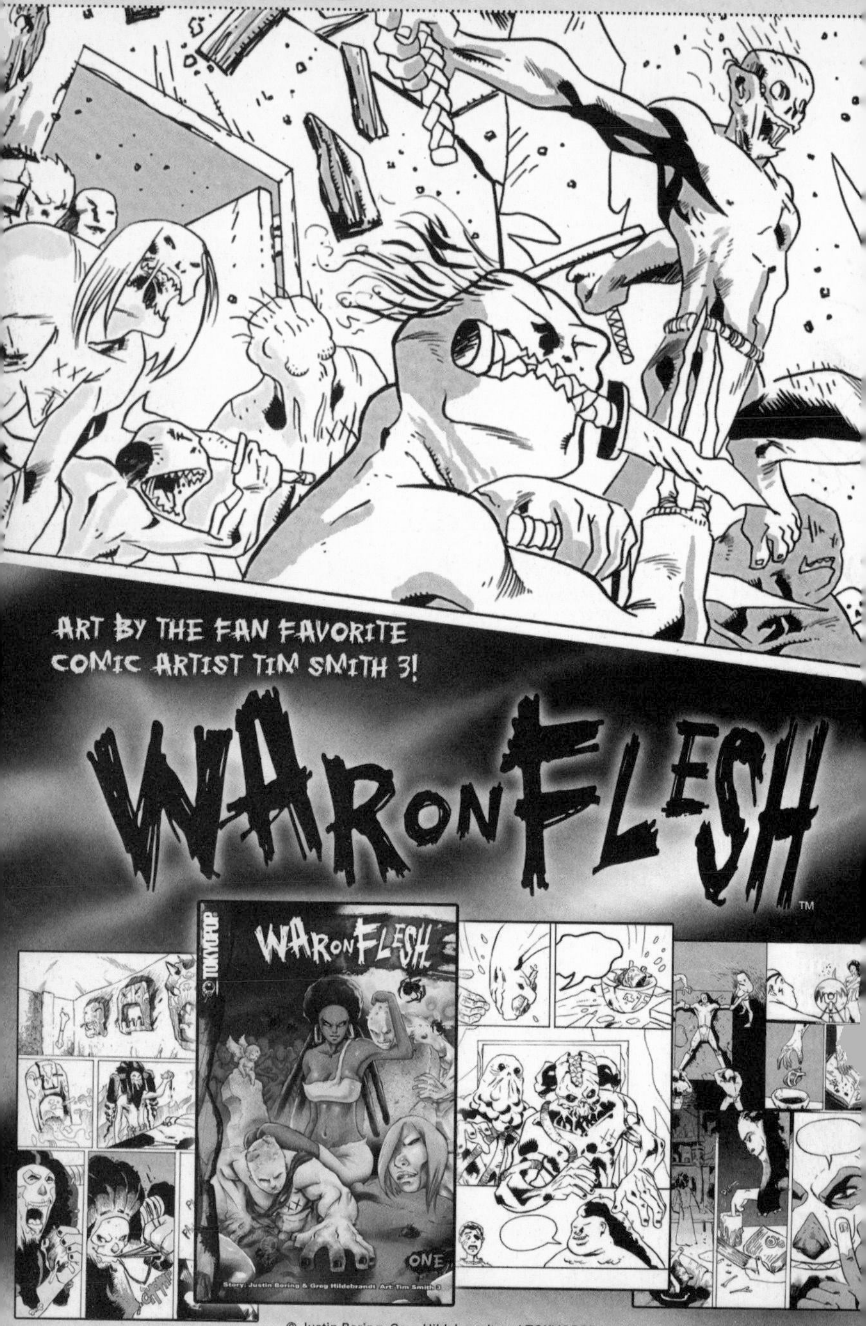
ART BY THE FAN FAVORITE
COMIC ARTIST TIM SMITH 3!
WAR ON FLESH™
TOKYOPOP
WAR ON FLESH
ONE
Story: Justin Boring & Greg Hildebrandt Art: Tim Smith 3

OT
OLDER TEEN
AGE 16+

In the deep South, an ancient voodoo curse unleashes the War on Flesh—a hellish plague of voracious Ew Chott hornets that raises an army of the walking dead. This undead army spreads the plague by ripping the hearts out of living creatures to make room for a Black Heart hive, all in preparation for the most awesome incarnation of evil ever imagined… An unlikely group of five mis-matched individuals have to put their differences aside to try to destroy the onslaught of evil before it's too late.

VOODOO MAKES A MAN NASTY!

PhD: PHANTASY DEGREE

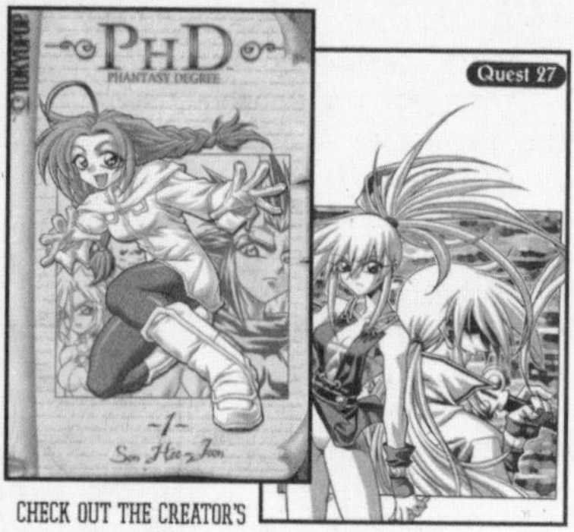
PhD
PHANTASY DEGREE
TOKYOPOP
-1-
Son Hee-Joon
Quest 27

CHECK OUT THE CREATOR'S *iD_eNTITY*

BY SON HEE-JOON

So you think you've got it rough at *your* school? Try attending classes at Demon School Hades! When sassy, young Sang makes her monster matriculation to this arcane academy, all hell breaks loose—literally! But what would you expect when the graduating class consists of a werewolf, a mummy and demons by the score? Son Hee-Joon's underworld adventure is pure escapist fun. Always packed with action and often silly in the best sense, *PhD* never takes itself too seriously or lets the reader stop to catch his breath.

~Bryce P. Coleman, Editor

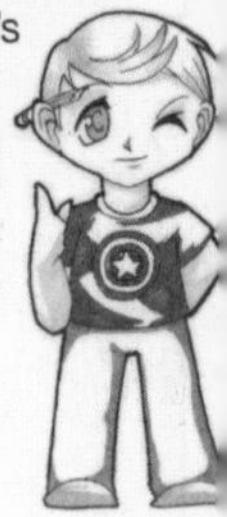

BOYS BE...

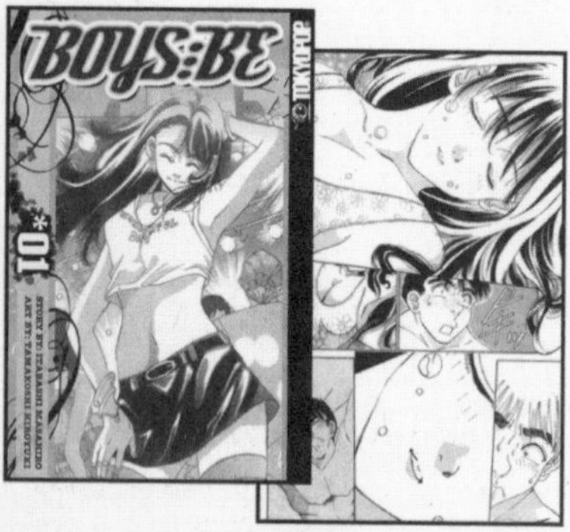
BOYS:BE
TOKYOPOP
01

BY MASAHIRO ITABASHI & HIROYUKI TAMAKOSHI

Boys Be... is a series of short stories. But although the hero's name changes from tale to tale, he remains Everyboy—that dorky high school guy who'll do anything to score with the girl of his dreams. You know him. Perhaps you *are* him. He is a dirty mind with the soul of a poet, a stumblebum with a heart of sterling. We follow this guy on quest after quest to woo his lady loves. We savor his victory; we reel with his defeat...and the experience is touching, funny and above all human.

Still not convinced? I have two words for you: fan service.

~Carol Fox, Editor

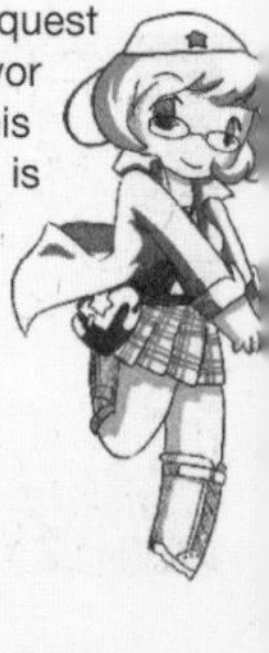

RIZELMINE
BY YUKIRU SUGISAKI

Tomonori Iwaki is a hapless fifteen-year-old whose life is turned upside down when the government announces that he's a married man! His blushing bride is Rizel, apparently the adorable product of an experiment. She does her best to win her new man's heart in this wacky romantic comedy from the creator of *D•N•Angel*!

Inspiration for the hit anime!

T TEEN AGE 13+

© YUKIRU SUGISAKI / KADOKAWA SHOTEN.

HONEY MUSTARD
BY HO-KYUNG YEO

When Ara works up the nerve to ask out the guy she has a crush on, she ends up kissing the wrong boy! The juicy smooch is witnessed by the school's puritanical chaperone, who tells their strict families. With everyone in an uproar, the only way everyone will be appeased is if the two get married—and have kids!

T TEEN AGE 13+

© Ho-Kyung Yeo, HAKSAN PUBLISHING CO., LTD.

HEAT GUY J
BY CHIAKI OGISHIMA, KAZUKI AKANE, NOBUTERU YUKI & SATELIGHT

Daisuke Aurora and his android partner, Heat Guy J, work with a special division of peacekeepers to keep anything illegal off the streets. However, that doesn't sit too well with the new ruthless and well-armed mob leader. In the city that never sleeps, will Daisuke and Heat Guy J end up sleeping with the fishes?

The anime favorite as seen on MTV is now an action-packed manga!

T TEEN AGE 13+

© Satelight/Heatguy-J Project.